Chicago Fundamentalism

Ideology and Methodology in Economics

Chicago Fundamentalism

Ideology and Methodology in Economics

Craig F Freedman

Macquarie University, Australia

World Scientific

NEW JERSEY • LONDON • SINGAPORE • BEIJING • SHANGHAI • HONG KONG • TAIPEI • CHENNAI

Published by

World Scientific Publishing Co. Pte. Ltd.
5 Toh Tuck Link, Singapore 596224
USA office: 27 Warren Street, Suite 401-402, Hackensack, NJ 07601
UK office: 57 Shelton Street, Covent Garden, London WC2H 9HE

British Library Cataloguing-in-Publication Data
A catalogue record for this book is available from the British Library.

CHICAGO FUNDAMENTALISM
Ideology and Methodology in Economics

ISBN-13 978-981-281-199-8
ISBN-10 981-281-199-0

Typeset by Stallion Press
Email: enquiries@stallionpress.com

Printed in Singapore by B & JO Enterprise

To Emily and Nicola who keep me grounded in the here and now;
and to Donna who inspires me to do more

Foreword

A Touch of the Billy Joels

Sing us a song, you're the ***piano man***
Sing us a song tonight
Well, we're all in the mood for a melody
And you've got us feelin alright
(*Piano Man* — Billy Joel)

It is hard to be straight faced when justifying an edited volume of one's own work. Most reasonable people would be quick to label it as some type of minor ego trip or at least one's own fanzine. Of course there is no reason that an author should feel the necessity for bringing out one's greatest hits. The usual excuse for this small plunge into self-indulgence is that many of the papers appeared in out-of-the-way, hard to find journals.[1] (To which vigilant critics will undoubtedly add, '... and thankfully so.') Certainly if ageing rock stars can do so, there is no reason for

[1] Most of these articles were submitted to specific journals by request. These did not represent placements defined by desperation. Thus it should hardly come as a surprise that a number of these articles appeared in the Australian journal dedicated to the History of Thought field. In any case, just to utter the categories 'History of Thought' or 'Methodology' makes it unnecessary to add the phrase 'not widely read journals'. This is practically definitional. Yet some of the places of publication will appear obscure even given the standards of the field.

ageing academics not to follow suit.[2] As an economist, I always have the market to serve as my convenient prop and rationale. *Let the market decide.* Publication will decide whether or not there is any demand for a collection of pieces that could be dismissed as mere history of thought and methodological pieces. Most economists caught up in current explorations where history seldom extends back for more than five years and reflection is something to be cured with sunglasses will look askance at so many articles given over to a decided backwater of the trade. Essentially these are viewed as the efforts of hobby farmers trying to catch the attention of the real thing. Given this understanding, such a volume represents only the author's thick skin and audacity.

I would hope though there is more here than a self-satisfied piano riff. If nothing else, I wanted to demonstrate to myself that I haven't been writing the same paper over and over again for more than a decade. Despite the temptation when compiling this volume, this collection is not just a series of pieces chosen at random from my past work. These represent the development of my thought over a number of years with the earliest piece being from 1992 and the most recent done this very year (2007). Forced to re-read the entirety of this work ('that was clever of me'; 'what could I have been thinking') a limited number of clear themes show up.[3] This implies that reading this book (and especially reading it in the selected order) makes it clear that those willing to embark on the journey are not being forced to take a random walk through unconnected pieces. The one underlying message to the discipline as a whole is more of a plea to learn to read which implies analyzing and thinking about what one usually only processes in the most superficial of manners. The plea is to take work seriously and to probe for the meaning within any piece. This

[2] Like so many 'Best of' albums, they are simply compilations of unrelated bits and pieces recycled in the hopes of squeezing out the last drops of glory from the dregs of properly forgotten work. Yet I have tried not to give in to the siren song represented by this encroaching debility that could be rightly labelled as succumbing to a touch of the 'Billy Joels'.

[3] What also unfortunately appears is some clumsy sentence construction and strained grammar. I have used this opportunity to correct faults that previously escaped my earlier editing efforts.

means rejecting oral traditions and lies our teachers told us. It is possible to get to the heart of any article if we don't start with preconceived ideas and read only to confirm our own prejudices.

The broader conclusion is that such advice doesn't only apply to those toiling in the backwaters of the profession. Even the most technologically narrow investigators need to approach their material with as fresh an attitude as possible. The greatest and most common sin to which economists fall prey is to know the results of their endeavours from the very beginning of their analysis. This creates a strong sub-theme evident in the rest of the work. Namely, one of the over-riding reasons for such ostensibly inexcusable behaviour. Ideology, as the volume's title reveals, is the other major concern that has obsessed my writing. The dangers of letting one's desires dictate one's results should be obvious. The corruption of the necessary separation of Church and State in the profession can only undermine the work of the profession itself. Economics in that case is reduced to rhetoric in aid of a preconceived objective.

To demonstrate these ideological pitfalls I look at the work of two of the great zealots of the trade, George Stigler and Milton Friedman. Two better economists would be hard to find. Yet their purpose exceeded that of simply discovering economic insights through more finer-honed analysis. They fought a greater battle, a struggle pitting darkness against light. But to do so they traduced the very underlying precepts of their profession as so many have done before. They are chosen not because they are an exception in resorting to ideological imperatives but rather because their great skill and economic intuition meant that they had greater and more long lasting impact on economic thought than their contemporaries or successors.

My hope then is that those who are strong hearted enough to work their way through this volume will come away a bit more thoughtful of what they do and what they say. If so, then my modest contribution to economics will not be without success. In closing let me just give deserved credit to Donna Joseph without whom this result would not have been possible.

Craig Freedman
December 2007

Acknowledgements

The editor and publisher would like to thank the following publishers who have kindly given permission for the use of copyrighted material.

The Economic History Network for the article: *A Review of Friedman–Stigler Correspondence. EH. Net*, 2006, September, http://eh.net/bookreview/library/1118.shtml

Heldref Publications for the article: *George Stigler as a Dissertation Supervisor.* **The Journal of Economic Education**, 2003, 34(3): 282–291.

History of Economic Theory Society of Australia for the articles: *Power without Glory — George Stigler's Market Leviathan.* **History of Economics Review**, 2005, 41 (Winter):19–48.*Countervailing Egos — Galbraith versus Stigler.* **History of Economics Review**, 1998, No 27(Winter), pp. 50–75. *Not for Love nor Money: Milton Friedman's Counter-Revolution.* **History of Economics Review**, 2006, 42 (Summer): 87–119. *When Truth is Not Beauty, Nor Beauty Truth — A Review Article of* **Econ Art** *by Rick Szostak.* **History of Economics Review**, 2001, 33 (Winter): 96–101. *Court Jesters, House Gadflies and Economic Critics.*

Istituti Editoriali e Poligrafici Internazionali for the article: *De Mortuis Nil Nisi Bonum — Milton Friedman, 1912–2006.* **History of Economic Ideas**, 2007, 15(2): 33–51.

Institut de Sciences Mathématiques et Economiques Appliquées for the article: *Shunning The Frumious Bandersnatch — An Unacknowledged Assumption of Coase's Theorem.* **Economie Appliqueè**, 1993, Vol. 46:2, pp. 81–100.

Macmillan Publishing for the article: *George Stigler.* In Darrity, William A. (ed.) **International Encyclopedia of the Social Sciences, 2nd Edition.** Farmington Hills, Michigan: Macmillan Reference USA, forthcoming.

Oxford University Press for the article: *In Defence of Footnotes — A clarification of A Misunderstanding of Keynes's Definition of Money.* **The Cambridge Journal of Economics**, 1993, 17(2): 241–244.

Southern Cross University for the article: *Economic Convictions and Prior Beliefs: Akerlof Wrestles with the Ghost of John Maynard Keynes.* **The Journal of Economic and Social Policy**, 2000, 4(2): 71–87.

Taylor & Francis Group for the articles: *Was George Stigler Adam Smith's Best Friend? Studying the History of Economic Thought.* **The Journal of History of Economic Thought**, 2007, 29(2): 213–228. *Why Economists Can't Read*, **Methodus [The Journal of Economic Methodology]**. 1993, Vol. 5:1, pp. 6–23. *Animal Spirits in His Soup: A Look at the Methodology and Rhetoric of The General Theory.* **The Journal of Economic Methodology, 1995,** Vol. 2:1, pp. 79–104.

Contents

Foreword: A Touch of the Billy Joels vii

Acknowledgements xi

Chapter 1 And Only I Was Left to Tell the Tale: Blindness as an Act of Will 1

Part I. Resurrecting the Chicago Revolution: The Cold War and the Economics Profession 19

A. George Stigler 20

Chapter 2 George Joseph Stigler (1911–1991) 21
Chapter 3 Power Without Glory — George Stigler's Market Leviathan 25
Chapter 4 Five Easy Pieces — George Stigler's Blueprint for a Counter-Revolution 71
Chapter 5 Countervailing Egos — Stigler versus Galbraith 111
Chapter 6 Was George Stigler Adam Smith's Best Friend? — Studying the History of Economic Thought 157
Chapter 7 Do Great Economists Make Great Teachers? — George Stigler as a Dissertation Supervisor 183

B. Milton Friedman **197**

Chapter 8 De Mortuis Nil Nisi Bonum — Milton Friedman 1912–2006 199

Chapter 9 Entre Nous — A Review of the Friedman–Stigler Correspondence 225

Chapter 10 Not for Love Nor Money: Milton Friedman's Counter-Revolution 231

Part II. Method or Madness — Why Methodology Matters **281**

Chapter 11 Why Economists Can't Read 283

Chapter 12 Shunning the Frumious Bandersnatch: An Unacknowledged Assumption of Coase's Theorem 321

Chapter 13 Animal Spirits in His Soup: A Look at the Methodology and Rhetoric of *The General Theory* 345

Chapter 14 In Defence of Footnotes — A Clarification of a Misunderstanding of Keynes's Definition of Money 379

Chapter 15 Economic Convictions and Prior Beliefs: Akerlof Wrestles with the Ghost of John Maynard Keynes 385

Chapter 16 When Truth is Not Beauty, Nor Beauty Truth: A Review of Econ Art — Divorcing Art from Science in Modern Economics 405

Chapter 17 Court Jesters, House Gadflies and Economic Critics 415

Chapter 1

And Only I Was Left to Tell the Tale: Blindness as an Act of Will

Listen to me. You mock my blindness, do you?
But I say that you, with both your eyes, are blind:
You can not see the wretchedness of your life,
Nor in whose house you live, no, nor with whom (Sophocles 1949: 21).

1. Picking Through the Methodological Slagheaps: How Not to be an Economist

Early toilet training in a simplistic view of child development is one of the keys to unlocking the future paths taken by the latter adult version of the much put upon infant. In a vaguely parallel fashion, for the budding academic, learning to read is an equally pivotal moment in moulding any subsequent career endeavours. I am not of course talking about basic literacy. But rather, I am focused on whether or not one is either capable or willing to comprehend what one reads.

By a quite innocent accident I was either favoured by fortune, or forever condemned, by learning to read as an undergraduate. As a result, I am apt to view those who remain unable to perform this essential act of scholarship as residing on the same level as those who have never quite mastered the intricacies of toilet training. It might go without saying that reading in this analytical, comprehensive way should pose no challenge to the typical academic. I cannot of course speak about either all academics or the typical one. My experience restricts me to those that forage within the occasionally barren fields of economics. But what has become increasingly obvious, and more so over the intervening years, is that economists are largely incapable of reading thoughtfully and unwilling to make the effort to do so. Economists cannot read and for the most part are quite self-satisfied with remaining within this state of scholarly illiteracy.

Most academics (not unlike most toilet trained children) are self-obsessed and more interested in telling others what they think than in trying to understand the thoughts of others. In some cases they simply seem incapable of doing so. Instead they find in each work exactly what they need to discover. If for instance they disagree with a given conclusion they will find that it is based on either flawed logic or faulty evidence ignoring all other indications to the contrary. It is not so much a case of conscious dishonesty as of having a priori beliefs determine one's analysis. This for me has always been one of the principal scourges of ideology. By reinforcing prior held convictions it closes off legitimate debate and investigation. Any approach antithetical to a desired conclusion is effectively filtered out.

Given a long standing tendency by economists to happily jumble together analytical and ideological concerns, the composition of this volume ceases to be quite so haphazard. In many ways the two halves actually fit quite closely together despite superficial appearances to the contrary. For both Stigler and Friedman, with eyes fixed on a more overarching target than mere economic theory, the humble objective behind economic analysis tends to be lost in the competitive shuffle to market one's own ideas[1]. If ideology tends to blind eyes and close

[1] Stigler was always aware of the need to market ideas. It was essential to Stigler that he triumph. As pointed out in this volume (Chaps. 3 and 4) more was at stake than a matter of theoretical correctness. At the core of the battle was a struggle between individual freedom and collectivist planning. Thus it was as crucial for George Stigler to convince his audience as it was for any true believing evangelist. Thus yielding on his core belief in competitive markets was simply not a feasible alternative. Like his close friend Milton Friedman, he was loathe to admit to any

minds, it is doubtful that a reader will be able to understand what he or she is reading. Respect for scholarly material becomes exceedingly difficult if the analyst's aim is only to gather support for one's own views and to demolish all viable opposition.

This is where a careful grounding in the history of economic thought can sometimes help an academic climb out of his or her solipsistic prison that is too prevalent in the trade. The approach taken in the history of thought articles reproduced within this volume attempts to demonstrate what meticulous analysis can achieve. In particular, it points to a simple but quite useful methodological approach which emphasizes a deep respect for the written word.

If this book has anything like a unifying theme it is best demonstrated by an early piece (Chap. 11), in which I pointed out that the reason why so much of economics was so poorly written was that economists were unfortunately unable to read. The article posits that no improvement could be expected in a discipline lacking concrete incentives to improve reading skills. In the many years since its publication (1993) an encouraging or noticeable improvement is hard to find. As a result, the articles included here when taken as a whole compose what can be seen as an increasingly desperate plea for economists to bite the proverbial bullet and make the effort to learn how to read. Perhaps each one can be seen as a sort of case study of how one goes about doing so. Each article attempts to reveal what a close and conscientious reading might yield, rewards that would otherwise go missing given more superficial attempts where sentences and meanings are taken out of context.

---

error. Instead, a single-minded repetition of ideas was more conducive to his objective.

> Another aspect of this salesmanship is the heavy use of repetition, perhaps the most powerful of arguments. ... Frank Knight another master of repetition, once replied to this charge in the course of perhaps his ninth repetition of his views in an article on capital theory, by quoting Herbert Spencer, "Only by constant iteration can alien truths be impressed upon reluctant minds." The method serves equally well with alien errors (Stigler 1988: 211–212).

Glancing over the table of contents it might appear that the work is presented in something resembling a logically reverse order. I suspect the ordering decision reflects my inherent doubt as to what level of abiding interest there ever is in work that has a clear methodological tinge[2]. So I reserve these not so much as an after thought but rather as a reflection on the previous history of thought material. Fortuitously, the reader may be drawn in by the preceding pieces to become more curious about the broader issues raised explicitly in these last set of articles. My initial examination of the Chicago counter-revolution (or perhaps counter-reformation) tends to be more coherent with key themes clearly etched through out these explorations. That this is true on rereading the pieces turns out to be something of a revelation to me, rather than a confirmation of some prior intention. Back in 1993 when I first started writing on this strange tribe inhabiting South Chicago I lacked any overarching plan. I stumbled from one small piece to the next until I started to glimpse the deeper connective tissue holding the Chicago enterprise together.

My fascination with the two great post-war Chicago guerrillas, the Don Quixote and Sancho Panza[3] of the Midway, who managed

---

[2] Like most other economists I have a bit of impatience with methodological discussions. A common impulse is to want to go ahead and do economic analysis rather than sit around nattering about how one might go about doing so. Even worse in my estimation is the tendency for such discussions to be overly prescriptive. The focus seems to linger on how economic analysis should be done rather than how such work actually gets done. My suspicion is that such prescriptions are never widely adopted because they are inherently unworkable. A very early example of this didactic tendency shows up in Descartes' *Rules for the Direction of the Mind.* These handy rules remain extremely uncongenial to most human minds. Of course Aristotle's pontifications, though not analytic, are equally unpalatable.

[3] A famous picture reprinted in Stigler's autobiography (1988: after p. 116) makes this comparison obvious. And in many ways their personalities fit as well. Friedman remained the ebullient and practical Panza while the sarcastic and close mouthed Stigler did a remarkable representation of the *knight of the mournful countenance.* This height difference formed the basis for one of Stigler's oft repeated jokes. (Several individuals in fact repeated it to me.)

> I have to tell you a story which probably Steve [George Stigler's son, Stephen Stigler] will tell you, because Steve told it to me. But it has to do

to launch their highly successful counter reformation, evolved quite accidentally and with a great deal of innocence. In the early nineties I became mystified by George Stigler's (1947/1951) inexplicable misreading of Paul Sweezy's (1937) simple 'kinked demand curve' model[4].

My attempt to figure out how such a good economist could get such a straight forward article so wrong succeeded in initiating my interest into the nature of the Chicago School project as well as its strategies and tactics. Over the years I have become increasingly convinced that in the words of that curious phrase left over from the Reagan years, both Stigler and Friedman saw themselves as more than economists. They saw themselves as freedom fighters. This may cause a younger generation of economists to stifle either a giggle or a yawn. But in the cold war era, economics had a moral edge to it. Questions were not limited to their theoretical or even empirical content. Each issue represented a potential battle between the forces of choice and those of collectivism. Or if we reduce them to their Chicago essences,

> with a time — I may be embellishing a little bit because I tell this story all the time and no-one stops me — let's say it's after he got the Nobel Prize [1982] and he is at a black tie dinner down town. The dinner has nothing to do with him, okay. But there he is, the recent Nobel Prize winner, present at this black tie event and so the MC says 'Here we have, in our audience, the recent Nobel Prize winner, George J Stigler, and George, would you please get up and take a bow and just say a few words?' So George gets up, takes a bow and says, 'Ladies and gentlemen, in my 40, 50-odd years of experience as a historian of economic thought, there is one generalization that to me stands out above all others. And that is, that all great economists are tall. To this generalization I only know of two exceptions. Milton Friedman and John Kenneth Galbraith.' (Conversation with Al Harberger, October 1997)

[4] This misrepresentation is extensively analysed in Freedman (1995). This article and a couple of other works demonstrating Stigler's strategic attacks on competing microeconomic models are not included in this volume. The look at the Stigler/Galbraith wars provides a flavour of this type of analysis. However my suspicion is that including more than a representative work would tend to distract from the main flow of argument that runs through these Chicago School articles.

economics became a battle zone representing an archetypal struggle between good and evil[5].

This is the tie in between ideology and methodology demonstrated consistently by this particular collection. A priori beliefs support a practically unconscious unwillingness to read, evaluate and understand sharply opposing views. The battle transcends theoretical issues or even the egocentric need to be right. With policy issues suggesting differences in fundamental values, among the first casualties is a concern for performing a painstaking analysis of economic literature. What we find is what we need to discover. This is illustrated by the approach consistently adopted by both Friedman and Stigler.

The result can be seen in the somewhat peculiar tactics adopted by these two eminent economists. As analysed in Chap. 6, Stigler proved ready and willing to dump the History of Economic Thought from the curriculum required for graduate students. Coming in the seventies this represented a body blow from which the field never fully recovered. This was a curious strategic decision since Stigler himself had long been a leading light in this pursuit and had produced a quite interesting dissertation under the legendary Frank Knight by looking at theories of production and distribution from a historical perspective[6]. The reason for

---

[5] The reflection of this Cold War attitude extended to those they were willing to promote and those who they were eager to defend. If the records were to be examined there was a remarkable correlation between work that they supported and the political views of the individual researchers. Not of course without exception but too high to be purely coincidental.

> They defended each other. Now, Aaron Director, for example, would never have written a good letter of recommendation for somebody who wasn't a staunch conservative, neither would Milton (Conversation with Paul Samuelson October 1977).

[6] George Stigler as noted in the included article "Do Great Researchers Make Great Teachers?", was one of the very few students who managed to survive doing a dissertation with Frank Knight. It is interesting to note that like Knight, Stigler himself attracted only a limited number of students. His insistence on treating graduate students the same as experienced academics made him a formidable figure. Even veteran economists were leery about running foul of that acerbic

abandoning this graduate requirement becomes clearer when Stigler points out that intensive study in this area risks having graduate students who are willing to consider too many sides of any given issue[7]. What he wished to produce are economists strongly wedded to a correct market vision of the world. His life long marketing tactic was to push a point as far as it could go and then to simply repeat it without alteration.

> You want to push it until it gets right up against a wall. So you want to push it everywhere and in every way, shape or form. That's the loyalty oath that you take to your profession. I don't think a lot of Economists do it. They don't have that sort of loyalty. You've got to take your ideas as far as you can. You've got to push them until they fail (Conversation with Sherwin Rosen, October 1997).

---

tongue. He could reduce grown men to tears and destroy them with a few well chosen words.

> Well, he was very intimidating in his critical approach. Your biggest fear was that he would make a joke at your expense. So one was always somewhat on guard (Conversation with Sherwin Rosen October 1997).

[7] History of Thought remained something of a guilty pleasure for George Stigler throughout his career. As always Milton Friedman was more direct in dismissing such study out of hand. History of Thought was essentially a hobby undertaken by economists to fill in slack periods of research.

> No, they just lost their productivity. I'm saying that there is sort of a balance wheel here. That if there are exciting things being done in a theory, an interesting and exciting thing to do with the structure of the body of economics, that's what will attract the top young economists. And then they'll be drawn away from the history of economic thought or similar such fields. On the other hand, if it's a dry period, so far as really adding to the structure of economic thought is concerned, then that's why, all of a sudden, everybody is interested in such things as the background of Stigler of Keynes, of Samuelson (Conversation with Milton Friedman, October 1977).

In fact, Stigler except for some exceptional cases seemed unwilling to tackle critics head on. Instead he favoured a strategic and devastating strike followed by silence or a glib put down[8].

> I don't know whether his first lecture [LSE in 1948] was half an hour or something like that and then he left. He also never answered criticism. I never understood that. That's just alien to my nature (Conversation with Paul Samuelson, October 1997).

It is thus hardly surprising that both Stigler and Friedman took the marketing of their theories and approaches to new heights[9]. Economics became a clearly adversarial game with a winner-take-all approach. It should come as no surprise then that economic history and statistical analysis degenerate into mere rhetorical tools given such a strategic stance. They exist to be used, to be rearranged in a

---

[8] An exception proved to be Gardiner Means. This was more the case of two similarly constituted combatants who couldn't let a dispute between them die a natural death. Both had strong *a priori* beliefs rooted in their own past experiences. Given their polemical bents and objectives, neither facts nor arguments were likely to sway them. In the never ending argument over administered prices, Stigler would always see market forces dictating prices while Means could only discern price setting in all major economic sectors.

[9] It might be legitimately claimed that one of the long lasting contributions that Friedman and Stigler made to the discipline was their emphasis on marketing their ideas as strongly as possible. Whether this adversarial approach was an unalloyed benefit is an issue that could be intensely debated.

> George Stigler, I remember when I was a young person, wired and said 'Selling is very important in your research. So write better. Work on writing because that is important. You've got to sell what you are doing. I think he's exactly right. You've got to sell what you are doing. It may be that in the long run good ideas do surface but they surface faster, if written in a persuasive fashion. Moreover, bad ideas may be put persuasively. And they may gain the necessary threshold. However, taking that same analogy in competition among ideas, there is a presumption, although not a certainty, that in the longer run, the good ideas are going to compete out the bad ideas. But that may take a long time and may not even always operate. There's nothing necessary about that. Nothing guaranteed about that (Conversation with Gary Becker October 1997).

manner that yields a desired result. What becomes clear in these pieces is that neither Stigler nor Friedman seemed consciously aware of what they were doing. Friedman (in the included review) tried to vanquish Keynes[10] by simply dismissing the importance of his work. Relegating him to the ranks of a minor Marshallian quantity theorist could achieve Friedman's objective without simultaneously elevating Keynes' work by taking it too seriously. Strategically this involved finding in *The General Theory* and his other writing on monetary theory, exactly the ideas that would support his claim. Friedman's obsession with 'liquidity traps' allowed him to see Keynes' originality as no more than performing a minor twist on mainstream theory.

This is in fact the point made in two of the earliest works published in the second or methodology section of this volume. The idea that somehow cash and money are synonymous in *The General Theory* is part of an oral tradition that was simply repeated in the post-war period, eventually finding its way into textbooks for decades. Despite being clearly erroneous, such blatant mistakes proved impossible to correct no matter how clearly they were demonstrated (nor for that matter, despite the greater usefulness of Keynes's actual construction). Corrections were simply politely ignored. Such simplicities are perpetuated due to the nature of the discipline. Though erroneous they are usually models that are easy to teach and easy to test. In lectures and more informally these commonplaces are replicated by each succeeding generation. They only seem to die through prolonged disinterest. A Stigler-inspired version of the kinked demand curve could be reproduced for decades in textbooks until finally killed off by professional ennui alone.

These are not entirely esoteric issues because the inability or refusal to read combined with fierce ideological objectives must eventually leach into the area of policy debates and decisions. Of course the Chicago counter-revolution intended not merely to

---

[10] Friedman's antics are examined at length in an endless review of the Friedman/Patinkin controversy. This ostensibly centred on the issue of a supposed Chicago oral tradition of the thirties. Certainly on Friedman's part the battle involved more than some simple fact finding issue.

change the profession's understanding of how the world worked but to change the nature of the world itself. Despite protestations, especially by Stigler, the point the Chicago stalwarts intended to make was not just that Keynesian macroeconomics or non-equilibrium economics were wrong, but that they were dangerous. Chicago's consistent failure to separate Church from State is what remains most dangerous. As displayed throughout these pieces, the discipline itself is undermined when economists decide that the objective of their profession is not so much to achieve understanding but rather to provide the foundations for pre-ordained theological goals.

2. Nobody Here But Us Chickens: The Unappreciated Importance of Ideology

> Another strong characteristic is the unity of this group who properly felt that they were lone voices crying in the wilderness. And that most of the profession was against them (Conversation with Paul Samuelson October 1997).

In examining ideology it is surprising how many economists seem deliberately blind to its influence and presence. (This might be labelled a 'no one here but us scientists' approach.) Perhaps in the case of Milton Friedman the polemical nature of much of his work is too obvious even for economists to ignore.

> And he [George Stigler], on more than one occasion asked me the question — he never gave the answer himself and I never knew how to answer the question myself — 'Did I think that Milton Friedman would be remembered most for his polemics on policy or his scientific work on things like the consumption function?' He never gave the answer himself and I didn't know what the answer to that question was. I still don't know what the answer to that question is, but he obviously thought about this issue. This was an issue in his view and I would have to infer from his own behavior that he was of the opinion regarding his good friend and respected colleague, that Milton's scientific work would be the hallmark by which he was most remembered. But that remains to be seen (Conversation with Harold Demsetz October 1997).

Certainly this tendency was noted by such erstwhile colleagues as Harry Johnson and Don Patinkin. Clearly they realised how Friedman strategically arranged his data and arguments to arrive with just the conclusions he desired.

> [Friedman] has frequently trapped and sandbagged critics of reputation and integrity by the technique of under-disclosure of analysis and evidence and apparent overstatements of the strength of his results (Johnson quoted in Leeson 2003: 261).

His many public appearances made it clear just where his ideological tendencies lay. (The point is not whether those *a priori* beliefs were good or bad but the influence that they exerted.)

Another story must be told when George Stigler's work is examined. In this case, economists whose memory extends far enough back to have some familiarity with his work ingenuously take Stigler's output at face value. Stigler clearly announces that ideology has no significant effect on economic theory. For many economists that is simply the end of the story. They seem happy to swallow such an announcement whole. By doing so, they fail to grasp the essence of the Chicago approach. Namely, economists must look to actual behaviour and actions rather than to specific pronouncements.

> There is this definite bias in Economics. You see what people *do,* not what they say. Because, you can never competently judge their motives, or what is in it for them [laughs]. You've got to study their behaviour, pure and simple (Conversation with Sherwin Rosen, October 1997).

The willingness however to believe that Stigler rose above the ideological frays of the Cold War period, lies in the fact of Stigler's integrity, subtlety of approach and refusal to seek the limelight. This is in stark contrast with the extroverted strategy embraced by Milton Friedman. However, as Milton Friedman himself points out in his own venture into methodology (the land of 'as if'), what people do is more important than what they say. Or in the classic phrase of economics, 'talk is cheap'. Clearly for both

Milton Friedman and George Stigler more than just economic theory was at stake.

> MF [Milton Friedman]: There's no problem. It's true, that George did want to change things.
>
> AD [Aaron Director]: But he preferred to study them, not to change them.
>
> MF: He preferred to say that he preferred to study them.
>
> AD: He preferred to study them. I should quit this argument.
>
> MF: It was partly a long-running difference between him and me.
>
> AD: You're right.
>
> MF: And he liked to stress, "I just want to understand the world and Milton wants to change it."
>
> AD: That's right. And predominantly I think that George was correct.
>
> RF [Rose Friedman]: You would have to have them both psycho-analyzed.
>
> AD: Yes. That's right.
>
> RF: Or hypnotized.
>
> MF: Added to that, well a lot of George's attitude came from Aaron. I think you had a lot of influence on what he said.
>
> AD: I don't think so.
>
> MF: Between you and me, you were more influential. But of course, you know, people get into patterns of what they say and it doesn't always correspond to what they do.
>
> AD: Yes (Conversation with Milton Friedman, Rose Friedman and Aaron Director August 1997).

But this is exactly the problem that is noted at length in the methodology section of this volume. Economists tend to take a superficial, if not naïve, attitude to complex articles. They are not inclined to dig deeper to unearth not only what authors are saying but why they are staking out certain positions. Economists lack the ability to read because there are few incentives that would make the effort worthwhile.

Instead of looking at Stigler's work as a whole, including the times in which he operated, these economists are willing to pick out just a few influential works and evaluate them in isolation.

What these innocents avoid is the Don Quixote aspect of much of his work. As has been so accurately stated, his lifelong goal was clearly to protect neoclassical price theory from being ravaged by any crude barbarian pretenders.

> Much of his work centered around saving the damsel in distress, neoclassicism, from her attackers: hence his work on the economics of information and his enthusiasm for the Coase theorem (Friedland 1993: 780).

This campaign had a two pronged approach. The positive aspect increasingly demonstrated a unified approach based on perfect competition (or as Melvin Reder (1982) notes in his perceptive piece, an unquestioning acceptance of a tight prior equilibrium[11]). Bits inherited from his teachers, such as theories of monopoly, tended to fall away. His break with Frank Knight became inevitable as Stigler gauged the reach of basic price theory to extend indefinitely.

> His views did become more consistent. I agree with you on that. Other people may not think so, but I think definitely that was true. He began to re-think some positions he had just inherited. Inherited you know, from his teachers and so on, or from the literature and he put it in a more consistent framework (Conversation with Gary Becker October 1997).

---

[11] Reder defines the Chicago approach focused on a Tight Prior Equilibrium as entailing the following procrustean operation:

> Any appropriate inconsistency of empirical findings with implications for the theory, or report of behaviour not implied by the theory, is interpreted as anomalous and requiring one of the following actions: (i) re-examination of the data to reverse the anomalous finding; (ii) redefinition and/or augmentation of the variable in the model, particularly the permissible objects of choice and the resource constraints; (iii) alteration of the theory to accommodate behaviour inconsistent with the postulates of rationality (constrained optimization) by one or more decision makers (resource owners); (iv) placing the finding on the research agenda as a researchable anomaly (Reder 1982: 13).

The other aspect of Stigler's work has an almost Grand Inquisitor characteristic. His ability to sniff out dangerous microeconomic heresies remains unrivalled. Notice that he only conducted his demolition derbies against those approaches that didn't implode quickly under their own theoretical inconsistencies. As demonstrated in his long running battle with John Kenneth Galbraith, the aim was total annihilation not reasoned debate. There simply could not be anything of value in the approaches adopted by Galbraith or others.

> MF: I don't think you're getting at any thing that is really specifically George Stigler. I think you're getting at something that is (a) the atmosphere at Chicago, and (b) intensified by Knight. That an academic is concerned not with being diplomatic, not with trying to avoid hurting people's feelings, but an academic is concerned with saying what's right. Telling the truth, or trying to get at it. And if you disagree with somebody you don't say, 'Well, now there may be something in what you say."
>
> RF: "You may be right."
>
> MF: You say, "That's a bunch of nonsense."
>
> AD: Exactly. That's not surprising (Conversation with Milton Friedman, Rose Friedman and Aaron Director August 1997).

To take such theory seriously would be to attach undue weight to it. The most efficient approach is inevitably to carefully construct a straw man argument which can be easily torched and destroyed. (This approach is detailed in the "Countervailing Egos" piece describing Stigler's conflagration of John Kenneth Galbraith.)

Given these two approaches characterising Stigler's career, the issue becomes the nature of his objective driving this consistent strategy. Understanding this becomes a two-step process. First, it is of crucial importance to locate the common element ruling Stigler's actions. Second, is to connect this ruling element to a congenial ideological imperative. This approach turns bits and pieces of a career into a coherent and consistent whole. Believing that Stigler was anything other than deliberate and conscious of what he was doing is to sell the man far too short. In a post war generation dominated by giants, he was able, based on the power of his economic intuition, to measure up against any of them.

> He was the smartest man I ever met, without doubt. The best working economist that there ever was. He was just the smartest, the very smartest man. ..... Think about it. How many times did he hit something on the head? It's just unbelievable all the things he managed to do that made a difference (Conversation with Sherwin Rosen, October 1997).

Here we need to revisit his graduate work, particularly his dissertation written under Frank Knight. Stigler more than his mentor was particularly drawn to distribution theories based on marginal productivity. Competitive markets eliminated debates over economic power and thus the ability to divert resources and returns to those exercising some crucial authority. Knight of course dismissed such a simple minded approach insisting that inheritance and fortune played roles of equal importance in matters of distribution.

What is unarguable is that alternative approaches focusing on non-equilibrium or multiple equilibrium outcomes could no longer sustain the same type of claims of either efficiency or equity. Thus those microeconomic alternatives which Stigler sought most strenuously to destroy all shared this common characteristic.

> Evidence of Stigler's attachment to neoclassical price theory is also given by that part of his work mainly critical of the work of others. Price rigidity, administered price inflation, the theory of monopolistic competition, and X-efficiency were prominent targets, and each of them denied the efficacy of the neoclassical analytical framework (Demsetz 1993: 800).

These alternatives in fact could be used to justify government regulated distribution. Stigler clearly was adamantly opposed to income redistribution. He felt that it blunted incentives for individuals to try to better themselves. In fact from a moral standpoint, such intervention encouraged people to degenerate by undermining the need for individual initiative.

> But we are persuaded that an economic system will not help us to move in the right direction unless it grants both opportunity and responsibility

> to the individual: the very uncertainty of our ultimate ethical goals dictates a wide area of individual self-determination. We are not able to supply a blueprint of the ideal life, but we are persuaded that even if it were known it would be ideal only for the person who individually and knowingly and voluntarily accepted it. It is not necessary, however, to know what is best; it is enough to know what is better (Stigler 1949: 8).

This line of thinking becomes apparent in the lectures delivered at the LSE in 1948. (See Chap. 4 in this volume.) What is also clear is having come through the first meeting of the Mt. Pelerin Society in the previous year; he saw such collective approaches and actions as dangerous to the foundations of freedom and liberty. The basic ideology that equated markets with choice and choice with freedom would in the decades that followed insure that all empirical results would favour the marketplace. Cradled in the cold war, Stigler's theoretical and empirical work would always be prefaced by this one unshakeable bit of economic faith. Markets work and the job of the economist was to demonstrate this unswerving faith to the sceptical public. Thus what on observation seemed to pose a problem to this one unarguable truth could be transformed, by the clever economist, into a reaffirmation of that faith.

> TP [Tight Prior Equilibrium] theorists are far less willing than others to accept reports of irrational or inefficient behaviour at face value, including money illusion, and typically seek to discredit or reinterpret such reports so as to protect the basic theory (Reder 1982: 15).

What this motley collection of musings hopes to do is to show the seamy side of fundamentalism when practised by the masters of the trade. The way in which economists can avoid such ideological traps is provided in the methodological articles in the back end of the volume. The one reliable approach that can break through oral traditions, assertions and lies passed on by our respected teachers is to learn to read carefully and critically. To do so is to break free of polemically driven economics where practitioners begin their investigations by knowing their results in advance.

References

Freedman, CF (1995). The economist as mythmaker — Stigler's Kinky transformation. *The Journal of Economic Issues*, 29(1), 175–209.

Johnson, H (2003/1971). The Keynesian revolution and the monetarist counter-revolution. In *Keynes, Chicago and Friedman,* R Leeson (ed.), Vol. 1, pp. 169–182. London: Pickering & Chatto.

Reder, MW (1982). Chicago economics: permanence and change. *Journal of Economic Literature*, 20 (September), 1–38.

Sophocles (1949). *Oedipus Rex.* D Fitts and R Fitzgerald (trans.). New York: Harcourt, Brace & World.

Stigler, GJ (1988). *Memoirs of an Unregulated Economist.* New York: Basic Books.

Stigler, GJ (1949). The economists and equality. In *Five Lectures on Economic Problems*, pp. 1–11. London: Longmans, Green.

Stigler, GJ (1947/1951). The kinky oligopoly demand curve and rigid prices. In *Reading in Price Theory*, KE Boulding and JS George (eds.), pp. 410–439. London: Allen and Unwin.

Sweezy, P (1937). Demand under conditions of oligopoly. *The Journal of Political Economy*, 47(3), 568–573.

Part I

Resurrecting the Chicago Revolution: The Cold War and the Economics Profession

Well, he [George Stigler] was a true believer. He wouldn't like that term. But put that in it because it's true. He was absolutely convinced that he was right. It wasn't a doctrinal battle, it was a battle of fact. I almost said of good and evil (Conversation with James Kindahl, October 1997).

A. George Stigler

Stigler had a knack for asking the right questions but the unfortunate habit of knowing the answers beforehand.

A student once asked me what was "beneath George Stigler's hard, sarcastic exterior." How could I resist answering "A hard, sarcastic interior"? (Friedland, C (1993). On Stigler and "Stiglerisms". *Journal of Political Economy*, 101 (51): 780.)

Chapter 2

George Joseph Stigler (1911–1991)

> As for George's caustic wit, he never let go one of his barbs for the sake of mere oneupmanship. They were always aimed at the target's ideas, not the target himself: even when a workshop speaker asked whether he should deliver his paper standing or seated and George responded, "With a paper like this, under the table would not be inappropriate (Friedland 1993: 781).

The post-war years saw a generation of remarkable economists who managed amongst themselves to remake the economics discipline and profession. Of this group, perhaps none possessed a better economic intuition or a keener economic mind than George Stigler. Though not as much of a public figure as his close colleague and long time friend, Milton Friedman, Stigler did as much, if not more, to form what became known as the Chicago School of Economics. It was at Chicago that Stigler would conduct research that not only gained him a Nobel Prize in 1982, but which ultimately changed the course of economic analysis. He had a rare talent for asking the right questions and putting forth provisional answers which inevitably provoked the profession and caused it to reconsider commonly held truths. At the same time, no economist was more a reflection of the ideological struggles of post-war America than George Stigler.

George Joseph Stigler was born in Seattle in 1911 to immigrant parents. His choice to attend the graduate program at the University of Chicago in 1932 was perhaps his most fateful decision. It was there that he formed a lasting friendship with Milton Friedman as well as becoming acquainted with Aaron Director, a young lecturer in the Department. These two would be among the very few who ever managed to significantly influence Stigler's thinking.

Despite his early and continuing contributions to the History of Economic Thought, his lasting contributions were in the fields of Industrial Organization and Government Regulation, two fields that he essentially helped to form. It is perhaps easiest to understand his life's work by grasping its essential consistency. In some sense he was a self-appointed white knight dedicated to defending the innocent damsel of traditional price theory against all and any attacks. He developed a knack for demonstrating the efficiency of markets despite and against all appearances to the contrary.

His pioneering work in Industrial Organization reinforced the core idea that markets work. Two noted works makes this amply clear. The *Economics of Information* (1961) analyses how markets use available information in the most efficient way. His *Theory of Oligopoly* (1964) essentially concludes that the traditional theories of perfect competition and monopoly could amply handle any issue dealing with market structure. (He would later push this further and eliminate the need for monopoly theory as well, indicating that competitive markets were sufficient to encompass the needs of economic analysis.)

If the first part of his post-war research helped to define the field of Industrial Organization by emphasizing the efficiency of markets, the second half demonstrated the inability of governments to improve outcomes through regulation. *What Can Regulators Regulate? The Case of Electricity* (1962) empirically indicated that government regulation of public utilities made no real difference in cost. What were then unexpected results helped to precipitate research that ultimately led to the deregulatory movement in public policy. In the same way, his analysis of the political market for government regulation, *The Theory of Economic Regulation* (1971), led to new research exploring how politicians operated and how and why government regulation became law. By ascribing narrow self-interest as motivating politicians, Stigler made a major contribution to the expanding field of Public Choice.

His final work on the role of government is perhaps his most controversial. Logically, political markets should resemble economic ones in that they are both under the sway of the test of time. If an existing arrangement is not the most efficient then this should create a situation where economic agents could benefit through improving the status quo. Therefore whatever is, must by definition be efficient. Otherwise it would change. Such an approach follows perfectly from Stigler's lifetime drive to become increasingly more consistent in his analysis. At the end of his career, he surveyed an economic world where competitive markets ruled and provided the only useful analytical key.

Unlike his close friend, Milton Friedman, he deliberately eschewed a public presence. Yet without him providing micro based research, Friedman and his counter-revolution against the forces of Keynesianism and other non-mainstream approaches would have failed to achieve its overwhelming success. George Stigler remained active and at his beloved University of Chicago from 1958 until his untimely death in 1991. He was a scholar of great but cutting wit who had a talent for forming either fierce friendships or lasting animosities. Anything lacking intensity was never his style.

References

Friedland, C (1993). On stigler and stiglerisms. *Journal of Political Economy*, 101(5), 780–783.

Stigler, GJ (1961). The economics of information. *Journal of Political Economy*, 69(2), 213–225.

Stigler, GJ and C Friedland (1962). "What can regulators regulate? The case of electricity". *Journal of Law and Economics*, 5(1), 1–16.

Stigler, GJ (1964). A Theory of Oligopoly. *Journal of Political Economy*, 72(1), 44–61.

Stigler, GJ (1971). The theory of economic regulation. *Bell Journal of Economics and Management Science*, 2(1), 3–21.

Stigler, GJ (1988). *Memoirs of an Unregulated Economist.* New York: Basic Books.

Chapter 3

Power Without Glory — George Stigler's Market Leviathan

> No arts; no letters, no society; and which is worst of all, continual fear and danger of violent death; and the life of man, solitary, poor, nasty, brutish and short. (Hobbes, 1914: 65)

All but the hopelessly naïve or perennially romantic understand that Nobel prizes are not a simple recognition of merit. Often they reflect the result of intense lobbying campaigns (rent seeking in economic terms) coupled with unstated political considerations (if not unsubtle and even blatant ideological concerns). Peace and sometimes literature awards are clearly prizes where such forces are identifiably at play. Even economics, replete with its own cast of rational self-seekers, is quite naturally tarred by the same brush[1]. A principled pillar of the

[1] Potential rewards are both psychological and material. There is international acknowledgment for one's work in a manner limited to a virtual handful of practitioners. As Stigler sardonically comments, 'I concede to Samuelson, nevertheless, that to a scientist educated hands make more melodious applause than ignorant hands, but too often the educated hands seem to be sat upon by educated asses' (1982b: 67). However, this cannot be entirely divorced from more mundane rewards. The type of wider name recognition earned translates into higher fees for appearances, whether as an expert witness or a conference speaker. Stigler himself saw his own rewards rise. It would be an economist of a saint-like disposition dominated by non-monetary objectives who would easily pass up all such offers.

profession like George Stigler, a Nobel laureate himself, campaigned unabashedly (though quite justifiably) on behalf of both Ronald Coase and Gary Becker.

Yet few amongst the far flung tribe of economists would be so petty as to grudge Stigler this particular award, even if the more cynical of us suspect that ideological considerations might have played a role in the actual choice. If the medal is intended to go to those who most influenced and changed the profession itself, then George Stigler would be automatically in the fore front for such honours, even when compared to his own remarkable post-war cohort.

Like many of that generation, Stigler used his rising status in the immediate post-war years to define and impose his vision on economics. He seldom passed up the chance to reinvent his beloved profession, seizing the strategic opportunities provided by an invitation to deliver a keynote address or give a specific set of lectures. A touch of missionary zeal often characterised such orations. Thus, his 1964 AEA Presidential address (1982f) to the assembled foot soldiers huddled together on the cold plains of Chicago was a call for all true economists to redeem their professional faith by means of testing, measurement and quantification[2]. Empirical work rather than theoretical faith could provide the one and only true path to salvation. But this ingrained reflex of rallying the troops at opportune moments had

---

[2] His position regarding quantitative methods always contained a whiff of the contradictory. Clearly, economics for Stigler, without empirical testing collapsed into sheer assertion. There is no reason then to cast doubt on his enthusiasm.

> It was just that he was so enthusiastic about quantitative measures. He thought that he was going to change the world ... I was sitting with Aaron Director at the time when he gave his Presidential address and we did look at one another at the time to try to see what each one thought about all of this. (Conversation with Ronald Coase, October 1997)

However, it can be argued whether he took empirical testing seriously, since his empirical results always seemed to verify his *a priori* beliefs.

> So, it doesn't seem altogether consistent ... he knew what the answer was going to be. He just regarded it [empirical evidence], as I say, as a way of persuading other people. (Conversation with Ronald Coase, October 1997)

a long history for George Stigler. A key and too often overlooked instance of this occurred in a series of five compact lectures given at the London School of Economics (1949), home in the past to such luminaries as Robbins and von Hayek. In these lectures, Stigler redefines the nature of economics and illuminates the direction that true faith must take during the post-war period[3]. This revealed credo remained remarkably constant throughout a long and fruitful career. The inner most heart of this vision is defined by a classic, if not austere, liberal philosophy. Stigler was a closet moralist, acting in much the same way as he conceptualised the motives and objectives of his early predecessors. "The desire for better men, rather than for larger national incomes, was a main theme of classical economics" (Stigler, 1949: 4).

Unfortunately, morality, while potentially an admirable quality, can permeate analysis in a less than desirable fashion if transformed into ideological imperatives. Despite his unquestioned skill as an economist and even as an original thinker, his bred in the bone classic liberalism ultimately left Stigler with a distinct blind spot. Not one that turned him into anything resembling a Homeric tragic figure, but perhaps someone more akin to Cervantes' Don Quixote, who needed to hold a few unvarying, if almost intentionally self-deceptive beliefs.

> ...most people will not be persuaded there ever were any knights-errant in the world. Now, sir, because I verily believe, that unless Heaven will work some miracle to convince them that there have been and still are knights-errant, those incredulous persons are too much wedded to their opinion to admit such a belief: I will not now lose time to endeavour to let you see how much you and they are mistaken. (Cervantes, 1993: Part Two 470)

It is this unyielding core, created by an unacknowledged ideology, which implicitly motivated the fierceness of his attacks on market critics.

---

[3] Readers have not noted sufficiently the singular interconnectedness of these lectures. The implicit assumption in their structure is that most of his audience would be returning during the course of the 5 days. These lectures then build on each other to provide a complex vision of economics. They should not be read as separate and complete lectures on quite distinct topics.

Yes, he viewed them as misguided and lacking in any substantial economic logic. But, he chose to dismiss, rather than discuss the issues these critics raised. In this, he was more of a St. Augustine banishing heretical views than a scientist sifting through empirical evidence. To discuss such clearly opposing views could only give them credence. More effective to dismiss out of hand these heretical views and those that formulated them.

Stigler was a true believer in market processes, a belief that was essentially *a priori* and unreachable by either logic or facts[4]. This belief in both the equity and efficiency of markets rested upon something more fundamental than any constrained economic objective. For Stigler, markets maximised freedom, at least freedom defined in terms of economic choice. It did so by removing economic power from the sphere of market decisions. Power, when exercised, limited choice and by doing so constrained liberty. Preserving liberty in the face of a constant threat from organised power required sacrifices, especially a determined resistance to government intervention[5].

---

[4] Let me emphasise that Stigler is not unusual in having ideological motivations, whether hidden or not. Robert Tollison could not resist using Stigler's death as an occasion for writing an obituary strongly imbued with Hegelian *End of History* overtones.

> Rational choice theory can explain politics in a predictable fashion. This was Stigler's lesson. Many have yet to learn it, but they will. All the voices to the contrary do not have the power to stop the onslaught of modern economic research which is pushing this paradigm further along each working day. We have probably come to the end of the history of economic thought. (Tollison, 1992: iv).

This is over the top, but at least somewhat reminiscent of Stigler's (1982f) 1964 *American Economic Association* presidential address which was not without its own 'Brave New World' flavour. Readers should keep in mind that this fervour does not restrict itself only to more conservative members of the economics profession. Self-styled left wing practitioners can be every bit as strident as their brethren on the right. It is Stigler's skill at demolishing his ideological opponents that sets him apart, rather than his pronounced adversarial approach to economics.

[5] It is always difficult to know when and to what degree Stigler resorts to tongue in cheek statements, in part to insure a response from his opponents. He thrived on controversy but shriveled when ignored. In a 1963 debate with Paul Samuelson, he fiercely markets his views by setting out the strongest aspect of any given one of his

Stigler viewed markets as providing a Hobbesian[6] bargain that could protect individuals from societal excesses, namely a misuse of economic power. In this sense, a compact is formed between the market as an institution and those individuals that compose that market. Individuals cede all economic power to the market and instead respond passively to market signals. They do so to avoid becoming a victim of unjustly applied economic power. Distribution then is no longer based on degrees of economic power but rather one's contribution to the economy. Given this perspective, marginal productivity theory, as developed since the time of JB Clark onwards, represents the objective solution to the age-old problem of distribution. Ricardo was amongst the first to raise the distributive issue of economic power when he focused on the question of which group retained property rights to key input factors. Clark's formulation essentially renders that question meaningless. Market forces determine outcomes and individuals respond to, instead of shaping, those issues. Rewards reflect individual efforts, leaving any fault residing firmly with the individual rather than with the governance system itself.

> ... it is of the essence of the good society that it permits individuals to behave as they wish provided they bear the consequences of their actions. (Stigler, 1949: 10)

---

positions. The context of course is the polarised presidential race of that year which reintroduced an ideological slant to debate. This slant, after the McCarthy era, had become more muted. Stigler's statements recall Goldwater's famous acceptance speech at that year's Republican convention (Extremism in the pursuit of liberty is no vice; moderation in defense of freedom is no virtue). Market inequities become the price one needs to pay for eternal vigilance.

To gain a feel for the dynamic tension between Stigler's classical liberalism and the increase and centralisation of state power in the post-war period read his defining essay 'The Economists and Equality', where he quotes de Tocqueville approvingly:

> Every central power, which follows its natural tendencies, courts and encourages the principle of equality: for equality singularly facilitates, extends, and secures the influence of a central power. (de Tocqueville quoted in Stigler, 1949: 11)

[6] For Hobbes, individuals cede political power to a monarch to protect themselves from the uncertainties and iniquities of power exercised capriciously by private individuals, the anarchic rule of nature.

Given Stigler's acolyte-like vision of liberty and the concomitant sacrifices due and demanded for its defence, any attacks that potentially undermined the legitimacy of this market compact required a response perhaps more frequently seen in the realm of knight errantry than in the more placid back alleys of academe. He was loath to admit error or back down from a deeply held position no matter how indefensible.

> But I think that he [Schumpeter] believed you go down in history books for what your ideas are. You don't admit a mistake, let's go down with all flags flying. And there was something of that, I think, in George. (Conversation with Paul Samuelson, October 1997)

His fiercest battles with Sweezy, Galbraith, Means, Chamberlin or Leibenstein, though superficially unrelated to one another, share this one common trait. Acceptance of any one of their positions would open up economics to debates that focused on economic power, exactly the type of debates which George Stigler deemed he had helped banish permanently to the nether world of economic reasoning. In the moral world inhabited by Stigler, this Grendel-like monster of greed and passion had to be forcefully chained to allow individuals the dignity of their own choice. Ever vigilant to prevent potential professional validation of theories embodying economic power, no quarter could be given to any opponent of the truth, omnipotence and inevitability of market forces. In practical terms, Stigler envisioned the potential for using a hypothesised existence of economic power to justify various forms of governmental intervention. In essence, any threat posed by the chimera of economic power would allow the forces of social engineering to substitute effective governmental power as a necessary countervailing force. At the very least, liberty would be heavily constrained with the growth of government bringing with it a list of expected ills:

> ... for those of us who believe that the result of this growth [in government] has been a large reduction in aggregate output, quite possibly with a deterioration in the moral quality of society. (Stigler, 1986: 337)

Only when George Stigler's long dormant ideology is revealed can a full understanding of his critical work commence[7]. Stigler is of course not unique in opting for such an ideological, winner-takes-all approach. Economists on all sides of any issue and particularly some of those who constituted his chief opponents tended to be similarly constrained. Stigler however was more skilled than most at conducting crusades and noticeably more successful. Ultimately his biggest conquest might have become his own objectivity as an economist. For these reasons alone, Stigler's almost forgotten battles deserve to be rediscovered. But before such evidence is provided I will need to sketch out briefly the long-running debate over economic power and distribution which Stigler was so keen to inter. This necessitates revisiting the often-debated economic framework so meticulously constructed by David Ricardo.

1. Ricardo's Wrong Track — Distribution and Power

> Political Economy you think is an enquiry into the nature and causes of wealth — I think it should be called an enquiry into the laws which determine the division of the produce of industry amongst the classes who concur in its formation. No law can be laid down respecting quantity, but a tolerably correct one can be laid down respecting proportions. Every day I am more satisfied that the former enquiry is vain and delusive and the latter only the true object of the science. (Ricardo quoted in Keynes, 1964: 4)

[7] Based on his unyielding ideological stance, McCloskey refers to Stigler as a Marxist, '...George Stigler, America's leading vulgar Marxist economist' (McCloskey, 1997: 361). It might be more accurate to designate him as a Stalinist for the sort of market fundamentalism he displays. Crude Marxists prefer to reduce the world to an economic rationale. Everything else can be dismissed as mere superstructure which simply reflects the underlying forces of production of any economy. In a not dissimilar way, all explanations for Stigler reduce to one of market forces. Just as an ideologically committed Marxist knows the answer to any question before commencing an investigation, so too did George Stigler. I suspect McCloskey used the Marxist term to describe Stigler, not only because of its accuracy in characterising an aspect of his scientific approach, but also because she is confident such a designation would have irked Stigler.

Distribution, rather than the Smithian problem of economic growth, dominated much of 19th century economics, but lingered on as only a partially recognised subtext in the 20th century. The inevitable link between distribution and economic power goes back at least as far as Ricardo. It is not far fetched to see Ricardo's concerns as a misguided focus that shunted economic analysis on to a rather unprofitable spur line[8]. His equally committed opponents largely responded to these distributional issues by diligently providing an efficiency rationalisation for any existing state of market outcomes. Starting then with Ricardo, the battle lines were drawn. The marginalist revolution, particularly the triumph of marginal productivity theory during the 1890s, finally succeeded in substituting market efficiency as the core explanation for distributive outcomes. But, while the Ricardian tradition emphasising economic power subsequently weakened within the profession, it did so without completely losing hold of the public imagination. It seemingly survived deliberate attempts to push this approach to the very fringes of the economic profession.

1.1. *Explaining rent*

> But in different stages of society, the proportions of the whole produce of the earth which will be allotted to each of these classes, under the names of rent, profit, and wages, will be essentially different ... To determine the laws which regulate this distribution is the principal problem in Political Economy. (Ricardo, 1923: 1)

Rent was essentially a windfall return based on controlling some key economic input. In this way, market prices could deviate significantly from more efficient exchange prices, or what Ricardo would call the natural price of a good or service. Under these circumstances, distribution need not be either efficient or equitable depending instead on the historical circumstances surrounding that key resource. Moreover, the key input itself could, and most likely would, change

---

[8] Though by itself an interesting question, it is peripheral to the focus of this paper. In this section, I find it useful to show that this type of debate did occur rather than trying to evaluate whether such an inquiry was or was not productive.

over time[9]. Controlling this economic resource defined the idea of economic power. Given the somewhat arbitrary nature of these distributive outcomes, a justification for countervailing government or public power came readily to hand. The dynamic underlying this controlling input and the analysis it nurtured can be simply grasped in Ricardo's own work.

Ricardo introduces as one of his focal points the concept of a return due to owning a scarce resource. For him the controlling factor in the distributive process was land. The difference between the natural price (or value) of a good and its market price reflected the degree of prevailing economic power. Under this framework, the landlord does no measurable work but receives this difference only to ensure access to his land[10]. The actual value of the corn raised on this land is its embodied labour[11]. For Ricardo, rent does not affect the value of a good. However, it definitely will change any distributive results.

Since land rent enters into the determination of the market price of food, the level of any required rental payments can to a degree determine and thus raise the natural price of labour without necessarily raising the value of the good produced. Profit is squeezed between these two immovable grindstones — wages and rent. Rent will rise

---

[9] What constituted a key resource was soon seen as something of a historical artefact by the time that Alfred Marshall published his definitive text.

> When Mill was growing up, England was still oppressed by the difficulty of obtaining raw produce and this was giving a bias to distribution in favour of those who own land, and against those whose income is derived from labour and who have many mouths to feed ... Since then it has dwindled; but Mill was always haunted by the fears which had oppressed Ricardo and Malthus. (Marshall, 1982: 316)

[10] The amount of rent depends on the fertility of land. The least productive or marginal piece of land receives no rent at all. In this case, the market price of any such produce equals its value. Since the value of the output is lower on the more fertile land, price and value must diverge.

[11] Ricardo adjusts this simple idea of embodied labour for differences in factor intensities, depreciation of capital and roundaboutness of production. None of this effects the basic ideas presented here.

with a growing population as more land is put into cultivation and the productivity of the soil falls. Rising rents translates into rising food prices that in turn cause higher wages and falling profits[12].

The landlord receives rent merely as the result of owning a piece of fertile land, the higher the fertility, the higher the rent. Ownership in and of itself affects the fertility of that land and thus the ultimate output not one whit[13]. Further, rent, by squeezing profits, seems to be a spoke in the wheel of accumulation. The solution for Ricardo is not of course the elimination of private property but the removal of land from its position as the key scarce resource by importing tariff free food from abroad.

Ricardian rent, as a return to a scarce resource can easily be generalised to any key input. In each case, payment is not in return for value added (marginal productivity) but simply for access. This viewpoint, in which certain property rights can earn 'something for nothing', can easily be extended to the role of the capitalist as well[14].

---

[12] It is clear for Ricardo that economic power derived from the ownership of key, scarce inputs, not only results in arbitrary and inefficient distribution patterns but taken to an extreme, erodes economic growth.

> ... long before this state of prices (zero profits) has become permanent there would be no motive for accumulation; for no one accumulates but with a view to make his accumulation productive, and it is only when so employed that it operates on profits. (Ricardo, 1923: 72–23)

[13] It might be argued that without the inducement of rent there would be less incentive to improve one's property. Such an analysis would indicate a basic confusion. As long as there is private property, one may reap the benefit of any improvements. These benefits, however, spring from the actual productive use of the land. Rent is the unadorned tribute paid for access to that land. The apparent confusion between the maintenance of property and the amount of rent paid is due to the potential separability between the reward provided strictly for ownership and the fact that the owner can also inhabit other, more productive roles.

[14] This whiff of Ricardian rents continued to persist even when Ricardo's own analysis remained largely a province of genteel historians of economic thought. Keynes saw interest earnings in much the same way as Ricardo saw rent.

> Interest today rewards no genuine sacrifice, any more than does the rent of land. The owner of capital can obtain interest because capital is scarce, just as the owner of land can obtain rent because land is scarce. (Keynes, 1964: 376)

Since Ricardo accepts the three great classes as given, he feels no need to rationalise the rewards each receives. But the exact distribution to these classes that each possibility embodies must ultimately affect the process of accumulation. Capitalists act as the engine of investment. The landed class, by controlling the key scarce resource, in Ricardo's era, interfered with the growth of societal wealth by thwarting the objective of the capitalist class.

However, this analysis is quite consistent with a very different distribution as Ricardo was willing to admit. Capitalists might be much like landlords. Both might be equally dispensed with. Writing to Francis Place he conceded,

> I believe that under such a system (of equality) mankind would increase much faster than it now does, but so would food also. A large proportion of the whole capital of the country would be employed in the production of luxuries, and thus we might go on, even with an increase of capital, without any increased difficulty, till that distant time, which because of its distance, Mr. Malthus says should not damp our ardour. Whether this would be a more happy state of society is another question which it is not now necessary to discuss. (Ricardo, 1973: 50)

Understanding Ricardo's analysis of economic power pinpoints its potential danger. By not feeling obligated to justify the existing distribution amongst the three immutable classes, David Ricardo provided an unintentional point of leverage for critics, reformers and revolutionaries.

1.2. *What the market has wrought let no man rent asunder*

> Labourers have been flattered and persuaded that they produce all. The Ricardo economists maintain that labour is the only source of wealth while others have even denied the right of capitalists to any share of the product. (Read, 1829: 56)

In Ricardo's description of economic forces lay the potential basis for a theory of class conflict and exploitation. There were those who were not slow to recognise this possibility. As presented, the interests of these three classes are always directly or at least indirectly opposed

(Ricardo's inverse relation between wages and profits). The landlord class appears to receive windfalls simply by existing (or more precisely, due to prevailing property rights and the concomitant political structure). Given this groundwork, the egalitarian or Ricardian socialists felt justified in calling for a general redistribution. Since profits are the leavings of wages, what need could there be for any share to go to the owners of capital let alone the landlords?

Ricardo's unintentionally insidious challenge to the economic *status quo* was unlikely to go unanswered. The owners of capital, for example, must also be shown to contribute something if a more radical agenda was not to dominate economic discussion. By accepting this Ricardian type of framework it then becomes insufficient simply to say that capitalists must be given something to induce them to leave go of their money. This would place the owners of capital on the same level with landlords, namely, unable to justify their own existence. The subsequent need to mount a compelling defence initially led to Nassau Senior's abstinence theory (otherwise known as a reward for waiting). Morality now makes its appearance on the opposing side as well, and we madly set sail on a sea defined by virtue and vice. Profit must be received not as the result of mere ownership of capital but as a reward for demonstrating self-control.

These feints and justifications merely form a set of preliminary skirmishes by self-appointed champions on both sides of the issue. The 19th century debate becomes full blown with Mill entering the lists on the side of redistribution. However, the issue by this time has shifted away from the rents earned by landlords to the profits earned by capitalists. Notice that the Ricardian framework still dominates. The issue is whether returns are determined according to some measure of value added or are simply a measure of economic power (ownership).

> If tools, buildings, and materials were the spontaneous gifts of nature, requiring no labour either in order to produce or to appropriate them; and if they were thus bestowed upon mankind in indefinite quantity, and without the possibility of being monopolized; they would still be as useful, as indispensable as they now are; but since they could, like air and the light of the sun, be obtained without cost or sacrifice, they would form no part of

> the expenses of production, and no portion of the produce would be required to be set aside in order to replace the outlay made for these purposes. The whole produce, therefore, after replacing the wages of labour, would be clear profit to the capitalist. (Mill, 1968: 94)

Though the exact basis of indemnification for co-ordinating and overseeing production can be questioned, the nature of the division is clear. One part of profit can be viewed as earned for services rendered. Interest however, in Mill's view, has no justification in the production process itself. Mill was never won over to Senior's waiting game argument. If waiting itself was the chief determinant, misers, French peasants, and hoarders of all hues and scents should expect more than a lumpier mattress from socking away most of their earnings. Mill clearly is making a traditional 19th century distinction between productive and unproductive returns.

Mill's approach, like Ricardo's, provides room to manoeuvre. There can be no logical reason for insisting on a unique distribution as corresponding to some unchanging prototype. Unlike the way that goods are produced, which is rooted in technology, a distribution pattern can mutate with changes in economic power. This must be true since the entirety of profits, according to Mill, are not justifiable. The payment of interest is the result of property relations which likely will vary as societal organisations change. Here lies the potential political danger. A distribution scheme with indeterminate foundations provides an ideal wedge for attacking traditional market capitalism.

> Unlike the laws of production, those of distribution are partly of human institution: since the manner in which wealth is distributed in any society, depends on the statutes or usages therein prevalent. (Mill, 1965: 21)

We should not be surprised to find that the synthesis of these two contrasting strands of British economic thought await only the deft hand and agile wrist of the great ameliorist, Alfred Marshall. The rules of the game by this time had been fairly well laid out. The labour process itself was beyond debate. Analysis of the distribution question had fallen into a predictable ritual. Once it was agreed as to how the pie was currently to be dealt out to the various economic players, the focus shifted to justifying such arrangements and determining how variable they might be. Marshall's major contribution here is a more careful delineation of the economic meaning of profit. In his analysis, a distinct cleavage appears. A trinity transmutes into four discernable classes. Not only land, labour and capital are allotted their shares of total output, but business ability, taken as a separate entity, demands recognition[15].

Entrepreneurs move to centre stage as the motive force behind any industrial system. If only implicitly, a drama filled with Ricardian passive players, has now gained a hero in the historical sense of that word. Marshall unfortunately fails to defuse in any definitive way the issue of economic power that he surreptitiously must confront, if only in his attempts to refute its importance. Given the chance to fudge or make a clear cut statement, Marshall's inborn cautiousness comes to the fore[16].

---

[15] Profits for Marshall cease to be an undifferentiated lump.

> Finally we may regard this supply price of business ability in command of capital as composed of three elements. The first is the supply price of capital; the second is the supply price of business ability and energy; and the third is the supply price of that organization by which the appropriate business ability and the requisite capital are brought together. We have called the price of the first of these three elements interest; we may call the price of the second taken by itself net earnings of management, and that of the second and third, taken together, gross earnings of management. (Marshall, 1961: 313)

[16] Ronald Coase (1994b) has an informative as well as delightful essay on Marshall's childhood. In particular he sketches the role played by his stern father, described by Alfred Marshall himself as exerting an 'extremely severe discipline' (Marshall quoted in Coase, 1994b: 125). Coase characterises this childhood as a partial explanation for Marshall's compulsive shying away from confrontation, for what might be characterised as an intellectual flinch.

> That was Marshall's character, which really wasn't very admirable. But it is understandable. I argue it's the way he was brought up by his father… I mean you can always hear the swish of the birch. (Coase conversation with author, October 1997)

He employs a two-step strategy, starting with a more easily defendable position of economically justifying the entrepreneur. If business ability is now the key resource, and thus the controlling factor, owners of this talent should be expected to exert themselves to insure a continuance of returns. To the extent that rewards are linked to the competitive market process, we escape any variation of the Ricardian windfall profit argument.

Marshall must employ a delicate piece of surgery to remove intact the return to capital from the realm of pure rent. Labelling a return as a rent is inordinately constraining as rents act as a force without a corresponding counter-force. They can be bestowed without requiring an equivalent sacrifice; not unlike an inheritance descending upon the first born. As such, there can be no justification of such arrangements without recourse to the theology of political theory. Positive interest rates and equivalent returns exist because capital is a scarce resource. Capital need not be the focal scarce resource in the Ricardian sense. The issue still arises since it remains a scarce resource that does earn a return. For Marshall, unlike some of his predecessors, capital constrained by these limitations does not grant automatic economic control in the market place. This creates the initial desired distance from Ricardo's insistence on rents paid to core inputs.

> Every attempt to establish this premise [labour theory of value] has necessarily assumed that the service performed by capital is a "free" good, rendered without sacrifice, and therefore needing no interest as a reward to induce its continuance. (Marshall, 1982: 587)

Marshall forces himself to envision a future where the ownership of capital is more dispersed with society inevitably shifting more indisputably into middle class comfort. In an unstoppable manner, old fortunes decay, the working class moves up the ladder with increasing education, frugality, and the acquisition of other commendable beliefs. The interest rate and similar pure returns to capital fall as this habit of restraint becomes more widespread. True to form, Marshall cannot resist the urge to have and eat his cake simultaneously. Interest is justified as a reward for the positive sacrifice of waiting. This promotion links Marshall to a familiar strand of British economic thought. But his own twist attempts to sidestep the inherent distributional disputes by assuming that this share of output, though justified, would steadily become insignificant. In a practical sense, an abstinence effort eventually would go unrewarded but its existence and theoretical validation would not logically disappear. Accepting this premise entirely marginalises economic power as a useful analytic tool.

Moreover, education, better opportunity and a growing economy would eventually "Diminish the toll which has to be paid by the working classes to those who organise the work of the community" (Marshall 1982: 225). Thus, entrepreneurship loses its special quality of a property right, transforming instead into a characteristic that appears with increasing regularity throughout the general public. This is of course Marshall's ultimately egalitarian social solution, a vision of a society composed entirely of the middle class.

We now have seen, via a fast forward tour through the musty attics of the history of economics, that there exists a forged link between seemingly distinct economic frameworks. Stigler's crusades all have this common denominator. They defend against any analysis that undermines a distributive market system based on marginal productivity factor shares. These alternative approaches all share the potential to provide a theoretical foundation for government intervention that can supplant individual choice.

1.3. *Stigler slices the Gordian Knot of economic power*

> What do I care about the law? Hain't I got the power. (Vanderbilt quoted in Josephson, 1934: 72)

In his first substantial work, Stigler looks critically at the triumph of marginal productivity theory which completed the work started in the 1870s by the marginal value revolution. With it comes the solution to the distribution problem in much the same way as the earlier contribution resolved the problem of price. The issue of economic power is not so much addressed as it is banished.

> The branch of economics which was in most urgent need of reformulation was, in fact, distribution. In 1870 there was no *theory* of distribution. Most

> English economists after Smith devoted separate chapters to rent, wages, and profits, but without important exception such chapters were only descriptive of the returns to the three most important social classes of contemporary England. Rent went to the landowners, wages to the labouring masses, and capitalists secured the "profits of stock." This type of analysis may have had its uses in the England of Ricardo and Mill, but its analytical shortcomings are obvious. Extended criticism is unnecessary at this point; the fundamental defect was clearly the failure to develop a theory of prices of productive services. (Stigler, 1941: 2–3)

This claim would not be quite so self-evident to either Ricardo himself or to others of the classical era. On closer reading it turns out that Stigler does not mean simply that Ricardo merely described existing distributions rather than explaining them. The key is that Ricardo never independently determined the basis for each reward rather than having some payment fall out as a simple residual. As shown previously, this implied that distribution seemed to depend on property rights, namely who gained control over the key resource and could extract rents. Such relationships are historical by nature. If then economic power could be exerted, government would have a rationale to limit through its own coercive power the worst of these imbalances. But power, no matter who exerts it, must by definition reduce choice. Limiting choice remained for Stigler the ultimate challenge to freedom and liberty.

This is the miraculous beauty of marginal productivity theory. If by giving each factor its contribution to output, the total product is exhausted, no residual thus remains. Lacking a residual, the exercise of private economic power is impossible. Market competition, under a given set of conditions, almost magically eliminated the core Ricardian problem. In other words, the closer markets resemble the conditions of perfect competition, the nearer one comes to dismissing problems of economic power.

> The completion of the marginal productivity theory of distribution was achieved only with the development of the proof that if all productive agents are rewarded in accord with their marginal products, then the total product will be exactly exhausted This exhaustion-of-product problem is of course unique to the general marginal productivity theory. (Stigler, 1941: 320)

However, as Stigler acknowledges, once the need is granted for an entrepreneur[17], residual payments once again must be introduced into economic analysis.

> Once uncertainly is introduced, the theory of distribution is altered greatly. Anticipations rule economic activity, and many of the anticipations must be erroneous because of the very fact of uncertainty. The entrepreneur becomes a residual claimant, and the exhaustion-of-product problem disappears. Anticipated marginal productivity becomes the basis for remunerating all productive services except entrepreneurship. (Stigler, 1941: 386)

The focus here on uncertainly does represent Knight's influence. Stigler himself would dismiss its importance in less than a decade's time[18]. But even with the entrepreneur's residual payment, it is clearly possible to avoid the Ricardian morass of economic power. The residual increase in productivity is due to entrepreneurial activity. Thus, the return to the entrepreneur has a basis that is not simply dependent on the application of pure property rights. As long as such

---

[17] As Stigler notes, the applicability of Euler's theorem to the distributional exhaustion of output coincides with a disappearance of the entrepreneur in a steady state economy.

> ... under what conditions does the entrepreneurial role disappear? It disappears, we know, in the completely stationary economy, where the stocks (not the rates of supply) of productive resources, the technology, and the tastes are rigorously fixed. In such an economy the same things are always done in the same way by the same men. Everything is reduced to routine; the captains of industry — and their innumerable adjutants — are in Nirvana. (Stigler, 1941: 384)

[18] Friedman and Savage in their 1948 article have a much different take on issues of uncertainly and risk. George Stigler would have accepted his colleague's view in this matter.

> I believe that the only theory of probability that can hold water is personal probability, the kind of thing that Jimmy Savage helped develop. If you take that approach, you can't distinguish uncertainty from risk. There's no break point. (Conversation with Milton Friedman, August 1997).

rewards are open to competitive forces, with residuals unsustainable over time, no threat to individual liberty can derive from private economic activity. The slippery slope that justifies government intervention and the subsequent limitation of choice is effectively salted down. Over the years, explicit concern for the entrepreneurial function would fade. Stigler, along with his colleagues and associates would dramatically push the applicability boundaries of perfect competition theory. The importance of this progression lies not only in its analytical usefulness but in its implicit support of individual choice.

2. Freedom as Choice

> The proximate reasons that the darkly pessimistic predictions of conservatives have not been fulfilled are two. First, the predictions were based on their special view of freedom: Freedom as consisting only of the lack of coercion by the state, so that the widening range of choices due to the growth of income and education is not an effective increase in freedom in Hayek's view, although it is in mine. (Stigler, 1988: 147)

There is more, however, than the mere accumulation of empirical evidence driving Stigler's life long insistence on marginal productivity as the underlying basis for distribution. As pointed out before, such an approach eliminates the vexing issue of economic power. If markets are perfectly competitive, no one is able to influence or more precisely coerce another person's choice. Individuals simply respond to market signals. This is at the heart of Stigler's orthodox liberal beliefs. Freedom, and by extension liberty, for him is defined as freedom of choice. It is not coincidental that his closest friend and colleague would title his most popular book *Free to Choose* (1980).

Contrast the freedom that flows from perfect competition with its alternative. Distribution as envisaged by Ricardo and his descendents depends on economic power. Given the indefiniteness that flows from the strategic employment of this power, governments can rationalise redistributive impositions as creating greater efficiency and/or equity. For Stigler such interventions were no more than the coercive use of state power motivated by rent seeking constituencies[19].

> Income redistribution is the hall-mark of any special interest group: gains in aggregate output will usually be shared with everyone, so the efficient use of political power usually involves income redistribution. (Stigler, 1982b: 63)

In this sense, the debate over marginalist ideas, the defence of the perfectly competitive model, is not a simple matter of economics but strikes at Stigler's core beliefs concerning a dearly bought freedom almost uniquely enjoyed by the American public. (George Stigler's enduring parochialism was hardly a well-kept secret[20].) In an exaggerated sense, these designated opponents to economic orthodoxy represent the thin edge of the wedge leading irresistibly down Hayek's (1944) *Road to Serfdom*[21].

---

[19] Stigler clearly disliked the ideal of income redistribution. This seems to flow from his belief in the ethics of productivity distribution. He agreed that:

> To hurt in any degree the interest of any one order of citizens, for no other purpose but to promote that of some other, is evidently contrary to that justice and equality of treatment which the sovereign owes to all the different orders of his subjects. (Smith quoted in Stigler, 1982e: 11)

[20] This is not particularly remarkable as it can be argued that this is a common American vice, even among academics.

> Another story about George, I've always found it to be a problem, which is how incredibly American he was. I used to be shepherding these Latinos through and here they would come to some question in his Price Theory examination. Explain something, something about the Dred Scott Decision. (Conversation with Arnold Harberger, October 1997)

[21] The idea is one of eternal vigilance. One wrong step takes history down a slippery slope inevitably leading to some form of totalitarianism.

> It might not be a perfect system; nothing was perfect; but what he objected to, was, the insertion of the wedge. Under the Prerogative Office, the country had been glorious. Insert the wedge into the Prerogative Office, and the country would cease to be glorious. He considered it the principle of a gentleman to take things as he found them; and he had no doubt the Prerogative Office would last out time. (Dickens, 1927: 481)

The idea of consumer sovereignty is more accurately seen as a presentation of market sovereignty. All must respond to the dictates of the market which is only the aggregate determination of a multitude of individual choices. In this sense, Stigler's joint paper with Becker (1977) is in its way a striking response to the increasingly critical stance to consumer sovereignty developed by John Kenneth Galbraith amongst others. In this critical approach, successful advertising produced market power by changing existing preferences and developing new ones, specifically those which redistributed income to corporate sellers. If instead, corporations appeal only to existing preferences, trying to convince potential customers that the flow of services provided will match inherent individual preferences, we return to a model where economic participants respond to market dictates. These markets neutrally represent no more than the resultant manifestation of individual choices. The possibility of market power is removed, as well as possible arbitrary redistributions of income due to any associated economic power.

What flows from such a defence of consumer sovereignty is a parallel insistence on a marketplace for ideas[22]. But taking the work of Stigler and Becker as our benchmark, the successful idea, like the successful product, is the one best suited to the existing set of consumers' preferences. Ideas, like other goods, are associated with flows of services and user costs. In this vision, ideas are marketed much like any good or service. Stigler's aim would be to persuade his targeted audience (other economists) that the ideas he presents provides the greatest service flows at the lowest associated user cost. Ideas that dominate

---

[22] Coase (1994) makes a strong case for identifying the market for ideas with the market for goods. He makes the point that the same people who urge a free market in ideas, tend not to support a similar free market in goods and services.

> The bulk of mankind will for the foreseeable future have to devote a considerable fraction of their active lives to economic activity. For these people, freedom of choice as owners of resources in choosing within available and continually changing opportunities, areas of employment, investment, and consumption is fully as important as freedom of discussion and participation in government. (Aaron Director quoted in Coase, 1994: 66)

are those which best appeal to existing consumer preferences[23]. Marketing, particularly selling one's ideas in a winner-takes-all fashion, inevitably must gain the upper hand. But this need not lead to the adoption of the best or even most correct views no matter what the objective measure chosen.

> I remember when I was a young person, George Stigler wired and said Selling is very important in your research. So write better. Work on writing because that is important. You've got to sell what you are doing. I think he's exactly right. You've got to sell what you are doing. It may be that in the long run good ideas do surface but they surface faster, if written in a persuasive fashion. Moreover, bad ideas may be put persuasively. And they may gain the necessary threshold. However, taking that same analogy in competition among ideas, there is a presumption, although not a certainty, that in the longer run, the good ideas are going to compete out the bad ideas. But that may take a long time and may not even always operate. There's nothing necessary about that. Nothing guaranteed about that. (Conversation with Gary Becker, October 1997)

The problem with a hard-sell approach is the need to simplify and not only in such land mark popular works like Milton Friedman's *Free to Choose* (1980). Identifying liberty with commercial choice (or the institution of private property) is at best a sloppy form of analysis and at worst the substitution of ideology for economics.

---

[23] The ideas underlying his 1977 paper with Becker are more clearly spelled out in a less scholarly work published soon after in *Ordo* (1979) and latter reprinted in *The Essence of Stigler* (1986).

> If deception by intellectuals were the motive force of social change, we would expect to observe numerous occasions on which a group of conservatives with large powers of persuasion had captured the public's fancy and succeeded in initiating a regime of declining governmental activity. After all, which socialist philosopher has been as profound as Hayek, which socialist propagandist has been as lucidly logical as Friedman? In fact, intellectuals largely — although not wholly — respond to the demands of their times: like Detroit, they produce to demand, rather than contrive that demand. Indeed, per educated person employed, Detroit may well turn out a larger variety of products. (Stigler, 1986: 340)

Consumers inevitably make choices no matter what the institutional framework, no matter what role government assumes in the economic process.

In the case of George Stigler, this brings us directly to the question of income distribution. He is quite correct in pointing out that discussions of this topic tend to be based on ethical considerations rather than positive economics.

> Such a positive theory would explain how the size distribution of income affected, and was affected by, developments such as rising wealth and education, the roles of taxation and other forms of political action, the institutions of inheritance, and the changing nature of the family. (Stigler, 1982e: 13)

However, it is at this point in any distribution discussion that admirable beliefs in freedom of choice can produce dilemmas. Stigler would have economists be what he sees as scientists, providing positive (non-ideological) analysis. Yet his own work with Becker tries to demonstrate the importance of selling one's ideas. Marketing by its very nature attempts to persuade others that a given flow of services meet fixed preferences rather than directly attempting to alter a set of those pre-existing ones. This inconsistent categorical imperative would have economists rise above their economic motives while ruled by those same every day incentives[24]. Stigler would have them lead in this manner despite granting them precious little impact on public choices. Inasmuch as economists remain scientists they are doomed to be ineffective (at least in Stigler's view). Using this same logic, the

---

[24] We often find Stigler in the strange position of pushing propositions beyond their empirical anchors.

> So he was very much this kind of a person who would say, 'I'll state this result as strongly as I possibly can, even if it's not completely justified by the evidence'. I mean I think at some level he said to himself, 'I'll make the strongest case I can and then see if that stirs people up'. In many ways he was using a bully pulpit that he had acquired from his stature in the profession. He was able to do that. (Conversation with Sam Peltzman, October 1997)

degree to which economists are effective measures the strength of their ideological objectives[25].

> The degree of popularity of a preacher does not necessarily measure his influence as a preacher, let alone as a scholar. In fact one could perhaps argue that unpopular sermons are the more influential — certainly if the opposite is true, and preachers simply confirm their listeners' beliefs, pulpits should be at the rear of congregations, to make clearer who is leading. Whether economic preachers lead or follow, they need an ethical system to guide their recommendations. (Stigler, 1982e: 13)

The need to resolve these fundamental incompatibilities, ultimately leads him to stand ideology on its head and turn assumptions and beliefs into testable hypotheses, an attempt made with varying degrees of success in his Tanner Lectures on Human Values, presented at Harvard University, 24, 25, and 28 April 1980.

> Man is eternally a utility-maximizer, in his home, in his office — be it public or private — in his church, in his scientific work, in short, everywhere... I believe it is a feasible and orthodox scientific problem to ascertain a set of widely and anciently accepted precepts of ethical personal behaviour and to test their correspondence with utility-maximizing behavior for the preponderance of individuals. My confidence that the

[25] The resolution ultimately is to raise the underlying market distribution from the narrow bound of efficiency to the more glamorous realm of equity and justice. With the fairness of marginal productivity theory reduced to a testable hypothesis, scientific objectivity is once again bleached free of any blatant ideological tint. At a more basic level, freedom is successfully defended against the encroaching forces of totalitarianism.

> He very much believed that the role of economists in formulating or moving policy was overstated. More than I do. It's not something I agree with him on. He would always take this very strong position. We were part of what Marx would call the superstructure. Bought by one side or another and we really didn't have an independent role to play in the evaluation of policy. And yet he had this belief that the world should be a certain way. It's clear. You know, he was a believer in markets. He didn't like the sugar subsidy for sure and I don't know how you really square it ultimately, with his position that this is the optimal way to redistribute. (Conversation with Sam Peltzman, October 1997)

> test would yield this result will be disputed by many people of distinction, and that argues all the more for making the test. (Stigler, 1982c: 35–37)

3. The Problem of Ideological Blinders

> The simplest way to test the role of ideology as a nonutility-maximizing goal is to ascertain whether the supporters of such an ideology incur costs in supporting it. If on average and over substantial periods of time we find (say) that the proponents of "small is beautiful" earn less than comparable talents devoted to urging the National Association of Manufacturers to new glories, I will accept the evidence. But first let us see it. (Stigler, 1982c: 35)

Ideology is dangerous in at least two manifestations. In the first, an economist knows the answer he or she desires to find and then puzzles out the most efficient and convincing way to reach that conclusion.

> It seems to me that when you get to his [Stigler's] later work, say with Becker, you know what the conclusion is going to be before you start the argument. In a sense, you're assembling arguments to support a conclusion. I mean that may be unkind and untrue but it's an impression. (Conversation with Ronald Coase, October 1997)

At first glance, the second approach appears to be indistinguishable from the first. Pick up research by a specific author. Given the topic, the reader knows the result beforehand. The only suspense comes from finding out exactly how the author reaches that preordained end. The difference with the first case lies in the degree of consciousness present. The researcher will claim that the facts speak for themselves even though the tune presented is always remarkably similar. Though it was almost inconceivable that George Stigler ever would reach a conclusion that undermined neoclassical theory, he would never deliberately (and consciously) fudge his analysis to reach a given result. He might overstate, or push a conclusion to an unwarranted extent, but this was more due to the need to market than any dishonourable impulse. (Whether marketing an idea in a strong arm manner is or is not dishonourable is quite another question.)

> It's not that he [George Stigler] ignored all the empirical work in making his decisions. He would come across empirical work which was contradictory to other empirical work. Somehow it always seemed to him that the empirical work which favoured his side was done better than the empirical work which didn't. But this is rampant in our profession. (Conversation with James Kindahl, October 1997)

For someone who insisted so strongly that ideology played little if no role in economic analysis, his strongest defence rested not on the revered Adam Smith of *The Wealth of Nations* but on the less congenial (to George Stigler) Adam Smith of *The Moral Sentiments*[26]. Ultimately, a strong sense of professionalism kept economists from degenerating into a morass of partisan arguments that was ideological by both nature and intent[27]. Only this countervailing imperative kept

---

[26] *The Moral Sentiments* moves away from simple self-interested actors and the anonymity of market relations. The role of trust starts to dominate. This though undermines the clean cut price theory supporting George Stigler's view of distribution. It introduces an unwanted element of ambiguity, antithetical to his objective. Throughout his career, George Stigler was at pains to separate decisively Smith's two great works.

> So in lots of ways, George Stigler was very dishonest, I don't know if he realised the extent, in never discussing the relation between these books. He should really have discussed it. It was part of Adam Smith's thought. If you want to understand Adam Smith, you have to try and understand how it is that he left these two books floating and gave you the job of relating them and I think it is very difficult. (Conversation with Mark Blaug, June 1998)
>
> You know my argument [about the relationship of *Wealth of Nations* and *Moral* Sentiments) is the opposite? He was sort of critical of Adam Smith in a way that I didn't think was justified. (Conversation with Ronald Coase, October 1997)

[27] Stigler violated his own narrow assumption of self-interest in his own actions. Not only was he a devoted family man, but he cared deeply about economics and the economics profession itself.

> He very much identified with the profession. He cared whether the profession moved ahead. So much of his work dealt with issues concerning the

economists from being ruled by narrow self-interest. Without such an escape route, it is difficult to imagine how one could analyse a profession composed of self-interested individuals that was not ruled in turn by those self-same passions[28].

Yet his insistence on the absence of ideology contrasts sharply with many of his actions and positions throughout his career[29]. His need to combat what he saw as the forces of collectivism arrayed

---

> profession. If you look at my catalogue, you'll see what I mean. There are a lot of categories under 'Profession'. He cared about the profession. He identified with it. He identified with the University of Chicago. He cared about this. Not just about his own progress. If it was good for the Department, he really cared. If the Department tried to get somebody, whom he thought would be good, he worked on it. If the Department was in danger of losing somebody, whom he felt would be a loss, he cared and he worked on it. He really had this funny identification. (Conversation with Claire Friedland, October 1997)

[28] Stigler had to make this assertion if ultimately market choice was to be defended with any degree of success. His economic arguments could not be distorted by desired ideological outcomes. Yet this role of economist as dispassionate scientist was asserted rather than proved. What evidence there is tends to move in the other direction.

> This is a popular Friedman view too. And it's wrong. I say that flatly. But it's interesting that just recently — I have somewhere a National Bureau Yellow Jacket manuscript of a research study by Richard Fuchs from Stanford University. Jim Poterby from this university, and Allan Krueger of the Woodrow Wilson School at Princeton. They did an extensive sampling of economists working in two areas of economics. Their finding is the opposite of Milton Friedman's. There was a very considerable degree of consensus on factual matters. However what they found was the difference in their policy recommendations were — I'm using your language, not their language — ideologically premised values. They were not fact driven. Now there are a few cases like the minimum wage or Ricardian comparative advantage where you can almost get certain unanimity, free of ideology. But these are exceptions in my opinion. (Conversation with Paul Samuelson 23, October 1997)

[29] As an eminent historian of economic thought he insisted that internal pressures of the profession defined the subjects for study.

> The dominant influence upon the working range of economic theorists is the set of internal values and pressures of the discipline. The subjects for study are posed by the unfolding course of scientific developments. (Stigler, 1965: 22)

against individual liberty brings a certain consistency to the paths he pursued and the strategies chosen to achieve his objectives[30]. That he took ideological stances in less formal arenas seems undeniable. If his statement about the price of freedom in a debate with Paul Samuelson cannot be categorised this way, it is hard to imagine what could.

> My basic answer to this painful problem is: In order to preserve the dignity and freedom of the individual in my society, I shall if I must pay the price of having some fail wholly to meet the challenge of freedom. I find it odd that a society which once a generation will send most of its young men against enemy bullets to defend freedom, will capitulate to a small handful of citizens unequal to its challenge. (Stigler, 1963: 19)

In place of academic exchange (a positive sum game), ideology offers only the adversarial combat of the courtroom (a zero sum game)[31]. No empirical evidence and certainly no logical argument could conceivably

---

[30] There is a strange contradiction lurking in the background here. Stigler's defence of liberty is conditional or at least has priorities. To fight encroaching collectivism, he is willing to see certain liberties curtailed. As Samuelson points out (Conversation with Paul Samuelson, October 1997), Stigler and his closest colleagues were ready to acquiesce to the version of McCarthyism sweeping university campuses in the 1950s (though not to its mirror image attempting to curtail more right wing opinion in the 1960s).

> And I remember for years after I left the University of Chicago, when they were contemplating influential appointments they would ask me about the person, 'Is he really sound?' In fact, Milton once showed his naïveté to me, but it wasn't about appointments. He said, 'Tell me the truth, is Galbraith a Commie?' (Conversation with Paul Samuelson, October 1997)

[31] Stigler (1988: 133–134) makes the convincing point that an economist that goes to Washington loses his credence as an economist. This extends to the role of expert witness. (Though he makes a point in his autobiography of his unwillingness to go to Washington he badly understates his willingness to perform in legal proceedings.)

> Is the expert honest? At very best, probably as honest as is possible in a process in which truth is sought by the vigorous presentations of opposing views, and where any admission by one side is heavily overemphasized by the other side. (Stigler, 1988: 133)

induce either one of these samurai paper warriors to make any but the smallest concessions to the opposing camp.

> Now, what you have to understand with somebody like Allen Wallis, and so to a degree those people who were in his circle [like George Stigler], is that Allen Wallis had the sharpest priors — I'm using the language of Bayesian probability — of anybody I ever knew. Almost no new data could change his view for this reason. (Conversation with Paul Samuelson, October 1997)

With most of his opponents however, Stigler adopted a basic hit and run policy. A devastating attack might then be followed up in an irregular fashion over the years with an occasional offhanded slap, as if chasing away a particularly annoying mosquito[32]. This reflected the level of irritation a given contending theory created as well as the longevity of an opponent's ideas. George Means represented one of the few (if not only) cases where Stigler was forced to hold his fire solely by the refusal of the *American Economic Review*[33]

The problem is Stigler does not either recognise or acknowledge that his adversarial approach to economic theory allows the same court room problems to intrude into academic life.

> For lawyers to write tendentious briefs in an adversarial environment presents few problems; no one expects, or demands, the truth from only one side. But for academics to twist facts, no matter how brilliantly, to fit the preconceived interest of their clients is disturbing. (Weinstein, 1992: 75)

[32] The classic example is an almost guerrilla war conducted against the kinked demand curve, one of Stigler's earliest campaigns and one that established him as a boots and all opponent. After his 1947 paper, he returned to the topic in one form or another. (Interested readers may dive anywhere into his irritated diatribe (1982a) or examine his footnote of scorn (1992: 456) for a good illustration of obsessive behaviour.) Sweezy for his part showed no interest in engaging in this debate. 'I haven't read it (Stigler's 1947 paper on the kinked demand curve). I don't think I ever did. I don't think I was aware of it actually. I didn't pay much attention to Stigler in those days. I was probably in one of my ultra-left moods, or something like that'. (Conversation with Paul Sweezy, October 1997)

[33] More precisely, both Stigler and Means would have carried on indefinitely. However, the then editor of *The American Economic Review*, George Borts, perhaps foreseeing the inherently irreconcilable differences between the two camps, ended the increasingly tendentious debate by offering to commission a third party to evaluate the state of the existing debate.

to continue the debate in print. Neither Stigler nor Means was capable of mounting a convincing attack upon one another since the debate revolved around articles of faith rather than empirically verifiable suppositions. Galbraith, though enjoying a similarly sustained debate with Stigler, developed a different pattern despite its ideological motivation. What at first was an intellectual struggle quickly transformed itself into something approaching a comedy routine; each new Galbraith book finding itself comfortably in range of Stigler's withering wit.

Ideology then continued to play a determining motivation behind George Stigler's work despite his explicit denials to the contrary. No other rationale makes such consistent sense of his critical work[34]. Otherwise the range and intensity of his battles remain merely rooted in his personality. In Stigler's case, the debates of the post-war era remain more revealing than any extensive excavation of his childhood. The exact nature of Stigler's underlying ideology can best be represented by three distinct but interconnected aspects. Taken together they form something of a *Reader's Digest* history of economics in the last half of the 20th century.

4. Stigler and Post-War Economics — The Three Pillars of Wisdom

> Lack of conviction has no inner connection with scientific objectivity. (Max Weber quoted in Stigler, 1941: v)

Never has it been any less than true that the current generation of economists stand on the shoulders of giants, or at least hyperactive

---

[34] I can only quote Stigler to defend my benchmark of consistency and comprehensiveness.

> The test of an interpretation is its consistency with the main analytical conclusions of the system of thought under consideration. If the main conclusions of a man's thought do not survive under one interpretation, and do under another, the latter interpretation must be preferred. (Stigler 1982g: 69)

dwarfs[35]. The remarkable post-war generation set the foundations for a modern discipline of economics as we now know it. The Keynesian revolution initiated a struggle for the very soul of the profession. Though the reaction against the new normative model of macroeconomics is more familiar, the accompanying struggle over the corresponding micro-basis of economic analysis was at least as important. Debate here, starting with the marginalist controversies in the immediate aftermath of the war, focused on the future role to be played by the model of perfect competition. Given the seeming triumph of the Keynesian approach to macroeconomics, a parallel microeconomic revolution focused on some model of imperfect competition seemed inevitable. The failure of this micro-alternative to take firm root led to a disparity between the dominant micro- and macro-paradigms. We can see this as eventually contributing to the micro-foundations debates of the seventies and the years to follow.

The post-war microeconomics debates came to define much of Stigler's approach to economics. Filtered through Stigler these issues formed what could be seen as the three pillars of post-war economics.

- Redistribution (economic power) versus market competition (marginal productivity theory).

> I guess he didn't like redistribution. He feels this down in his gut. That's all I can tell you. (Conversation with Sam Peltzman, October 1997)

This holds the key to understanding Stigler's critical work. In his gut he knew that rationalising redistribution posed a threat to individual choice and hence to individual liberty. However, his drive for consistency within his own theoretical position meant that he could not attack redistribution as inefficient. If it was, then over time incentives would exist for it to change. A given distribution would lose its political viability. Yet he felt compelled to find some basis to undermine

[35] This well-known quote by Voltaire seems largely forgotten by the current generation of economists who almost believe that they have bootstrapped their way to enlightenment.

redistributive arguments which served only as a persistent abrasive to his liberal disposition[36].

For this reason, he reserved his most scathing attacks for those economists offering frameworks that detoured from the orthodoxy of perfect competition. In particular, he focused on those alternatives that offered multiple equilibria or non-equilibrium solutions. This is the common thread running through the analysis offered by such a diverse group as Sweezy, Chamberlin, Galbraith, Means and Leibenstein. At first glance these economists seem more distinguished by their differences than their similarities. However, each championed an economic approach which signalled the demise of unique equilibrium market solutions.

This becomes important only when examined in light of Stigler's core beliefs. Each alternative placed in peril the marginal productivity approach to distribution long championed by Stigler. The focus starts with his dissertation under Knight[37]. I would contend that it

---

[36] Stigler's professional standards demanded that he adopt a consistent position to this crucial issue. Resolving the problem of arguing against redistribution without falling back on standard market inefficiency statements proved to be a problem with a very elusive solution.

> But look, if you're going to regulate, conditional on wanting to redistribute income, I can't tell you that this is wrong. So, if I don't like it, if I tell you it's wrong, it has to be because I don't like the redistribution. Or you can argue on global grounds. If you have a lot of this in society, it may have global effects on efficiency. You and I can fight over a cookie, but if everybody's doing it, it is spending a lot of society's resources, that kind of argument. But that's a more subtle basis on which to oppose these things then economists usually do by saying it's inefficient. (Conversation with Sam Peltzman, October 1997)

[37] Marginal productivity as the basis for distribution remained the clearest break that Stigler made from his revered teacher, Frank Knight. Stigler's refutation of Knight's (1976) famous essay 'The Ethics of Competition' could not be clearer.

> When I first read this essay a vast number of years ago, as a student writing his dissertation under Professor Knight's supervision, you should not be surprised to hear that I thought his was a conclusive refutation of "productivity ethics." When I reread it a year or so ago, I was shocked by the argumentation. (Stigler, 1982d: 18–19)

remained as the driving forces behind his defence of orthodoxy. Not only is a reward proportional to marginal productivity the most efficient form of income distribution but ethical as well. '… I wish only to assert that the appeal of productivity ethics for income distribution commands wide support not only from the public but also from the economists when they are watching their sentiments rather than their words' (Stigler, 1982d: 19). Ethics, like everything else, becomes driven by utility maximising behaviour. For Stigler this had to be a testable hypothesis rather than the sort of convenient assumption typically employed by most economists. '… I believe that it is a feasible and even an orthodox scientific problem to ascertain a set of widely and anciently accepted precepts of ethical personal behaviour, and to test their concordance with utility-maximising behaviour for the preponderance of individuals' (Stigler, 1982c: 36).

As Stigler characterises the post-war period, questions of distribution had come to dominate policy and economic questions as they had never done before.

> Most recently the desire for greater equality has grown strong. Every policy is scrutinized for its effects on the distribution of income, and the results of this scrutiny weigh heavily in the final judgment of the desirability of the policy. A growing number of economists, indeed, implicitly argue that no other injustice equals in enormity that of large differences in income. (Stigler, 1949: 1)

It is just this insistence on equality of results that causes Stigler's unbending liberal heart the most anxiety. The moralist buried deep within sees this type of redistribution as undermining the soul of a good society.

> … we are persuaded that an economic system will not help us to move in the right direction unless it grants both opportunity and responsibility to the individual: the very uncertainty of our ultimate ethical goals dictates a wide area of individual self-determination. … On the liberal philosophy, it is necessary that all contestants begin the race at the same point, but it is fatal to require that they reach the finish line simultaneously. (Stigler, 1949: 8–9)

- Market efficiency (exemplified by Koopmans (1957) essays) vs. economic growth (Beveridge and Galbraith)

> Well, I'll eat it, said Alice, and if it makes me grow larger, I can reach the key- and if it makes me grow smaller, I can creep under the door: so either way I'll get into the garden, and I don't care which happens! (Carroll, 1956: 9–10)

In the immediate post-war period, public memory retained the images of market failure as represented by the great depression. These contrasted sharply with the collective triumph that government had achieved in waging and winning World War II, an intervention verging well into the neighbourhood of social engineering. Growth became the prime imperative ensuring employment and economic stability. Given these requirements, issues of efficiency took a decided backseat. Trade-offs of efficiency for growth were seen as necessary sacrifices to prevent the collapse of post-war economies (and keep them insulated from the collective vision of communism). The manifestation of this, articulated industry policy, became attached to a variety of programs with varying objectives often justified by convenient, if not always rigorous, economic thinking.

In all cases, however, such proposed policies have been connected directly or indirectly with the concept of economic growth. The fact that discussions of industry policy are to some degree another way of discussing growth policy explains where the core of the problem is. Growth, as a subject to be tackled, has long been an issue assiduously avoided by many well-known economists. Growth and the reasons for it was the motivation behind Smith's *Wealth of Nations*[38]. His policy was a prescriptive policy for unshackling the potential of the English economy. Ricardo successfully deflected the focus of economics onto issues of distribution, a direction that economists found difficult to abandon entirely. This position continued to dominate, in spite of a general recognition that explaining

---

[38] For discussion of growth theory during the formative years of economics see Brewer (1995).

economic growth, particularly insofar as it reduced poverty, remained the chief duty of any economist[39].

Modern growth theory, in the immediate post-war period, did not find its roots in a rediscovery of Smith's questions, but in one of market co-ordination. It raised the Keynesian question in a dynamic framework. In their work, Harrod (1948) and Domar (1947) point to the lack of any fundamental endogenous mechanism which might prevent recurrent large swings in unemployment and capacity utilisation. Given the assumptions of their model, steady-state growth was unlikely. The model suggested that growth could be boosted by increasing the investment to output ratio. But this was hardly the point of the work done by Harrod and Domar. Solow's (1956) solution spoke to the co-ordination difficulty since the policy implications were not at the forefront of the debate[40]. Given the nature of the questions raised it hardly comes as a surprise that after an initial flurry of interest in the early- and mid-sixties, interest in growth models largely waned. The questions that naturally follow from accepting the earlier, more historical analysis of economic growth bear obviously on questions of industry policy both as regards existing and potential manufacturing sectors.

Shifting growth theory, so that it nestled comfortably within the confines of the debate characterising economic efficiency, removed issues of distribution to the periphery of research. Efficiency replaced the more institutional requirement of political stability as the necessary

---

[39] We often forget the number of economists that were first drawn to the subject by their desire to aid the less fortunate.

> The question [of the elimination of poverty] cannot be fully answered by economic science. For the answer depends partly on the moral and political capabilities of human nature, and on these matters the economist has no special means of information: he must do as others do, and guess as best he can. But the answer depends in a great measure upon facts and inferences, which are within the province of economics; and this it is which gives to economic studies their chief and their highest interest. (Marshall, 1982: 3)

[40] See Solow (1994) for a good summary of his understanding of the debate and what he was attempting to do in his work.

basis for economic growth. Without the need to maintain a countervailing force against the use of private economic power, the rationale for government intervention dwindled. The coupled threat to individual choice was largely neutered. The two-step process seems clear in retrospect. First, Stigler, and his colleagues, in all their work extended the applicability of neoclassical analysis, particularly the reach of competitive markets[41]. His work (1968) on oligopoly effectively eliminated that theoretical middle ground by vanquishing this lingering distraction inhabiting an ill-defined region between monopolistic and competitive markets. The next strategic step set its sights on demolishing the importance of monopoly theory[42]. Once markets

---

[41] Part of Stigler's idea of marketing an idea was to push it to its extreme. He would nail his flag to an extreme position and relish any subsequent attacks. For him, the worst response was no response.

> He was a bit of a provocateur. He liked upsetting people. I told you he wrote that column for Business Month. After a year went by, nobody had criticized it. They didn't get any letters to the editor. And you know, he had said so many outrageous things, that insider trading is really OK, that sort of thing. He said things meant really to try to upset people. Well, he gave it up. He wasn't having any fun. He wanted people to criticize his ideas and then he wanted to come back with his rejoinders. You know, he wanted to have a little fun. (Conversation with Claire Friedland, October 1997)

[42] In his autobiography, Stigler describes (1988: 91–122) his journey from embracing the commonly accepted wisdom of the profession (and of his teacher Henry Simons), to believing that issues concerning monopoly power were at most only of minor importance. He came to describe antitrust actions as largely wasted effort. In this sense, an economist simply had no professional role to play in the political process.

> I conclude — and perhaps I am alone in concluding — that when the economist goes to Washington, he deserves no more credence, and no less, than any other political appointment, and it is mildly deceptive to address him as Doctor or Professor. (Stigler, 1988: 135–136)

Stigler's whole-hearted embrace of Harold Demsetz' work on regulation (1968) fails to surprise given this context. This approach undermines the attention paid to the issue of natural monopolies by providing competition in bidding for contractual rights as an effective substitute to competition within the marketplace. Stigler does

are established firmly as widely competitive, the motivations and costs of government intervention can only undermine economic efficiency and growth. If government cannot improve economic outcomes, the undeniable analytic imperative becomes to explain why governments nonetheless do intervene. It is unsurprising that George Stigler's work moved from pioneering empirical and theoretical pieces in industrial organisation to path breaking insights in the field of government regulation[43]. This happened not according to some premeditated grand strategy but rather evolved from the natural unfolding of his professional interests. My point is that these interests were always guided by a core and unalterable belief in freedom of choice as the foundation of liberty and morality.

- Collective choice (Samuelson and public goods) versus individual choice (von Mises and private goods)

> Now trends of evolution can change, and hitherto they almost always have changed. But they changed only because they met firm opposition. The prevailing trend toward what Hilaire Belloc called the servile state will certainly not be reversed if nobody has the courage to attack its underlying dogmas. (von Mises, 1980: 179)

Just as the Protestant Reformation inevitably called forth a regrouping and reaction by the forces of Catholicism, the widespread acceptance

---

not deny the existence of monopolies but raises his ever sceptical voice in terms of the attention economists have lavished upon them.

> The strength of the competitive force does not imply that there are no monopolies or that they are always transitory, although in century-long periods they are indeed transitory. What is implied is that the processes of obtaining, defending, sharing, and eliminating monopoly positions are more important and interesting than the exercise of monopoly power. (Stigler, 1988: 164)

[43] Given his passion for consistency, Stigler was forced to argue for the efficiency of the political marketplace. In this sense, economists had no more justification to meddle in political outcomes than in market results. See his posthumously published work (1992), "Law or Economics?" for a clear exposition of this position.

of collective action by mainstream economists and the public at large was bound to create something of a backlash. Friedrich von Hayek viewed the need for strategic regrouping amongst the considered voices of conservatism as urgent to brake the ever-creeping encroachment on individual liberty. At his urging, thirty-six intellectuals, mostly economists, met at a resort hotel on Mont Pelerin, Switzerland, 10 April 1947. Amongst the invited group were two rising young economists (Stigler and Friedman)[44] who had become friends and sometime colleagues as graduate students in Chicago and later in Washington DC during the war[45]. This conservative vanguard issued a resulting statement of aims that conveys an almost alarmist tone.

> The central values of civilization are in danger. Over large stretches of the earth's surface the essential conditions of human dignity and freedom have

---

[44] Friedrich von Hayek relied on Aaron Director's recommendations when issuing invitations. (Hayek himself owed the publication of his *Road to Serfdom* (1944) to Director's intervention that persuaded the University of Chicago to publish it.) It was Director who recommended that the list includes his brother-in-law, Milton Friedman and George Stigler. Aaron Director would remain one of the most influential (and among the very few) intellectual influences on Stigler. He essentially supplanted Frank Knight in this role. Director himself had made his own journey from hard left to hard right ideology. He had originally arrived at Chicago in 1927 to study with Paul Douglas. One of his few publications is a co-authored book with Paul Douglas (1931). However, under the influence of Jacob Viner, his intellectual stance shifted radically, so much so that he once jokingly referred to his brother-in-law, Milton Friedman, as 'my radical brother-in-law'. In 1962, Director helped to found the Committee on a Free Society at the University of Chicago, which was established to 'clarify and reinforce the tradition of individual liberty in its economic, political, historical and philosophical dimensions'. This and other information can be found in the obituary released by The University of Chicago News Office (13 September 2004).

[45] Stigler was consistently conservative in all that he did. As his long-time research associate, Claire Friedland pointed out, 'He was the only person in Chicago during the late sixties still wearing a homburg' (Conversation with Claire Friedland, October 1997). The consistency of his political positions does seem to point to a specific ideological stance.

> I never heard George make jokes about Ludwig von Mises' extremism, although there were a lot of jokes made at the time, but George was generally on the right side of most issues. (Conversation with Paul Samuelson, October 1997)

> already disappeared. In others they are under constant menace from the development of current tendencies of policy. The position of the individual and the voluntary group are progressively undermined by extensions of arbitrary power. (Mont Pelerin Society, 2003: 1)

Seen in the context of the cold war, there was a clear ideological battle for the proverbial hearts and minds of mankind. It was not only the clearly professed collectivists of the Soviet Union that together posed an imminent danger, but also intellectuals of western democracies that were too understanding or too accommodating to dangerous alternatives. In this environment, a new, Keynesian inspired textbook, like the one produced by Paul Samuelson, and seen as innocuous today, could generate a firestorm around those institutions that chose to adopt it[46]. Economists like Samuelson and Arrow, in their attempts to formalise large sections of economic theory, seemed determined to find limitations and faults with competitive markets.

The traditional liberals, represented at Mont Pelerin, firmly believed that a free economy was necessary for a democratic society[47]. Given

---

[46] Textbook debates within a department or university seem driven by ideology or perhaps theoretical issues that matter to economists more as professionals than as teachers. Thus, the new wave of post-war Keynesian textbooks met resistance from the old guard as well as politicians and businessmen keen on sniffing out anti-free market (communist) influences.

> I [Carolyn Bell] occasionally met a student who asked if it was true that the book [Samuelson] was communistic and if she would be required to read that radical, Keynes. Like the parents who prompted these questions, many economics faculty condemned the new approach, sometimes in a destructive power struggle. One highly thought of institution was still having difficulty in recruiting in the early sixties because its senior members had for so long adamantly refused to consider appointing anyone using Keynesian analysis. (Bell, 1988: 147)

[47] Much of this account of that first Mont Pelerin meeting comes from the PBS produced program *Commanding Heights*. The show interviewed some of the surviving original participants. Milton Friedman remembers it as a meeting of 'good eggs'. He also recalled a heated debate on distribution where von Mises turned on the other participants by denouncing them as 'a bunch of Socialists'.

what they uniformly viewed as a dangerous and almost unrecognised drift towards collectivism, they, like their socialist opponents, saw no other viable option than to embrace the underlying courage of their ideas. They needed to find the courage to be idealistic. The extent of the leap taken, from this position to that of a full-fledged ideologue, is hard to measure. A few steps in this direction need not lead to a deliberate attempt to slant research to achieve a given set of preconceived outcomes. Stigler himself was never as crude as that. Nor did he ever consciously try to achieve results that fit with his deeply held beliefs. But someone who believed so unequivocally in a certain goal would inevitably find evidence to support what he knew (in an almost *a priori* way) to be correct. It is hard to imagine what data, research, or evidence could have moved Stigler to fundamentally change his views about markets. To lose his faith would have fatally undermined the basis of his moral precepts.

For these reasons, Stigler would not surrender his precept that the Trojan horse of beneficial state services ruthlessly advanced collectivist aims at the expense of liberty. But unlike other clearly confessed ideologues, Stigler refused to rest his case on some simple statement of faith or acknowledge that it might be no more than a claim based on anecdotal evidence. Consistent with his methodology, the assertion of imperilled liberty must be transformed into a testable hypothesis.

> The proof that there are dangers to the liberty and dignity of the individual in the present institutions must be that such liberties have already been impaired. If it can be shown that in important areas of economic life substantial and unnecessary invasions of personal freedom are already operative, the case for caution and restraint in invoking new political controls will acquire content and conviction. (Stigler, 1975: 18)

5. Cold Warriors Fade Away — The Cost of Ideology

> I dare say, I think that would have been Milton Friedman and George Stigler's attitude to McCarthy. One would have wished he didn't do it so loudly, didn't do it so vulgarly, but they would have said that he was essentially

> right. In the same way that a lot of people said you know, you have to put up with McCarthy to keep communism in check. Stigler would have regarded McCarthyism as not being a threat. (Conversation with Mark Blaug, June 1998)

For George Stigler, ideology had to remain an unacknowledged, guilty secret. By his own reasoning, actions springing from this set of beliefs and imperatives were outside economic analysis. Such an avowal could only undermine the integrity of the discipline like a worm burrowing from within.

> An ideology ... is a commanding set of beliefs, beliefs that are probably not grounded upon self-interest or are related to the interests of the holders in so subtle and obscure a manner as to make it more useful to treat the beliefs as data. (Stigler, 1988b: xiii)

If though, these sets of beliefs and preferences determined George Stigler's world view, his professional conclusions could not remain unmarked by his ideological inclinations. Like any other economist, Stigler did not come to his data with a blank slate. Even with the best will in the world, some influence must necessarily remain despite all his insistence on empirical testing. Facts do not speak for themselves. They need interpretation. The very nature of such interpretation cannot by definition be entirely objective. At least some slight residue of spin will be detected by the careful researcher.

Ideology subtly undermines the work of even the very best researcher. In George Stigler's case, we can most clearly see this influence in his critical work. He strapped on his battered armour and levelled his lance only in defence of his bedrock beliefs. When defending the major tenets of neoclassical economics he inevitably resorted to the adversarial legal tactics of the courtroom[48].

---

[48] The irony is that a bare knuckled brawler like George Stigler could characterise his beloved profession as a gentlemanly pursuit. The example set by the Chicago school should have been sufficient to undermine any such assumption.

> ... it is fair to say that indignation and outrage have disappeared from economics. This is no doubt the reason economics is at the moment

George Stigler's overriding concern was to demolish opposing, and inherently dangerous, heretical doctrines. This led to a pattern of misrepresenting these doctrines, not with the intention to deceive but rather driven by an overwhelming need to triumph. He was a partisan, but an honest and ethical one. The problem comes with simply being a partisan, even when that describes a great economist stooping to conquer. The temptation to yield to these matters of the heart is great, but there is little evidence that yielding generates either research or insights.

> It cannot be doubted that economists have imported egalitarian values into economics from the prevailing ethos of the societies in which they live, and that they have not been important contributors to the formation of that ethos. (Stigler, 1982e: 13)

References

Bell, CS (1988). The principles of economics from now until then. *Journal of Economic Education*, 19(2), 133–147.

Brewer, A (1995). The concept of growth in eighteenth-century economics. *History of Political Economy*, 27(4), 609–638.

Cervantes, M (1993). *Don Quixote*. Ware Hertfordshire: Wordsworth Editions Limited.

Coase, R (1994a). The market for goods and the market for ideas. In *Essays on Economics and Economists*, pp. 64–74.

Coase, R (1994b). Alfred Marshall's mother and father. In *Essays on Economics and Economists*, pp. 119–129.

Commanding Heights (2003). Hayek's Mt Pelerin Conference. From episode 1 of *Commanding Heights* (PBS), http://www.pbs.org/wgbh/commandingheights/shared/minitextlo/vid_miltonfriedman.html, 2 December 2003.

Demsetz, H (1968). Why regulate utilities? *Journal of Law and Economics*, 11(1), 55–65.

> highly respectable and ... lacking in promise of basic influence on policy in the future. I do not know whether it is an occasion for pride or for regret that the economist is using Marquis of Queensbury arguments in an arena where emotional brass knuckles continue in fashion. (Stigler, 1965: 27–28)

Director, A and P Douglas (1931). *The Problem of Unemployment*. Chicago: University of Chicago Press.

Domar, E (1947). Expansion and Employment. *American Economic Review*, 37(1), 343–355.

Dickens, C (1927). *David Copperfield*. London: Macmillan and Co.

Friedman, M and R Friedman (1980). *Free to Choose*. Melbourne: Macmillan.

Harrod, RF (1948). *Towards a Dynamic Economics*. London: Macmillan.

Hayek, FA (1944). *The Road to Sefdom*. Chicago: University of Chicago Press.

Hobbes, T (1914). *The Leviathan*. London: JM Dent and Sons.

Josephson, M (1934). *The Robber Barons*. New York: Harcourt, Brace.

Keynes, JM (1964). *The General Theory of Employment, Interest and Money*. New York: Harcourt Brace Jovanovich.

Knight, FH (1976). The ethics of competition. In *The Ethics of Competition, and Other Essays*, pp. 1–24. Chicago: University of Chicago Press.

Koopmans, TC (1957). *Three Essays on the State of Economic Science*. New York: McGraw Hill.

Magnusson, P, F Balfour, M Shari, M Kripalani, D Roberts, G Smith and N Mangi (2003). Where free trade hurts. *Business Week*. 15 December pp. 22–26

Marshall, A (1982). *Principles of Economics Eighth Edition*. Philadelphia: Porcupine Press.

Marx, K (1967). *Capital Volume III*. New York: International Publishers.

McCloskey, D (1997). The rhetoric of economics, revisited. *Eastern Economic Journal*, 23(3), 359–362.

Mill, JS (1968). *Essays on Some Unsettled Questions of Political Economy*. New York: Augustus M Kelley.

Mill, JS (1965). *Principles of Political Economy*. Toronto: Macmillan.

Mont Pelerin Society (2003). Short history and statement of aims. *The Mont Pelerin Home Page*, http://www.montpelerin.org/aboutmps.html, 2 December 2003, p. 1.

Read, S (1829). *The Political Economy*. Edinburgh: Printed for the Author.

Ricardo, D (1923). *The Principles of Political Economy and Taxation*. London: JM Dent.

Ricardo, D (1973). Letter from Ricardo to Francis Place. In *The Works and Correspondence of David Ricardo, Volume IX — Letters July 1821–1823*, P Sraffa and M Dobb (eds.), pp. 49–54. Cambridge: Cambridge University Press.

Solow, R (1956). A contribution to the theory of economic growth. *Quarterly Journal of Economics*, 70(1), 65–94.

Solow, R (1994). Perspectives on growth theory. *The Journal of Economic Perspectives*, 8(1), 45–54.

Sowell, Thomas (1993). A Student's eye view of George Stigler. *Journal of Political Economy*, 101(5), 784–791.

Stigler, GJ (1941). *Production and Distribution Theories*. New York: MacMillan.

Stigler, GJ (1947). The Kinky demand curve and rigid prices. *Journal of Political Economy*, 55(3), 432–449.

Stigler, GJ (1949). The economists and equality. In *Five Lectures on Economic Problems*, pp. 1–11. London: Longmans, Green and Co.

Stigler, GJ (1954). Ricardo and the 93 per cent labour theory of value. *American Economic Review*, 48(3), 357–367.

Stigler, GJ (1963). A dialogue on the proper economic role of the state (with Paul A Samuelson). *Selected Papers*. no. 7, pp. 3–37. Chicago: University of Chicago Graduate School of Business.

Stigler, GJ (1965). The influence of events and policies on economic theory. In *Essays in the History of Economics*, pp. 16–30. Chicago: University of Chicago Press.

Stigler, GJ (1968). A theory of oligopoly. In *The Organization of Industry*, pp. 39–66. Chicago: The University of Chicago Press.

Stigler, GJ (1975). Reflections on liberty. In *The Citizen and the State — Essays on Regulation*, pp. 14–19. Chicago: The University of Chicago Press.

Stigler, GJ (1982a). The literature of economics: The case of the kinked oligopoly demand curve. In *The Economist as Preacher*, GJ Stigler (ed.), pp. 223–243. Oxford: Basil Blackwell.

Stigler, GJ (1982b). Do economists matter? In *The Economist as Preacher*, GJ Stigler (ed.), pp. 57–67. Oxford: Basil Blackwell.

Stigler, GJ (1982c). The ethics of competition: The unfriendly critics. In *The Economist as Preacher*, GJ Stigler (ed.), pp. 27–37. Oxford: Basil Blackwell.

Stigler, GJ (1982d). The ethics of competition: The friendly economists. In *The Economist as Preacher*, GJ Stigler (ed.), pp. 14–27. Oxford: Basil Blackwell.

Stigler, GJ (1982e). The economist as preacher. In *The Economist as Preacher*, GJ Stigler (ed.), pp. 3–13. Oxford: Basil Blackwell.

Stigler, GJ (1982f). The economist and the state. In *The Economist as Preacher*, GJ Stigler (ed.), pp. 119–135. Oxford: Basil Blackwell.

Stigler, GJ (1982g). Textual exegesis as a scientific problem. In *The Economist as Preacher*, GJ Stigler (ed.), pp. 68–71. Oxford: Basil Blackwell.

Stigler, GJ (1986). Why have the socialists been winning? In *The Essence of Stigler*, KR Leube and TG More (eds.), pp. 337–346. Stanford: Hoover University Press.

Stigler, GJ (1988a). *Memoirs of an Unregulated Economist*. New York: Basic Books.

Stigler, GJ (1988b). Preface. In *The Chicago Studies in Political Economy*, G Stigler (ed.), pp. ix–xviii. Chicago: University of Chicago Press.

Stigler, GJ (1992). Law or economics? *The Journal of Law & Economics*, 26(2), 455–468.

Stigler, GJ and G Becker (1977). De gustibus non est disputandum. *American Economic Review*, 67(1).

Tollison, RD (1992). George J Stigler: Chicago political economist. *Public Choice*, 73(4), iii–iv.

University of Chicago News Office (2004). Aaron director, founder of the field of law and economics. http://www-news.uchicago.edu/releases/04/040913.director.shtml, 13 September, 1–4.

Von Mises, L (1980). Trends can change. In *Planning for Freedom*, pp. 173–179. South Holland, IL: Libertarian Press.

Weinstein, M (1992). Economists and the media. *Journal of Economic Perspectives*, 6(3), 73–77.

Chapter 4

Five Easy Pieces — George Stigler's Blueprint for a Counter-Revolution

Waitress: I don't make the rules.

Dupea: OK, I'll make it as easy for you as I can. I'd like an omelette, plain, and a chicken salad sandwich on wheat toast, no mayonnaise, no butter, no lettuce. And a cup of coffee.

Waitress: A number two, chicken sal san, hold the butter, the lettuce and the mayonnaise. And a cup of coffee. Anything else?

Dupea: Yeah. Now all you have to do is hold the chicken, bring me the toast, give me a check for the chicken salad sandwich, and you haven't broken any rules.

Waitress (spitefully): You want me to *hold* the chicken, huh?

Dupea: I want you to hold it between your knees. (Scene from *Five Easy Pieces,* 1970)

1. A Time and a Place

How many goodly creatures are there here!
How beauteous mankind is! O brave new world,
That has such people in't. (Shakespeare, *The Tempest*, act5, sc. 1: 1)

With the end of World War II, there was a generally held popular belief that the world would henceforth be a better place with greater opportunities for all within a broader political environment of equity and fair play[1]. The victorious allies had overcome the depths of the Great Depression while defeating the totalitarian threat to liberty and democracy[2]. The idea that planning for a brighter future was the key to these objectives seemed unarguable given the wartime experience[3].

Events had also radically altered the contours of the economics profession. In an analogous fashion, the urge to create a better world permeated many academic endeavours during the post-war period. In this most ideological of centuries, economists were unlikely to remain immune. From being largely a church based on market principles, the Keynesian revolution had taken root and substituted active government policy for unfettered market forces[4]. The embrace of these Keynesian principles, which seemingly had been tested by the events of the thirties and by the subsequent war, was as rapid as it was widespread.

---

[1] Allied governments and especially that of the United States nurtured this belief during the war. This is exemplified by a series of seven documentaries directed by Frank Capra and collectively known as *Why We Fight.*

> To be inspired with the will to win, Capra told his associates as they embarked on this work, Americans needed to be shown that they were fighting for the existence of their country, and at the same time were carrying the "torch of freedom" for a better post-war world — a world in which conquest, exploitation, and economic evils had been eliminated and peace and democracy prevailed. (Dower, 1986: 16)

[2] The irony that this democratic triumph would not have been possible without the collaboration of the Stalinist Soviet Union seemed lost to many at the time (and often forgotten today). Pragmatic cold warriors could subsequently invoke strategic amnesia on the issue or confess the periodic need for flexible pragmatism.

[3] Like those corporate interests who came away from World War I with a similar idea of economic planning (see Weinstein, 1968), these latter day planners tended to disregard a basic difference in a wartime economy. Namely, in such an economy demand for output is virtually guaranteed in the form of necessary munitions. Producing for an unpredictable market (the standard peace time condition) is not analogous to producing for a given wartime demand.

[4] It is easy when working within the Anglo-American tradition to over generalise the existence of market driven economics. The German Historical School or that of the American Institutionalists certainly took radically different departures from this mainstream price theory approach.

Fears of another economic depression had shaken any unquestioned faith in the benevolence of market driven results. In a parallel fashion the work of Chamberlin, Hall and Hitch, Lester and others had thrown doubt at least on the universal employment of a marginal approach or the unique equilibrium results of perfect competition as the most useful framework for microanalysis[5]. It seemed inevitable that the brave new world of quantity adjusted aggregates, championed by the dominant Keynesians, would soon find an equally non-traditional microfoundation to serve as its theoretical anchor.

Success unfortunately, often carries within it the seeds of its own demise. The faith in planning, intrinsic in the new consensus economics of this era, would eventually put the Keynesian approach, as well as alternative micro-theories, on the wrong side of the Cold War divide[6]. Planners become synonymous with the collectivism promoted behind the Iron Curtain. Markets, on the other hand, would become identified with the ingrained individualism which formed the basis for freedom and liberty[7]. *Free to choose* (1980), as unfolded by the master

---

[5] Freedman (1995) points out that the immediate post-war period witnessed a struggle to maintain the marginalist micro-framework against alternative approaches. Ultimately this failure to provide micro-foundations for the Keynesian revolution would provide a perfect Achilles heel for more neoclassical economists to aim at in the seventies.

> This lack of compatibility between the two systems of economics was due to the failure of either side during the decades of the thirties and forties to achieve complete victory. The forces of each camp won conditional strategic battles. Perhaps the traditional price theorists surreptitiously occupied the high ground since they denied the Keynesians a dominant microeconomics compatible with their model. The Keynesian position was left with an inherent vulnerability. (Freedman, 1995: 202)

[6] It can be argued that Keynes saw responsibility for economic policy to depend on a small group of highly intelligent and well-trained professionals with the virtues exemplified by him and his Cambridge associates.

[7] In a broadcast with BBC radio aired shortly before his death (16 November 2006) Milton Friedman when asked how he would like to be remembered answered, 'As a friend of freedom'. He went on to explain that he meant both economic freedom and political freedom. Political freedom was a requirement (usually though not always) for economic freedom.

story spinner Milton Friedman, would become the *sine qua non* of true democracy and individual rights. The Chicago School's attempt to revive classic liberalism, of the type defined by Smith, de Toqueville and Mill, would have at its core a strongly ideological basis. This would remain a defining characteristic despite the fact that one of its founding members, George Stigler, would consistently maintain the ineffectiveness of ideology and the peripheral nature of outside events and debates on the evolution of economic theory[8].

Friedman can be accurately viewed as arriving at Chicago with an ideological imperative that served to shape his subsequent career[9]. George Stigler, though a member of Columbia University until 1958, when he joined his close friend and ally at Chicago, shared common concerns with his former classmate Milton Friedman. For both, a counter-revolution in the field of economics needed to be launched if men and women were to remain moral beings able to bear the full responsibility for their decisions and actions. In a sense, this ostensible battle for the minds of the economic profession was in fact

---

[8] For someone so wedded to the perceived classical liberalism of Adam Smith, George Stigler demonstrates a noticeable blind spot to the way these early economists perceived analysis. Economic theory remained policy driven and quite concrete. The purpose of such explorations was closely wedded to the changing policy debates of the 19th century. Stigler choses to trivialise such a relationship rather than coming to terms with the way in which the policy tail could wag the theoretical dog.

[9] Friedman stuck with Chicago despite initially being awarded the position only when the preferred candidate, George Stigler, was deemed too quantitative by University of Chicago President Cowell. As an underpaid associate professor he was tempted to accept a more generous offer from John Hopkins. 'Tell me, from the fullness of your experience, together with my indifference curves, how large a price ought I to pay for the privilege of being at Chicago?' (Hammond and Hammond, 2006: 80). In those early days he also despaired that he and his allies at Chicago were losing too many battles to the dark forces (the Keynesians).

> The dep't has voted to make Samuelson an offer. We don't yet know the end of the story. But whatever it is, I am very much afraid that it means we're lost. The Keynesians have the votes & mean to use them. Knight is bitter & says he will withdraw from active participation in the dep't. Mints, Gregg, & I are very low about it. (Letter from Milton Friedman to George Stigler in Hammond and Hammond, 2006: 46)

a desperate struggle for their souls. A fortuitous series of lectures in 1948 by George Stigler carefully laid out his tactical blueprint for the forthcoming struggle. This paper attempts to analyse this now only vaguely recollected event and how Stigler's tour de force came to be implemented in the following decades.

2. A Good Egg Gives Some Lectures — The Background

> Now trends of evolution can change, and hitherto they almost always have changed. But they changed only because they met firm opposition. The prevailing trend toward what Hilaire Belloc called the servile state will certainly not be reversed if nobody has the courage to attack its underlying dogmas. (von Mises, 1980: 179)

Sometimes serendipity seems to direct the flow of historical events. There is an utter inevitability in retrospect, but the rather unromantic mechanics of every day life requires a number of individual items to fall into place before a given outcome appears in the role of destiny's child. That George Stigler, who was a relatively rare traveller outside the bounds of the United States[10], found himself in London in March of 1948 seems inextricably linked with a book that had difficulty finding a publisher, though not an audience.

> Near the end of World War II, in 1944, Hayek wrote a small book, *The Road to Serfdom*. In it he argued that the western democracies were proceeding down the same road that fascist Germany and Italy and communist

[10] In this he departed from his close friend Milton Friedman who would turn up almost anywhere on the face of the earth to promote his particular economic agenda. Stigler maintained an almost provincial outlook which is in some ways distinctly American.

> Another story about George, I've always found it to be a problem, which is how incredibly American he was. I used to be shepherding these Latinos through and here they would come to some question in his Price Theory examination. 'Explain something, something about the Dred Scott Decision'. (Conversation with Arnold Harberger, October 1997)

> Russia had already taken, and that that road led inevitably to the loss of individual freedom. The book had been rejected by numerous publishers but was finally accepted by the University of Chicago Press after being strongly supported by Aaron Director. (Stigler, 1988: 140)

According to Stigler in his autobiography the unexpected success of the book in the United States translated into cash from the Volker Foundation to help von Hayek underwrite a meeting of conservative intellectuals in Switzerland (Stigler, 1988: 142). Just as the Protestant Reformation inevitably called forth a regrouping and reaction by the forces of Catholicism, the widespread acceptance of collective action by mainstream economists and the public at large created something of a backlash. Friedrich von Hayek viewed the need for strategic redeployment amongst the considered voices of conservatism to be urgent if the ever creeping encroachment on individual liberty was to be slowed. At his urging, thirty-six intellectuals, mostly economists, met at a resort hotel at Mont Pelerin, Switzerland, 1–10 April 1947. Amongst the invited group were two young economists[11] who had become friends and sometime colleagues as graduate students in Chicago and later while working in Washington D.C. during the war. The Society's resulting statement of aims has an almost alarmist tone to it.

> The central values of civilisation are in danger. Over large stretches of the earth's surface the essential conditions of human dignity and freedom have already disappeared. In others they are under constant menace from the development of current tendencies of policy. The position of the individual and the voluntary group are progressively undermined by extensions of arbitrary power. (Mont Pelerin Society, 2003: 1)

Given the company he kept, it is hard to imagine that at some stage the young George Stigler (and his close friend Milton Friedman)

---

[11] Though Stigler claims not to have met von Hayek before the gathering at Mont Pelerin it is clear that he exchanged correspondence prior to that date.

> Hayek writes: A junket to Switzerland in April is contemplated, to save liberalism. I assume you & Aaron would go. If this comes off, (1) train Aaron on bridge, and (2) let's find a fourth liberal; and teach him. (Letter from George Stigler to Milton Friedman in Hammond and Hammond, 2006: 49)

would not have found himself drawn into the field of attraction surrounding Friedrich von Hayek[12]. However, timing in a career, as well as in matters of the heart, is everything. The subsequent lecture series in London, arising from this fateful meeting in Switzerland, not only allowed George Stigler a more international audience at an earlier stage in his career, but provided the opportunity for him to construct and present an integrated research program. This program would become part of the framework supporting a successful counter-revolution against the post-war Keynesian dominance.

Thus, the trajectory; from the London School of Economics, to the University of Chicago, then over to Switzerland and back again to the LSE, describes the forces that fortuitously brought George Stigler, as a rising star of his profession, over to London to deliver a series of five lectures at the home of Robbins and von Hayek[13]. The London School of Economics at that time was one of the few academic bulwarks standing against the tide of Keynesianism sweeping the post-war landscape. Given the stated agenda of von Hayek, and

[12] That Stigler became regarded by this conservative intellectual elite as a good egg, can be traced to his relationship with Aaron Director and indirectly to his then closer ties to Frank Knight. Hayek would have quite naturally invited Director to such a meeting, if for nothing else than to reciprocate the help provided in publishing his book. Director, who was one of Knight's protégés and close friends, would have brought Knight along as well as his brother-in-law, Milton Friedman. Stigler, who was close friends with Friedman and the student of Knight, would have almost automatically completed the four innocents journeying abroad. Much of the account of that first Mont Pelerin meeting comes from the PBS produced program *Commanding Heights*. The show interviewed some of the surviving original participants. Milton Friedman remembers it as a meeting of 'good eggs'. He also recalled a heated debate on distribution where von Mises turned on the other members denouncing them as 'a bunch of Socialists'.

[13] Friedrich von Hayek would himself shift in 1950, from the London School of Economics to the University of Chicago, becoming a professor in the Committee on Social Thought (he was barred from entering the Economics department because of his Austrian economic views by one member whom he would not name and many speculate was Frank Knight). (See article in Wikpedia on Hayek for these and other details.) It is hard to know the exact series of events leading to the lectures Stigler presented at the LSE. Letters from Hayek to Stigler stored at the University of Chicago may prove to elucidate the missing links.

the clear direction that Stigler's work had taken in those years following the war, it can hardly be described as purely accidental that Stigler found himself presenting his economic manifesto before such a potentially congenial group.

> That hostility to collectivist restrictions on personal freedom, as well as the liking for a competitive order, were somewhat stronger in the University of Chicago's economics department than at most other places (except, and especially, the London School of Economics). (Stigler, 1988: 139)

3. Conservatives of the World Unite — How the LSE Manifesto Created an Economic Framework

> I am writing mainly to swell your head — though God knows it must be big enough already. Hayek reports that your lectures were 'brilliant' & successful. Indeed, he said yours were by all odds the most successful series of lectures they had ever had. I didn't realise the state of English Economics had sunk so low — though, come to think of it, Hayek was including prewar experience, so I guess I'll just have to take it to mean that the English are still smart enough to agree with the rest of us. (Letter from Milton Friedman to George Stigler, 7 April 1948 in Hammond and Hammond, 2006: 80)

The use of the word 'brilliant', except when modifying a star or a diamond, tends to make any cautious academic inherently uneasy. The term smacks, especially today, of exaggerated praise. In these times when everyone is above average, a brilliant lecture may only be one which prevents you from easing into sleep. Even in 1948, years before the Hollywoodisation of the language, to call a lecture brilliant would seem more than a bit overboard, especially coming from the traditionally reserved English. Hayek of course was not English but also was not known to give way to gushing. However, if Stigler's five lectures delivered at the LSE were not brilliant, they were certainly incisive, displaying a masterful control of the mechanics of presentation. But it is not rhetorical skill alone or even the ostensible content of these lectures that sets them apart. Rather a careful reader needs to look for the underlying coherence of the blueprint presented as well as the persistent moral objective inherent in Stigler's goals.

It is rare when an economist telegraphs the professional creed by which he or she is willing to live, but this was Stigler's fearless aim in these nearly enigmatic discourses. It is then all the more a shame that they seem largely forgotten today. A few economists may still be aware of his lecture on monopolistic competition, but no one appears to have pointed out that these five individual presentations formed an integral part of a larger whole. Similarly lost to discussion is what Stigler's overall objective might have been when he made so bold as to lecture some of England's most distinguished economists.

The published version plays against expectations. The entire five lectures compose barely sixty pages even when expanded with charts and notes. They each would have been no more than 30 min in length when actually presented. Conciseness did tend to be symptomatic of most of his written as well as his oral presentations[14]. To assume that Stigler would present five unrelated lectures on topics of interest badly underestimates his ability, objectives and mode of operation. He never wasted his time or that of his audience.

> About forty-five minutes into the class hour I found myself at the end of my notes! I was filled with consternation. I might last out the first session, but what about the rest of the quarter? I believe that this is not an unusual experience for new teachers, but I must admit that I have never reached the abundance of knowledge that made the time in the classroom seem inadequate. (Stigler, 1988: 39)

By the time of these lectures, Stigler had already established his reputation as one of the hard men battling a dominant Keynesian stream characterised by economic planning, with many of these opponents based at Harvard (and later at MIT)[15]. He had played a key role in

---

[14] To get some sense of this, compare his text on price theory (any edition) to contemporary texts of the day.

[15] The battle was fought by Chicago stalwarts as a no quarter offered, winner-takes-all affair. For instance, Milton Friedman himself played no small role in detaching the Cowles Commission from its post-war home in Chicago. (It re-established itself at Yale where it has been ever since.) The sort of theorists laying the foundations of General Equilibrium theory and the new science of econometrics tended towards

holding back the micro-counterpart of the Keynesian revolution during the marginalist debates[16]. His LSE lectures were in fact a blueprint, building upon an interconnected approach that provided a basis for refounding the discipline. Stigler's objective was clear. The rationale for government intervention, so popular in this immediate post-war period, needed to be effectively closed off. Economic analysis had to be put on a tighter leash and refocused. This invitation to speak was a chance for Stigler not merely to react to and attempt to push back the forces of darkness but to establish a 'city on the hill' for the economics profession, an alternative to the current aims and objectives of those toiling within the discipline. It was in fact a very moral view harking back to the classic liberalism of Smith, Mill and de Tocqueville.

Few economists today would claim that their subject had any intrinsic relation with morality. Certainly, in the post-Friedman/Stigler era, Chicago economics, as represented by Steven D Levitt, seems determined to veer towards much more modest aims. The discipline has come to reflect a need for solving specific problems rather than building general systems. The key issue, given this more narrow view,

---

grand theory and abstraction. Friedman always styled himself as a follower of Marshallian partial equilibrium. Moreover, such theorising by economists like Kenneth Arrow led to an emphasis on market failure instead of market success. The Cowles Commission represented an attempt to establish a more rigorous framework for Keynesian economics, itself anathema to both Friedman and Stigler.

> On the whole, I admit I was wrong on Colin. He is not the man you or I would want in that perfect University Arthur [Burns] wants to found, but he is personally nice, many of his instincts are on the right side, and he's much more interesting and provocative, and fundamentally no sloppier, than Kuznets or some other people in NY or Chicago. And he would be marvellous in infuriating the Cowles boys, although probably not your equal. (Letter from George Stigler to Milton Friedman, December 1947 in Hammond and Hammond, 2006: 73)

[16] This can be seen in those works attacking the labour demand approach of Richard Lester and the price setting analysis of Hall and Hitch. (See Stigler, 1946; 1947a; 1947b). For a retrospective look at the marginalist debate from the viewpoint of the marginalist forces see Machlup (1967).

becomes one of devising a method for testing a given hypothesis without any a *priori* judgements clouding the interpretation of results[17].

---

[17] Some attitudes in the profession never change. Economist within the profession like to take pot-shots at Levitt, sneering at the notoriety earned for his popular work *Freakonomics* (2005). Stigler himself sneered at popularisers, even shaking his head at his close friend Milton Friedman who he judged was too interested in making policy pronouncements

> Aaron Director (AD): But he [Stigler] preferred to study them, not to change them.
> Milton Friedman (MF): He preferred to say that he preferred to study them.
> AD: He preferred to study them. I should quit this argument.
> MF: It was partly a long-running difference between him and me.
> AD: You're right.
> MF: And he liked to stress, "I just want to understand the world and Milton wants to change it."
> AD: That's right. And predominantly I think that George was correct.
>
> (Conversation with Milton Friedman, Rose Friedman and Aaron Director, August 1997).

His longest entrenched feud was with John Kenneth Galbraith. Each new book by Galbraith would inevitably elicit a withering review by George Stigler even in later years when Galbraith's fame and popularity had waned. Galbraith perhaps came too close to the bone, when he implicitly pointed out this nettle in Stigler's professional achievements.

> As Galbraith related the story, Stigler had said on more than one occasion that it was a tragedy of our time that so many had read Galbraith and so few had read Adam Smith. Galbraith replied, the deeper tragedy is that no one much read Stigler at all. (McCann and Perlman, 1993: 996n)

The Chicago School approach to economics as instituted by Stigler and Friedman emphasised empirical testing of all hypothesis. Stigler's presidential address (29 December 1964) to the assembled conclave of economists at the annual AEA convention is to some extent a visionary look at the quantification of economics. In this sense someone like Levitt is in fact carrying on this longstanding tradition. However, Stigler himself sometimes strayed from standards of impartiality when judging his own statistical results.

> He would come across empirical work which was contradictory to other empirical work. Somehow it always seemed to him that the empirical work which favoured his side was done better than the empirical work which didn't. (Conversation with James Kindahl, October 1997)

Today it would be reasonable to assume that most in the profession would not see the objective of economic understanding to lie in moral action. Yet Stigler had broader goals in mind. Perhaps he was never a moralist to the same degree as Smith, Mill or Marshall. But if he doubted that economics could produce more moral men, he hoped it could insure that men were not made worse by means of government coercion. Planning and regulation inevitably led to a redistribution of income by forcibly changing contractual terms. Such intervention distorted individual choice by shifting the level of individual responsibility and accountability. For Stigler, moral action required that individuals bear the full weight of their decisions and choices. This involved the classical difference between license and liberty or freedom and coercion. Stigler did not want to prescribe moral behaviour but rather to allow individuals to achieve it. Given such an outlook, the only safeguard against collective tyranny was the marketplace. Markets ensured that power could not be exercised by any given individual. In a Hobbesian type of agreement, individuals ceded power to the market in order to achieve freedom of choice.

Stigler journeyed to London to substitute the liberating potential of markets for the heavy hand of government. Given this unarguable starting point, economics by necessity had to be structured so as to reflect this one self-evident fact. The five lectures are stepping stones in sketching out Stigler's vision of research. For the remainder of this section I will briefly demonstrate how each lecture contributed to this one overwhelming objective.

3.1. *Banking on a moral imperative*

> The maxims are, first, that the individual is not accountable to society for his actions, in so far as these concern the interests of no person but himself. … Secondly, that for such actions as are prejudicial to the interests of others, the individual is accountable, and may be subjected either to social or to legal punishment, if society is of the opinion that the one or the other is requisite for its protection. (Mill, 1947: 95)

As befits a crusade, the core of these lectures is a moral one. In his first lecture Stigler refers to the moral aims of the classical economist, namely to produce better men[18].

> Why, then, did the classical economists display such great and persistent concern with policies that maximize output? Their concern was with the maximizing, not with the output. The struggle of men for larger incomes was good because in the process they learned independence, self-reliance, self-discipline — because, in short, they became better men. (Stigler, 1949a: 4)

The first lecture superficially seems concerned with economic equality. In particular, it puzzles over the fact that classical economists appeared to have little concern for the topic in contrast to the post-war fixation by Stigler's contemporaries[19]. This point is exaggerated to heighten the contrast.

> More recently the desire for greater equality has grown strong. Every policy is scrutinized for its effects on the distribution of income, and the results

---

[18] The problem of a discipline that aims to make better men was clearly pinpointed by Milton Friedman. Given a draft of the lecture, he responded by worrying what such an objective might be in more concrete terms.

> Re your solution? "the improvement of the individual" is about as ambiguous a touchstone as "equality". I don't know how to define either. You cite Marshall. In him, "the improvement of man" equals the remaking of other peoples into the image of the Englishman, which is warning enough that this slogan has danger of leading to the narrowest kind of presumptuous provincialism. (Letter from George Stigler to Milton Friedman, February 1948 in Hammond and Hammond, 2006: 78)

[19] For effect, Stigler overstates his claims in this lecture as he does in the others as well. Perhaps something of what Stigler has in mind is reflected in a later presentation provided by Galbraith (1954). Ironically, this was a session in which Stigler (1954) himself gave a rather savage rejoinder to what he perceived as Galbraith's overstatements.

> To many of us the notion that one individual shall be in position to control the real income of others remains more than slightly obscene. We react to it much as a Puritan to Professor Kinsey — adultery exists no doubt, but how much better not to talk about it. (Galbraith, 1954: 5)

> of this scrutiny weigh heavily in the final judgment of the desirability of the policy. A growing number of economists, indeed, implicitly argue that no other injustice equals in enormity that of large differences in income. (Stigler, 1949a: 1)

The underlying theme, however, is that calls for government intervention imply a basic unfairness in market distributions of income[20]. Stigler's ruling assumption equates distribution based on marginal productivity as necessarily flowing from equilibrium-adjusted competitive markets. Where individuals receive compensation equivalent to their proportional economic contribution the outcome must be both efficient and equitable. Economists then must cease to support social engineering policies that lack either theoretical or empirical justification. For these reasons the classical moral imperative is superior to present day concerns with income distribution. Economics cannot state what that moral objective might be but assumes that it can best be facilitated through the individual responsibility inherent in any competitive market.

> There is not and cannot be agreement on the precise character of man we seek to achieve ... But we are persuaded that an economic system will not help us to move in the right direction unless it grants both opportunity and responsibility to the individual: the very uncertainty of our ultimate ethical goals dictates a wide area of individual self-determination. We are not able to supply a blueprint of the ideal life, but we are persuaded that even if it were known it would be ideal only for the person who individually and knowingly and voluntarily accepted it. It is not necessary, however, to know what is best; it is enough to know what is better. (Stigler, 1949a: 8)

Economic analysis is therefore equilibrium analysis which provides the basis for distribution according to individual marginal productivity[21].

---

[20] Ironically, classical economists do have quite a bit to say about income distribution. Ricardo starts a tradition whereby property rights (in the ownership of land) create a vestigial power which determines income distribution. Such distributions do not by necessity encourage either economic or moral growth.

[21] Stigler maintained a career long interest in questions of income distribution, in particular, the efficiency and morality of those generated by markets. As one of the few graduate students ever to complete a dissertation under Frank Knight, his work focused on what would continue to be in an implicit sense, the underlying theme of

Government intervention should aim at removing obstacles to competitive markets rather than dictating specific outcomes.

> The policy of ignoring inequalities of resources and battling vigorously against inequalities of income is a wanton subsidy to psychiatrists. Our concern should be much more with the ownership of resources that leads to the wide difference in income. We should seek to make labour incomes more equal by enlarged education systems, improvements of labour mobility, elimination of labour monopolies, provision of medical care for poor children, and the like. (Stigler, 1949a: 10)

His first lecture then is less narrow than may originally appear. It is very much a 'back to the future' approach which calls on economists to return to the values underlying classical analysis. An economic system must encourage self-improvement. Markets represent the governance structure that allows individuals to achieve such a goal. It is then unsurprising that Stigler buttresses his lecture by sprinkling it so liberally with quotes from Alexis de Tocqueville[22]. In particular, he ends his first piece with an extended quote from Tocqueville. Its purpose is to underline the parallel

---

his economic analysis. Stigler maintained that *Production and Distribution Theories* (1941) was far too heavily influenced by Knight. Stigler's introduction of uncertainty is definitely a deliberate bow to Knight and seems in line with what a disciple of Knight might conclude. But even at a rather early age, Stigler's future break from his teacher is foreseeable. For Stigler, Knight's central concern with uncertainly need not seriously distort market outcomes, nor call for a planned policy of income redistribution. Market outcomes may still remain efficient as well as equitable.

> Once uncertainly is introduced, the theory of distribution is altered greatly. Anticipations rule economic activity, and many of the anticipations must be erroneous because of the very fact of uncertainty. The entrepreneur becomes a residual claimant, and the exhaustion-of-product problem disappears. Anticipated marginal productivity becomes the basis for remunerating all productive services except entrepreneurship. (Stigler, 1941: 386)

[22] Alexis de Tocqueville, like Adam Smith, has become one of the icons of self-styled classical liberals. Like all those with strong ideological predilections it is sometimes difficult to discern how much such people really understand of their idol's work. A recent biography of Alexis de Tocqueville (Brogan, 2006) questions the degree to which Tocqueville was a Tocquevillian.

drawn between the fixation with equality and the greater centralisation of power. With the Cold War soon to build up to the Berlin Blockade in 1948, Stigler would see this threat to freedom as palpable. Stage one of reforming economics by establishing a counter-revolutionary vanguard was to question the assumption that income equality should be a concern of economists, theoretically or as applied to policy directions. The invidious acceptance of such an assumption only sold out individual freedom for a spurious gain in material equality.

> But, the only thing I can remember him [George Stigler] saying or writing, he wrote it somewhere but I can't remember where, was that he favored a capitalistic oriented system. He favored it because it created the kind of person that he'd like better to live with. And that kind of person was somebody who felt responsibility for himself, and not one who thought that others were responsible for him. (Conversation with Harold Demsetz, September 1997)

3.2. *A gorgon's look at monopolistic competition*

> He [Edwin Chamberlin] found the school to be distinguished "by the zeal with which the theory of monopolistic competition has been attacked", and called it the Chicago School of Anti-Monopolistic Competition. What was a minor recreational activity for us was the raison d'être to him! (Stigler, 1988: 150)

The objective behind George Stigler's second lecture is also clear. The theory of Monopolistic Competition must be destroyed and Stigler was just the man to deliver a body blow to the theory. This gunslinger position was of course nothing new to Stigler. Part of the Chicago counter-revolution was to maintain the profession's belief in price theory while undermining Keynesian economics. The latter could be left to the tactics of his comrade in arms, Milton Friedman. But it was largely George Stigler's responsibility to defend the basis of neoclassical theory. He does after all come to the task of levelling his aim at Monopolistic Competition with a few battles already under his belt. The most important of these was his (1947b) successful war waged against the 'kinked demand curve', which would be the basis for his subsequent approach to torching all non-equilibrium alternative systems[23].

There were two reasons that compelled Stigler to attempt a 'seek and destroy' mission of Chamberlin's work[24]. In many ways monopolistic competition had a similar status within micro-economics that Keynesianism did within macroeconomic analysis. It was a threat to standard market theory both because it did not fit into a customary equilibrium analysis and because it had gained widespread credibility throughout the profession.

> My recollection is not worth much, but for what it's worth is that the Robinsonian emphasis on the individual firm's economics, the analysis of marginal revenue and marginal cost, fitted in very well with what we were otherwise thinking. There were no problems about that. But the Chamberlinian attempt to make it into a theory of general equilibrium was not. The attempt,

---

[23] See Freedman (1995) for an analysis of Stigler's approach. Essentially the method was to create an ersatz version of the original theory and then destroy his own purposefully crafted straw man. As was the case with Monopolistic Competition, the kinked demand curve provided something of a micro-foundation for the Keynesian approach to macroeconomics. In the case of the kinked demand curve it established a justification for labor market outcomes within such a quantity adjusted system. Stigler was sufficiently successful in the case of kinked demand curves as to replace Sweezy's (1937) original version with his ersatz variant in the professional literature.

[24] There was also a very personal reason as well. Chamberlin (1947) had reviewed Stigler's textbook *The Theory of Price* (1946b). This represented Stigler's first attempt to expand his more limited text *The Theory of Competitive Price* (1942a) beyond the narrow confines of a perfectly competitive market structure. Chamberlin's review was rather scathing. Chief of the book's insufficiencies seems to have been a lack of regard and space for Chamberlin's own theory of monopolistic competition. Though offered a right of reply by *The American Economic Review*, Stigler declined. His LSE lecture represents his far more deadly and effective response.

> I am not inclined to do this [write a reply] because
>
> (1) of a general feeling against replies to reviews, and
> (2) the inappropriateness of a short note in dealing with this matter (and the disinterest in a long one). All I gain by a reply is creation of doubts in the minds of those economists (numerous, alas) who think Chamberlin is a great man. (Letter from George Stigler to Milton Friedman, August 1947 in Hammond and Hammond, 2006: 61)

> as it were, to discuss about closer or less close substitutes in different markets, that kind of thing, trying to talk of an industry of imperfect competitors was not. Now maybe it's only that I'm really going back to George's later discussion, but I think from the very beginning that we got on very much less well with that general approach and those preconceptions. (Conversation with Milton Friedman, August 1997)

How Stigler intended to destroy the theory's credibility is to some degree telegraphed in a restrained but angry letter that he had written to Chamberlin in response to a critical review (1947) of Stigler's (1946b) text on price theory.

> In any event, it is not a sin to reject your orientation; in this I have very illustrious companions. I am prepared to argue (1) that your theory is indeterminate, and (2) that it is not useful (often in realistic analysis). I do not recall a single consistent application of it to a real problem, and this is the ultimate failure of a theory. (Letter from George Stigler to Edwin Chamberlin August 1947 in Hammond and Hammond 2006: 62–62)

This is not the place to do anything like a detailed analysis. However, the attempt throughout is to dismiss Chamberlin's theory as both unworkable and trivial. Once a theory becomes the target of a convincing act of demolitions, there is virtually no path to redemption having once landed in this hellish scholarly category. Stigler starts by indicating that only exceptional times would have seen such a theory being given any sort of credibility. The shock to accepted belief that the Great Depression represented, a veritable perfect storm of circumstances, provided acceptable camouflage for an essentially hollow theory. '... because it was the 'thirties', they were enthusiastically received' (Stigler, 1949b: 12). Note that the undertone is that this was a decade when all sorts of dangerous heresies were accepted because of the desperate times[25]. Rational analysis became overshadowed as events somehow clouded the judgement of otherwise reasonable

[25] Stigler makes such departures from price theory a clear aberration by ironically referring to the Great Depression as 'that chasm between darkness and light' (Stigler, 1949b: 12). As Coase (1994) points out, the acceptance, in the thirties, of the theories put forward by Chamberlin (1933), Robinson (1933) and Keynes (1937) has very little to do with their ability to predict as yet unobserved phenomena. The thirties

economists. Stigler could point to (what was for him) indisputable economic nonsense as typified by the administered pricing work of Gardiner Means, the kinked demand curve of Paul Sweezy and other similar theories that attempted to change the basic microeconomic framework of received wisdom. This occurred as frequently as the more successful attempts to transform macroeconomic beliefs. Notice the way in which he could simply dismiss Joan Robinson's work as needing no critical evaluation because he recognised, quite correctly, that her approach presented no dangerous departure from standard price theory. Stigler even at this relatively early stage of his career had what was probably the best nose for dangerous heresy within the profession[26].

> Her volume marks no break with the tradition of neo-classical economics; indeed it contains I think, too uncritical an acceptance of the substantive content of orthodoxy. (Stigler, 1949b: 12–13)

To Stigler 'Professor Chamberlin was a true revolutionary' (Stigler, 1949b: 13). No harsher condemnation can be made by those seeking to defend market freedom against the incursion of regimented planners.

---

represented a crisis for economic theory and these systems both seemed to offer a way out of the existing problems.

> These books were certainly an instant success, and their contents were quickly absorbed and used by economists interested in price theory. ... These new books by Chamberlin and Mrs Robinson, which started the analysis with the decisions of the individual firm and used new tools such as the marginal revenue schedule, seemed to offer the way out. (Coase, 1994: 22)

[26] George Stigler had the same attitude to heretics as any religious fundamentalist. Such apostates hadn't simply gone astray. There could not be a scintilla of anything good or useful in such a doctrine.

> I think you're getting at something that is (a) the atmosphere at Chicago, and (b) intensified by Knight. That an academic is concerned not with being diplomatic, not with trying to avoid hurting people's feelings, but an academic is concerned with saying what's right. Telling the truth, or trying to get at it. And if you disagree with somebody you don't say, "Well, now there may be something in what you say". (Conversation with Milton Friedman, August 1997)

Stigler points out that Chamberlin stresses the heterodox nature of markets, emphasising what makes markets different from one another and the interdependencies of those markets and the firms within them. Stigler by necessity must stress the similarities in markets to insure that efficiency and equity flowed from individual choice. Moreover, for Stigler, in no other way but by abstracting and generalising was it possible to generate a productive theory, one that could generate a testable hypothesis.

> Well George did not think that differences were so important for economic analysis. You wanted to understand prices, demand and supply? You could use the same kind of model no matter where you applied it and you didn't have to have a really special model for it. I think that was why he was not a fan of the 1930s and 1940s industry studies. They thought every industry was unique. I think that was one of the consequences of the Chamberlin monopolistic competition model and he didn't see any useful generalization coming out of that. He was always interested in generalizations. And he was not interested in explaining the particular as much as he was in the generalization that you could deduce. (Conversation with Harold Demsetz, October 1997)

The lecture is of additional interest for plugging an important whole in the fabric of price theory. What somehow finds its way into this effective demolition job of Chamberlin is a concluding and unexpected plunge into the uncongenial world of methodology. The approach sketched is remarkably similar to that which his friend, Milton Friedman (1953), would bring out as path-breaking work a few years later. (And serve much the same purpose for Friedman as for Stigler.)[27] It is ironic, but strategically appropriate, that Stigler uses a

---

[27] Methodological discussions between Stigler and Friedman arose from Stigler's reaction to Chamberlin's review (1947). In fact, Milton Friedman in conversation with the author freely admitted his debt to George Stigler. To some degree, as related to the author by his former student, Mark Blaug, Stigler felt he had never been accorded recognition for the positivist approach to economics.

> I should like to offer the general proposition that every important scientific hypothesis almost inevitably must use assumptions that are descriptively erroneous. It is of the very nature of a really important scientific generalization that

methodological argument to dismiss further discussion of methodology. These discussions had become fraught given that the charge of 'unrealistic assumptions' had been increasingly used as a lever to try to dislodge standard price theory.

Stigler notes that Chamberlin's vision was clearly a legitimate way of looking at economic life. One may even argue that it was more congruent with untutored observation, and in this sense more 'realistic'. The importance of this alternative approach is immediately wiped away since Stigler claims quite emphatically that this is completely irrelevant on theoretical grounds. Instead, such a characteristic only explained why it was accepted so readily. This criticism makes only partial sense since the realism of assumptions may be, by themselves, insufficient, but only if they do not lead to a useful theory that makes observations more comprehensible. Similarly, predictions alone are certainly not sufficient either since the goal is to gain understanding rather than simply predictions. Stigler sidesteps this issue by focusing instead on the question, 'Does a theory incorporating this viewpoint contain more accurate or more comprehensive implications than the neoclassical theory?' (1949b: 33) Notice the leeway this provides Stigler since he gets to define what the vague term 'accurate' and 'comprehensive' might mean.

Clearly the conclusion of this second and particularly vivid sermon is that 'Thou shalt have no other price theory before you'. Competitive markets eliminated market power and left individuals 'free to choose'. Only such an approach provided an effective bulwark against the planners who threatened ultimately to remove not only economic but political freedom. Systems lacking a competitive equilibrium could be used to opportunistically legitimise arbitrary distribution systems and thus provide a rationale for government intervention. Market systems made these dangerous justifications vanish.

---

it provides a simpler rationalization of a mass of facts than was available before. It is likely to obtain its objective by an inspiration about the particular basic elements of the situation that are important and by discarding what after the event can be shown to have been irrelevant complicating assumptions. In a way, the better the hypothesis the greater the extent to which it simplifies, the more sharply will its assumptions depart from reality. (Letter from Milton Friedman to George Stigler, November 1947 in Hammond and Hammond, 2006: 65)

3.3. *Redeeming the classical economists*

> I just don't dare send you an article on how smart the classical economists were, or you'll give up completely. (Letter from George Stigler to Milton Friedman, November 1947 in Hammond and Hammond, 2006: 67)

At this stage (lecture three) in Stigler's 1948 reconstruction of economics, time was ripe to point out to all the sinners among the congregation the always grave danger of backsliding when it came to government intervention. How better to do this than through case studies involving clear, if convenient economic history, especially if by doing so the bogeyman of unintended consequences could be cleanly demonstrated[28]. Under such a scenario, what counts are not the good intentions of the planners, but the economics that drive the results.

The lecture itself is ostensibly an attempt to rehabilitate classical economists given the then commonly held prejudices. (Today, the profound lack of awareness of such individuals as Senior, Leslie or McCulloch, would make the issue of rehabilitation moot.)

> For how little those venerable men knew. They did not know of marginal revenue and marginal cost, of marginal product and marginal propensity … They did not know that one can draw economical diagrams … nor that one can distil the essence of economics in the heat of the differential calculus … Nor were the deficiencies merely terminological and expositional. The classical

[28] The quality of Stigler's recounting of this slice of 19th century economic history strays beyond the bounds of this discussion. The temptation to embellish history, including intellectual history, is a shared weakness among economists who hold objectives to be far more critical than the path leading to them. The most polemical are often those most prone to this failing. This would include Stigler's close colleague Milton Friedman as well as their bete noire, John Maynard Keynes.

> As a historian of thought in areas in which he was emotionally involved as a protagonist and prophet, Keynes seemed to me to be seriously lacking in the unexciting but essential qualities for the intellectual historian of objectivity and of judiciousness. Even when he was engaged in selecting those upon whom to bestow laurels for having in some degree anticipated his discoveries, his selection seemed to me then, and still seems to me now that I have acquired more knowledge of the older literature, often to have been random when not eccentric. (Viner, 2003: 418)

> economists did not know that the demand curve is terribly important. They did not even know that competition is imperfect, and that monopolists do not charge all they may. (Stigler, 1949c: 25)

The claim is clearly ironical, since what Stigler intends to show is that they were able economists in terms of practical application and problem solving. This being the rightful aim of economics, the fact that retrospectively we can snub their theoretical apparatus as crude, should not provide the decisive measure with which to evaluate their work.

> The discrepancies between pronouncements and practice are notorious in the field of methodology[29]; can it not be so also in the theory of value? In writing their treatises, may not the classical economists have employed an apparatus which is different and in modern eyes inferior to that which they employed to analyse concrete problems? (Stigler, 1949c: 25–26)

Whether Stigler's audience, or subsequent readers, were convinced that the implicit, but unspecified working methods of these early economists were more sophisticated than their explicit treatises is not without interest, but a step removed from the underlying purpose of Stigler's third sermon. As might be expected given the nature of 19th century debates, the issue chosen to illustrate the wisdom of these classical economists involved a policy controversy. This should hardly come as a surprise given the strong tradition that for these practitioners, policy debates were very much intertwined with theoretical issues. Their modern counterparts are liable to forget that the economics of the time was heavily policy driven, certainly from the time of Adam Smith, but prior to his monumental work as well. However, what is more relevant in understanding the purpose behind Stigler's five lectures is how this particular one advances the overall objective of his performance at the London School of Economics.

---

[29] In light of Stigler's methodological announcement in his second lecture and his subsequent adherence to such practise, his statement here is to some degree an indictment of his own work and that of Milton Friedman (1953) who formulated this version of positivism to a greater extent.

The given example describes a situation that would touch familiar chords within the listeners of 1948, especially with the Great Depression as a shared recent experience. The introduction of the power loom had to varying degrees impoverished skilled weavers after the Napoleonic wars in England. Skilled weavers being independent contractors (via the putting out system) found it difficult to compete with power loom factories. The almost inevitable result was a general exploitation of family members to stay afloat. The governmental response (a not unfamiliar one), was to appoint a Royal Commission.

> Their reports, published in 1839 and 1840, provided a wealth of material and confirmed the fact that the weavers were in pitiful circumstances. (Stigler, 1949c: 27)

A portion of the labour market is in dire straits. The immediate issue for government officials is to ascertain the cause of such a condition and based on such investigations to consider whether any specific policy could improve their lot. Not surprisingly, a key conclusion (supporting Stigler's own predilections) is that such workers needed to shift out of this particular superseded occupation. Unfortunately, labour combinations in other trades ultimately blocked entry to these viable alternatives. Any government solution therefore must necessarily focus on removing such restraints to trade. Intervention should focus on removing these impediments to market operations. In addition, such a solution could explore whether it might be possible to increase competitiveness within the industry by boosting productivity. However, methods which seem to protect these workers from the rigor of competition; minimum wages, taxes on power looms or on imports, not only hurt other sectors of the economy but ultimately impoverish the very group it seeks to serve[30].

Unintended consequences must almost inevitably undermine the best intentions of planners. Besides this consistent conclusion, Stigler is also able to introduce an important sub-theme in this middle

[30] For Stigler's modern day version of similar issues, see his discussion on minimum wage legislation (1947a). Certainly this debate would have been fresh in his mind while devising his resurrection of the classical virtues.

lecture which would form the keystone to Stigler's own version of the Chicago School counter-revolution, namely the need for quantification and testing. This would be the visionary call of his AEA Presidential Address in 1964 (1982). One can hardly argue with his own conclusion concerning the overriding importance of applied, empirical work. Though the parishioners listening to this sermon would be well advised to recall Stigler's own warnings about the discrepancy between pronouncements and practice (1949c: 25).

> No intelligent person can fail to modify and adapt his general position to suit its peculiarities. There are obviously important pieces of evidence, and he must take account of them ... There are indisputable developments, and his theory must give an account of them. The theorists' eternal, and proper, striving for generality is disciplined by the facts. These, I repeat, are the effects of analysis of concrete problems. (Stigler, 1949c: 35–36)

3.4. *On being mathematically dysfunctional*

> On Samuelson's definition, I suppose, one writes an essay on mathematics; on the conventional definition, one writes an essay on economics. (Stigler, 1949f: 100)[31]

There was a deeply held conviction developing within the Chicago School counter-revolution at this time that ran directly counter to the

[31] At about the same time as Stigler was dismissing Samuelson in print with a well-phrased aside; he was privately consigning him to the dustbin of economists at rather a tender age. (At the time Samuelson was no more than 34 years of age.)

> Rumor has it that Samuelson was quite the unsuccessful suave chairman, a la Schumpeter, at the meetings. Solomon Fabricant said he referred to you as an altar boy or something of the sort; I would have relished being there to see your reaction. It may merely be prejudice, but I'm inclined to write him off as an economist. Two of his recent jobs (the Survey article and his essay in the Hansen festschrift were pure mathematical exposition, as is also his current *Economic* item (which, by the way, has already been done better by Wold), and his textbook suggest that he doesn't know anything that hasn't appeared in the *Survey of Current Business*. (Letter from George Stigler to Milton Friedman, January 1949 in Hammond and Hammond, 2006: 97)

Cowles Commission which in this post-war period also chose Chicago as its working base. In fact such department members as Jacob Marshak or Don Patinkin split their time, also serving as researchers with the Commission. This fourth sermon by Stigler, in his role of evangelical prophet, scourges the sin of mathematisation. The use of mathematics is of course by itself no sin. Stigler is in no way math phobic. However, in the same way that eating is an innocent necessity while gluttony is a sin, mathematics obediently serving economics is admirable, while mathematics as an end in itself derails the entire enterprise of economics.

> The increase of mastery over mathematics, however, is not free. The budget equation of the mathematical economist applies also to himself: he purchases mathematical literacy with economic illiteracy. An economist, after all, is not an unemployed mathematician. (Stigler, 1949d: 44)

Following the lead of Friedman, the Chicago School, at least in the decades following the war, is deliberately Marshallian. Partial equilibrium analysis, while clearly unrealistic, proves far more serviceable for applied work than a Walrasian general equilibrium approach. (Notice the clear application of the methodological foundation articulated by Stigler in his second lecture.) The Marshallian approach also sternly suppresses mathematical exposition. The Chicago translation of this approach is that mathematics must remain consistently subservient to economic intuition and analysis.

> Because the mathematical method is so powerful and beautiful, and its possession still sufficiently rare to command distinction, the mathematical economist is under constant temptation to use it just for the sake of using it. (Stigler, 1949d: 43)

All of this is quite true. If anything, the contrast with the overuse of mathematics emphasises the essential point of the previous sermon, namely the importance of empirical work. On a surface level the discussion is a warning against such economists as Gerald Debreu who confuses ends with means. But perhaps a deeper purpose is revealed in the fact that one of the few contemporary economists he bothers to name in the lecture is one of his persistent targets. Samuelson appears in a cameo role to provide a rendition of Poisson's idea that 'mathematics has no symbols for confused ideas' (Stigler, 1949d: 39). The appearance allows Stigler to dismiss the way in which Samuelson has utilised mathematical tools.

> The Poisson view is objectionable not merely because it is untrue, but because it is almost the opposite of the truth. It is an insulting restriction on the usefulness of mathematics to credit it with the ability to deal only with clear concepts. The history of science gives us good reason to believe that every concept of modern science will be found to be ambiguous at some future time. Therefore a snobbish mathematics would be unusable at present. It is as if one were to assert that language is only for the expression of pure thoughts: we have also mathematical pornography. (Stigler, 1949d: 30–40)

As pointed out previously, Stigler had an exceptionally fine nose for sniffing out heresy. This pertained not only narrowly to neoclassical theory but to any approach that surreptitiously undermined the efficiency of markets and promoted government intervention. Perhaps then the problem was not solely with the methods mathematical economists used but also with the work such economists did. Those at the Cowles Commission who were not simply developing econometric theory seemed determined to place the Keynesian approach into a more rigorous general equilibrium framework. Optimality itself seemed purposely constructed to point out market failures rather than market efficiency. In the hands of Paul Samuelson or Kenneth Arrow (Cowles Commission) theoretical results could all too easily translate into policy demands. Innocent recreation in the form of abstract theoretical constructions when manipulated by Keynesian economists would become transformed into an unambiguous basis for demanding greater government intervention. These perhaps unconsciously dangerous planners had captured the high ground offered by burying economic intuition under a barrage of symbolic expression. Mathematics as a weapon of shock and awe mesmerised opponents with its Gorgon like glance. A successful counter-revolution would need to initially neutralise the effect of such a potentially commanding weapon.

> This is almost the way George would be talking if he was sitting here. 'Having you and your six friends argue about a lemma, that's progress!' He wouldn't be indignant. He would be laughing. He would be dismissive. He'd say, 'You're dopes. You're dopes'. What should you do with them George? 'Exile them to Samoa'. He'd dismiss them with a wave of the hand. (Conversation with Sam Peltzman, October 1997)

3.5. *An economist plays a game of monopoly*

> He once wrote an article about monopoly, that you should break up companies. He eventually abandoned that theory. And the reason he abandoned the theory was very interesting. In those days he thought, you could tell the government what to do and the government would do it; but his later view was, no. He adopted the view that there are politics and politics is worse than monopoly, or can be worse than monopoly. So he changed, drastically changed his point of view on that. And he began to take this view that you are better off having a rotten something that doesn't work perfectly in the market than having the government get involved. (Conversation with Gary Becker, October, 1997)

The idea of monopoly has always been the open sesame of government intervention. It had been the driving force behind antitrust legislation in the United States as well as other countries. Stigler would have been well aware that Gardiner Means' (1939) contention of an America ruled by administered prices basically posited a monopolised economy. For Means, such a structural defect accounted for the seeming unending length of the Great Depression. In developing an economic blueprint for professional work that would staunchly minimise the requirement for planning or intervention, the obsession with monopoly needed to be rendered benign.

His required five sermons to the English devout needed to reflect his own long journey of escape from the old Chicago School of Knight and Simons. Stigler started to change his views on the issue of monopolisation between the years of 1942 and 1949. It is not that his basic belief in the competitive nature of most industries changed, but rather his reading of the evidence did. His 1942 piece is very open ended, explaining the limitations of available techniques and data. By 1949 his use of many of the same studies became a battering ram applied to the views of rival theorists. Something does happen; post-war, to George Stigler's professional approach. Seemingly he came to fear that neoclassical price theory was under serious attack. For its proponents, compromise or even the smallest concession, would be equivalent to surrender.

In 1942, the question of how competitive an economy as a whole might be, held no real meaning for Stigler. Certainly it was not a question that could be quantitatively answered.

> The second major problem is concerned with the much discussed question: How competitive is the economy as a whole? Despite the frequency with which dogmatic answers are given to this question, it is doubtful whether any meaningful answer is attainable ... it is difficult to find any important purpose in asking how competitive an economy is. There is some intellectual curiosity in knowing how much smaller national income is than it would be under workable competition (where practicable!), but the curiosity does not merit huge expenditures for a crude and unsatisfactory answer. (Stigler, 1942: 4)

Stigler questions whether any of the methods employed resolve the problem. Workable competition could only be ideally rather than practically used. As Stigler points out

> ... we do not yet possess the information to classify industries accurately as workably competitive or otherwise ... and more important, we do not know how far the monopolistic industries depart from workable competition. (Stigler, 1942: 5–6)

For this reason, though he considers Wilcox's (1940) efforts at classification to be admirable, it yields no definitive answers. Certainly to Stigler (1942), concentration ratios are ambiguous since there is no established relationship between any such ratio and a level of competitiveness.

Stigler in his fifth and final lecture repeats his belief that these estimates have little if any scientific value. He does, however, let the proverbial cat out of the theoretical bag by admitting that such figures seem to have an unfortunate effect on social policy. This is what distinguishes his 1942 remarks from those of 1949 and gives a thoroughly accurate trajectory to where his views would evolve as the decades advanced in his career. By 1949, he is engaged in an open battle with an opposing blueprint for the economics profession as well as for consequent policy.

> There is no necessary relationship between one's views on the extent of competition and on the type of economic policy that should be pursued. One can believe that the economy is 99% monopolized, and still argue for policies designed to revive competition and private enterprise; or one can believe that the economy is 99% competitive and still argue for syndicalism or socialism. Such positions, however, are not popular ... Most economists would probably change their policy views if they were convinced that their appraisal of the relative roles of competition and monopoly was fundamentally wrong. (Stigler, 1949e: 46)

Given the role that he is assuming in this lecture, he has no trouble leaning on the very same Wilcox (1940) study he previously regarded with some scepticism. It is clear that this has become a purely rhetorical battle where nuances are considered self-imposed hindrances to one's argument[32].

At this point his series of sermons draw to a close. He has indicated the necessary direction economics must take if it is not to become the unwilling dupe of totalitarianism but remain aligned to

---

[32] Stigler would reassert much the same argument at the AEA convention of the same year (1949).

> Free entry ... may be defined as the condition that long-run costs of new firms if they enter the industry will be equal to those of firms already in the industry ... With this understanding, free entry seems a valid characterization of most American industries. One may concede this and still argue that, because of the large capital requirements necessary to establish a new company of minimum efficient size, free entry is often difficult, and firms in industries with (absolutely) large capital requirements have a sheltered position. I have as little basis for my scepticism of this argument as its many adherents have given for supporting it. (Stigler, 1950: 27)

the forces of freedom. He has done so by eradicating the five plagues afflicting modern (*circa* 1948) economics.

- Sacrificing growth and efficiency for ersatz equality.
- Focusing on more realistic but fundamentally useless non-equilibrium alternatives.
- Ignoring the law of unintended consequences.
- Sacrificing economic content for mathematical eloquence.
- Obsessing over the monopoly phantasm.

4. Future Directions — How These Lectures Influenced Stigler's Future Work

> I don't know how important ideology is, but think it is unimportant. You don't know how important it is, but think it is important. My position is better because I try — feebly and so often unsuccessfully — to use a trusted theory of human behaviour to explain social phenomena. Your position is worse because you try — with marvellous ease — to explain the mysteries by a *deus ex machine*. (Letter from George Stigler to Milton Friedman, 29 March 1984)

The blueprint sketched out in his London School of Economic lectures is uncannily accurate in foreshadowing the course of Stigler's own career as he set about over turning the commonly held wisdom of his day. In this, he worked the micro-economic seams of the counter-revolution leaving the more macro-aspects to his team mate, Milton Friedman. The thesis of his work, as developed in those five lectures, stated that government intervention into market economies represents incursions against individual choice and thus liberty. In a Hobbesian like compact, competitive markets remove the issue of private power. To convince the economic profession (and the wider public) of the validity of his thesis he had to perform three distinct labours, not quite up to the rigours demanded of Hercules, but still a daunting task.

- The initial task required a demonstration that competitive markets are pervasive. Given the freedom of choice, efficiency and growth generated by such market structures, any justification for government intervention is forestalled.

- He next had to demonstrate that the stated objectives behind government intervention could not be substantiated. This implies that not only isn't such interference necessary but it is incapable of accomplishing its presumed goals.
- Last, given that government interventions are not motivated by social welfare concerns, he had to locate such objectives within the self-interest of government agents such as politicians or bureaucrats. In this case, not only does such interference fail to raise the general well being but it instead aims at redistributions that lower overall social benefits.

The years George Stigler spends after this sermon, given as a still somewhat youthful preacher, fulfils his stated agenda. Until the early sixties he focuses mainly on those aspects of economics that reinforce his vision of a world dominated by competitive markets. This culminates in two of his key (and perhaps best) articles. With his "Theory of Oligopoly" (1964), Stigler is able to demonstrate that no such theory need be developed. Any attempt to limit competition, if successful, in the short run would tumble over into the realm of monopoly. While in the far more likely case of a failure to maintain such limits, the market returns to its naturally competitive status. He had only to wait for Harold Demsetz (1968) to demonstrate that even monopoly markets are essentially competitive. Competition for the market could effectively replace any competition within the market itself. Next, by tackling information, Stigler deliberately took on such noted economists as Kenneth Arrow head on. Economists in the fifties and early sixties widely came to believe that information, or more accurately the lack of accurate, reliable information produced market failures. Inevitably, given this starting point, the peculiar nature of information yielded imperfect markets. Stigler's approach and that of the Chicago School emphasises not what makes these markets differ but rather what these economists see as the remarkable similarities between all such governance structures. Starting from the assumption that a market is a market, Stigler is able to demonstrate that the market for information is not different than any other market and thus does not provide the occasion for government intervention[33].

The second stage of his career parallels the change in the sixties of political regimes with the Democrats replacing Republicans and the subsequent Washington migration of many of Stigler's traditional foes from Harvard and MIT. Given that such a changed environment brought with it more aggressive antitrust enforcement and other calls for a more activist government, what could be a more appropriate conservative response than demonstrating, with hard facts, the clear futility of expecting that government objectives could be achieved? Stigler, with the help of Claire Friedland (1962), does this by reopening questions that had seemingly been too obvious to investigate. Does regulation, for instance, of public utilities yield benefits to consumers? The surprising finding that such regulation had no effect roused the profession from its dogmatic sleep and spurred it to investigate additional regulatory aspects[34]. Some of these were done by Stigler himself (1975).

[33] To do this Stigler limits his concerns to simply the case where information is available but needs to be found. In his day one might refer to this as the 'Yellow Pages' approach to information search or today to information as a problem in 'Googling'. Though this application of standard techniques to describe information search is both clever and useful it cannot be considered sufficient in and of itself. It leaves out too many important aspects of information that differentiates this market from those of standard commodities. This indeed may be one of those cases where differences rather than similarities are more important for useful analysis.

> And that's what makes it powerful and that's, at the same time, what has in it in my mind, some defects. Because, doing it that way, says that there's nothing peculiar about information. You could treat it like the supply and demand for wheat. Whereas I think there are some things that are peculiar about information, for example the public goods aspects of information and maybe some other things about it, that merits treating it somewhat differently. But his treatment of it was a clear extrapolation of the neoclassical toolkit. (Conversation with Harold Demsetz, October, 1997)

[34] As mentioned before, this work comes at approximately the same time as Stigler is making his visionary speech whereby the future lies with greater empirical work, with a profession that depends on evidence for its conclusions.

> I think one of the respects in which he himself was critical of neoclassical economics and which he viewed, maybe not as an option but as a supplement to

In the seventies, with the Vietnam War and the coming of age of the baby boom generation serving as the occasion to mount a panoply of demands for radical reform in the economy (and in the economics profession), Stigler responded with the concluding chapter of his blueprint. Since governments are nothing but a collection of self-interested agents, government intervention via the regulatory path will serve special interest groups and associated politicians at the expense of general welfare measures. At the height of the call for revolution in the country, Stigler (1971) brings out 'A Theory of Regulation', to demonstrate the exact opposite. If his previous work displayed the futility of government intervention, he would now explore why governments were so fixed on passing regulations that

---

> neoclassical economics, was his great love of imaginatively gathering evidence bearing on propositions. The neoclassicals were not at the forefront of providing evidence for their ideas. He definitely felt that this was needed and that these principles could not stand on their own feet, that inevitably, they had to be either defended or attacked on the basis of evidence gathering. So he was a great respecter of quantitative work and perhaps more than he should have been. In his presidential address to the American Economics Association he was almost romantic about the possibilities of bringing data to bear on various propositions. I'm sure that he later realized that you weren't able to get your bearings or pull yourself out of dilemmas solely by looking at the data. (Conversation with Harold Demsetz, October 1997)

The irony is that Stigler and Friedland's (1962) early and dramatic findings on regulation were based on a flawed statistical analysis whereby some of the data entered was a decimal off. (See Peltzman (1993) for details.) Though making no change in the statistical significance of the results, the size of the effects would have dramatically altered. Serendipity had no small part to play in driving the beginning of this attack on received wisdom. Interestingly enough, when informed of this discrepancy many years later, Stigler chose to sweep the facts conveniently under the rug. How this practise coincided with his 1964 Presidential sermon on the coming age of evidence remains a challenge for any serious researcher.

> And George's answer was that there was no point in making a big fuss about this mistake because it was twenty years ago and nobody cares anymore. And there has been a mountain of research on this topic. It is much more sophisticated than ours. Ours was *very* crude by comparison. (Conversation with Claire Friedland, November 1997)

did not achieve those objectives. With any abiding fortune, this would put the nail in the coffin of government regulation. All such action could be reduced to an elementary economic drive to further self-interest. Again, under Stigler's analysis, a market is a market[35]. Thus, a political market may best be analysed by the standard economic methodology of supply and demand. The very simplicity of the approach is effective in driving home Stigler message of non-intervention.

> He often convinced himself they were actually true. Like when he was confronted with some fact about regulation, he would say 'Ah, you're going to find some Congressman was bought off. [laughter] You are actually going to find that. That's what you're going to find. Are you sure that you didn't find that this Congressman...?' You know, that kind of writing, that kind of a very strong view. (Conversation with Sam Peltzman, October 1997)

Stigler then presents the relatively rare case where the unfolding of his career can be clearly discerned in his visionary statement to those

[35] This would lead him, in the final stage of his career, to push the idea of market efficiency to its logical conclusion. Political markets over time must reflect consumer preferences. Sugar subsidies are clearly inefficient from a narrow economic viewpoint, but if they are maintained over time, they must reflect the public's preference for income redistribution. Otherwise such an arrangement would change. (See Stigler's (1993) retrospective article.) The consequence, however, is that given the efficiency of political markets there is little left for the economist to do in terms of policy. There is a responsibility to better understand the workings of the market and to persuade those within the economics profession. But, it is essentially a misuse of a valuable resource (time) to try to influence policy makers or the public.

> Herewith a quote that seems to encapsulate the difference between you [George Stigler] and Aaron [Director], on the one hand, and me, on the other:
>
> Alexander Hamilton "had come to profess the 'pessimistic' view of man, maintaining that people are governed by 'passion and prejudice' rather than by 'an enlightened sense of their interests'; and yet throughout his career he expended more energy and talent in appeals to the intelligence and virtue of common citizens than did any other American in public life. So much stronger was his natural optimism than his acquired pessimism". (Letter from Milton Friedman to George Stigler, 24 December 1987)

gathered at the LSE in 1948. The four decades that followed clearly refined that vision and put it into practise. Time may have made him more consistent but did not shift him from his self-allocated task.

> I think he went to a more satisfactory position, absolutely. The earlier view, as you say, he picked up, that was the literature, he hadn't really thought it through. I mean, you know, he hadn't thought through everything at that point, and he hadn't really thought it out. As he thought through more and more, I think he came to a more satisfactory thesis on the issue. I think you're absolutely right, he did. ... But his views did become more consistent. I agree with you on that. Other people may not think so, but I think definitely that was true. He began to rethink some positions he had just inherited. Inherited you know, from his teachers and so on, or from the literature and he put it in a more consistent framework. (Conversation with Gary Becker, October 1997)

5. The Race is to the Swiftest — What has Chicago Wrought?

> The way to freedom was to unleash the millions of individual actions that made up a working economy, and never to seek to control them. (*The Economist* commenting on Ralph Harris, 2006: 92)

Because so much was at stake, not only personally but morally as well, the marketing of ideas dominated Stigler's professional strategies. Debates and academic discussions transmuted into an adversarial or winner-takes-all approach. The discipline became akin to the legal battlefield of the courtroom where opposing lawyers search for a winning rather than a correct argument.

It often seems that economists when following this approach are quick to note each others' attempts to sermonise but slow to acknowledge their own. The corrosive effect of preaching and the way it closes off rival theologians from considering alternative approaches is clearly exemplified by George Stigler's own career. Not that Stigler was unusual in practising such exclusion but rather that even the best of economists are afflicted with this failing. His extended contests with Gardiner Means and John Kenneth Galbraith display these traits to an embarrassing degree. For instance, charges of theology and dogma are swapped equally between Galbraith and Stigler. To an extent it is true about both. Stigler is determined to see competition as the dominant market structure while Galbraith stands steadfastly for market power as his prevailing doctrine. It is nearly impossible to think of any evidence that would change their respective stands. (The same can be said of his sustained battle with Gardiner Means.) Stigler is intent on measuring percentages of dominated markets. Galbraith allows that many markets are competitive but that a number of key markets are dominated by only a few firms. There is no common ground for debate or any effort to reach shared terms of discussion. Ideology inevitably trumps any empirical evidence. Thus, the most useful conclusion to be drawn after evaluating the type of evangelical barnstorming perfected by the Chicago School is that economics, like all disciplines, requires a clear separation between Church and State. Economists should decide whether the objective of their profession is to achieve understanding or to provide the foundations for preordained theological goals.

> Men cannot live without an economic theology — without some rationalization of the abstract and seemingly inchoate arrangements which provide him with his livelihood. For this purpose the competitive or classical model had many advantages. It was comprehensive and internally consistent. By asserting that it was a description of reality the conservative could use it as the justification of the existing order. For the reformer it could be a goal, a beacon to mark the path of needed change. Both could be united in the central faith at least so long as nothing happened to strain unduly their capacity for belief. (Galbraith, 1957: 17)

References

Brogan, H (2006). *Alexis de Tocqueville: Prophet of Democracy in the Age of Revolution — A Biography.* New Haven: Yale University Press.

Chamberlin, EH (1947). Review of *The Theory of Price* by G. Stigler. *The American Economic Review*, 37(3), 414–418.

Coase, R (1994). How should economists choose? In *Essays on Economics and Economists,* pp. 15–33. Chicago: The University of Chicago Press.

Dower, JW (1986). *War Without Mercy.* New York: Pantheon Books.

Economist (2006). Ralph Harris, 4th November 1992.

Freedman, CF (1995). The economist as mythmaker — Stigler's Kinky transformation. *The Journal of Economic Issues*, 29(1), 175–209.

Friedman, M (1953). The methodology of positive economics. In *Essays in Positive Economics*, pp. 3–43. Chicago: University of Chicago Press.

Friedman, M and R Friedman (1980). *Free to Choose — A Personal Statement.* Melbourne: Macmillan.

Galbraith, JK (1954). Countervailing power. *The American Economic Review Papers and Proceedings*, 44(2), 1–6.

Hammond, JD and CH Hammond (eds.), (2006). *Making Chicago Price Theory: Friedman-Stigler correspondence 1945–1957.* London and New York: Routledge.

Levitt, S and S Dubner (2005). *Freakonomics: A Rogue Economist Explores the Hidden Side of Everything.* New York: William Morrow.

McCann, CR Jr and M Perlman (1993). On thinking about George Stigler. *The Economic Journal*, 103 (July), 994–1014.

Machlup, F (1967). Theories of the firm, marginalist, behavioral, managerial. *American Economic Review*, 57(1), 1–33.

Means, G (1939). *The Structure of the American Economy. Part 1 Basic Characteristics.* Washington: US Congressional Reports.

Mill, JS (1859/1947), *On Liberty.* New York: Appleton-Centruy-Crofts.

Mont Pelerin Society (2003). Short history and statement of aims. *The Mont Pelerin Home Page* http://www.montpelerin.org/aboutmps.html, 2 December 2003, p. 1.

Peltzman, S (1993). George Stigler's contribution to the economic analysis of regulation. *The Journal of Political Economy*, 101(5), 818–833.

Robinson, J (1933). *The Economics of Imperfect Competition.* London: MacMillan.

Stigler, GJ (1941). *Production and Distribution Theories.* New York: MacMillan.

Stigler, G (1942a). *The Theory of Competitive Price.* London: Macmillan.

Stigler (1942b). The extent and bases of monopoly. *The American Economic Review Paper and Proceedings*, 32(2), 1–22.

Stigler, GJ (1946a). The economics of minimum wage legislation. *The American Economic Review*, 36(1), 358–365.

Stigler, GJ (1946b). *The Theory of Price.* London: Macmillan.

Stigler, GJ (1947a). Professor lester and the marginalists. *The American Economic Review*, 37(1), 154–157.

Stigler, GJ (1947b/1951). The Kinky oligopoly demand curve and rigid prices. In *Reading in Price Theory*, KE Boulding and GJ Stigler (eds.), pp. 410–439. London: Allen and Unwin.

Stigler, GJ (1949a). The economists and equality. In *Five Lectures on Economic Problems*, pp. 1–11. London: Longmans, Green and Co.

Stigler, GJ (1949b). Monopolistic competition in retrospect. In *Five Lectures on Economic Problems*, pp. 12–34. London: Longmans, Green and Co.

Stigler, GJ (1949c). The classical economics: An alternative view. In *Five Lectures on Economic Problems*, pp. 25–36. London: Longmans, Green and Co.
Stigler, GJ (1949d). The mathematical method in economics. In *Five Lectures on Economic Problems*, pp. 37–45. London: Longmans, Green and Co.
Stigler, GJ (1949e). Competition in the United States. In *Five Lectures on Economic Problems*, pp. 46–62. London: Longmans, Green and Co.
Stigler, GJ (1949f). A survey of contemporary economics. *The Journal of Political Economy*, 42(2), 93–105.
Stigler, GJ (1950). Monopoly and oligopoly by merger. *American Economic Review Papers and Proceedings*, 44(2), 7–14.
Stigler, GJ (1954). The economist plays with blocs. *The American Economic Review Papers and Proceedings*, 44(2), 23–34.
Stigler, GJ (1961). The economics of information. *The Journal of Political Economy*, 69(2), 213–225.
Stigler, GJ (1964). The theory of oligopoly. *The Journal of Political Economy*, 72(1), 44–61.
Stigler, GJ (1965/1982). The economist and the state. In *The Economist as Preacher*, pp. 119–135. Chicago: The University of Chicago Press.
Stigler, GJ (1964/1975). Public regulation of the securities market. In *The Citizen and the State*, pp. 78–100. Chicago: University of Chicago Press.
Stigler, GJ (1988). *Memoirs of an Unregulated Economist.* New York: Basic Books.
Stigler, GJ (1993). Law or economics. *Journal of Law & Economics.*
Stigler, GJ and C Friedland (1962). What can regulators regulate? The case of electricity. *The Journal of Law and Economics*, 5(1), 1–16.
Sweezy, P (1937). Demand under conditions of oligopoly. *The Journal of Political Economy*, 47(3), 568–573.
Von Mises, L (1980). Trends can change. In *Planning for Freedom*, pp. 173–179. South Holland, Illinois: Libertarian Press.
Weinstein, J (1968). *The Corporate Ideal in the Liberal State 1900–1918.* Boston: Beacon Press.
Wilcox, C (1940). *Competition and Monopoly in American Industry*, Monograph 21. Washington: T.N.E.C.

Chapter 5

Countervailing Egos[1] — Stigler versus Galbraith

> I am reluctant to reply to Professor Stigler for I could seem to be urging the claims of my book against those of a very great classic. And I could conceivably be missing the deeper cause of Professor Stigler's sorrow which may be not that so many read Galbraith and so few read Smith but that hardly anyone reads Stigler at all. (Galbraith quoted in Hession, 1972: 89)

In the sixties, only a colleague at Chicago would have placed their money on George Stigler to prevail in any future economic match-up against John Kenneth Galbraith. Stigler seemed to be the champion of a discredited theoretical framework, though this was only true if viewed from a popular, rather than professional standpoint. At the

---

[1] This paper focuses on the rhetorical skills of George Stigler and his propensity to misrepresent the ideas of his opponents. He was not of course the only economist of his generation adept at savaging his adversaries and misrepresenting opposing views. From opposite sides of the economic spectrum, both Milton Friedman (conversation with the author on 28 August 1997) and Geoffrey Harcourt (conversation with the author on 27 September 1995) note that no one could be as devastating as Joan Robinson. Galbraith himself matched Stigler in ferocity, ego and height. But Stigler was ultimately more influential in shaping the economics profession than all his opponents combined.

coalface where theoretical gnomes, like Stigler, toiled away at micro theory, perfectly competitive models had hardly vanished. Galbraith, policy adviser, ambassador and novelist, held sway in the court of public opinion. His domain never extended significantly into academic confines. Whatever limited influence Galbraith could command would dissipate as the Keynesian consensus broke apart upon the rocks of stagflation in the seventies. The Chicago School of Economics would gain dominance during this period, thanks in no small part to the multifaceted talents displayed by its *eminence grise*, George Stigler.

Throughout his career, Stigler kept up a relentless flow of sniper fire aimed squarely at any economic models that distanced themselves from the Chicago belief in a *tight prior equilibrium* (Reder, 1982). That he did respond tenaciously is not remarkable. Despite a pose of academic detachment, theories reflect the economist as much as the problem investigated. A challenge, whether intended or not, is taken somewhat personally. One might say that much of the trench warfare Stigler engaged in was for the heart and soul of the profession. To those deeply engaged, this was no trivial matter. What separates Stigler from the rest of the combatants is neither his dedication nor his ferocity, though it is hard to imagine greater ferocity than he often displayed; nor was it his cleverness or skill in attacking opposing views, though here again his talents were great. What stands out is the way Stigler consistently misrepresented alternative arguments. This apparent strategy was not due to any intentional resolve or lack of integrity, but rather the result of the tendentious nature of his criticism. The ability to distinguish what we want to perceive from what we actually perceive is rare. It seems to have skipped George Stigler completely[2].

For Stigler, a theory could never be a simple starting point for mutual inquiry. Economic arguments had to be fully articulated, each one encased in its own impregnable carapace. This made it relatively

[2] It is far from uncommon for economists to find in a work exactly what they expect. Prejudgement is a widespread vice. What I am interested in is not Stigler's intentions but the consequences of the approach he adopted.

simple to find nothing of value in theories he identified as essentially opposed to his own[3]. His misrepresentations attempted to shift the terms of debate on to more congenial territory where any further conversation would seem pointless. By dismissing critics like Galbraith, Stigler successfully helped to limit economic acceptability to a narrow range of topics and methods in which adversarial debate rather than the give and take of discussion prevailed. Stigler can be seen, as pioneering a form of economic correctness, meaning the elimination of certain approaches, methods, and theories from the profession that he found distasteful. These he would damn as consisting of imprecise thinking based on anecdotal evidence[4]. Allowing for the validity of such criticism, still, Stigler's insistence on precision in an ambiguous world moves dangerously close to preferring the precisely wrong to the approximately right. This clearly comes through in his obvious distaste for the work of John Kenneth Galbraith[5]. By examining an early but decisive clash between these two economists, we can gain a better understanding of Stigler's methods in undermining opposing views. By stubbornly refusing to entertain alternatives, by adopting an adversarial style of debate more suited to the

---

[3] Evidence of Stigler's attachment to neoclassical price theory is also given by that part of his work mainly critical of the work of others. Price rigidity, administered price inflation, the theory of monopolistic competition, and X-efficiency were prominent targets, and each of them denied the efficacy of the neoclassical analytical framework. (Demsetz, 1993: 800)

See Freedman (1995a, b) for an in depth discussion of the way in which Stigler misrepresented the work of Sweezy (1939) and Berle and Means (1932).

[4] This is particularly ironic given his own casual approach to empirical work. A reader comes away from tasting Stigler's particular pudding well aware of a basic disregard for its ingredients. See Freedman (1995b) for an account of his rather cavalier approach to statistical analysis.

[5] One suspects that this distaste filtered down to a personal level. Both are given short shrift in each others' autobiographies. In a letter to Gardiner Means, Galbraith describes Stigler as:

> ...a superficial man who regrets his inability to command any general interest and attention for his work. If somebody gets satisfaction defending past error, I don't think it should be denied to him. (Galbraith, 1970)

court room[6] than to the common rooms of economic discussion, Stigler did the profession he so loved a lasting disservice.

1. Matter and Anti-Matter

> To many of us the notion that one individual shall be in position to control the real income of others remains more than slightly obscene. We react to it much as a Puritan to Professor Kinsey — adultery exists no doubt, but how much better not to talk about it. (Galbraith, 1954: 5)

It seems strange that so much of our fears, hates and jealousies can sometime find a physical manifestation, something that would otherwise only exist in the alternative world of our imagination. Yet if we lived in a truly Hegelian world, we could find no better concrete embodiment of the logic of an underlying dialectic than Galbraith and Stigler. Without the one, the other could not have existed, so much did each help to define where and for what his opponent stood. As a result, it is hard to prevent a discussion of personality from creeping into any analysis of the long battle they fought from opposing trenches of the economics profession. It is of course a cliche to say that the acorn does not fall far from the tree. But it is hardly surprising that George Stigler and John Kenneth Galbraith consistently ended up on the opposite side of any issue. Genes may not be destiny nor environment alone conclusive, but taken together the two do seem to get the job done.

Economists, and certainly this includes George Stigler, like to sneer at what they call anecdotal evidence. But to do so is to wilfully ignore the way we come to believe that something holds true. We have convincing experience only of the anecdotal. Deep down we believe fully only that which accords with our own experience. Battalions of statistics are all unavailing when compared to a contrary personal experience. Though Stigler explicitly rejected as half-baked, any theory that could not stand up to rigorous and detailed attack, it

[6] Deirdre McCloskey has remarked that given Stigler's temperament, his interest in Law and Economics was hardly surprising (conversation with McCloskey, 5 July 1996).

is his own intuition about markets that shaped his arguments over the years. What empirical evidence could ever convince Stigler to fundamentally change his mind, to find grievous faults with the working of the price system? In his autobiography Stigler (1988a: 210) does cite a few noteworthy conversions, economists who changed their minds and embraced new ideas. A similar conversion by Stigler would have been no less likely to occur than the pope's public embrace of Islam[7].

Stigler (1988a) was the only son of immigrant parents. Unlike most first generation children, Stigler was never forced to work. His only brush with manual labour was a three-week stint picking apples. Galbraith (1981), one of four children, grew up on an Ontario farm that had been in his family's hands for several generations. Like any farm boy, he put in long hours doing chores. Stigler grew into a theorist who did not believe in getting his hands dirty, who in a sense had no interest in finding out how things worked. His dislike of survey material, or the use of case studies in the style of Joe Bain, was pronounced[8]. The Chicago compulsion to look for unifying models that could apply generally, always prevailed. Details were applied more for their expositional convenience than for their evidence, to help in

[7] A second and related trait of scholars is that they seldom change their minds. We must remember that we are discussing scholars with good minds, and they would usually lose in a swap of minds. It was most unusual when Keynes's *General Theory* led Alvin Hansen, a hitherto conservative economist of mature years, to abandon his previous scientific position and become a vigorous exponent of Keynesian doctrine. (Stigler, 1988a: 210)

Notice the subtle undercurrent of incredulity here as if the aged and respected local vicar had suddenly converted to scientology after reading *Dianetics* by L Ron Hubbard. It might also be added that not only was Stigler predictably consistent, but that throughout his life he refused to ever admit an error no matter what the evidence. Galbraith, despite his evident egotism, admits in his autobiography (1981: 284–285) that history judges and finds economic theory, including parts of his own, wanting. When his facts changed he was, no matter how grudgingly willing to admit error. Not only did Stigler not concede error, but he was still intent on castigating his opponents decades after the battles had been fought and won. He used the occasion of a Nobel Prize to deliver a few such parting shots. (Stigler, 1983: 536).

[8] See Stigler (1988a: 162) for his own thought of the Mason group at Harvard.

telling a likely story. Though Stigler wanted to be a businessman (1998a: 15) and went so far as to get a MBA from Northwestern, he displayed little real interest or particular knowledge of business. Industrial organisation, to which he devoted much of his career in the post-war period, was for him simply applied price theory.

> His method was to learn enough about the industry, and perhaps only just enough, to help fashion a statistical test. (Demsetz, 1993: 796)

For all the stated passion he expended on measurement, his consistent and almost sole objective was to extend the reach of price theory. His tests were in a sense only rhetorical devices to support the *a priori* conclusions of his theory[9]. Thus, he was often given to claim more for his results than was empirically justified.

Stigler's concern was that of a classic liberal, one who valued individual choice over all else, believing that the market provided the best basis for individual self-realisation.

> ... we are persuaded that an economic system will not help us to move in the right direction unless it grants both opportunity and responsibility to the individual: the very uncertainty of our ultimate ethical goals dictates a wide area of individual self-determination. (Stigler, 1949c: 8)

Galbraith, the farm boy, saw collective choice as complementing decentralised decision-making. The sort of corporate and government planning that he regarded as a natural function of the growth and development of capitalism, Stigler found abhorrent and unnecessary. To say that these views are a mere reflection of their formative years would strike most economists as cheap pop psychology (assuming there is any other kind). Yet as Stigler himself admits (1982a: 63), we all interpret abstract propositions in highly personal terms. It is hard

[9] Given his agenda it is easy to see why Coase's (1937) article on the firm had no interest for him. The internal organisation of the firm was largely irrelevant, in his mind, when compared to his concentration on markets.

> The omission, I believe, was due to Stigler's disinterest in the internal organization of the firm. (Demsetz, 1993: 798)

to imagine how those personal terms can be divorced from our experiences[10]. Stigler's and Galbraith's were so totally opposed that it is hardly surprising that the theories which rang nearest the truth to one were incompatible with the predilections of the other. Stigler as a fervent Roosevelt New Dealer strikes one as an absurdity not only in retrospect, but also peering through the eyes of the teenage George Stigler.

In one decisive sense, these two long time sparring partners were nonetheless similar. They were both outsiders, provincial boys who scrambled their way out of obscurity. Perhaps as his long time associate says of George Stigler, shyness was ultimately at the heart of each one's abrasiveness.

> George, on being introduced to an individual, a small group, or a large audience, would *always* make a joke. He never failed. I hardly dare suggest that there was a certain shyness behind this disarmament with wit. (Friedland, 1993: 783)

They both had that touchiness of the somewhat gauche young man, afraid of being slighted or even worse ignored. Perhaps both provincial boys suffered from a certain self-conscious touch of inferiority, a fear of being overlooked. This might explain the tendency that both had for showing off, for never refraining from the clever remark, regardless of the hurt it might cause.

> I suffered from a problem in personal relations that I never quite overcame. This was not so much from being more versatile, more diligent or perhaps

---

[10] Schumpeter, less concerned with the polite conventions of the economics profession knew this. Though, even he felt at times embarrassed in bringing sociological concerns into his work, pursuits only appropriate for economists past their glory days.

> Could we confine ourselves to Pareto's contributions to pure theory, there would be little need for glancing at the man and his social background and location. But into everything that was not a theorem in the pure logic of economics the whole man and all the forces that conditioned him entered so unmistakably that it is more necessary than it usually is in an appraisal of scientific performance to convey an idea of that man and of those forces. (Schumpeter quoted in Smithies (1950: 634).

> more able than my colleagues. Such can be tolerated. The damage arose from my fear, which I earlier indicated and which I never quite suppressed, that my superiority would not be recognised. (Galbraith, 1981: 18)

Stigler found a home in the rough and tumble of Chicago's economics department, which for many years defined itself in terms of being the maverick of the profession, a place full of ambitious young economists on the make. Galbraith, for all his acquired charm, his ease with the movers and shakers of the world, never felt completely comfortable at tradition-bound Harvard. Given their combative natures and their beliefs, any meeting between the two could not possibly be amiable.

> Not everyone enjoyed and appreciated George Stigler as much as all those who knew him well. Kenneth Galbraith, for instance, had the bad judgment to engage in public debate with George a couple of times. Thereafter Ken was quoted to the effect that he would not demean himself by appearing on the same platform with a character so disreputable and contemptible as to have been mentioned favorably in the *National Review*, as Stigler had been. Later, to be sure, Galbraith apologized — to the editor, Bill Buckley. (Wallis, 1993: 778)

2. A Survey of Contemptible Economics

> To be sure, for half a century economics has been a kind of trial of wits between those who sought to perfect this doctrine of ultimate harmony and those who-citing inequality and its perpetration by inheritance, external economies, immobility of resources, and other inhibiting forces-sought to limit it. But the doctrine was only completely vulnerable at one point and that was where monopoly entered — the defenders and attackers entirely agreed that monopoly (*cum* oligopoly) was deeply subversive of the competitive model. And, since oligopoly was stubbornly resistant to incorporation in a new system, at least by the old methods, it destroyed without leaving anything in its place. (Galbraith, 1948: 109)

In Westerns, the classic gunslinger remains Jack Palance in *Shane*. Hired by local ranchers to drive out newly arrived dirt farmers, impeccably dressed in black, he sneers at them, insulting their manhood, and defying them to fight back. He knows that not a single one is his match. Without pushing this analogy to the point of filling the other film roles, it is clear that whatever his sartorial proclivities might be, George Stigler was Chicago's hired gun (employment more as a labour of love than motivated by the strictly monetary rewards of a contract killer). Though physically at Columbia University during his major tussles with Galbraith, his heart and intellectual commitment never wandered far from Chicago. He had already savaged Lester (Stigler, 1946, 1947b) and Sweezy (Stigler, 1947a), beating back the attempts of those two Easterners to attack and replace Chicago doctrine. Underlining these two counter-attacks was a near compulsion to defend the theoretic and empirical validity of marginal productivity theory, the subject matter of his dissertation under Knight (1938), of his first major published paper (1939)[11] as well as his first book (1941). In much the same way, marginal productivity theory lay behind his savage dissection of a 1948 collection of essays *A Survey of Contemporary Economics* (see Appendix A).

The book itself seems innocent enough, an attempt by the American Economic Association to examine the field of economics over a 15 year period from 1930 to 1945. There are 13 surveys covering a variety of fields. The attempt was to give the non-specialist in those fields an idea of recent developments. (Even then the dangers of economics becoming too narrowly specialised were apparent.) The coverage was not meant to be comprehensive.

> Finally, the choice of contributors and, in turn, their selection of subjects and substance answer to no grand design for a unified method or philosophy of economic thinking. The purpose of the book is not to impose an artful scheme upon the interpretation of recent analysis and policy, nor to

[11] To concede to oligopoly theory a degree of legitimacy would be to undermine the basis for marginal productivity theory. See Freedman (1995a, b).

> At a more sophisticated level, the new work did strike a blow at the concept of inherent order in capitalist behavior: the doctrines of imperfect and monopolistic competition ran sharply counter to what Professor Roll has called the 'optimal distribution of resources prejudice'. (Galbraith, 1948: 99–128)

> influence their future course, but to review their substance and appraise their significance. (Ellis, 1948: vii)

The selection of contributors does lean toward the liberal Harvard/Berkeley nexus of that era[12]. (See Appendix A) That may in part reflect the post-war composition of the profession, especially among its younger members. Yet their brief is to present rather than evaluate the work (though some do overstep this boundary in their enthusiasm for some particular line of investigation). Moreover, each survey was reviewed by two critics, as they are called in the volume. The published works supposedly reflect their authors' response to those suggestions. The critics include many conservative voices including a number from Chicago and even from Harvard (Schumpeter and Haberler).

For those at Chicago, the problem seems to be that in many key areas of price theory (Value and Distribution, Employment Theory and Business Cycles, Monopoly and The Concentration of Economic Power, Price and Production Policies, Federal Budgeting and Fiscal Policy, Economics of Labor) the survey challenges the orthodox view. Common to all these essays is an enthusiasm for the then popular Keynesian line, which in Chicago was equivalent to being wrong by definition. Harvard at this time embodied a source of conservative frustration. It served as the transmission centre for a heretical infestation that was devouring

---

[12] A second volume published four years later, dealing with topics not covered in the first, corrects the liberal/conservative balance, perhaps reflecting the criticism evidenced by reviewers of the earlier book. Moreover, the reviewers (or critics) of each survey are allowed a short comment compared to this absence in the first volume (supposedly due to limitations of space). The reviewers are referred to by Robertson as, "self-effacing prenatal critics". (Robertson, 1950: 1)

In contrast to Stigler, it is interesting to note that Viner (1950), in his review of the volume, while also judging the range of views presented as being too narrow, saw these views as representing a consensus of the profession as it then existed.

> The contributors, moreover, were chosen predominantly, perhaps wholly and deliberately, from among the safe, middle-of-the-road members of the profession, with respect both to their policy-attitudes and their methodological predilections. The result is that the volume is representative only of the patterns of value-judgment and the methods of analysis adhered to by the center portion of our profession. (Viner, 1950: 651)

the sound foundations of economic science. Galbraith boasted that 'the Keynesian revolution entered the United States and went on to Washington by way of Harvard.' (1981: 91). A doctrine which proclaimed non-clearing markets and which was scorned by his revered teachers (such as Knight and Viner[13]), would hardly be given a fair hearing by Stigler. 'Keynes produced a bundle of paradoxes and heresies in the *General Theory of Employment, Interest, and Money.*' (Stigler, 1988a: 213)

Stigler's role in this context is clear. Review articles are usually commissioned. *The Journal of Political Economy* was Chicago's house journal. The article is the lead one for April issue of 1949. For a review to be so featured is unusual[14]. One can only conclude that the editor, Earl Hamilton, and the others connected with the journal at that time, felt that it was imperative to reply to this collection of heresies. Moreover, one does not normally choose George Stigler if the goal is simply to extol the virtues of a recent work[15]. Stigler accordingly was commissioned not so much to simply review but to destroy this well publicised collection of surveys. That others, outside of the Chicago circle, recognised this is indicated by a 1952 *AER* companion volume. The new editor, Bernard Haley, one of the writers attacked by Stigler in the first volume, refers to reviews by Viner (1950) in the *AER* and by Robertson (1950) in the *QJE*. What sticks out is the absence of the other top US journal which is studiously ignored, the *JPE* issue containing Stigler's search and destroy mission. Yet in many ways this second volume is a reflection of Stigler's harsh demands for more conservative voices. The lesson learnt by those at Chicago was that such savagery worked.

Given Chicago's propensity for hand to hand combat, it is not surprising that Stigler took every opportunity available to undermine the value and even the integrity of that survey volume. The basic premises held by these two groups of contending economists were

---

13 See Viner (1936) and Knight (1937). Both are particularly critical reviews of Keynes' *General Theory.*

14 This indicates something of the importance with which the volume was received. A quite different review article (in spirit and approach) by Dennis Robertson led the February 1950 issue of the *Quarterly Journal of Economics.*

15 Those who like to believe that people mellow as they age will do well to peruse Stigler's (1988b) incisive demolition of *Palgrave's Dictionary of Economics.*

located at opposite ends of the economic spectrum. The majority of survey writers saw the fifteen years from 1930 to 1945 as a period of theoretical and empirical breakthroughs. Those whose hearts beat in rhythm with Chicago's saw these years as a detriment to the advancement of the economics profession[16].

> The plain fact is that the economic theory of 1948 is much the same as that of 1930 — a little better here and a little worse there. If the contributors had taken Ellis' 'main ideas' and 'fifteen years' at all literally, the volume would have run to fewer pages. (Stigler, 1949a: 101)

Judged as a critical review, Stigler's article fails[17]. This is not to say that room for ample criticism does not exist. A case can be made that some of the authors of the surveys display an unnecessary bias and enthusiasm for the work they chose to review, even if the bias represents a popular consensus of that era. They then can justly be accused of falling short of an ideal standard.

> The ideal performance would call for a large measure of self-abnegation, of objective reporting of what was prevalent, even if what prevailed was not wholly approved of by the contributor, but with aid provided to the non-specialist so that he could reach some judgement of his own as to the merits of recent developments in the various fields. (Viner, 1950: 650)

---

[16] Though scathing about this period in his 1949 review article, he applies quite another characterisation to this same era when addressing a University of Chicago Trustee dinner in 1962.

> Economics, for example, has had two golden ages in the last century, from 1870 to 1900, and from 1935 to 1950, in the latter case with time out for a war. (Stigler, 1963b: 40)

Stigler seems to be tailoring his statements according to the point he wishes to make and the audience he wishes to persuade. There is nothing remarkable about making strategic evaluations. But such an approach does tend to produce far from helpful exaggerations.

[17] Compare Robertson's (1950) critical but more thoughtful and amiable *QJE* article. Robertson is of course of an older generation and brought up in the Cambridge tradition. Perhaps though the difference that counts most is that Stigler professes to be a Marshallian, Robertson is.

Stigler, on the other hand, seems more concerned that they lack the proper bias. An even-handed approach would be unlikely to win Stigler's plaudits.

> He (Haley) has performed this summarizing function with skill, and his essay is an excellent contribution to analytical bibliography. With such a purpose, however, the essay cannot rise much above the literature with which it deals. Where the literature is wrong, Haley is wrong with it. (Stigler, 1949a: 93–94)

Stigler clearly signals his intention in his opening paragraphs. His aim is not so much to review the volume but to argue that it is a one-sided look at the direction in which economics is headed.

> I shall argue that, on the whole, the *Survey* has failed in its announced purpose of supplying informative summaries of the recent literature of economics but that it is a somber success in conveying the essential character of the literature. (Stigler, 1949: 93)

Stigler is clearly claiming that the failings of the volume (the unscientific, vacuous nature of the discussion) are a reflection of the material that the authors insist on including and equally on that which they choose to exclude[18].

---

[18] This is most evident in his evaluation of Reynolds' look at the labour literature (Reynolds, 1948). He savages Reynolds for arguing that wage differentials (at least their upper limits) are largely a matter of custom. Such a statement is in direct conflict with marginal productivity theory. As such, a hypothesis of this sort should, in Stigler's usual formulation, simply be a matter of fact which can be empirically verified. Stigler, however, simply dismisses it as so self-evidently wrong as to need no comment. This is a rhetorical trick that Stigler would learn to perfect during his career (see Freedman 1995a, b). By heaping scorn on an idea, he shifts the terms of inquiry to a level where asking for an explanation would amount to a self-confession of ignorance of the most woeful sort (failing to see the obvious). Such rhetorical flourishes are meant to stop further questioning rather than encourage discussion.

> I do not wish to digress on an appraisal of this particular view, which simply defies credulity. I do wish to emphasize that this is dogmatic theorizing and that it is at the unscientific, not the 'prescientific', level at which one does not bother to verify his theory. (Stigler, 1949a: 99)

Stigler's deepest intuition was that markets delivered the goods. He took this to mean not only at a material but at an ethical level as well[19]. Arguments starting from any other point of departure were dismissed rather than analysed. He deemed that allowing such heresies even a foothold into generally accepted discourse was unwise, unnecessary and unnerving. Though steadfastly insisting on empirical verification, rather than the sort of *a priori* reasoning which he describes as endemic to, as well as the defining measure of Keynes and his cohorts, it is ironic that all of Stigler's statistical work merely confirmed his own preconceptions[20]. While Keynes was known for his sometimes infuriating ability to change his opinion as available data changed[21], Stigler proved over the decades to be impervious to any set of facts.

Throughout his career, those he vociferously attacked were for the most part Harvard habitués. This is not so much a coincidence as a predictable response. In the post-war era, both the dominant schools of industrial organisation, that of Edward Chamberlin and of Edward Mason, were centred at Harvard. Both clearly deviated from standard price theory. Market outcomes under these approaches were not necessarily unique or efficient. The work of Sweezy, Means, and Galbraith, both before and after the war, tried, whether explicitly or not, to develop a micro-economics consistent with the growing Keynesian trend in macro-economics[22], in each case relying on some

---

[19] See Stigler (1949c, 1982b, c) for his ethical views.

[20] Typically, his statistical work tends towards the expedient rather than towards painstaking analysis. He consistently claims more from his analysis then is justified. A good early example of this approach is clearly shown in his 1947 attack on Sweezy's kinked demand curve. Throughout his career, Stigler claimed that his arguments demolished any rationale to take Sweezy's model seriously. See, however, Freedman (1995a) for an alternative view.

[21] I do not think it is any more an economic law that wages should go down easily than that they should not. It is a question of facts. Economic law does not lay down the facts, it tells you what the consequences are. (Keynes quoted in Skidelsky. (1992: 349)

[22] See Freedman (1995b).

form of oligopolistic industrial structure. This ran counter to Stigler's Chicago traditions as well as to the trend that price theory was taking there. In this respect, Harvard succeeded in defining itself as the enemy camp.

> The emerging Chicago tradition challenged both of these ruling views. It proceeded from the assumption that modern price theory is a powerful weapon in the understanding of economic behavior, not simply a set of elegant theoretical exercises suitable for instruction and the demonstration of one's mental agility. In particular, primarily under the influence of Aaron Director, we moved away from the assumption that monopoly was almost ubiquitous in modern economies. This Chicago orientation had three main facets. The first was that the goal of efficiency is pervasive in economic life, where efficiency means producing and selling goods at the lowest possible cost (and therefore the largest possible profit). This goal is sought as vigorously by monopolists as by competitors, and monopoly power is of no value in explaining many phenomena which have efficiency explanations. (Stigler, 1988a: 162–163)

The selection of surveys, out of a possible total of 13, which Stigler chooses to evaluate, is hardly a matter of chance given his agenda and his in-bred aversion to Harvard-style doctrine. It is best then to discount his claims of expediency and his ready professions of limited knowledge. These are rhetorical devices to avoid any discussion of selection bias. Six of the seven[23] articles reviewed are linked by their common violation of core Chicago price theory.

His treatment of Galbraith's own effort (his is one of the seven stigmatised selections) exemplifies Stigler's approach and allows us a

[23] For those who have forgotten, the relevant six essays are: Value and Distribution, Employment Theory and Business Cycles, Monopoly and The Concentration of Economic Power, Price and Production Policies, Federal Budgeting and Fiscal Policy, Economics of Labor. (See Appendix A for further details.) The odd man out is Paul Samuelson. Stigler's quarrel here has more to do with methodology or perhaps the subject matter of economics itself. In a sense it is a more basic argument but one that is peripheral to his real target.

> On Samuelson's definition, I suppose, one writes an essay on mathematics; on the conventional definition, one writes an essay on economics. (Stigler, 1949a: 100)

useful insight into the emerging conflict between these two figures. Galbraith's survey concentrates on oligopoly theory. The emphasis is on the way in which such market structures affect market outcomes. It can be seen as a warm up exercise for his 1952 book on countervailing power. While in other cases Stigler damns the survey writers with faint praise, when it comes to Galbraith, Stigler foregoes the faint praise. But the volley Stigler fires across Galbraith's bow does not speak to the points Galbraith makes. Stigler uses the formal devices of a lawyer to reframe and destroy his arguments. Galbraith himself inadvertently sums up the point of contention between the two.

> To concede that a businessman should orient his price policy to social norms is to assert that the single-minded pursuit of profit is presumptively anti-social. It admits of a rule of private collectivism that accords important legislative functions to the private entrepreneur. Conservatives and liberals alike found the idea unappetizing. The implied alternative, namely that price behavior had become a fit area for state intervention, also had disagreeable overtones. (Galbraith, 1948: 112)

As Galbraith points out, critical theory, starting with Sraffa's 1926 paper, opens the way for economic models lacking a determinate solution. The claims then for market efficiency fall to the ground. The issue between Galbraith and Stigler becomes whether or not competitive markets with flexible prices dominate the US economy or oligopolistic markets with administered prices. Stigler is not so naive to claim that the US economy actually consists of the classic large number of independent firms, none dominant in size. (Stigler, 1949b: 47). The frequent criticism of theoretical, and especially classical, economists that they are or were not aware of this fact reveals both a distressing ignorance of the literature and a lack of understanding of scientific methodology. (Stigler, 1942: 1–2). Stigler however clearly sees, as does Galbraith, that the real issue is not literally one of industrial structure but of price and output.

For Galbraith, industries where a few firms produce the bulk of market output (high concentration ratios) have interdependent choices to make. Once an individual firm's decisions affect the market price, it would be ingenuous to suppose that firms make those decisions without giving thought to the decisions of rival large firms. Such interdependence may or may not lead to competitive market prices. But it does seem obvious that collusion is far more likely the fewer the firms there are to collude. Supported by, what is to him, convincing studies on the price behaviour of such firms, Galbraith sees this issue as settled and obvious.

Oligopoly is a structural problem that Stigler had to struggle with before finding a solution conducive to his own ends. Stigler would eventually tackle the problem of interdependent decisions by focussing on collusion and particularly the costs of cheating on a collusive arrangement. If one combines his work on the economics of information (1961) with his work on collusion amongst oligopolies (1962), the solution is evident. Given that collusive agreements are difficult to maintain, competitive prices should be the rule rather than the exception. Stigler would wait until 1970 to empirically demonstrate that prices were indeed flexible rather than rigid. Following this string of logic backward from the established frequency of flexible prices, one could then safely conclude that the problem of interdependent decisions has no serious consequences for economic analysis.

> In Stigler's confrontation with the oligopoly problem, he avoids the very aspect of it that others saw as its central feature and that neoclassical economics fails to deal with: interdependence of decision making. He does this by *assuming* that this problem, in some unspecified way, is solved simply because it is in the interest of firms in the industry to solve it. (Demsetz, 1993: 805)

Stigler starts to change his views on the issue of monopolisation between the years of 1942 and 1949. It is not that his basic belief in the competitive nature of most industries changes, but rather his reading of the evidence does. His 1942 piece is open-ended, explaining the limitations of available techniques and data. By 1949 his use of many of the same studies becomes a battering ram applied to the views of rival theorists. Something does happen in the post-war era to George Stigler's professional approach. Whatever generosity he might once have wished to extend to his opponents vanishes. There is a parallel here with the rising Cold War tensions of the late forties and early fifties. Certainly, Stigler as a founding member of the Mt. Pelerin Society[24] would consider classic liberalism to be under serious threat from collectivist doctrine. When taken in combination with the prevailing political environment, any concession yielded by the proponents of neoclassical price theory would have been the equivalent of an ignominious surrender.

In 1942, the question of how competitive an economy as a whole might be, held no real meaning for Stigler. Certainly, it was not a question that could be quantitatively answered.

> The second major problem is concerned with the much discussed question: How competitive is the economy as a whole? Despite the frequency with which dogmatic answers are given to this question, it is doubtful whether any meaningful answer is attainable ... it is difficult to find any important purpose in asking how competitive an economy is. (Stigler, 1942: 4)

For this reason, though he considers Wilcox' (1940) efforts at classification to be admirable, it yields no definitive answers. Certainly to Stigler (1942), concentration ratios are ambiguous since there is no established relationship between any such ratio and a level of competitiveness.

Stigler in his 1949 LSE Lecture on 'Competition in the United States' repeats his belief that these estimates have little if any scientific value. He does, however, let the proverbial cat out of the theoretical bag by admitting that such figures seem to have an unfortunate effect on social policy. This is what distinguishes his 1942 remarks from those of 1949. By 1949 he is engaged in an open battle with an opposing blueprint for the economics profession as well as for consequent policy.

> There is no necessary relationship between one's views on the extent of competition and on the type of economic policy that should be pursued. One can believe that the economy is 99 per cent monopolized, and still argue for policies designed to revive competition and private enterprise; or one can believe that the economy is 99 per cent competitive and still argue

[24] See Hartwell (1995) for an account of the reasons behind the founding of the Mont Pelerin Society.

> for syndicalism or socialism. Such position, however, are not popular... Most economists would probably change their policy views if they were convinced that their appraisal of the relative rôles of competition and monopoly was fundamentally wrong. (Stigler, 1949b: 46)

Given the role that he is assuming in this lecture, as well as that played in his review article (1949a), he has no trouble leaning on the very same Wilcox (1940) study he previously regarded with scepticism. When battling for leverage, nuances serve only as self-imposed hindrances to one's argument[25]. Can we then take the accusation that Stigler makes against Galbraith seriously?

> He [Galbraith] possesses a view of industrial organization that seems to me independent of the empirical studies which he cites, I have used the same studies, and in more detail, to derive the opposite view of our industrial organization. (Stigler, 1949a: 96)

Here Stigler is talking about the same Wilcox (1940) study, which Stigler had previously viewed as highly ambiguous. The nature of

---

[25] He would reassert much the same argument at the AEA convention of the same year.

> Free entry ... may be defined as the condition that long-run costs of new firms if they enter the industry will be equal to those of firms already in the industry ... With this understanding, free entry seems a valid characterization of most American industries. One may concede this and still argue that, because of the large capital requirements necessary to establish a new company of minimum efficient size, free entry is often difficult, and firms in industries with (absolutely) large capital requirements have a sheltered position. I have as little basis for my skepticism of this argument as its many adherents have given for supporting it. (Stigler, 1950: 27)

This concession to monopoly would cease once Demsetz (1968) provided an argument allowing competition to rule despite long-run costs. One might remark that Stigler did not need empirical evidence to find such an argument convincing. In fact Stigler would also ignore elements in this work that sounded suspiciously similar to Galbraith's hypothesis of countervailing power.

> If we allow buyers access to the same technology of collusion, the market will be characterized by bilateral negotiations between organized buyers and organized sellers. (Demsetz, 1968: 271)

ambiguous data is that investigators are likely to draw whatever conclusions they want from it. It is not surprising that Galbraith and Stigler reach opposite ideas given their initial opposite preconceptions. This is no more a cardinal sin on Galbraith's part than on Stigler's.

The rest of Stigler's indictments are of much the same character. Stigler picks items out of context to facilitate his attack. At no time is there an attempt to judge Galbraith's survey on its own merits, the objective the author sets for himself. He mocks Galbraith's claim that the US economy is dominated by oligopolistic markets.

> ... he turns to the low-quality literature on giant corporations and concentration ratios, with which he is much more satisfied. (Stigler, 1949a: 95)

One must not forget that Galbraith is surveying the recent literature on the subject. Much of the work of that time, starting with the effort by Berle and Means (1932), leaned heavily on the non-competitive nature of the US economy. Part of this involved the sort of concentration ratios that are the object of Stigler's scorn. While non-competitive pricing may be more likely given fewer firms involved in the market, there is, as previously stated, no conclusive evidence of a strong relationship between industry concentration and a lack of price competition. But Galbraith does not merely focus on this one-structural aspect. Stigler misleads the reader by emphasising this issue. What is at stake is not simply whether an industry is highly concentrated but whether competitive pricing does or does not prevail in the given market. Galbraith cites Means' (1939) work on inflexible or administered prices as well as the work of Mason (1938), Humphrey (1937), Wallace (1936) and Galbraith (1936). Stigler fails to mention this aspect but instead hoots at the more dismissible work on concentration ratios. This is not the crux of Galbraith's contentions. Galbraith clearly supports the view that oligopoly is the dominant market structure. But given the available research on the subject, this predilection is at least equally as plausible as a strongly held, but opposite, belief in competitive markets. It is reasonable to chide Galbraith for presenting this as a settled issue. There is a little basis for deriding such a conclusion as purely spurious.

Taking a more dispassionate view, it is reasonable to suggest that neither side of this debate supported their claims with compelling evidence. Concentration ratios fail to compel belief, no matter how tailored. The work on price flexibility was not conclusive except to hardened partisans. One thing only is clear. Neither side of the debate sufficiently distinguished how an oligopolistic as opposed to a competitive market would look and operate. Until such a standard could be firmly agreed upon, many of these arguments, whether empirical or theoretical by nature, would continue to have a, 'your mother wears army boots', tone about them. Wilcox (1950), reiterating his 1940 monograph, may think only 20% (at most) of the economy is not price competitive. The fair-minded must tend to agree with Stigler's (1942) claim that this is a rhetorical rather than an empirical point. We can look at specific markets but the aggregation process conveys insufficient information. Ideally, what we need to know is whether firms in a particular market deviate significantly from marginal cost pricing or not. Even a rough approximation would be difficult.

Demsetz claims that Stigler wore his passion for measurement on his sleeve (1993: 795). The one common thread running throughout Stigler's work is that economic questions are basically the questions of fact. Issues that were meaningful could be decided empirically. If this is not the case, economics is reduced to so much talk. Stigler, in fact, castigates the economics of the thirties and forties for taking the easy road of empty theorising.

> Thus the dominant characteristic of the dominant type of economic theorizing in the period under review is well brought out by the essay: this has been the period of the clever gadget and the plausible surmise — the age of the easy answer. The tedious and difficult work of testing theories by a comparison of their predictions with evidence not incorporated in the formulation of the theory — that is, by noncircular tests — and careful interpretation and generalization of inductive studies have been deemed unnecessarily circuitous paths to knowledge and to social welfare. (Stigler, 1949a: 104)

This is a ringing condemnation but one applicable to any period of economics. The idea that empirical findings are unlikely to be disputed reveals either an ingenuous nature or one which finds ambiguity to be uncongenial[26].

> An inconvenient *a priori* argument can always be eroded or blunted by challenging its exclusion or inclusion of some assumption, but economists find it difficult to resist well-established *empirical* findings. (Stigler, 1982c: 23)

The problem is that it is hard to think of one case where empirical findings convinced Stigler to change his mind. He often quoted studies that he found to be convincing, but these were findings that agreed with his preconceived ideas and opinions.

Galbraith's survey became the occasion for these two opponents to clearly stake out their positions, foreshadowing the offensive weapons they were wont to employ. It represents one out of many preliminary rounds in which the Chicago School attempted to rescue economics from those who had shaped the dominant view of the subject in the thirties and forties. It was to be expected that Stigler would be the point man for the attack on Galbraith's first major work. This time the confrontation would be face to face at the 1953 AEA convention.

3. An Economist Plays with Blocs

> At the end of 1953, the American Economic Association scheduled a special session to consider it. A newspaper reporter covering the meeting heard one young scholar tell another, 'It's time to go and hear them destroy

---

[26] Coase (1994) argues against the standard Stigler/Friedman methodological approach in which empirical evidence is assumed to be conclusive.

> Some articles, of course, involve the testing of alternative theories, and this means that some theories are bound to come out worse. But I doubt whether such studies have often led to a change in the views of the authors. My impression is that these quantitative studies are almost invariably guided by a theory and that they may most aptly be described as explorations with the aid of a theory. In almost all cases, the theory exists before the statistical investigation is made and is not derived from the investigation. (Coase, 1994: 26)

> Galbraith.' The effort was undertaken with enthusiasm and competence by David McCord Wright, then of the University of Virginia, and George Stigler of the University of Chicago. Neither approved new thought, however plausible. (Galbraith, 1981: 283)[27]

Galbraith gained economic notoriety through his first popular work[28]. In many ways, *American Capitalism* forms a natural progression from the ideas expressed in Galbraith's (1948) survey article. Though still known for its theory of countervailing power, the persistent reader confronts that particular idea only in the last half of the book. Galbraith first lays out his understanding of post-war American capitalism, both how it works and how it had changed. The book can best be described as an extended meditation on the nature of private economic power since the turn of the century. According to Galbraith's view, oligopolies have shaped American markets rather than vice versa. As a consequence, an economist's traditional lullabies were out of tune with the reality of current industrial structure.

In standard analysis, power could not enter as an issue since the core neoclassical model assumed that firms were too small to affect

---

[27] To be more exact, his two inquisitors were George Stigler, then of Columbia University and John Perry Miller of Yale University. David McCord appeared as a discussant of these three presentations.

[28] His attempt to write a book for his fellow economists was less than a total success.

> I have always thought *A Theory of Price Control* one of my more important books. No other combines such technical competence as I possess in economics with such experience in the subject. It was so regarded by its reviewers. But there were few of these and, initially, few readers of any kind. The experience persuaded me that one could spend one's life producing professionally well-regarded books that would go extensively unread. And one could be even less fortunate. In the natural course of events, one's books come to those reviewers, the established specialists in the field, who are the strongest defenders of the established view. It is a system that selects an adverse jury for all inclined to innovation. I decided that henceforth I would submit myself to a wider audience, a decision that, in contrast with some others, I have not regretted. (Galbraith, 1981: 175)

market prices[29]. They were forced to adapt to market dictates as best as they could. In the absence of private power, the check of government intervention is unneeded. Consumers exercising their right to choose can effectively meet their needs and in so doing force firms to strive for efficient operation. Galbraith sees this reign of price competition as belonging to times long past. Firms had hijacked pricing power by regulating competition. As evidence, Galbraith cites available studies based on the best existing data.

> The critics of the figures [industry concentration figures] have, with a few exceptions, been men who are deeply devoted to the economic and political system identified with the competitive model as an economic and political goal. They have been in the always equivocal position of the man who must testify to the virtue of a well-loved mistress. (Galbraith, 1954: 37)

Yet, despite the prevalence of monopoly power, despite the automatic links between saving and investment turning out to be a mirage, the post-war economy, for all the widespread foreboding which greeted it, had performed effectively. According to Galbraith, it maintained and promoted a desperately required level of social harmony[30] largely without government assistance.

---

[29] Competition mitigates economic power by making the behaviour of any participant in the market contingent on the behaviour of other and like participants. It makes sellers subject to the independent actions of other sellers, and buyers subject to the independent action of other buyers. The undoubted effect is to limit or dissolve the opportunity for arbitrary, or self interested, or perhaps any effective use of market power which would limit or lower the real income of others. (Galbraith, 1954: 1–2)

[30] It is easy to forget the turbulence of the thirties. The sustained depression years did threaten the social fabric of many countries as both extreme right and left wings of the political spectrum offered their own particular solutions to these problems. Sporadic violence was not uncommon. In the immediate postwar period the fear of another deep depression was wide spread. Memories of those unsettled times were still quite fresh.

> In accordance with a surprisingly well-observed convention, the American Business spokesman does not often express his fear of depression in public. To express the fear is, perhaps, to invite the fact — and perhaps also to inspire the interest of the state in measures to counter the threat. Few others have

> The task of this and the chapters following is to examine in turn the circumstances which have kept social inefficiency, private power, government intervention and unemployment from ruining us in the recent past. (Galbraith, 1957: 85)

Galbraith, like Stigler, is convinced of the need for decentralised and rapid decision-making in the productive sector[31]. Galbraith suggests that even in the absence of competition the existing set of dominant market structures are still self-regulating. Using a Newtonian analogy, he concludes that the rise of concentrated market power eventually generates an opposing power structure which checks abuse. In this way, gains are shared and social harmony maintained. The only role left to the government is one of promoting the formation of opposing blocs in those cases in which transaction costs otherwise might hinder them (labour and farmers are a case in point). This is not far removed

---

> been under such a ban. Farmers, workers and intellectuals, in the years since the war, have made no secret of their fear of depression. Before World War II ended it was taken as accepted that there would be a post-war collapse with unemployment ranging upward from seven, eight or ten millions. (Galbraith, 1957: 6)

Robertson's (1950) review of *A Survey of Contemporary Economics* (1948) anticipates Galbraith's emphasis on this issue.

> Perhaps the consumers of the United States can now afford to pay a good deal of ransom to insure the stability of her free enterprise system — a stability which has become of outstanding importance to us all. Poorer nations, under pressure to earn their overseas bread, may be called upon to face the risks of instability involved in taking a tougher line with the spirit of 'live and let live'. (Robertson, 1950: 10)

[31] This is not the case for bureaucratic structures, like government agencies. For Galbraith, it is questionable whether this should be the case. Governmental objectives, and the best means for accomplishing them, necessarily differ from those of the private sector.

> The process of decision-making has two dimensions, timing and quality. For relatively simple and undifferentiated types of production — the production of electric power, for example — the quality of the decision is normally more important than its timeliness. There the administrative problems of public management can be solved. Quite the reverse is true of consumers' goods. A poor decision is normally to be preferred to a late one. (Galbraith, 1957: 171)

from the basic Smithian idea that given the proper environment, markets will operate effectively. However, these environments may sometimes need to be created, they will not necessarily create themselves. But once in place, continuing intervention is minimal. There is unfortunately an inherent danger as well[32]. If one accepts Galbraith's re-conceptualisation of the market as power blocs, then the potential for a wage/price spiral seems obvious. Linking himself to Keynes, Galbraith sees the in-built inflationary tendency of this market structure as being more of a political problem than anything else.

Once saving and the certainty of its utilisation in investment became suspect, Galbraith, like so many others of that era, saw the necessity of providing a macro founded micro-economics reflecting both the reality of the existing industry structure as well as the new Keynesian understanding of the economy. The doctrine Keynes presented raised uncomfortable questions about income distribution and profits. Galbraith's response was to provide an answer based on relative bargaining power. Extending his 1948 analysis, Galbraith concluded that the need for government intervention, in terms of anti-trust actions, was rapidly dwindling. Removing government from performing this pivotal function should have found favour with Stigler's own penchant for such a limited role. But Stigler is not so easily lured by this particular prospect of a self-adjusting market based economy. Accepting Galbraith's simple proposal is equivalent to defining power as the basis of economic analysis.

An analytic core so defined is antithetical to the sort of market faith commonly held in Chicago[33]. Power relationships have the distinct

[32] None of the book is couched in the deadly serious, formal, come rigorous manner beloved by economists. This is after all a book deliberately aimed at a broad public audience. Its goal is not to repel or to bore. We also need to remember that the push for economically correct rhetoric was only slowly gathering steam for its eventual triumph. A look through the journals of that era sees a number of different styles and procedures coexisting quite comfortably. See Freedman (1995a) for an exploration of this issue.

[33] One sees this clearly in the 1972 paper by Alchian and Demsetz. Their core proposition is that authority has no role to play even within the confines of the firm. The sphere of voluntary exchange is extended to embrace labour relations.

disadvantage of yielding no unique equilibrium. They are consequently at odds with Stigler's unwavering adherence to the lasting validity and general applicability of marginal productivity theory[34]. Where power relations dominate economic activity, factors of production are rewarded with their marginal product only by chance. Relative power, not market forces, determines income distribution. This remains the compelling problem at the heart of any oligopoly theory. Whatever else its virtues may be, capitalism, defined by market power, is not synonymous with economic efficiency. Faced with this alternative, Stigler must forcefully reiterate the dominance of competition. His first step is to aggressively attack the opposing hypothesis of industrial concentration.

Galbraith's book cavalierly dismissed the hardcore price theory forming the basis of George Stigler's intellectual life. In effect, Galbraith was presenting Chicago, and Stigler, with a black bordered condolence card. In doing so he appears to shed the same sort of sympathetic tears over the demise of standard price theory that the Walrus spared for his esteemed oyster friends.

> The comparative importance of a small number of great corporations ... cannot be denied except by those who have a singular immunity to statistical evidence or striking capacity to manipulate it. (Galbraith, 1957: 109)

Given their earlier exchange (1948–1949), and the nature of Galbraith's hypothesis, Stigler has no option, but to slash and burn in his well honed and familiar fashion. This he proceeds to do at the 1953 AEA meetings despite the incongruity of Stigler taking an ostensibly more interventionist approach than Galbraith[35].

A book like *American Capitalism* that was an avowedly popular work was for Stigler a sufficient self-confession of guilt. 'Popular' was

---

[34] See Yordon (1992) for a very useful discussion of Stigler's unshakeable belief in productivity theory, the basis of his doctoral dissertation (Stigler, 1938).

[35] Stigler's enthusiasm for vigorous anti-trust enforcement flagged under the influence of Aaron Director and convincingly ended when Demsetz (1968) indicated that even supposedly natural monopolies could be shown responsive to competitive forces.

a shorthand for a lazy piece of journalism peppered with assertions rather than reasoned arguments backed by empirical evidence. It is true that Galbraith's arguments are far from tightly reasoned and his evidence more impressionistic than overwhelming, but that in a sense is part and parcel of most popular writing. The point of such writing is to focus and stir debate rather than rivet each element of a model firmly in place. By appealing to the public at large, Galbraith hoped that the ensuing debate would be one that professional economists could not avoid.

In Stigler's eyes a populariser was no better than a witty entertainer, plying a trade which had more to do with the art of a novelist than the science of a practising economist[36]. This narrowing down of debate provides a rationale to exclude those whose rhetoric strays from the established norm. Galbraith, like Veblen before him, would gradually be marginalised for this as well as for other sins. Stigler then needs no prodding to go into action. The nature of his response is telegraphed by the title chosen ('The Economist Plays with Blocs'). Clearly Stigler has no intention of restraining himself.

Galbraith's popular appeal seemingly had its desired effect. Organisers of the 1953 AEA meetings scheduled a session devoted to discussing, or more accurately eviscerating, this new theory of countervailing power. Stigler rose in response to Galbraith's opening remarks. Galbraith had taken the opportunity to respond to a number of objections raised since the publication of his work. Stigler proceeded to raise all the same objections as though Galbraith had spent the last thirty minutes discussing the novels of Jane Austen. There is no recognition of Galbraith's remarks, no change in his set critique. This adds something sour and carping; an unnecessary note of petulance, to what would otherwise be legitimate objections. Despite speaking so soon

---

[36] The fact that Galbraith would go on to write a novel as well as numerous literary essays only confirmed the suspicions of most economists.

> ... a gifted satirist seeking to penetrate our complacency and force us to re-examine long accepted views and using the long-accepted methods of exaggeration, caricature and gross omission appropriate to this jester role (Stigler quoted in Hession (1972: 158)).

after Christmas there is a want of generosity in Stigler approach[37]. It is an unreformed, grinch-like, George Stigler that faces the audience.

> To sum up this stage of our analysis, we may say that Galbraith's notion of countervailing power is a dogma, not a theory. It lacks a rational development and must be accepted or rejected without reference to its unstated logical antecedents. (Stigler, 1954: 10)

These rough remarks[38] could equally be applied to Stigler's own efforts[39]. Neither ironic self-recognition nor even-handedness appears

---

[37] I want to close with an apology for the consistently negative attitude I have felt compelled to take with respect to Galbraith's theory. One would like to speak well of so urbane and witty a presentation. Especially at this season one would like to avoid expressing doubts that a mysterious, benevolent being will crawl down each and every chimney and leave a large income as well as directions to the nearest cut-rate outlet. Yet even at this season, Galbraith cannot persuade us that we should turn our economic problems over to Santa. (Stigler, 1954: 14)

[38] In his autobiography, Galbraith recalls this session as an attempt to demolish his work. Stigler's efforts are not described. He is instead misidentified as being affiliated with Chicago. Though that might remain his spiritual home, in 1953 he was a staff member of Columbia University and would not return to Chicago until 1958. Galbraith's studied lack of comment may be symptomatic of the mauling received at those hands.

[39] Charges of theology and dogma are swapped equally between Galbraith and Stigler. To an extent it is true about both. Stigler is determined to see competition as the dominant market structure while Galbraith stands steadfastly for market power as his prevailing doctrine. It is nearly impossible to think of any evidence that would change their respective stands. Stigler is intent on measuring percentages of dominated markets. Galbraith allows that many markets are competitive but a number of key markets are dominated by a few firms. There is no common ground of debate or any effort to reach such shared terms of discussion.

> Men cannot live without an economic theology — without some rationalization of the abstract and seemingly inchoate arrangements which provide him with his livelihood. For this purpose the competitive or classical model had many advantages. It was comprehensive and internally consistent. By asserting that it was a description of reality the conservative could use it as the justification of the existing order. For the reformer it could be a goal, a beacon to mark the path of needed change. Both could be united in the central faith at least so long as nothing happened to strain unduly their capacity for belief. (Galbraith, 1957: 17)

to have a role to play when the aim is to demolish rather than to evaluate a theory. Galbraith did not sufficiently detail the conditions under which countervailing power would arise. This does not imply that the work is fundamentally wrong and should simply be discarded. What Stigler was hoping to do is not to force Galbraith or possibly other supporters of countervailing power to clarify their ideas but rather to close off the discussion before it became too widespread. As pointed out previously, the session itself was a response by the mainstream of the profession to the popular interest Galbraith's book generated. The very speakers at the session seem to have been chosen for their varying ability to overwhelmingly reject rather than discuss the work.

Stigler starts, as always, from a non-controversial premise. He lists three bases of Galbraith's theory, all of which, he concedes, are commonly held by a number of economists.

- The American economy is currently efficient and progressive.
- The American economy is dominated by large business concerns.
- The American economy is characterised by powerful sellers faced by powerful buyers.

Stigler does raise the quibble that there is a seeming contradiction between the first two points. Monopolised economies, he declares to be necessarily inefficient. In doing so, he ignores his implicit assumption that resources are equally employed in both cases. In the post-Keynes era, many economists would not be willing to accept this assumption at face value. Galbraith chooses to advance instead a Schumpeterian line that large firms, being capable of devoting more resources to R&D, produce more innovative economies. Considered dynamically, a monopolised economy can in this sense be more efficient. Stigler ignores this possibility. Instead, he resolves his own hand-crafted contradiction by pointing out that the US economy is superior to those of Britain, France and Germany. These countries have more concentrated industries. Hence he concludes that the US economy is ahead because it has more competitive markets. Stigler here seems to accept what he has so vociferously rejected before; the link between concentration ratios and competition. By doing so he allows his audience to make a natural extension of his reasoning by implicitly suggesting that the US economy would be even more vibrant were concentration ratios to fall further. Galbraith's logic is set on its head. This though is a parlour trick not a reasoned argument. To hone in on concentration ratios as the sole basis for explaining growth rates cannot be taken seriously[40].

This is merely a warm up for Stigler. He is ready to attack the Achilles heel of Galbraith's position, the rather striking claim that countervailing power leads to the sort of competitive result familiar from welfare economics. It is understandable how one might think that Galbraith is referring to the standard maximisation of surplus (consumers and producers) familiar to all practising economists. Galbraith makes a muddle of this. Careful reading, however, indicates that for the most part, he is referring to a state of social stability where rewards are shared somewhat equitably. It is doubtful, in the absence of competitive markets, that oligopolies would be willing to respond to consumers' demands at the lowest possible price. Galbraith however assumes that the mutual tolerance between different economic sectors makes it worthwhile to pay a bit more for one's purchases[41]. It would be possible to argue that the absence of such disruptions may even make this approach more cost-effective. Whatever may be the case, Galbraith acknowledges his original lack of clarity on this point. Stigler responds by ignoring this confession. Galbraith further admits that competition must be assumed somewhere down the line if, for example, a supermarket's

---

[40] Stigler conveniently overlooks the war damage these European countries had suffered. One then wonders what response Stigler made when both France and Germany, with no change in market structure, charged ahead of the United States growth figures in the latter part of the fifties. Perhaps by that time he had characteristically forgotten those earlier claims. Stigler's remarks here are largely gratuitous, reflecting a debating strategy rather than a point of discussion.

[41] In many ways Galbraith's emphasis on social stability seems more in the Japanese than the United States tradition. Certainly, the sort of balance of power that Galbraith sees as the definitive nature of a modern economy seems a better fit with how the Japanese market structure would evolve in the post-war period.

countervailing power vis á vis suppliers is to produce tangible consumer benefits.

> I suspect they are right. I am sure that I was more than a little reluctant, at this particular stage in my argument, to confess a reliance on competition. After all, it is a bit embarrassing after one has just murdered his mother-in-law to disinter the lady and ask her to help do the cooking. (Galbraith, 1954: 4)

Stigler again gives little indication that he has heard these remarks.

Galbraith's failure to explain why countervailing power comes into existence is Stigler's most telling criticism. This leads him to claim that Galbraith eschews rational explanation. But in fact Galbraith's brief explanation is no more irrational than the explanation of self-generating competition. No one likes to be on the losing end of a power struggle. Once you grant that markets are dominated by oligopolies it is logical to wonder what the response would be of those on the receiving end of oligopoly power. If possible, provided the costs are not too great, some attempt will be made to respond by gaining a better bargaining position. Franchisees form organisations to better negotiate with the franchiser. Increased concentration amongst car part suppliers shifts the nature of negotiations between them and the large car companies. Relative bargaining strengths determine income distribution. The motivation to develop opposing blocs is clearly present. Since Galbraith posits substantial barriers to entry (first mover advantage, learning by doing, firm specific knowledge) it is not surprising that he does not see these shared profits as bringing new competitors into the field. The real issue is whether arrangements of this type do occur[42].

---

[42] Stigler makes a rather curious criticism of Galbraith's explanation that excess aggregate demand will undermine the stability derived from countervailing power by igniting inflation. In such a case pricing power is not blocked but rather augmented by the ability of each bloc to pass on increased costs. That countervailing power fails to hold under these circumstances does not destroy the logic of the argument. Galbraith is not claiming the sort of universality for his approach that Chicago academics would put forward for price competition.

> ... as the demand functions become generally inelastic, there is an opportunity for coalitions between those whose interests are otherwise opposed in

This is where, by Stigler's own empirical methodology, the work of an economist must lie. Stigler turns to the evidence at hand.

Stigler sees two potentially testable areas in Galbraith's proposition:

- Power begets offsetting power.
- Bilateral monopoly of this sort yields beneficial results.

He begins by constructing a multi-pronged attack on the first issue. Stigler's approach is flawed from the start. Galbraith never implies that power necessarily begets off-setting power. Finding a few counter-examples would not do. Ideally, playing according to Galbraith's rules, Stigler must demonstrate that countervailing power has only a trivial impact on observed economic outcomes. This is exactly what Stigler does not do. He instead opts to craft a counter-example. Ironically even this highly limited case fails to convince. Stigler contends that labour unions were incapable of achieving any degree of countervailing power without distinct government assistance. As evidence of this claim, he looks at unionisation in 1929 prior to the Great Depression. 'As all would agree this was ... a year in which government was not particularly favourable to unions and so the natural emergence of countervailing power might be better displayed.' (Stigler, 1954: 11) Contrary to Galbraith's supposition, the largest unions of that time (those most capable of exerting countervailing power) were not located in industries that were recognisably concentrated. Stigler concludes that in this instance, power clearly did not beget power. Does this undermine Galbraith's contentions?

Unfortunately, Stigler's argument will not bear weight. A little knowledge of the US labour movement is sufficient to dismiss it. The period chosen represents a low water mark for the American labour movement during the first half of the twentieth century, the least conducive environment for countervailing power to be displayed.

---

bargaining, and the inflationary process is accelerated ... In conceding the imperfections or malfunctioning of countervailing power I am apparently made responsible for it. Such criticism, in effect, requires that the social phenomenon described be both universal in application and socially benign in effect. This is silly. (Galbraith, 1954: 5)

Industry-wide unions had faded and would not be revived until the thirties when the CIO under John Lewis and the UAW under Walter Reuther gained strength. In 1929 the surviving large unions were all craft unions. They were only large relative to those existing at that time, not in any absolute sense. Craft unions by definition tend to be organised in industries where very little if any market power holds sway. Stigler must know that even the smallest slice of historical information is sufficient to undermine his example. One can only suppose that Stigler makes the attempt for its rhetorical effect, rather than as a means of clarifying any inherent weakness in Galbraith's argument.

It is true that the government's intervention in the thirties would make it more feasible for labour to oppose large oligopolies. But since the time of Adam Smith, economists have recognised that attempts by labour to organise and bargain were apt to fail, given the intrinsic balance of power between employers and employed. The New Deal government stepped in to even up the odds, motivated as much by a desire to reduce the ongoing strife between the new industry-wide labour unions and big business. As stated before, a one off assistance by the government to boost a group over a difficult barrier is contained within Galbraith's elucidation of his theory. By itself, such a necessity does not prevent a system from subsequently becoming self-regulating. Stigler is on firmer ground when he questions the supermarket and department store as arising in response to the concentrated power of the producers of that era. There are probably other reasons, including transaction cost explanations, that better account for their initial success and latter expansion. Yet countervailing power should not be entirely dismissed. It can provide insight into the ongoing relations between supermarkets and their suppliers. Imagine an alternative market where Proctor and Gamble, Néstles and Lever Brothers sold to small corner stores[43].

Stigler's second point is more important. It is the hardest question to respond to of any in his scattershot attack. This is the 'so what?' question. Countervailing power may redistribute income, but

[43] Until very recently this accurately described Japanese distribution channels and the subsequent high prices of consumer goods.

why should this be desirable? No obvious answer can be advanced. Galbraith's defence is more political than economic in nature. One sided power would in the US inevitably bring forth a call for increased government intervention to rectify the imbalance. This in turn would tend to decrease economic performance. Ironically this is not inconsistent with the type of political economy reasoning Stigler himself favoured[44]. As Stigler very correctly points out, all of these organised groups will not gain equal bargaining power. The problem is that Galbraith makes no such claim. He merely suggests that individuals in these groups will do better for themselves, on average, than if they remained unorganised. Each and every participant may not gain financially. A few might have bargained more effectively had they been on their own. For the vast majority, this will not be the case.

In his autobiography, Galbraith (1981) considers that he had been overly optimistic in seeing countervailing power as a widespread solution[45]. In the years to come it would not prove to be a defining economic mechanism. Countervailing power would in many cases fail to develop. Balances of power (between labour and big business) would shift. Galbraith, as he would in his later writing, suffered here from what Schumpeter (1951) termed the English disease, extrapolating from a time and place specific case to an all encompassing theory. However, useful discussion was not promoted by Stigler's remarks since they only attempted to focus attention away from the issues Galbraith actually raised. That is, exactly the problem with Stigler's approach. Seeking to shut down debate only leads to an intellectual dead end.

---

[44] The problems of rent seeking described by Stigler (1971) in his own seminal work on regulation arise only due to some particular government intervention. Stigler's solution is implicitly to downsize government to prevent such possible intrusions.

[45] ... in 1952, carried away by the idea, I made it far more inevitable and rather more equalizing than, in practice, it ever is. Countervailing power often does not emerge. (Galbraith, 1981: 284)

4. The Blocs Come Tumbling Down

> The stiletto concealed in his humor was reserved for ideas or policies and was never ad hominem — unless "An Economist Plays with Blocs," his brilliant title for an article on John Kenneth Galbraith's theory of countervailing power, can be so interpreted. (Friedman, 1993: 771)

Most of Galbraith's constructive work has fallen out of favour these days, though some of his populist notions remain. You hear echoes in the recent debate over corporate callousness. For the most part, the reality remains that barring the coining of a few terms (techno-structure, countervailing power) Galbraith has bequeathed little of lasting value, at least as judged by the economics profession. Ironically, neither Stigler's nor Galbraith's position on oligopoly has triumphed, judging by published work in the leading journals. Game theory takes into account the interdependence of corporate decisions. The work of transaction cost analysis focuses on the inner working of the firm. Stigler never felt either one was a useful approach to economic analysis.

On the other hand, Galbraith's contribution as a critic is similar to that of the one economist he most resembles. Thorstein Veblen also railed at mainstream economics and wrote for a larger audience than his fellow economists. But without a rigorous system of easily digested models, those mainstream economists who he rejected, in turn rejected him. Galbraith might have been indulging in self-description when he said of Veblen,

> He was not a constructive figure; no alternative economic system and no penetrating reforms are associated with his name. There was danger here. Veblen was a skeptic and an enemy of pretense. Those who drank too deeply could be in doubt about everything and everybody; they could believe that all effort at reform was humbug. I've fought to resist this tendency, but in other respects Veblen's influence on me has lasted long. (Galbraith, 1981: 30)

What remains in looking back at the battles staged by these long time opponents is that Stigler misrepresented Galbraith as he misrepresented all those who took up the cudgels of oligopoly and interdependence. His vision of the classic liberal society, where individual self-realisation through market choice is prized above all else, relied on the precise distribution of income represented by the tenets of marginal productivity theory. Bargaining indicated a realm of private power and a subsequent limiting of choice. It invited government intervention to rectify or at least counterpoise that exercise of unregulated power. Stigler (1949c), early in his career, quotes de Toqueville on the tendency of government to continually encroach individual liberties in the name of protecting the equal rights of its citizens[46].

> Every central power, which follows its natural tendencies, courts and encourages the principle of equality; for equality singularly facilitates, extends, and secures the influence of a central power. (de Toqueville quoted in Stigler (1949c: 11)

Whatever the validity of Stigler's views, the real issue here is how we go about reading an article or listening to a fellow economist speak. Do we read and listen only to find something wrong? To do so we zero in on loose details or badly represented links of a model and ignore the idea itself. Do we ridicule what others have put forward in good faith, or do we treat opposing views with due respect? By stamping on a partially nourished idea we may lose much that is valuable. Do we try to shut off debate, to silence opponents, or do we search for possible common ground? The adversarial approach of the courtroom remains the wrong model for economists to embrace. This is not a question of being nice. Niceness has absolutely nothing to do with this. The issue is a respect for ideas, even those which may clash with your own.

Many economists, not only those influenced by the combativeness of the Chicago seminar, defend this quasi-legal approach by speaking of a 'market place of ideas' which somehow tests the truth of ideas on the anvil of reason, or some metaphor to that effect. Stigler obviously believed in such a marketplace. In the continual struggle between contending camps, the soundest ideas, in this view, ultimately prevail. Starting from this assumption, it can only follow that current ideas

---

[46] Income redistribution allows a dominant group, like the middle classes, to use the coercive power of the state for its own benefit. See Stigler (1970).

must inevitably be superior to those of the past. Given his deeply held belief in market competition and the versatility of the price mechanism, what else could Stigler believe and advocate? Though we may be no more than midgets standing on the shoulders of giants, the working theorist need only keep his gaze focused upward. This struggle however, with its emphasis on ongoing and inherent progress, owes more to the Social Darwinism propounded by Herbert Spencer than to anything that Darwin himself cared to claim. There is no random and impersonal mechanism at work, which can match environment to idea in the way indicated by evolutionary struggle. The various sellers of those ideas are simultaneously active in attempting to construct an environment entirely conducive to their own particular merchandise. An assumption of objective progress in the march of ideas must be ingenuous at best. As always, the victors get to write the accepted historical accounts and define the terms of progress.

It is highly debateable whether faulty economic ideas eventually, under the extreme scrutiny of ambitious academics, are swept into deserved oblivion. Arguments prevail which best respond to what listeners want to hear. Perhaps economists are essentially conservative as Stigler (1959) long claimed, leaving them vulnerable to more powerful methods for restating their core beliefs. Stigler's emphasis on precision accompanied by empirical verification seemed to promise more than the discursive method traditionally favoured by English economists or by their American counterparts like Veblen. It seemed in tune with the idea of adopting scientific methods and approaches that was sweeping the post-war US.

Stigler was a master of the hard sell, manipulating his opponents' views to turn them to his own advantage[47]. Though he conquered, his compulsion to shut down rather than encourage debate,

[47] Whether Stigler saw himself as unfairly representing others' work is another matter, but one unfortunately that must remain a mystery given the lack of any reported deathbed confession. It is both more convenient and equally likely that Stigler saw himself as playing hard but fair. Even academics generally justify what they do in order to live with themselves. Evidence that Stigler ever acted dishonourably is absent, nor is there any reason to suspect that he did.

caste a pall over the profession which has in no way lessened. "Stigler's revered teacher Frank Knight claimed that the basic principle of science — truth or objectivity — is essentially a moral principle, in opposition to any form of self-interest. The presuppositions of objectivity are integrity, competence and humility." (Knight, 1937b: 244). Though most if not all economists would grant Stigler a high degree of integrity and competence, how many would extend humility to that list[48]? We are all, in our own way, fools. Those who so pointedly refuse to suffer fools lightly[49], who by doing so indulge their own sense of importance, are at some level rejecting only themselves. We need to tolerate the shortcomings of one another, not excoriate them.

> Never did they [ideas] arrive, he said with the hard edges that later critics came to attribute to them when trying to define their terms. Ideas were apt to be like fluffy balls of wool with no fixed outline and the relationship between concepts when first perceived was likely to be equally woolly. Keynes mistrusted intellectual rigour of the Ricardian type as likely to get in the way of original thinking and saw that it was not uncommon to hit on a valid conclusion before finding a logical path to it. (Cairncross, 1996: 87)

---

[48] Stigler was not alone in resorting to tendentious arguments to shut off opposing views. Whether Stigler's point of view was ultimately correct or at least more correct than his opponents is not at issue here. But Stigler did set the tone for the profession by his acknowledged skills and his deadliness in any debate. This is true even if Stigler himself had moments of self-doubt.

> When we strive to solve a scientific problem, is ambition for our own professional status completely overshadowed by our love of knowledge? ... When we write an article to demonstrate the fallacies of someone else's work, is our hatred for error never mixed with a tiny bit of glee at the display of our own cleverness. (Stigler, 1963: 92)

[49] As Milton Friedman so eloquently stated, Stigler's attitude was Let the chips fall where they may, my task is to be objective, accurate, and interesting. (McCann and Perlman, 1993: 1012)
Stigler was undoubtedly interesting. Objective and accurate are a bit harder to accept.

Appendix A. Contents of a Survey of Contemporary Economics

Value and Distribution
Author: Bernard F. Haley (Stanford)
Critics: E. H. Chamberlin (Harvard)
J. M. Clark (Columbia)

Employment Theory and Business Cycles
Author: William Fellner (UC Berkeley)
Critics: Gottfried Haberler (Harvard)
Alvin Hansen (Harvard)

Monopoly and the Concentration of Economic Power
Author: J. K. Galbraith (Harvard)
Critics: R. A. Gordon (UC Berkeley)
A. D. H. Kaplan (Brookings Institute)

Price and Production Policies
Author: Joe S. Bain (UC Berkeley)
Critics: Joel P. Dean (Columbia)
Donald H. Wallace (Princeton)

Federal Budgeting and Fiscal Policy
Author: Arthur Smithies (Harvard)
Critics: James K. Hall (University of Washington)
Lawrence H. Seltzer (Wayne University)

The Theory of International Trade
Author: Lloyd A. Metzler (Chicago)
Critics: James W. Angell (Columbia)
Jacob Viner (Princeton)

Economics of Labor
Author: Lloyd G. Reynolds
Critics: Clark Kerr (UC Berkeley)
Sumner H. Slichter (Harvard)

Development and Use of National Income Data
Author: Carl S. Shoup (Columbia)
Critics: M. A. Copeland (Cornell)
E. E. Hagen (Bureau of the Budget)

Monetary Theory
Author: Henry H. Villard (Hofstra College)
Critics: Edward S. Shaw (Stanford)
Elmer Wood (Missouri)

Dynamic Process Analysis
Author: Paul A. Samuelson (MIT)
Critics: Friedrich A. Lutz (Princeton)
Fritz Machlup (Johns Hopkins)

Econometrics
Author: Wassily Leontief (Harvard)
Critics: Joseph A. Schumpeter (Harvard)
W. Allen Wallis

Socialist Economics
Author: Abram Bergson (Harvard)
Critics: Frank D. Graham (Princeton)
A. P. Lerner (Roosevelt College)

The Prospects For Capitalism
Author: David McC. Wright (Virginia)
Critics: Frank H. Knight (Chicago)
Paul M. Sweezy (Wilton Centre, N.H.)

References

Alchian, AA and H Demsetz (1972). Production, information costs, and economic organization. *The American Economic Review*, 84(3), 488–500.

Bain, J (1956). *Barriers to New Competition*. Cambridge: Harvard University Press.

Berle, AA and G Means (1932). *The Modern Corporation and Private Property*. New York: The Commerce Clearing House.

Cairncross, A (1996). Keynes the Man. (20 April 1996). *The Economist*, p. 87.

Chamberlin, EH (1933). *The Theory of Monopolistic Competition*. Cambridge: Harvard University Press.

Coase, R (1994). How should economists choose? In *Essays On Ecomnomics and Economists*, pp. 15–33. Chicago: University of Chicago Press.

Cohen, GA (1978). *Karl Marx's Theory of History — A Defense*. Princeton: Princeton University Press.

Demsetz, H (1993). George J. Stigler: Midcentury neoclassicalist with a passion to quantify. *The Journal of Political Economy*, 101(5), 793–817.

Demsetz, H (1968). Why regulate utilities? *The Journal of Law and Economics*, 11 (April), 55–65.

Ellis, HS (1948). Preface. In *A Survey of Contemporary Economics*, Vol. I. HS Ellis (ed.), pp. v–viii. Homewood, Ill.: Richard D Irwin.

Freedman, C (1995a). The economist as Mythmaker — Stigler's kinky transformation. *Journal of Economic Issues*, 29(1), 175–209.

Freedman, C (1995b). No end to means — George Stigler's profit motive. *Macquarie Economics Research Papers*, No. 15/95.

Freedman, C (1993). Why economists can't read. *Methodus*, 5(1), 6–23.

Friedland, C (1993). On Stigler and Stiglerisms. *The Journal of Political Economy*, 101(5), 780–783.

Friedman, M (1993). George Stigler: A personal reminiscence. *The Journal of Political Economy*, 101(5), 768–772.

Galbraith, JK (1981). *A Life In Our Times*. Boston: Houghton Mifflin Company.

Galbraith, JK (1970). Letter to Gardiner C. Means — August 19, 1970. *Gardiner C. Means Papers, Series VI A, Stigler on Industrial Prices*.

Galbraith, JK (1957). *American Capitalism — The Concept of Countervailing Power* (Revised Edition). London: Hamish Hamilton.

Galbraith, JK (1954). Countervailing power. *American Economic Review Papers and Proceedings*, 44(2), 1–6.

Galbraith, JK (1952a). *American Capitalism — The Concept of Countervailing Power*. Boston: Houghton Mifflin.

Galbraith, JK (1952b). *A Theory of Price Control*. Boston: Houghton Mifflin.

Galbraith, JK (1948). Monopoly and concentration of economic power. In *A Survey of Contemporary Economics*, Vol. I, HS Ellis (ed.), pp. 99–128. Homewood, Ill.: Richard D Irwin.

Galbraith, JK (1936). Monopoly power and price rigidities. *Quarterly Journal of Economics*, 50(2), 456–475.

Hartwell, RM (1995). *A History of the Mont Pelerin Society*. Indianopolis: Liberty Fund.

Hayek, F (1944). *The Road to Serfdom*. Chicago: Chicago University Press.

Hession, CH (1972). *John Kenneth Galbraith & His Critics*. New York: New American Library.

Humphrey, DH (1937). The nature and meaning of rigid prices, 1894–1933. *The Journal of Political Economy*. 45(4), 651–661.
Knight, FH (1937a). Unemployment and Mr. Keynes' revolution in economic thought. *The Canadian Journal of Economics and Political Science*, 3(1), 100–123.
Knight, FH (1937b). *Freedom and Reform*. New York: Harper & Brothers.
Mason, ES (1938). Price Inflexibility. *Review of Economics and Statistics*, 20(1), pp. 53–64.
McCann, Jr. CR, and M Perlman (1993). On thinking about George Stigler. *The Economic Journal*, 103(July), 994–1014.
Means, G (1939). *The Structure of the American Economy*. Part 1 *Basic Characteristics*. Washington.
Reder, MW (1982). Chicago economics: Permanence and change. *Journal of Economic Literature*, 20(3), 1–38.
Reynolds, LG (1948). Economics of labor. In *A Survey of Contemporary Economics*, HS Ellis (ed.), Vol. I, 255–288. Homewood, Ill.: Richard D Irwin.
Robertson, D (1950). A revolutionist's handbook. *Quarterly Journal of Economics*, 44(1), 1–14.
Robinson, JV (1933). *The Economics of Imperfect Competition*. London: Macmillan.
Schumpeter, J (1951). *Ten Great Economists from Marx to Keynes*. New York: Oxford University Press.
Skidelsky, R (1992). *John Maynard Keynes — Volume Two: The Economist as Saviour 1920–1937*. London: Macmillan.
Smithies, A (1950). Memorial. *The American Economic Review*, 40(4), 628–645.
Sowell, T (1993). A student's eye view of George Stigler. *The Journal of Political Economy*, 101(5), 784–792.
Sraffa, P (1926). The laws of returns under competitive conditions. *Economic Journal*, 36 (December), 535–550.
Stigler, GJ (1988a). *Memoirs of an Unregulated Economist*. New York: Basic Books.
Stigler, GJ (1988b). Palgraves' dictionary of economics. *Journal of Economic Literature*, 26(4), 1729–1736.
Stigler, GJ (1983). Nobel lecture: The process and progress of economics. *The Journal of Political Economy*, 91(4), 529–545.
Stigler, GJ (1982a). The economist and the state. In *The Economist as Preacher*, pp. 119–135. Chicago: The University of Chicago Press.
Stigler, GJ (1982b). The ethics of competition: The friendly economists. *The Economist as Preacher*, pp. 14–26. Chicago: University of Chicago Press.
Stigler, GJ (1982c). The ethics of competition: The unfriendly critics. *The Economist as Preacher*, pp. 27–37. Chicago: University of Chicago Press.
Stigler, GJ (1982d). The economists and the problem of monopoly. *The Economist as Preacher*, pp. 38–56. Chicago: University of Chicago Press.
Stigler, GJ (1982e). *The Pleasures and Pains of Modern Capitalism*. London: The Institute of Economic Affairs.

Stigler, GJ (1975). The economists' traditional theory of the economic functions of the state. In *The Citizen and the State*, pp. 103–113. Chicago: University of Chicago Press.

Stigler, GJ (1971). The theory of economic regulation. *Bell Journal of Economics and Management Science*, 2(1), 3–21.

Stigler, GJ (1970). Director's law of public income redistribution. *Journal of Law and Economics*, 13(1), 1–10.

Stigler, GJ (1963a). A theory of oligopoly. *The Journal of Political Economy*, 72(1), 44–61.

Stigler, GJ (1963b). *The Intellectual and the Market Place*. New York: Free Press.

Stigler, GJ (1961). The economics of information. *Journal of Political Economy*, 69(3), 213–225.

Stigler, GJ (1959). The politics of political economists. *Quarterly Journal of Economics*, 73(4), 522–532.

Stigler, GJ (1954). The economist plays with blocs. *American Economic Review Papers and Proceedings*, 44(2), 7–14.

Stigler, GJ (1950). Monopoly and oligopoly by merger. *American Economic Review Paper and Proceedings*, 40(2), 23–34.

Stigler, GJ (1949a). A survey of contemporary economics. *The Journal of Political Economy*, 42(2), 93–105.

Stigler, GJ (1949b). Competition in the United States. In *Five Lectures On Economic Problems*, pp. 46–62. London: Longman's, Green and Co.

Stigler, GJ (1949c). The economists and equality. In *Five Lectures On Economic Problems*, pp. 1–12. London: Longman's, Green and Co.

Stigler, GJ (1947a). The kinky oligopoly demand curve and rigid prices. *The Journal of Political Economy*. Reprinted in *Readings in Price Theory*. KE Boulding and GJ Stigler (ed.), pp. 410–439. London: Allen and Unwin.

Stigler, GJ (1947b). Professor Lester and the Marginalists. *The American Economic Review*, 37(1), 154–157.

Stigler, GJ (1946). The economics of minimum wage legislation. *The American Economic Review*, 36(3), 358–365.

Stigler, GJ (1942). The extent and bases of monopoly. *The American Economic Review Papers and Proceedings*, 32(2), 1–22.

Stigler, GJ (1941). *Production and Distribution Theories*. New York: Macmillan.

Stigler, GJ (1939). Production and distribution in the short run. *The Journal of Political Economy*, 47(2), 305–327.

Stigler, GJ (1938). The development of modern distribution theory out of the theory of subjective value 1870–1895. Ph.D diss., University of Chicago.

Stigler, GJ and J Kindahl (1970). *The Behavior of Industrial Prices*. New York: Columbia University Press.

Sweezy, PM (1939). Demand under conditions of oligopoly. *The Journal of Political Economy*, 47(3), 568–573.

Viner, J (1936). Mr. Keynes on the causes of unemployment. *The Quarterly Journal of Economics*, 51(2), 147–167.

Viner, J (1950). A survey of contemporary economics. *American Economic Review*, 40(4), 649–653.

Wallace, DH (1936). Monopoly prices and depression. In *Explorations in Economics*, DH Humphrey (ed.), pp. 349–367. Cambridge: Harvard University Press.

Wallis, WA (1993). George J. Stigler: In memoriam. *The Journal of Political Economy*, 101(5), 774–779.

Wilcox, C (1950). On the alleged ubiquity of oligopoly. *American Economic Review Paper and Proceedings*, 40(2), 67–73.

Wilcox, C (1940). *Competition and Monopoly in American Industry*, Washington: T.N.E.C. Monograph 21.

Yordon, WJ (1992). Stigler's adaptable and indivisible plan and the micro/macro schism. *The History of Political Economy*, 24 (Summer), 455–470.

Chapter 6

Was George Stigler Adam Smith's Best Friend? — Studying the History of Economic Thought

> There is a well-known story, still worth retelling, about a word game George invented for young children. He would give them, he said, a million dollars if they correctly answered three questions. The first, "Who was buried in Grant's tomb?" and the second, "Whose head was on the Lincoln penny?" inspired great confidence in the child for a prospective life of luxury and leisure. Invariably, all hopes were dashed with the third question: "Who was Adam Smith's best friend?" Except one time the son of a friend responded, "Why, you are, Uncle George." (Rosen 1993: 809–810)

At times economists seem to treat research into the history of their profession as a guilty pleasure, equating it with 'the love that dares not speak its name', to steal an expression from Oscar Wilde. As a field of research it retains at best an equivocal position. Should real economists waste their time amusing themselves with such a completely irrelevant and non-applicable field? This at best ambivalent attitude by most of the profession meant that the establishment of the first journal dedicated to this area of endeavour (*History of Political Economy*) served as the eagerly awaited signal for the most prestigious general journals to stop publishing articles of this nature. By the 1970s, the subject's relegation to the backwaters of the discipline translated into a generalised move to drop history of economic thought (as well as economic history) as a requirement of graduate education.

> ... history of thought, like all other fields, is well enough served by its own specialists. These were the reasons why Stigler proposed and supported the decision of the Economics Department at the University of Chicago to abandon its history of thought requirement in 1972, before many other departments did. (Rosen 1993: 811)[1]

As one of the chief pall bearers of the subject, George Stigler remained largely unable to come down authoritatively on either side of the question. This lack of definitive response is very atypical for such a professional academic warrior. In many ways, despite his great love of the subject and the foundation role it played in establishing his own career, George Stigler had an ambiguous attitude to the subject. Arguably, the foundation of Stigler's own career had at its base his life long interest in the history of his own beloved discipline. These issues are a constant theme of his intellectual development from work done while acquiring a master's degree at Northwestern to the

---

[1] Ironically, Sherwin Rosen toned down this strong position in a conversation I had with him. However, he stressed the point that the marginal product derived from teaching History of Thought was simply too low to continue the requirement.

> Now, I don't know if he [George Stigler] was a *leader* [in abolishing HET], but he was certainly in *favour* of it. I don't know how that issue first came up. I think it came up because most young Economists had lost interest in it and it was just a big tax on everyone's energy. No-one was working on it. It wasn't really much of a research field. I think it's had a slight come-back but it's still pretty small. Even now, you see very few PhD's with that particular interest. There's also been a general laissez faire attitude around here about graduate degree requirements. So I think that's how it came up for discussion. In the same way, there was an Economic History requirement which I don't think we have anymore either. That was also dropped. So I don't think he was in favour of putting artificial restrictions on a degree. That was probably his motivation. But I don't know. I don't think *any* of us were too happy about that move. (Conversation with Sherwin Rosen, October 1997)

thesis he undertook under the guidance of Frank Knight. Direct research in this area continued throughout his career. But history of thought provided him with more than a potential field of research. I would suggest that it helped form his approach to economics as well. Yet he continued to do an uncharacteristic straddle in evaluating the importance of this endeavour. In a very self-deprecating way, he often seemed on the verge of asking the profession to forgive him these untamed idiosyncrasies.

> The study of the history of economics has escaped all the forces that have transformed the character of economic research in the twentieth century. Neither foundation nor government is at all interested in intellectual history, so it is perhaps the last unsubsidized research area in economics. It has escaped any serious quantification, and research assistants can seldom be used — why, even committees are scarce in the field! (Stigler, 1965a: v)

As an innocent form of merriment indulged in by economists past their prime or even toying with senescence, history of thought need not be given any special consideration. It is simply an endeavour low on the pecking order of the profession[2]. Restricted to this framework it matters little if economics has a useful past or not. The response to Stigler's question would simply be 'Who cares?' But this misses the more essential issue that Stigler has in his sights. What Stigler is actually attempting is a preview of the debate that would exile history of thought to the back blocks of graduate education for decades to come (As far as I can tell, the years of exile continue). This defines the central issue that Stigler attempted to tackle in his own short piece. A field of study may be worthwhile for two potential reasons. It may

---

[2] Even before the subject was sidelined in graduate programs and before Stigler himself wondered if it was worth studying, history of thought had fallen into disrepute. One of the major practitioners in the area (Mark Blaug) complained to his former dissertation supervisor, George Stigler:

> ... the low state of repute in which the subject has fallen in the United States discourages me from pursuing that interest any further. People positively jeer at you when you state your specialty ... it should be a side line, they argue. (Mark Blaug letter to George Stigler, December 20, 1961)

have some intrinsic value and demand study in and of itself. This provides room for the specialist to flourish. Areas like labour, public finance and monetary economics easily meet this criterion. Other fields, while providing challenges for potential specialists, also provide salutary basic approaches to understanding the discipline itself. The collective wisdom of the profession prescribes minimum doses of microeconomics, macroeconomics and econometrics swallowed with persistent regularity by all graduate students to gain at least a limited proficiency of their subject. Here, it is as much the way of dealing with material, as the material itself, which is important.

Ironically, Stigler was the antithesis of a specialist[3]. Once he had his initial insight and did preliminary work to establish the worth of that insight, he moved on to other areas. He left the grubbier work of developing a rich seam to others who lacked his mercurial temperament. Consistency within his work lies in his market concerns, his attempts to extend the authority of market relations and his approach to the subject.

We can then eliminate the more uninteresting aspect to George Stigler's question since clearly he had no intention to justify an interest in the subject whether indulged in by him or any other economist. The issue revolves around an approach to economics rather than the

---

[3] George Stigler was never one to follow up his breakthrough ideas and intuition. The more plodding work, the work of the technician and specialist, he left to others.

> He was a guy with a lot of ideas and yet impatient. George had an impatient personality. Even in playing tennis, if he didn't get the point in two shots you could tell he really tried for a hard shot, he didn't want to just sit and hit it back and forth. He was a good tennis player, particularly when he was younger, but he had a real impatience. And that was true intellectually too. He wouldn't sit with one problem for five years as some people might do. And so in his papers, he has an idea and he tests it. So there are a lot of good ideas in his work but he doesn't sit and stay with a problem for a long time. I think that's true. In that I think that he's substantially different from Milton, you know his work on money or his work on consumption functions were longer ventures, he took longer periods of time. He had more patience. George was not the most patient researcher. (Conversation with Gary Becker, October 1997)

value of a specific field of study. Whether or not it is a speciality more honoured in the breach than in assiduous practice is a narrower issue. The question that concerned Stigler is whether or not a very model of the modern economist need trouble him or herself with the history of his or her discipline. Did in fact the history of economics have anything to offer to the profession in general?

1. Field Versus Foundation

> Some historians of economics — Schumpeter is an eminent representative — believe that an understanding of the evolution of a science helps to understand its present structure. This claim may be conceded and restated as the plausible hypothesis that correct knowledge never has a negative marginal product. Nevertheless, one need not read in the history of economics — that is, past economics — to master present economics. (Stigler, 1982e: 107)

This puts into perspective the key issue if we want to measure the usefulness of any enforced scholarly requirement. Stigler fails to sufficiently define what it means to master economics. Or to be more precise, he sets his benchmark in a rather superficial way. "The young theorist, working with an increasingly formal, abstract, and systematic corpus of knowledge, will seldom find it necessary to consult even a late-nineteenth-century economist." (Stigler 1982e: 107)

Such a statement is essentially irrefutable if we identify being an economist in a limited and highly technical fashion. Such training is inescapable given the inevitable specialisation of the discipline. But being a good mechanic, though a necessary achievement, is not sufficient to yield anything more than a pedestrian academic with little insight into his or her own endeavours. Being a good scholar demands the development of a minimum level of economic intuition. At its most basic, this is equivalent to an ability to analyse and interpret research results, both one's own and that of others. In educating, rather than merely training, graduate students, these objectives should dominate. Decisions need to be made in terms of the minimum requirements to achieve competency as an economist versus research decisions concerning specialisation. These two very different objectives define core versus field courses. Thus, when left to the practising specialist, no justification is required. Any field which catches some scholar's interest is worthy of pursuit. Much more is required to become the common fare for all aspiring economists. Thus, Stigler's question, 'Does Economics Have a Useful Past?' involves issues of general nutrition rather than the appeal it may have for some palates such as his own.

The parallel issue of economic history is in its way an easier one to argue despite the current disrepute of that specific study[4]. As Frank Knight claimed:

> Historical economists have also been more ready to think of change, as contrasted with finality, in the pattern of economic history, which is valuable both in itself and as a complement to economic theory. (Knight, 1956: 18)

If economics is something more than a rather uninteresting branch of applied mathematics, then it needs to be grounded as "a study of mankind in the ordinary business of life." (Marshall, 1982: 1). The raw material of economics must remain embedded in past economic events[5]. Citing specific economic outcomes does not conclusively demonstrate a given functional relationship. But knowing what happened in the past provides us with the intuition and inspiration necessary to form sensible hypotheses. A good economist is always an economic tourist, to use that

---

[4] Those interested in the role of history in the study of economics should start with the article "Does the Past Have Useful Economics?" written by Stigler's then colleague Donald McCloskey (1976). And yes, the reference to Stigler's article is deliberate. For a more recent publication that evaluates the role of history in economic analysis see Hodgson (2001).

[5] Curiously enough, while professing a lifelong interest in the history of his own discipline, Stigler never seemed to extend that interest to the broader field of economic history. Such an interest is certainly not present in his written work. What amounts to an indifference to this particular area of study has its antecedents in his graduate education, the days when the study of economic history was not optional.

> Chester Wright taught economic history from 4 to 6 each afternoon, with a ten-minute break at 5 P.M. for the Social Science tea. The course was competent but unexciting so I invariably attended only half of each session. (Stigler, 1988: 26)

fortunate phrase of Deirdre McCloskey[6]. Our curiosity is aroused by economic events and the desire to make sense of them. We supplement our own experiences with those of others throughout the ages. (Economic history remains essentially an analysis of past experiences). It should be explicitly obvious that such knowledge, though of intrinsic use to any economist is not acquired through core courses in micro or macroeconomics and certainly not through a thorough grounding in econometrics. That the study of economic history is complementary to that of economic theory, providing the needed experience to flesh out the bare bones of more abstract reasoning, should be sufficient to provide a rationale for its common study[7].

---

[6] McCloskey uses this phrase to describe Armen Alchian, a younger member of the Stigler circle though based at UCLA. "Armen Alchian, who is more Catholic than the Pope, who never went to the University of Chicago, but is a real Chicagoan." (Conversation with Paul Samuelson, October 1997). It is meant to convey someone who can remain a stranger in his or her native land, looking at society with fresh and curious eyes.

> When he [Armen Alchian] talks about the housing market you discover soon that he is holding vividly in mind the first house that he and his wife Pauline bought in Los Angeles. When he talks about the subsidization of the middle class implicit in the distinction between California State at Fullerton and the University of California at Los Angeles you can hear his experiences with his own children or echoes of an argument decades ago with a University administrator, not an economist. Armen has gone through life as a tourist in his own economy, noting with wonder the existence of transactions costs, the expensiveness of establishing property rights, the strange rhetoric of vested interests. (McCloskey 1996a: 365–366)

[7] A recent article by McGrattan and Prescott (2004) demonstrates the power of applying modern techniques to economic history. The authors revisit the often cited issue of Irving Fisher's mistake. On the eve of the 1929 stock market crash, Fisher claimed in a headline article (*New York Times*, 22 October 1929) that stocks were undervalued. The authors conclude that contrary to common belief, Fisher was right. What is important here is not whether or not the conclusion is correct but the implications such studies have for broader issues. How is the value of a company measured? To what degree is that valuation reflected in its share price? If undervalued shares can collapse, what other factors drive stock exchanges? Without such historical studies, economics can remain at a level of abstraction where any result is possible depending on the assumptions initially made.

> They [general principles] afford serviceable approximations to partial, but important, aspects of the truth; the study of history and factual data yields other true and important generalizations. (Knight, 1956: 28)

Is there then something approaching a parallel argument for history of economic thought? Here, we need to look more closely at the analysis provided by George Stigler, some four or five years before he helped drive the study into the graduate wilderness in which it has remained ever since.

2. Sheltered Workshops

> These matters belong to scientific history, and the history of science bores most scientists stiff. A great many highly creative scientists ... take it for granted, though they are usually too polite or too ashamed to say so, that an interest in the history of science is a sign of failing or unawakened powers. (Peter Medawar quoted by Stigler 1982e: 107–108)

Stigler as mentioned, almost summarily dismisses the need to study history of thought to master present day economics (though never defining what is needed for such mastery, let alone what qualifies as present day economics[8]. To be fair, he does backtrack and put the subject on trial. Since Stigler's verdict assisted in the subject's exile, the evaluation of its place in economics can be served by examining Stigler's own reasoning on the matter.

Stigler starts from the premise that economics is a science like the physical sciences. He is then drawn to agreeing with those sciences

---

[8] To underscore the point, Stigler is willing to push this idea to the extreme. The logical extension would claim that any knowledge of past economics is completely superfluous. What is more, given that time is a highly limited resource, pursuing such interests inevitably reduces the capacity to do original research. This puts history of thought into the more onerous classification of distraction rather than the innocuous category of being an innocent amusement.

> A young economist who believes that Adam Smith was the Smith who founded the Mormon faith will only provide innocent amusement outside of Utah, at no cost to his professional status. (Stigler, 1988: 215)

that essentially sneer at forays into the history of their subject. "... these scientists are usually right in dismissing the history of science as a research weapon ... The economics of 1800 like the weather forecasts of 1800, is mostly out of date[9]." (Stigler, 1982e: 108). A complement to this argument is that "... the discipline of the history of economics [is] the study of earlier economics with a purpose other than the understanding of the workings of an economic system." (Stigler, 1982e: 108). In other words, it serves to a certain degree as a substitute for the real work of an economist. This idea is put forcefully by Stigler's old friend and colleague, Milton Friedman, in an attempt to explain a reviving interest in the subject.

> I'm saying that there is sort of a balance wheel here. If there are exciting things being done in a theory, interesting and exciting things to do with the structure of the body of economics, that's what will attract the top young economists. And then they'll be drawn away from the history of economic thought or similar such fields. On the other hand, if it's a dry period, so far as really adding to the structure of economic thought is concerned, all of a sudden, everybody is interested in such things as the background of Stigler, of Keynes, or of Samuelson. (Conversation with Milton Friedman, August 1997).

The questionable assumption on Stigler's part is the forced parallel between a science like physics or chemistry and the study of economics. Not too much is claimed these days for the ideas relating to phlogiston. But it is harder to identify the progress of economic theory with the discarding of set systems or ideas. Without too much exaggeration it might be said that there is hardly any theory, no matter how seemingly half-baked that has not witnessed a comeback given enough time. It might be a new and improved model embodying more of the latest glitz in terms of technique, but at its heart not such a departure from the

[9] Notice he does not say that studying the actual weather of 1800 is out of date. Much can be learned by examining past weather patterns. In this we get a reaffirmation of the study of history as a complement to the study of economics.

original[10]. This leads to a different view of the role played by the history of economic thought.

> Now take an economics textbook. It's more or less the same. Exposition improves, techniques improve. There is a lot more illustrative material that didn't exist before. The empirical work doesn't seem to have changed its vision, or at least it hasn't in economics. It's very tricky, this whole business of how ideas emerge and subjects change, and so on. But it is striking; I think you could still learn something from Adam Smith. How many 18th-century chemists would be worth reading today? (Conversation with Ronald Coase, October 1997)

But perhaps to understand Stigler's point it may be useful to simply concede temporarily Stigler's point. It turns out not to be as drastic as it appears at first glance. The history of the subject may not have any direct use in feeding current research, but it is in the more indirect and subtle avenues that shape the thinking within economics that this area of research may find its ultimate value. Stigler then sets up his courtroom at this more distant site and proceeds to weigh the worth of the subject.

Stigler's curious defense of his first love has as its basis a variation on a previous rationale provided by Schumpeter. "Some historians of economics — Schumpeter is an eminent representative — believe that an understanding of the evolution of a science helps to understand its present structure." (Stigler, 1982e: 107). Stigler manages in a rather contradictory way to acknowledge the validity of this argument while simultaneously dismissing it as trivial. "This claim may be conceded

[10] In the immediate post-war period the profession as a whole accepted the posted death notices of Say's law only to witness it's revivification in the 1980s with New Classical economics. In economics, announcements of any internments are likely to be a gross exaggeration.

> *In his autobiography, George Stigler refers to monopolistic competition as dead and buried.*
> A bit premature.
> *Never pronounce a death sentence on anything.*
> No, that's right.
>
> (Conversation with Harold Demsetz, October 1997).

and restated as the plausible hypothesis that correct knowledge never has a negative marginal product." (Stigler, 1982e: 107). Schumpeter is unlikely to have intentionally stooped to utter such banalities. Stigler, throughout his career, could not always remove the implicit sneer from all of his comments. What emphasises the somewhat gratuitous nature of this initial remark is that Stigler then proceeds to use much the same argument in defending history of thought[11].

However, he chooses not to tackle this justification head on but rather by providing an umbrella structure. This reduces to the proposition of teaching Edwina Economist how to read. By providing three advantages that History of Thought yields in this instructional objective, evolution becomes just one rationalisation carrying no more weight than the other two. Before considering the most persuasive of his three arguments, looking at Stigler's other proposed alternatives at least provides a sense of completeness. His overall justification, if true, is unarguable. Most economists, as he points out, do not know how to read. "Most professors do not know how to read a scientific work well, and this skill is developed only with purposeful practice." (Stigler, 1982e: 108). Without offering any compelling formal or empirical evidence, the examples of economists doing this are nearly inexhaustible. Many economists seem to read papers with prior expectations as though already knowing what will be there. Or they read in a carping, mean spirited way, trying to find some error, no matter how strained, that they can point out[12].

---

[11] Strangely enough, Stigler ignores the remarks of his teacher, Frank Knight. This is not unrelated to the evolutionary position mentioned by Stigler and later co-opted by him. Basically, the hypothesis is that it helps economists avoid wasting time reinventing the wheel.

> Frank Knight's claim for studying the past, to avoid previous error, has much to say for it; though, like the exceedingly rare statement in economics, it seems better in theory than in practice. (Rosen, 1993: 810)

If we treat this as a testable hypothesis, it might be difficult to demonstrate this beneficial restraining nature in the works of those with a command of the history of their subject.

[12] See the paper by Freedman (1993) on this subject and compare it with what McCloskey (1985, 1992) has to say on this topic.

If a comprehensive study were to be done of referee reports, many, if not a majority, would fall into this category[13]. As Stigler himself so usefully points out[14]

> The second requirement in reading an economist with comprehension is a certain measure of detachment of even sympathy. Even the best of men is a strange mixture of truth and error, of insight and partial blindness, of careful and slovenly thought and writing. One may proceed over the man's work with an analytical microscope, examining each sentence, phrase, and word with scrupulous care — and yet never understand what he is trying to say. (Stigler, 1982e: 109)

There is then no argument to make against Stigler's description of the value of learning to read well or his criteria of comprehensiveness and consistency when interpreting a given work. However, it is not clear that reading the classic works of economics better serves the objective of learning to read, than does any other more recent set of articles. Here, George Stigler lets his own readers down a bit since his own defense tends to depend on a particular adversarial model of academic life which he, himself, consistently exemplified through out his career.

---

[13] For those interested in empirical work in this area, see Mackie (1998: 88–128) who discusses survey results.

[14] The irony here is that this sensible practice was honoured almost entirely in the breach by Stigler. It would be more accurate to say that he read the work of others like a lawyer pouring over a deposition given by an opposing witness. A reader is struck by the similarity of this bit of good sense by Stigler with what Keynes had to say. (Keynes came a bit closer to actually following his own dictum in this case.)

> This means, on the one hand, that an economic writer requires from his reader much goodwill and intelligence and a large measure of cooperation; and, on the other hand, that there are a thousand futile, yet verbally legitimate, objections which an objector can raise. In economics you cannot *convict* your opponent of error; you can only *convince* him of it. And, even if you are right, you cannot convince him, if there is a defect in your own powers of persuasion and exposition or if his head is already so filled with contrary notions that he cannot catch the clues to your thought which you are trying to throw to him. (Keynes, 1973: 740)

This could best be exemplified as a clear focus on the marketing aspect of research[15].

> Scientific literature is to a considerable degree controversial literature. New ideas are sold very much the way new automobiles are sold: by exaggerating their superiority over the older models. There is a difference

[15] It is not difficult to construct an argument attributing part of the Chicago School's post-war success to its superior ability to market its idea. This does not imply that these economists succeeded in selling the profession shoddy goods. But the marketing aspect of the Chicago approach does at least put into play whether the ideas they professed were intrinsically better. What is undeniable is that academics like Stigler and Friedman were masters of the marketing side of the business as well as more than able economists. The end result of their foray into hard nose competitive selling of ideas is to cause others to imitate their style lest they be unable to compete.

> If you happen to have a product that is no good you might market it well but it's going to fail. So I do think marketing is very important when undertaking an intellectual activity. It's probably more important *now* than it was before. The market is much bigger for one thing. You have people making serious money out of marketing ideas and getting reputations from successfully doing that. But it's not only the money. It's the associated prestige and all kinds of other things as well. It seems to me that there's a lot more score keeping these days. Unlike in previous days, Economists are now reckoned to be in a pretty interesting discipline. So to succeed, you've got to be able to sell your ideas somehow. How you do that? I don't really know. Maybe you do attack other people. That's been done over the years, but it doesn't always work. It doesn't work if there's nothing behind your attack. (Conversation with Sherwin Rosen, October 1997)
>
> Part of it is the persuasion. There's no question. I mean George Stigler, I remember when I was a young person, wired and said 'Selling is very important in your research. So write better. Work on writing because that is important. You've got to sell what you are doing. I think he's exactly right. You've got to sell what you are doing. It may be that in the long run good ideas do surface but they surface faster, if written in a persuasive fashion. Moreover, bad ideas may be put persuasively. And they may gain the necessary threshold. However, taking that same analogy in competition among ideas, there is a presumption, although not a certainty, that in the longer run, the good ideas are going to compete out the bad ideas. But that may take a long time and may not even always operate. There's nothing necessary about that. Nothing guaranteed about that. (Conversation with Gary Becker, October 1997)

> in the method of salesmanship, however: a new theory may be more important eventually than even its inventor believes and claims, but the value of the older theories is invariably greater than he acknowledges. Scientific innovation proceeds more by disparagement of rivals than by excessive self-praise, perhaps because it appears more modest. (Stigler, 1982e: 111)

If you accept this courtroom vision of academic research, much of Stigler's remaining argument falls into line. Classic works then provide better training for young economists in learning how to read since the reader will not take such a partisan view to the work. In other words, the reader will more likely be willing to work through the author's meaning rather than focus on either ripping it to shreds or defending it[16].

But it is Stigler's approach to the evolutionary nature of knowledge that is most interesting. Again, this evolution is viewed from an adversarial framework where theories are tested in the fire of hostile reaction. As such, reading of past controversies leaves the careful student more humble, less willing to be so self-assured about positions taken in current controversies. However, for Stigler the second half of this lesson is far more important, namely ignore the first.

> The more subtle lesson is that it does not pay to learn the first lesson: the temperate, restrained, utterly fair-minded treatment of one's own theories does a disservice to these theories as well as to one's professional status and salary. The scientist is loath to buy new models which have not been well advertised. (Stigler, 1982e: 111)

Stigler's defense of his first love, though not lacking in useful arguments, is a case of imposing a deliberate handicap where none was needed. He would eventually acquiesce to the idea that a strong enough case could not be made for history of thought. The dangers associated with the study of the profession's intellectual history have

---

[16] A second reason for History of Thought as a training ground for critical reading supplied by Stigler is that readers will be less likely to waste valuable time on less than valuable articles.

lurking within it serious dangers that may override any potential benefits.

> Economics, I thus believe, has a useful past, a past that is useful in dealing with the future. Many useful commodities and services are not produced in a society because they are worth less than they cost: it remains the unfulfilled task of the historians of economics to show that their subject is worth its cost. (Stigler, 1982e: 118)

This is really a contingent question. Unless we accept the adversarial framework, which according to Stigler is forging economic truth, our calculations are unlikely to be the same as his. George Stigler's own arithmetic became clear a few years later in 1972 when his best estimate was that the cost made required study not worthwhile. In this, George Stigler may have miscalculated his weightings. I would argue that banning this alleged dangerous source of ambiguity ultimately sapped and limited the vitality of future committed armies of economists. Narrowness of focus may have brought with it conviction and certainty but at the cost of intuition and breadth of knowledge.

3. Adam Smith's George Stigler Problem

> I have long been a good friend of Smith, though I have no right to claim priority in his circle. I do not believe that my friendship will distort the judgments I shall propose. (Stigler, 1982a: 146–147)

The title of one of George Stigler's collected works is hardly an accident. The common thread of *The Economist as Preacher*, is that all the essays contained in the volume are attempts by Stigler to preach to the brethren of the economics profession. "Almost all the essays in this volume are concerned with questions of intellectual influence." (Stigler, 1993b). The relevant question here is whether Stigler's urge to preach in some cases influenced his own analysis. More specifically, did his intense study of the intellectual history of his beloved profession make him more aware of the ambiguities of argument or did his implicit desire to preach to the congregation affect to some extent his analysis of the acknowledged masters of the trade?[17] A quick feel for these issues can be gathered by examining an aspect of his study of Adam Smith. What the German scholars have compulsively labelled *Das Adam Smith Problem* lays bare many of the competing issues involved.

> Well, you know my argument is the opposite? No, he [Stigler] was sort of critical of Adam Smith in a way that I didn't think was justified. (Conversation with Ronald Coase, October 1997)

He did follow his own dictum to read Adam Smith the same way that he read all economic literature. "At no point in this discussion of how to read scientific works has the word "past" been used: the correct way to read Adam Smith is the correct way to read the forthcoming issues of a professional journal." (Stigler, 1982e: 110) Unfortunately,

---

[17] George Stigler's one area of disagreement with Milton Friedman was over the role of an economist in policy formation. This was not an area where Stigler felt that economists had any influence.

> And he, on more than one occasion asked me the question — he never gave the answer himself and I never knew how to answer the question myself — 'Did I think that Milton Friedman would be remembered most for his polemics on policy or his scientific work on things like the consumption function?' He never gave the answer himself and I didn't know what the answer to that question was. I still don't know what the answer to that question is, but he obviously thought about this issue. This was an issue in his view and I would have to infer from his own behaviour that he was of the opinion regarding his good friend and respected colleague, that Milton's scientific work would be the hallmark by which he was most remembered. But that remains to be seen. (Conversation with Harold Demsetz, October 1997)

Yet his untiring attempts to preach to the economics profession seem to have been unbounded.

> He wrote all of those books. They're not exactly academic pieces but terrifically interesting. I loved those pieces. There is really no room for that type of writing any more. Maybe some people just do it as a hobby [laughs]. I just don't know. By the time I really knew him he wasn't doing much of that. (Conversation with Sherwin Rosen, October 1997)

this meant that he found within works like *The Wealth of Nations* exactly what he was expecting to find[18].

Stigler essentially reduced Smith's economics to fit a pattern contiguous with his own beliefs.

> Smith had one overwhelming important triumph: he put into the center of economics the systematic analysis of the behavior of individuals pursuing their self-interest under conditions of competition. This theory was the crown jewel of *The Wealth of Nations*, and it became, and remains to this day, the foundation of the theory of the allocation of resources. (Stigler, 1982a: 147)

Few who have read Smith with the slightest care would deny the importance of self-interest to his economic framework. But Stigler's need to adopt an adversarial framework in all of his analysis, to market his views as strongly as possible led him to dismiss the economic significance of Smith's *Theory of Moral Sentiments.*

> In fact Smith's professional work on psychology (in the *Theory of Moral Sentiments*) bears scarcely any relationship to his economics, and this tradition of independence of economics from psychology has persisted despite continued efforts from Jennings (1855) to Herbert Simon and George Katona to destroy it. (Stigler, 1965b: 28)

---

[18] Like others, Stigler admires those elements of Smith that agree with his own ideas. This allows economists with diametrically opposed views to call on the wisdom contained in the *Wealth of Nations* to advance their own ideas.

> Is it possible that Homer meant to say all they make him say, and that he lent himself to so many and such different interpretations that the theologians, legislators, captains, philosophers, every sort of people who treat of sciences, however differently and contradictorily, lean on him and refer to him: the general master for all offices, works, and artisans, the general counselor for all enterprises? Whoever has needed oracles and predictions has found in him enough for his purpose. It is a marvel what wonderful correspondences a learned man, and a friend of mine, draws out of him in support of our religion; and he cannot easily let go of this opinion, that this was Homer's purpose (yet he is as well acquainted with this poet as any man of our century). And what he finds in favor of ours, many of old had found in favor of theirs. (Montaigne, 1963, 442–443)

This assertion seems based more on Stigler's requirements than an unbiased and careful reading of the work involved[19]. As Coase points out:

> It is wrong to believe, as is commonly done, that Adam Smith had as his view of man an abstraction, an "economic man," rationally pursuing his

[19] This insistence on a purely self-interest rational decision-maker ultimately put Stigler at odds with some of his closest theoretical allies. Ultimately, his most influential teacher was Viner, but as Viner makes clear:

> The important thing for the interpreter of Smith is to note how low down ... reason enters into the picture as a factor influencing social behaviour. The sentiments [that is, the instincts] are innate in man ... Under normal circumstances, the sentiments make no mistake. It is reason which if fallible. (Coase, 1994: 16)

Even such a dependable intellectual ally like Harold Demsetz is unable to accept Stigler approach in this area unswervingly:

> I don't know any more about why George would have believed in those suppositions, why he would have been such a strong believer. I do have my own beliefs on this which are available in a presidential address called 'The Primacy of Economics' an explanation of its imperial success in the social sciences. It appeared in *Economic Enquiry* a couple of years ago. Well, when I gave this paper, this presidential address, one of the questions I was asked was about this Adam Smith characterization. Whether he had two different people in his world, one who populated the *Theory of Moral Sentiments* and the other who populated *The Wealth of Nations.* I said 'no'. He had one person for two different contexts in which decision making was taking place. I think that is the case. I think that is perfectly consistent between these two volumes. (Conversation with Harold Demsetz, September 1994)

Deirdre McCloskey, though hardly an admirer of George Stigler, quotes Smith himself which can serve as a refutation Stigler's narrow insistence.

> Here's what Smith would say about the numbero uno, country-club Republicanism that elevates selfishness to a philosophical axiom: "Though, perhaps, it never gave occasion to more vice than what would have been without it, [it] at least taught that vice, which arose from other causes, to appear with more effrontery, and to avow the corruption of its motives with a profligate audaciousness which had never been heard of before" [Adam Smith, *The Theory of Moral Sentiments*, 1759, VII.ii.4.13] (McCloskey 1996b: 98).

> self-interest in a single-minded way. Smith would not have thought it sensible to treat man as a rational utility-maximiser. He thinks of man as he actually is: dominated, it is true, by self-love but not without some concern for others, able to reason but not necessarily in such a way as to reach the right conclusion, seeing the outcomes of his actions but through a veil of self-delusion ... if one is willing to accept Adam Smith's view of man as containing, if not the whole truth, at least a large part of it, realization that his thought has a much broader foundation than is commonly assumed makes his argument for economic freedom more powerful and his conclusions more persuasive. (Coase, 1994: 116)

Stigler's rejection of the sort of ambiguity that the study of history of thought promotes meant that political agents, like economic ones, had to be motivated solely by self-interest. This is where Stigler's marketing imperative in the world of ideas runs off the rails. When engaged in History of Economic Thought, considered analysis rather than boldness yields greater returns. Stigler saw the modesty that the subject could induce as dangerous, but perhaps a more accurate representation would acknowledge that ambiguity can be successful in restraining the bombast that adversarial approaches often bring.

Thus, Stigler evaluates Smith on the legislative market and finds him wanting[20]. After the exacting elimination work of 1971 in *A Theory of*

---

[20] Stigler takes Smith to task for failing to apply self-interested behaviour in a rigorous fashion to the political marketplace. In a subtle way Smith is being found wanting for not being more like George Stigler.

> It may appear that Smith's failure to apply the organon of self-interest to political behaviour requires no explanation. Political science had been a normative literature for 2300 years before Smith wrote and had continued to remain normative to the present day ... Yet it is uncomfortable to explain Smith's failure by the failure of everyone else, for he is a better man than everyone else. His ability to examine the most pompous and ceremonial of institutions and conduct with the jaundiced eye of a master economist — and the evident delight he took in such amusement — is one of the trademarks of his authorship. The "uniform, constant, and uninterrupted effort of every man to better his condition" (I, 364 [326]) — why was it interrupted when a man entered Parliament? (Stigler, 1982d: 143–144)

Regulation, only rational actors remained, creating political market efficiency. Stigler's own work of 1971 meant that Smith had to be taken to task for not reducing political activity to simply another type of self-interested action. Even reducing supplementary explanations to mere extenuating circumstances was not good enough for Stigler. Self-interest had to be the sole, not only the dominant, motivation of political legislation[21]. This is not what Adam Smith has to teach us.

> He often would take these very strong positions which he convinced himself were actually true. Like when he was confronted with some fact about regulation, he would say 'Ah, you're going to find some Congressman was bought off. [laughter] You are actually going to find that. That's what you're going to find. Are you sure that you didn't find that this Congressman ...?' You know, that kind of writing, that kind of a very strong view...
>
> I don't think it was clear in his mind what the distinction was, between stating a powerful position that covers a lot of the cases, and what happens in a particular event. When confronted with a particular application he literally almost believed it.
>
> He wouldn't back off and say 'Well, look, that's part of the remaining 10 or 20 percent, which is doing better than explaining just fifty percent — tossing coins — that's just part of the noise. Methodologically he understood that but in his gut I don't think he really understood that.
>
> Yet he would often criticise others. I know he would often criticise people for trying to explain every observation and not accepting the fact that

[21] The insistence that everything had to reduce to self-interest in the political market did not seem to be motivated by theoretical imperatives. To make sense of the hard edge way in which Stigler marketed his political framework we may need to resort to ideological considerations.

> We're talking about the political world, the political market as opposed to the economic one. But in interpreting the political market, George very consistently, interprets the political market as a resolution of opposing self-interests and tended to give very little attention to the extent to which it arose, out of the desire of the people involved in government, to promote the public interest. (Conversation with Milton Friedman, August 1997)

> there was a certain degree of error. But when in the middle of a lunch time conversation, if you confronted him with something like that, with some anomaly, he could have just said, 'Look, that's the error. Let's just go on and talk about the substance'. But he would in fact say, 'No. You're going to find that some interest was in there on the political front. You'll find it if you look hard enough.' You wouldn't find it. (Conversation with Sam Peltzman, October 1997)

4. The Advantage of Having a History

> Only a brilliant mind can make a brilliant mistake. (George Stigler quoted in Friedland, (1993: 781))

Despite his worry about ambiguity induced by a careful study of the history of economic thought, along with the dangers of retaining an open mind, Stigler himself seems to prove that lifetime immunity to this particular siren's song is possible[22]. If the other side of an argument ever whispered to George Stigler while in quiet repose or thought, all available evidence would seem to demonstrate that a selective deafness continued to define all such dialogues.

However, without the discipline of a close reading of the acknowledged past masters of the trade, we can never have any great hope of ridding the professions of the myths and unchallenged oral tradition that riddles economic thinking. So much of what an economist thinks he or she knows is formed in the classroom or during informal conversations with teachers or classmates. All too often the simple questions are never asked. Teaching itself can be done in a mechanistic

---

[22] George Stigler seemed to maintain the Vince Lombardi doctrine that in economics, as in football, winning is everything. Having an open mind could only prove a handicap for the ambitious young academic.

> One attribute of able economists that I learned early is that they seldom admit or correct a mistake. Of course an able economist shouldn't (and perhaps is not allowed to) make many mistakes, at least the kind of mistakes that are easily correctible, but even the few correctible mistakes are seldom admitted. (Stigler, 1988: 208)

manner with the material taught dominated by demonstrations and techniques that lend themselves to easy lecturing and is similarly easy to test, whether or not what is taught is at all credible[23]. One hope that History of Thought holds out is as a lever to shatter some of those long-standing myths or at the very least bring them to trial. In which case open mindedness can lead to more critical thinking, not in the sense of conducting search and destroy missions against competing theories, but maintaining a proper scepticism to each and every framework. It stops us from prejudging others' work as well as our own results.

> It seems to me that when you get to his [Stigler's] later work, say with Becker, you know what the conclusion is going to be before you start the argument. (Conversation with Ronald Coase, October 1997)

These days it is quite possible to have what many would characterize as a productive career as an economist, while lacking the most

---

[23] Certainly, many in the trade simply repeat commonplaces without reflecting too long on whether their statements would bear even the most superficial of examinations. Attribution is as dubious here as the use of Latin tags among modern day lawyers.

> One historian of economics, D.H. MacGregor, said that Say's Law (a proposition, not really due to J.B. Say, only partially summarized by saying that there cannot be overproduction of all commodities at one time) should be called Hearsay's Law. Jacob Viner ... once told me that the average modern reference to the classical economists is so vulgarly ignorant as not to deserve notice, let alone refutation. (Stigler, 1988: 214)

Equally, textbooks serve to formalise some of the worst aspects of the oral tradition. Stigler looks at the persistence to the 'kinked demand curve' as representative of this retrograde tendency.

> A second hypothesis is that the textbooks of a discipline play a powerfully conservative role in the transmission of doctrine ... The writing of textbooks is apparently not a thought-intensive activity: the modal number of changes of any sort between editions of a textbook in its discussion of the kinked demand curve is zero. (Stigler, 1982b: 238)

basic knowledge of what defined the economics profession in even the near past.

> ... it is possible to obtain a PhD in economics without ever hearing of Friedman's irrelevance of assumptions thesis, the marginalist controversy, the aggregation of demand problem, the Cambridge capital controversies, doubts concerning the relevance of constant returns to scale, or U-shaped average cost curves, or questions regarding the relevance of IS-LM analysis. (Schiffman, 2004: 1091)

Economists reared on a diet of watery gruel may never be able to transcend conventional thinking, the mere run of the mill. The generation of economists that defined the immediate post-war period, Friedman, Stigler, Samuelson, Arrow and others, all shared a level of economic intuition that appears to have dissipated in each succeeding generation. "He had an intuition that was always very good. And I think it particularly helped when he was dealing with the history of economic thought." (Conversation with Ronald Coase, October 1997)

This is admittedly only an impressionistic response to this question, but a proposition that cannot be easily dismissed without some serious investigation. As knowledge of this intellectual history has faded in turn with each succeeding post-war generation it may not be mere coincidence that we have witnessed the simultaneous blunting of intuition. We may be well on our way to producing superior technicians but measurably impoverished thinkers among our latest crop of academics.

We are running out of giants and must needs make do instead with the shoulders of ambitious dwarves. Those who do not thoroughly understand from whence we came will have trouble finding their way forward.

References

Coase, R (1994). Adam Smith's view of man. In *Essays on Economics and Economists*, pp. 95–116. Chicago: University of Chicago Press.

Freedman, C (1993). Why economists can't read. *Methodus [Journal of Economic Methodology]*, 5(1), 6–23.

Friedland, C (1993b). On Stigler and Stiglerisms. *Journal of Political Economy*, 101(5), 780–783.

Hodgson, GM (2001). *How Economics Forgot History: The Problem of Historical Specificity in Social Science*. New York: Routledge.

Keynes, JM (1973). *The Collected Works of John Maynard Keynes Vol. X11I*. London: MacMillan.

Knight, FH (1956). Economics. In *On the History and Method of Economics*, pp. 3–33. Chicago: University of Chicago Press.

Mackie, CD (1998). *Canonizing Economic Theory*. Armonk, New York: M.E. Sharpe.

Marshall, A (1982). *Principles of Economics*. Philadelphia: Porcupine Press.

McCloskey, D (1976). Does the past have useful economics? *Journal of Economic Literature*, 14(2), 434–461.

McCloskey, D (1985). Economical writing. *Economic Inquiry*, 24(2), 187–222.

McCloskey, D (1992). Writing as a responsibility of science: A reply to Laband. *Economic Inquiry*, 30(4), 689–695.

McCloskey, DN (1996a). Economic tourism. *Eastern Economic Journal*, 22(3), 365–368.

McCloskey, DN (1996b). Economic tourism. *Eastern Economic Journal*, 22(1), 97–100.

McGrattan, ER and EC Prescott (2004). The 1929 Stock Market: Irving Fisher was right. *International Economic Review*, 45(4), 991–1009.

Montaigne, M de (1963). An apology for Raymond Sebond. In *The Complete Essays of Montaigne*, pp. 318–457. D Frame (trans.). Stanford: Stanford University Press.

Rosen, S (1993). George J. Stigler and the industrial organization of economic thought. *Journal of Political Economy*, 101(5), 809–817.

Schiffman, DA (2004). Mainstream economics, heterodoxy and academic exclusion: a review essay. *European Journal of Political Economy*, 20, 1079–1095.

Stigler, GJ (1965a). Preface. In *Essays in the History of Economics*, P. V. Chicago: University of Chicago Press.

Stigler, GJ (1965b). The influence of events and policies on economic theory? In *Essays in the History of Economics*, pp. 16–30. Chicago: University of Chicago Press.

Stigler, GJ (1971). The theory of economic regulation. *Bell Journal of Economics and Management Science*, 2(1), 3–21.

Stigler, GJ (1982a). The successes and failures of professor Smith. In *The Economist as Preacher*, pp. 146–159. Chicago: University of Chicago Press.

Stigler, GJ (1982b). The literature of economics. In *The Economist as Preacher*, pp. 223–240. Chicago: University of Chicago Press.

Stigler, GJ (1982c). Preface. In *The Economist as Preacher*, p. vii. Chicago: University of Chicago Press.
Stigler, GJ (1982d). Smith's travels on the ship of state. In *The Economist as Preacher*, pp. 136–145. Chicago: University of Chicago Press.
Stigler, GJ (1982e). Does economics have a useful past? In *The Economist as Preacher*, pp. 107–118. Chicago: University of Chicago Press.
Stigler, GJ (1988). *Memoirs of an Unregulated Economist.* New York: Basic Books.

Chapter 7

Do Great Economists Make Great Teachers? — George Stigler as a Dissertation Supervisor*

President Reagan fared much better than the student who came to George complaining that he didn't deserve the "F" he'd received in George's course. George agreed but explained that "F" was the lowest grade the administration allowed him to give. (Friedland, 1993: 782)

In the eleven years that George Stigler laboured at Columbia University he had exactly one dissertation student[1]. That number did not radically increase during his subsequent first eleven years at

* In recognition of my mother's attempts to transform me into a well-mannered child, I wish to thank the following people for helping to make this article possible. William E. Becker (Indiana University) who suggested the topic to me a number of years ago. Gary Becker (University of Chicago), Mark Blaug (University of Rotterdam), Arnold Harberger (UCLA), Paul Samuelson (MIT) and Sam Peltzman (University of Chicago) for their kindness in taking time out from their own busy schedules and talking to me about George Stigler. All of those mentioned can be expected to eschew any and all responsibility for what I have produced subsequently.

[1] Mark Blaug was the only graduate student with enough confidence to take on Stigler as his supervisor. They remained good friends and Stigler was consistently supportive of Blaug despite obvious political as well as methodological differences.

Chicago, though it did in fact at least double[2]. Stigler was an economist of great ability, skill and influence, arguably one of the best economic minds of his age. (This is a rather remarkable statement given compeers like Friedman and Samuelson.) Though he clearly thought teaching to be a lesser activity, an adjunct to research, George Stigler took his teaching very seriously (as he did all activities associated with his professional life). His influence on his colleagues in particular and the profession in general is unmistakable. Friends and foes alike (there were few, if any, who knowing George Stigler did not fall into one or the other category) conceded his ability to persuade whether in written or verbal form. The puzzle then is why such a formidable figure who contributed so much to economics, was not sought out more as a dissertation advisor by the many graduate students passing through the economics department in Chicago? The answer reveals not only something about George Stigler himself (which might then remain on the purely idiosyncratic level), but also about graduate education in economics and more specifically about student supervision.

1. Good Teacher/Good Researcher

One way to simply dismiss this question is to conclude that the parallel between communicating to one's peers and to one's students is simply spurious. In a field where the division of labour (returns to specialisation) is the benchmark, there is simply no reason why the skills that make a good teacher (or supervisor) should be closely associated with those which set apart the research of an economist. It is true that communication and persuasion are needed in both cases, but again, the audience or market is different[3].

---

[2] Sam Peltzman completed a dissertation in the field of industrial organisation, while Tom Sowell's work involved History of Thought. However, the Sowell/Stigler effort was more the result of a shotgun wedding than a willing partnership. George Stigler's opinion of Sowell's abilities remained critical throughout the remaining years. Other students included John Hause and James Feguson. Students like David Levy fall outside this initial 11 year limit.

[3] Whether economists are good communicators in any sense of the term is entirely another issue. But it is not an issue particularly germane to the problem at hand.

Stigler himself did not accept this view. He could not imagine a good teacher of economics not being at the same time a competent and published researcher. Stigler distinctly believed that only good researchers were qualified to develop and sustain rigorous standards within the economics profession. On a surface level at least, this would seem to contradict his insistence on specialisation, his stern condemnation of the generalist (see Stigler, 1963a: 10). Why should not individuals specialise in teaching while others focus on research? Stigler could not accept this premise since he saw successful teaching as a joint product arising out of research and as such inseparable[4].

> He [the teacher] is to acquire knowledge and construct ideas — and keep them a secret. It is improbable scientifically: it asks a man to be competent in his understanding of work that he has had no part in constructing. (Stigler, 1963a: 14)

This, of course, does not argue for a symmetric flow of causality. All good teachers must under Stigler's dictum be good researchers. It does not necessarily follow that good researchers turn into good teachers. Nor, though Stigler states his argument with great assurance[5], it is far from clear that his premise is relevant for undergraduate education (an area remote from Stigler's concerns for most of his career (see Stigler, 1963b: 80)). Graduate and undergraduate education, as they are both currently constituted, seem to have quite

---

[4] Certainly, Stigler's insistence (1963a) that not only active research, but published research, is a necessary requirement for good teaching seems excessive. Aaron Director has published precious little but has had a large influence at Chicago, especially on George Stigler himself. On the other side of the Atlantic, Arnold Plant was similarly reluctant to publish yet influenced students at LSE including Ronald Coase, Arthur Lewis, Basil Yamey, Ronald Fowler and Arthur Seldon among others. What might be said is that today, a research economist who seldom published would be unable to retain a position at a major research institute. This would be the main constraint limiting his or her effectiveness as a teacher.

[5] This was all part of Stigler's strong belief in a need to market one's theories by presenting them in the strongest and most positive way possible, whether or not entirely justified by the empirical evidence available.

distinct objectives[6]. Graduate training prepares them [the students] only to do abstract research within a framework that only a few fellow graduates can understand. (Colander and Brenner, 1992: 6–7). To the extent that Stigler is accurate in terms of effective teaching, his logic is much more applicable to graduate teaching and especially to supervision.

Nor are there any signals, especially from research institutions, that teaching (particularly undergraduate teaching) is taken at all seriously. Until very recently, graduate students were left unexposed to teaching techniques[7]. Given time as a scarce resource, investing in teaching, to augment future income flows, would not bear up under any serious scrutiny[8]. No one ever taught Stigler (or most economists) how to teach. Instead, the training of an academic economist

---

[6] Colander (1991 (see especially pp. 75–80), 2001) argues convincingly that undergraduate and graduate teaching inhabit two quite separable worlds. The skills needed for success in one region are distinct from that required in the other. The argument is sensibly based on the difference in the relevant markets.

> It is only when they are faced with the reality of teaching students who are completely indifferent to what the teachers are doing that they acquire, through on-the-job training, a knowledge of economic institutions sufficient to get by in the classroom. But it's no thanks to their graduate training. Graduate economics students receive little useful training for teaching undergraduates. (Colander, 1991: 77)

[7] The process is very much a 'learning by doing' procedure. Sceptics will wonder whether under such circumstances any noticeable learning curve can be detected.

> Even for individual graduate departments running their own programs as offshoots, the attitude appears to be that there are only 'some incidental benefits for the graduate instructors' current (undergraduate) students. (Becker, 1997: 1362)

[8] This has been a consistent finding of all and any attempts to engage in either anecdotal or empirical analysis of the profession (see Colander and Klamer (1987) on this point.)

> Teachers discover, at least at the elite institutions, that the rewards and respect are reserved for the researchers. Teaching is not a topic of conversation among the movers and shakers of the profession. (Klamer, 1992: 55)

(especially in the major US departments) bears the closest resemblance to the sort of personal and professional relations characterising medieval guilds. Education is part of a socialisation process. You learn to do by imitating those professors that have gained the most success in the discipline and/or those you most admire. When time comes to pick up the chalk and begin, you revert to the memories (and class notes) of your own instructional experience[9]. This perpetuates a tradition of 'chalk and talk' that still continues as a substitute for what educational theorists might think of as effective teaching. The simplest option has always been to replicate the past whenever possible[10].

Such arguments, however, fail to get to the heart of graduate teaching, especially an economist's role as mentor and supervisor. The question of whether good economists can be bad teachers is not one that can be resolved by simple empirical evidence involving numbers of PhD students, class enrolments or course evaluations. Measurement confusion reflects a supposition that each relevant market under examination is to a large degree homogeneous. But the slightest reflection will reveal the demand for and supply of dissertation supervisors to be clearly heterogeneous. In an obvious way, the interests of the graduate students themselves will vary. Some may select a specific economic department in the hopes of working with a particular staff member. Others may be less sure of their aims. But these are not the

---

[9] If we were dealing with the field of research, charges of plagiarism might arise. Perhaps as an indication of the low esteem in which it is held, such practices in the field of teaching are seen as simply carrying on a particular (and honoured) tradition. Uncritical homage, of this type, also propagates and sustains myths in the profession as well.

> Larry Neal's Presidential Address to the Economic History Association is entitled, "A Shocking View of Economic History." Early on he pays "Tribute to the spirit of Alexander Gerschenkron because, sitting through repeated lectures by first Paul David, then at Berkeley by Albert Fishlow, and finally Henry Rosovsky, I heard Gershenkron's most memorable lectures at least three separate time!" (Saffran, 2001: 256)

[10] See Becker's (1997) article on this point.

differences I wish to emphasise. Though Stigler himself was loath to allow psychological constraints to enter into explanations, it is exactly those clearly psychological determinants that shed the most light on this issue[11].

2. Protestant Fathers/Renegade Students

As previously mentioned, supervision harks back more to the medieval guilds than to simple markets of exchange. It is as much an issue of human relationships as of intellectual problem solving. The ability to bring a dissertation topic to fruition has to be constrained by the largely implacable barrier of personality. For most students, Stigler did not appear to be a sympathetic figure. A man who even his own colleagues found to be formidable would have little appeal for most graduate students. To an extent, this was due to Stigler's idiosyncratic approach to people. More than is perhaps appropriate, he treated students and especially those he supervised as equals. This meant that his standards were as demanding of these apprentice wannabes as they were for the journeymen and masters of the discipline. For most professional economists, being on the receiving end of George Stigler's caustic wit was not unlike an immersion in an acid bath. Remarkably, the pH level of the bath remained largely unchanged for students, especially at the graduate level. His standards for analytical reasoning did not adjust

---

[11] George Stigler certainly had no room for individual psychology in his own research (see Stigler, 1963a: 12, one among many places). He steered strictly clear of the type of hubris so clearly displayed by Oedipus (at least as depicted by Sophocles). For him there was always a clear division between the public man and the private individual. Throughout his life Stigler made a concerted and successful attempt to keep them apart. (To such an extent that the private man remained hidden from view for most, if not all his colleagues.) He firmly believed that biographical details shed no light on intellectual ideas.

> I am a strong supporter of the view that a knowledge of the life of a scholar is more often a source of misunderstanding than of enlightenment about his work. (Stigler, 1997: 111)

for experience or ability. He refused to suffer fools gladly, no matter what their stature[12].

This did not make him a poor supervisor, unless the definition of a good performer is tied to generating the greatest utility for the greatest number of students. True, making Stigler the benchmark for all graduate education would greatly decrease the numbers of newly minted PhDs (though it might raise the quality). But no one is suggesting Stigler as representing any sort of aspirational benchmark in supervision. Instead, the very heterogeneity of the market could make him just the person to supervise a distinct minority of aspirants (and by no means those with the most negligible potential).

> In my view, the good teacher is not distinguished by the breadth of his knowledge, by the lucidity of his exposition, or by the immediate reactions of his student. His fundamental task is not to dispense information, for in this role he is incomparably inferior to the written word. His task is to fan the spark of genuine intellectual curiosity and to instill the conscience of a scholar — to communicate the enormous adventure and the knightly conduct in the quest for knowledge. (I realize that this view of the teacher's function will strike many as austere. They will emphasize the need for sympathetic development of the utmost in each individual, and turn teaching into coaching. I think they do a disservice to mediocre as well as to good minds.) (Stigler, 1963a: 14)

Stigler in this quote is quite clearly describing his own, much admired teacher, Frank Knight[13]. Despite subsequent differences with Knight

---

[12] It is impossible to speak to anyone who knew him, however slightly, without having them relate the scars Stigler could inflict by using his all too ready wit. One economist I spoke to in Chicago (October 1997) recalled that meeting Stigler was the only time he had been gratuitously insulted in his life. Or as Gary Becker put it, 'Given the choice of making a smart remark or not hurting someone's feeling, Stigler would always choose to make a smart remark'. (Conversation with Becker, October 1997)

[13] Too much reverence for a supervisor can prove equally dangerous for a graduate student. In Paul Samuelson's opinion, the very awe in which some students at Chicago held Knight, undercut their own efforts.

> In fact, Knight's major influence at that time resulted in the view that Knight had done everything and there was nothing left to do. So, he was the cause that a pretty important generation of Chicago economists never got their PhD degrees. (Conversation with Paul Samuelson, October 1997)

on economic matters, he clearly remained Stigler's idol through out all his life. As Blaug puts it, he remained in awe of the man (in much the same way that despite his differences, Blaug remained nervous and in awe of Stigler). It seems clear that to a certain degree, Stigler did model himself in the classroom after Frank Knight, adding, however, an unfortunate element that bespoke more of Jacob Viner than of anyone else. Stigler himself relates the way in which during one of his own graduate courses, Viner mentally flattened a fellow student (see Stigler, 1988: 20).

> Today's fashionable notions of teacher–student relations present a warmer, almost cuddly, picture. This was not Stigler's vision.
>
> "When I was a student," he said, "I never threw my arms around Jacob Viner. He would have killed me if I tried!"
>
> I know of no student who wanted to throw his arms around George Stigler but I am sure the consequences would have been equally dire. (Sowell, 1993: 792)[14]

Most students would have found the cost of working with Stigler to be prohibitive. In a sense, like Frank Knight, he expected his students to write something meaningful. For the average PhD student, the dissertation period is sufficiently traumatic under the best of circumstances. The temptation to substitute a more congenial, and ready at

[14] This points out a clear contradiction in George Stigler as an individual. His public face (what Sam Peltzman refers to (Conversation with him, October 1997) as projecting an image of the 'Protestant Father' figure) contrasted with a privately generous individual. He for some reason felt driven to remain publicly consistent with his own economic model (if that is not a too far-fetched interpretation to suggest).

> When George was skeptical as I said about the altruism issue I said, 'Look George, look how generous you are to your children. Are you doing that out of self-interested motives? Who are you kidding? You're not doing it out of that.' And he looked at me and he didn't answer. He knew he was not doing that out of self-interested motives. (Conversation with Gary Becker, October 1997)

hand, alternative[15] can dominate even the most noble of intentions. It is the successful completion of a dissertation that garners rewards rather than an ambitious project that fails to reach full fruition.

> He was non-directive in an era where you had very powerful people like Milton Friedman and Al Harberger who were the opposite. In the case of Friedman, this was the era of the money demand function. And if you were a graduate student in money, you did a demand for money study. Greg Lewis, in labour economics, very closely supervised, in painstaking detail, the research of his students. Al Harberger did the same thing at that time. It was investment and durables. George was not like that at all. (Conversation with Sam Peltzman, October 1997)

However, given the heterogeneous nature of graduate students already noted, this low cost alternative would not necessarily be a high yield strategy for each and every student[16].

> Had my Chicago exposure been limited to the likes of Jacob Viner and Milton Friedman, both of whom were also my teachers there, I doubt that I should have ever emerged from the familiarly large ranks of Ph.D's with no or few publications. Jacob Viner, the classically erudite scholar whose self-appointed task in life seemed to be that of destroying confidence in students, and Milton Friedman, whose dominating intellectual brilliance in argument and analysis relegated the student to the role of fourth-best imitation — these were not the persons who encouraged students to believe that they too might eventually have ideas worthy of merit. (Buchanan, 1997: 173–174)

---

[15] Miller's (1962) article on the Chicago school makes this point indirectly. Most Chicago students did dissertations with those members of the faculty that closely supervised (lowered the cost of doing) a dissertation.

> In the year 1959–60 … Chicago students showed substantially less interest in the fields of industrial organization, public finance and fiscal policy, economic history and development and international economics, that their counterparts at Harvard or Columbia, separately or together. Two-thirds of the thesis subjects fell in the three fields of land economics, labor economics, and monetary economics. (Miller, 1962: 68–69)

[16] Frank Knight had only a handful of students, but three of them were Henry Simons, George Stigler and James Buchanan.

If you look at three of his well-known students Mark Blaug, Sam Peltzman and Thomas Sowell, their common denominator is a clear sense of self-direction and self-confidence. They were all capable of standing up to Stigler, of giving as good as they got[17]. This was no different than the way in which he treated other academic economists. To gain his respect, you had to prove yourself capable of returning his serve (to hark back to Stigler's tennis playing days)[18].

> He slaughtered his students. Right at the beginning of our conversations together, I realized (I don't know whether I grasped this consciously) that you always had to give back as good as he gave. (Conversation with Mark Blaug, June 1998)

He was then the right supervisor for a very unusual group of students. The vast majority wisely stayed away. Moreover, he looked after those few students he did shepherd. He was instrumental in both Blaug and Sowell receiving Fellowship and Scholarship funds to see them through their degrees[19].

---

[17] This would explain the 'odd couple' friendship with Robert Solow. Both men could be described as being extremely witty, intelligent and capable of expert verbal sparring.

[18] There is no evidence whatsoever that Stigler was ever deliberately malicious. He never intended to hurt someone intentionally. As his friends and colleagues point out, his criticism was never personal. But his words could have a devastating effect on established academics (reducing them to tears), let alone students. He never adjusted his rules of engagement to those of lesser ability. George Stigler displayed no real respect for individuals who were unwilling or incapable of playing according to his own hard nose methods. Here you do tread a very fine line, since by destroying opposing arguments in his inimitable scorched earth fashion; he left whoever was at the receiving end feeling stupid, inadequate and angry. Had Stigler's motives been focused at a more personal level, which they were not, the results still would have appeared to be much the same.

[19] He continued to be supportive of both Blaug and Peltzman throughout their subsequent careers. To some degree he regarded Peltzman as his protégée and pushed for his appointment at Chicago, even to the point of putting up research money from his own (Walgreen) account. It was a different story with Thomas Sowell who in many ways Stigler found wanting. Being a man who never minced his words, Stigler made his view of Sowell clear whenever he was asked for a recommendation. In his own reminiscence of George Stigler, Sowell (1993) hints at the underlying strife, but generally chooses to adopt a more discreet and politic 'de mortuis nil nisi bonum' approach.

3. Open Season on Ideas/Open Season on Students

As a graduate teacher, Stigler was not particularly effective in any conventional sense of the term. We could say of Stigler what he in fact said of Frank Knight. Knight was both a great and an absurd teacher. The absurdity was documented by his utterly disorganised teaching, with constant change of subject and yet insistent repetition of arguments. (Stigler, 1997: 97).[20] Knight appealed to the more exceptional students, a Don Patinkin (see Patinkin, 1973) or his brother-in-law Lester Telser, even though neither one ultimately worked under him. The average graduate student had quite a different experience[21]. Knight's great gift to students was the instillation of a sceptical, irreverent approach to established theories. 'The big job of economics is to divest people of prejudices — to have them see the questions as they are'. (Knight quoted in Patinkin (1973: 791))

Stigler did continue this aspect of Knight's tradition. 'One lesson I learned, or possibly overlearned, was that of scepticism toward received beliefs and authoritative reputations. ... I suspect that we heard the word "nonsense" too often. I certainly came away believing that the popular acceptance of an idea was little support for its validity'. (Stigler, 1988: 26–27). In subsequent years, Stigler's Chicago course in Industrial Organisation became an occasion to ridicule a particular, almost cherished set of his own Harvard Bete Noirs (as well as others).

> It was the perfect place for Stigler to conduct a Demolition Derby. Nor was he hesitant about the task. Theories like "monopolistic competition" and

---

[20] Note the parallel to Mark Blaug's comments concerning George Stigler:

> I don't think he was a particularly good lecturer. But the lectures were like a lot of his articles. Lots of sarcastic jokes, very arrogant, quite cynical. (Conversation with Mark Blaug, June 1998)

[21] Don Patinkin relates his initial failure at first attempting to take Knight's class.

> ... leaning on the back of a chair, occasionally puffing on a corn-cob pipe — and rambling on in a high-pitched voice and in a disjointed manner on mysterious issues that certainly cast no light on the newly revealed truth which was then being enthusiastically explicated everywhere ... after a few such bewildering experiences, I gave up in despair. (Patinkin, 1973: 788)

> "countervailing power," which were treated reverently at Harvard (where they originated), were eviscerated by Stigler. (Sowell, 1993: 787)

While such an approach will amuse the best students (and confuse the rest), it is not clear that an unrestricted diet of Demolition Derbies builds strong minds or healthy economists. Demolition Derbies have no rules of engagement. You bash into an opponent, choosing the perceived weakest spot of his vehicle. (I am not in a position to know whether female drivers have in more recent times taken up the sport.) The last car standing wins. Victory goes not necessarily to the sturdiest car but to the driver best skilled at manoeuvring. When extended to economic teaching and discussion, it is far from clear what most students gain by watching a clever teacher eviscerate an opponent. They are often not in a position to dispute such cleverness. It is even less obvious how productive such an approach would be at an undergraduate level.

Stigler certainly never attempted to reach out to his students. This deliberate distance might produce only a limited number of consequences at the graduate level, but would more likely generate serious and unfavourable outcomes when applied to large undergraduate lectures. Such students are bound to have much wider ranges of ability and interest in the subject. At this level, a key characteristic becomes an ability to approach economics afresh from the vantage point of an average student with no prior background in economics. This is no mean feat for a consummate economist for whom economics has become an intuitive way of thinking. For most students, economics is painfully non-intuitive. But, Stigler saw no reason to compromise. He unequivocally spoke in the shorthand of his profession, refusing to make links obvious. Like his teachers before him, Stigler expected his own students to battle their way to his level[22]. To use a more modern

---

[22] This extended to using parochial examples that would fail to register in the minds of foreign students.

> I used to be shepherding these Latinos through and here they would come to some question in his [Stigler's] price theory examination. 'Explain something, something about the *Dred Scott Decision*.' It drove me up the wall. How could he bear to ask a question like that when more than half the students were from abroad? (Conversation with Arnold Harberger, October 1997)

term, he was distinctly 'user unfriendly'. His own textbook is a clear example of this tendency. It is written not for the struggling student, but for someone who already understands (to some extent) price theory. It is written for the instructor rather than the student[23].

> This book (*The Theory of Price*) is probably the least readable thing Stigler ever wrote. It was not a matter of convoluted writing or confused thought ... but of excessive condensation that required painstakingly slow pondering over every concentrated thought. If the book had been three times as long, it could have been read in half the time. (Sowell, 1993: 785)

Can one conclude anything about teaching using George Stigler as a case study? Those who most benefited from George Stigler were to a large degree self-selected. This is why he provides a less than optimal model for undergraduate teaching. Good, even great economists do not necessarily make successful teachers at this level[24]. In contrast, graduate work and particularly locating an appropriate supervisor is more like a search for a congenial marriage partner. There is no precise formula to describe the necessary chemistry or the correct

---

[23] Stigler was certainly never long winded, whether in his publications, the classroom (or in destroying an opponent). But demanding that others fill in the links or follow up the implications of a brief sketch of an argument does not seem a widely effective approach to teaching.

> I had carefully prepared by outlining the first five or six weeks of the twelve-week quarter. About forty-five minutes into the class hour I found myself at the end of my notes! I was filled with consternation. I might last out the first session, but what about the rest of the quarter? I believe that this is not an unusual experience for new teachers, but I must admit that I have never reached the abundance of knowledge that made the time in the classroom seem inadequate. (Stigler, 1988: 19)

[24] John Hicks is one of a number of renowned economists who fit into this category.

> Whether the subjects on which he lectured did not really interest him or for some other reason, Hicks failed to inspire his undergraduate audience. However, Hicks's standing at LSE soon underwent a dramatic change. In 1931, at Robbins's instigation, in part because he had some mathematical training, Hicks began to give lectures on advanced economic theory and his power as a theorist was immediately apparent. (Coase, 1994: 210)

approach to adopt. There are too many exceptions to provide sufficiently hard and fast rules. What George Stigler demonstrates is that no matter what the number of graduate students an academic attracts, a clear passion for the subject coupled with the quality of his or her own research abilities will over time produce the best results.

References

Becker, WE (1997). Teaching economics to undergraduates. *The Journal of Economic Literature*, 35(3), 1347–1373.

Buchanan, JM (1997). James Buchanan. In *Lives of the Laureates*, W Breit and RW Spencer (eds.), pp. 95–112. Cambridge MA: MIT Press.

Coase, R (1994). Economics at LSE in the 1930s: A personal view. In *Essays on Economics and Economists*, pp. 208–214. Chicago: University of Chicago Press.

Colander, D (1991). *Why Aren't Economists as Important as Garbagemen?* Armonk, NY: M.E. Sharpe.

Colander, D (2001). *The Lost Art of Economics*. Cheltenham, UK: Edward Elgar.

Colander, D and A Klamer (1987). The making of an economist. *The Journal of Economic Perspectives*, 1(2), 95–111.

Friedland, C (1993). On Stigler and Stiglerisms. *Journal of Political Economy*, 101(5), 780–783.

Klamer, A (1992). Academic dogs. In *Educating Economists*, D Colander and R Brenner (eds.), pp. 49–61. Ann Arbor: University of Michigan Press.

Miller, HL Jr. (1962). On the Chicago School of Economics. *Journal of Political Economy*, 70(1), 64–69.

Patinkin, D (1973). Frank Knight as teacher. *American Economic Review*, 63(5), 786–810.

Saffran, B (2001). Recommendations for further reading. *The Journal of Economic Perpectives*, 15(2), 255–262.

Sowell, T (1993). A student's eye view of George Stigler. *Journal of Political Economy*, 101(5), 784–792.

Stigler, GJ (1963a). Specialism: A dissenting opinion. In *The Intellectual and the Market Place and Other Essays*. G Stigler (ed.), pp. 9–17. London: Collier-Macmillan.

Stigler, GJ (1963b). Elementary economic education. In *The Intellectual and the Market Place and Other Essays*, G Stigler (ed.), pp. 73–85. London: Collier-Macmillan.

Stigler, GJ (1988). *Memoirs of an Unregulated Economist*. New York: Basic Books.

Stigler, GJ (1997). George Stigler. In *Lives of the Laureates*, W Breit and RW Spencer (eds.), pp. 95–112. Cambridge MA: MIT Press.

B. Milton Friedman

I sometimes think some of the Chicago people are hopeless. Well, I wouldn't include Milton as among the hopeless because he was smart enough to punch his way out of a paper bag sometimes. But in the end he didn't want to do so. (Conversation with Paul Samuelson, October 1997)

Chapter 8

De Mortuis Nil Nisi Bonum — Milton Friedman 1912–2006

Craig Freedman

*Macquarie University**

> People in our profession have always been kind of scared of Milton Friedman as a polemicist. So, he gets away with a certain amount of murder. And when he's safely dead and when they've salted his grave against any revival, the daggers will come out. I'm flogging the point. That doesn't change his overall status. (Conversation with Paul Samuelson, November 1997)

Death acts as a perennial handsome prince to reputations no matter how questionable they might have been while the person was still among the living. A simple kiss bestowed by that dark angel while gathering in his own, miraculously washes away all the stains and grime that accumulates during a lifetime. Obituaries gush with a list of accomplishments and sparkling moral qualities. The transformations can be stunning to behold. We could all choose our favourite figures of disparate ideologies, dubious deeds and diverse professions

---

* My appreciation to all those interviewed in 1997 during research conducted on my George Stigler project. They showed me unrestrained and undeserved patience. Any disappointment they may feel at the result is not entirely unexpected.

who have undergone a similar sandblasting until they are barely recognisable. An almost unprecedented flow of warm, effusive praise greeted the death of Milton Friedman:

> Nonetheless, like many others I feel that I have lost a hero — a man whose success demonstrates that great ideas convincingly advanced can change the lives of people around the world. (Summers, 2006: 2)
>
> "Among economic scholars, Milton Friedman had no peer," Ben S. Bernanke, the Federal Reserve chairman, said yesterday. "The direct and indirect influences of his thinking on contemporary monetary economics would be difficult to overstate. (Noble, 2006: 1)

I am strongly tempted, of course, to stroll down this predictably comforting path and do the same. 'Of the dead, do not speak ill' commands the old Roman saying. Or, as those of us who were forced to bump along amidst the ubiquitous baby boom generation in the United States were admonished by our mothers, 'If you can't say something nice about someone, then it's better to say nothing at all.' But, where's the fun in that? Warts and all pictures are always more interesting than ersatz plastic saints. Asked to write such an obituary for a journal dedicated to the History of Economic Thought, the most rewarding, and only revealing approach would be to deal with the life and times of Milton Friedman as we would deal with any other major figure in the field now long dead. The aim should never be to do a hatchet job on the man and provide some welcome schadenfreude for inveterate Friedman haters[1] but to provide a balanced view of his accomplishments.

---

[1] This group is not composed solely of his ideological opponents. He had a habit, or perhaps a perfect genius, for constantly shifting his terms of debate. When his gladiatorial counterpart thought he had been safely hemmed into a particular corner of the ring, Friedman would suddenly pop up unexpectedly having changed the rules of engagement. However, accusing him of deliberate obfuscation and distortion is quite another matter. A true believer, he saw the world and all of its available data through a set of inflexible, critical glasses.

> When I used to debate him he would rebut almost everything I said on which we might disagree with statistics that he quoted. One day I realized that he was faking his information and his statistics were as phony as a 3 dollar bill!

Personally, I only met the man once when I interviewed him regarding his close friend George Stigler in August 1997. He was accompanied by his long-time wife Rose and his brother-in-law, Aaron Director[2]. I was alerted before the meeting that husband and wife were quite short. And true to that warning, husband and wife were both quite diminutive[3]. But he had one of the largest personalities I had ever run across. His ebullience and personality filled the room. What was most noticeable was his restless intellectual curiosity where

---

> I whipped him from then on by bringing source books on the statistical evolution of the American economy to each and every debate! He didn't know the most fundamental facts about the evolution of the U.S.A.!
>
> He was a theorist who made up his theories as he went along and to suit his prejudices. His book on money propounded the theory that (I am simplifying) all you needed to do to control inflation was to control the growth of money supply. For about a decade that theory was propounded by almost every economist in the United States. But there were economists who knew it to be simplified nonsense and tried to rebut it but to no avail. The business media loved Friedman to death since it was so simple to control the economy; control the money supply and you have it made. (Rinfert, 2000: 1)

[2] Aaron Director is perhaps the eminence grise of the Chicago School. Little has been written about his achievements or influence. Yet in the post-war counter-revolution against the planners and collectivists, his hand can often be recognised in many of the key events of the time, however faintly. He is the figure always lurking in the background of any photo. From his role in assuring the publication of von Hayek's *Road to Serfdom* to his successful efforts in establishing a Chicago School of Law and Economics, Director always served as something of an intellectual consigliore to those forming the more public face of the movement. He was the conservative lodestone keeping his brother-in-law on task and one of the few voices that greatly influenced George Stigler.

> But, Aaron Director was extremely conservative. Why, I don't know. By the time I knew him he was already like that. And he was an iconoclast. But he didn't develop new data with respect to industrial organisation. He didn't develop and articulate new theories. He just said that the conventional belief wasn't so. (Conversation with Paul Samuelson, November 1997)

[3] There is a wonderful photo reproduced in Stigler's (1988) autobiography displaying a rear view shot of the two dynamos of the Chicago School (Stigler and Friedman) walking down a path. The association shifts quickly to drawings by Daumier of Don Quixote and Sancho Panza.

any statement automatically had to be questioned, analysed and debated. Unlike his fallen compatriot, George Stigler, he gave off an air of benevolence. Those who had been trounced in a debate might think otherwise, but I ended up quite charmed by the man.

> Mr. Friedman loved to argue. They say he was the greatest debater in all of economics. As improbable as it sounds, given Mr. Friedman's small frame and thick glasses, few who saw him would deny that he had an astounding amount of charisma. It probably explains why he was so successful on television. (Goolsbee, 2006: 1).

Much has been made quite rightly about his impact on the economics profession and on the world more widely. He had a quicksilver mind and no one was faster on his feet then Milton Friedman. He is not known to have come off second best in any debate. But there is more to Milton Friedman than the Nobel Prize winning economist who revitalised the field of monetary economics. He was most of all a sublime polemicist. The only other figure that could potentially operate at a similar level was the man whose ghost Friedman set out to exterminate, John Maynard Keynes. Both were deeply committed men determine to move their countries to moral objectives. To do so, details of data, history or results, often got lost in the ensuing struggle. Friedman was a holy crusader battling to retain a classical liberal's view of the world against the forces of planning and collectivism. In Friedman's view, only freely operating competitive markets could protect against the coercive power of the state and guarantee freedom through individual choice. It might be fair to say that Friedman's professional output always remained in service to his moral imperatives.

> I'd like to be remembered as a friend of freedom, both economic freedom and political freedom. (Milton Friedman interviewed by the BBC WorldWide, 17 November 2006)

1. Bliss was It to be Young

One's childhood seems to leave an indelible mark on all our future years. Milton Friedman's unshakeable belief in the power of economic markets was perhaps as much influenced by his own formative experience as by any of his subsequent research. As his close friend and colleague, Stigler (1982a: 63), was forced to admit, we all interpret abstract propositions in highly personal terms. Milton Friedman was the fourth and youngest child of immigrant parents who went from working in New York sweatshops to owning a clothing store in Rahway, New Jersey. The death of his father while in his last year at high school meant that the young Friedman would need to supplement his scholarship to Rutgers by working as a waiter and clerking in stores during the Depression years (Noble, 2006: 3). Having pulled himself through by his own determination, hard work and intelligence, it would be far from unusual for him to come away from such an experience assuming that failure was largely, if not entirely, the responsibility of the individual[4]. Having both Homer Jones and Arthur Burns as teachers during his undergraduate years at Rutgers undoubtedly also steered him towards both a conservative course and one that emphasised the importance of money in economics as well as the necessity of undertaking detailed empirical work[5].

Though Milton Friedman is forever identified with the University of Chicago, many in the economics profession might be surprised to discover that his PhD was earned at Columbia under Simon Kuznets and not awarded until 1946. He did spend time as a graduate student in Chicago, entering in the Fall of 1932 and returning after a year spent at Columbia in the Fall of 1934. However, it was his time

[4] It is possible to contrast Friedman's experience with that of John Kenneth Galbraith, also one of four sons who grew up working on his father's farm in Canada. Galbraith saw the value of collective choice as well as the decentralised decision-making of the marketplace.

[5] Homer Jones was himself a graduate of Chicago who would establish the St. Louis Fed as the bulwark of Monetarism in the United States during his long tenure there (1958–1971). Burns would become Chairman of the Federal Reserve (1970–1978) after working extensively with Wesley Clair Mitchell both as his PhD student and then as his colleague at the National Bureau of Economic Research.

at Chicago that would prove influential in a number of senses. He met his match in both size and intellect in the shape of Rose Director, the sister of staff member Aaron Director, who would remain his wife until his death. The influence of Rose on her husband or her intellect should not be underestimated although she held no formal academic post. He also at the same time met George Stigler and Allen Wallis who would remain close friends and sometime colleagues throughout his long career. Unlike his two friends, Friedman did not come under the spell of Frank Knight[6] to the same extent that Stigler, Wallis, or his brother-in-law Aaron Director did. Instead, the greatest influence on his work was undoubtedly Jacob Viner[7] who converted him to a view of price theory and market efficiency that was later characterised by Reder (1982) as an unswerving belief in a Tight Prior Equilibrium.

Despite an acknowledged reputation as one of the best of a rising group of young economists, Milton Friedman initially would have difficulty in finding employment. This was not solely due to a lingering degree of Anti-Semitism that remained in academic

---

[6] Avoiding a complete fascination with Frank Knight probably assisted Friedman in the long run. Though his friend George Stigler managed to write a dissertation under him and to later break with Knight's core teachings, others ran into greater difficulties.

> In fact, Knight's major influence at that time resulted in the local view that Knight had done everything and there was nothing left to do. So, he was the cause that led to a pretty important generation of Chicago economists never getting their PhD degrees. (Conversation with Paul Samuelson, November 1997)

[7] Friedman would in fact teach the graduate course in price theory, the basic boot camp for aspiring Chicago graduate students. In this, he followed the tradition established by Jacob Viner.

> The careful and persistent use of modern price theory, the third area to which Milton also made major contributions, has a different source: Viner's famous course in economic theory was surely the origin of this part of tradition. Primarily by a rigorous exposition of price theory, Friedman instructed generations of students in its use. (Stigler, 1988, 156–157)

departments but also a reaction to his argumentative nature if not outright abrasiveness. Milton Friedman was a born salesman in the days when hard nose selling was not a recognised academic virtue. In this, Friedman once again was to prove prescient and ahead of the academic pack. His unparalleled ability to sell his ideas, not only to an academic audience but to the wider world, would eventually make him the most influential economist of the second half of the 20th century.

> Milton had certain troubles, because of two things. Anti-Semitism, but also people were afraid of him, his corrosiveness and so forth. Gottfried Haberler wanted Milton Friedman to be appointed to Harvard and somebody like Ed Chamberlin, who was a very conservative person, was the department member most violently opposed. This was because the Chicago School hated both the theories of Imperfect and of Monopolistic Competition. (Conversation with Paul Samuelson, November 1997)

His return to Chicago, the citadel from which he would launch his counter-revolution against Keynesianism, came in 1946 as the result of the misfortune of his close friend George Stigler[8] who had been the department's preferred choice for the position. As Stigler (1988) relates the event:

> In the spring of 1946 I received the offer of a professorship from the University of Chicago, and of course was delighted at the prospect. The offer was contingent upon approval by the central administration after a personal interview. I went to Chicago, met with the President, Ernest Colwell, because Chancellor Robert Hutchins was ill that day, and I was vetoed! I was too empirical, Colwell said, and no doubt that day I was. So the professorship was offered to Milton Friedman, and President Colwell and I had launched the new Chicago School. (Stigler, 1988: 40)

---

[8] Although George Stigler made light of the incident in later years, some trace of injury and bitterness perhaps always remained. In part this explains why Stigler subsequently fended off all offers to return to Chicago until 1958 when backed by private funding (the endowed Walgreen Professorship of American Institutions) the offer simply became overwhelmingly attractive.

Milton Friedman would arrive at Chicago with an ideological baton in his knapsack[9]. He would battle the forces of collectivism represented by the then dominant Keynesian theology and replace it with an individualistic, market-based approach. In the immediate cold-war era this represented not simply a quarrel over competing academic theories but what Friedman saw as a death struggle pitting freedom and individual choice against totalitarian collectivism. When he departed Chicago some 30 years later, he would leave largely triumphant.

> The great thing about the free enterprise system is that it prevents anyone from having too much power. (Milton Friedman in his PBS series *Free to Choose* 1980)

However, he faced an initial struggle, not only from the profession at large who tended to dismiss his claims as eccentric but from within the Keynesians and mathematical theorists within the Chicago department itself.

> The Samuelson matter was again forced to a head — by Douglas — & thanks mainly to his efforts we lost badly. The dep't has voted to make Samuelson

---

[9] This ideological imperative would eventually cause a rift between Friedman and his one time colleague Don Patinkin. In a posthumously published essay, Patinkin … stated that in his judgment, Friedman returned to Chicago in 1946 'to continue the school's fundamental ideological advocacy of free-market economic liberalism'. (Leeson, 2003b: 2). That Friedman had managed to raise the ideological temperature after 1946 seems clear, at least through the eyes of a particularly apt eye-witness.

> It was not until after I left Chicago in 1946 that I began to hear rumors about a "Chicago School" which was engaged in *organized* battle for laissez faire and "quantity theory of money" against "imperfect competition" theorizing and "Keynesianism". I remained skeptical about this until I attended a conference sponsored by University of Chicago professors in 1951. The invited participants were a varied lot of academics, bureaucrats, businessmen, etc., but the program for discussion, the selection of chairmen, and everything about the participants were so patently rigidly structured, so loaded, that I got more amusement from the conference than from any other I ever attended. Even the source of the financing of the Conference, as I found out later, was ideologically loaded (Jacob Viner quoted in Patinkin (2003a: 112)).

> an offer. We don't yet know the end of the story. But whatever it is, I am very much afraid that it means we're lost. The Keynesians have the votes & mean to use them. Knight is bitter & says he will withdraw from active participation in the dep't. Mints, Gregg, & I are very low about it. (Letter from Milton Friedman to George Stigler in Hammond and Hammond (2006: 46))

He also faced an uneasy cohabitation with the Cowles commission whose economists seemed to represent everything that Friedman did not, general instead of partial equilibrium, highly mathematical approaches and an attempt to make the Keynesian system more rigorous in its structure[10]. Added to this, despite his stature in the profession, Friedman was originally hired as an associate professor at a non-competitive remuneration.

> Machlup was pressing me to consider Johns Hopkins. As you doubtless know, Smithies turned them down for Harvard. I don't know whether to think about it seriously or not. They would offer 8,000 which with 3,000 to 5,000 from the Bureau makes an enormous differential over the 7,500 plus 4E contract I am scheduled to get next year (7,000 this year). Tell me, from the fullness of your experience, together with my indifference curves, how large a price ought I to pay for the privilege of being at Chicago? (Letter from Milton Friedman to George Stigler in Hammond and Hammond (2006: 80))

It is important, however, to keep in mind that in the forties, Milton Friedman was still very much a product of the first Chicago School as well as of his old mentor Arthur Burns. Although quite conservative for its time, it was nowhere equivalent to the approach that Friedman and his close ally George Stigler would create at Chicago.

> That first Chicago group was conservative by standards of the time and less so by standards of today's time. But still, as a group, they were on the

[10] The struggle with the Cowles Commission would end with relocation to the Yale University campus.

> On the whole, I admit I was wrong on Colin. He is not the man you or I would want in that perfect University Arthur wants to found, but he is personally nice, many of his instincts are on the right side, and he's much more interesting and provocative, and fundamentally no sloppier, than Kuznets or some other people in NY or Chicago. And he would be marvellous in infuriating the Cowles boys, although probably not your equal. (Letter from George Stigler to Milton Friedman, December 1947 in Hammond and Hammond (2006: 73)).

> conservative side. It was no way as conservative as the second Chicago School of Director, Friedman, if you had to skip all names but one; I think Friedman's name should be the one you should keep and Gary Becker's. (Conversation with Paul Samuelson, November 1997)

The defining work which Friedman would do came out in the fifties with some subsequent material tumbling into the sixties. This became Milton Friedman's addition to the theoretical base that defined the Chicago school. Certainly, his letters makes it clear that his approaches and material of the fifties existed in an incipient form in the late forties. Still, in the forties, Friedman had not yet made his break with the ideas of his teachers or completely disassociated himself with mainstream Keynesian thought.

> He was 'shocked' to re-read his wartime essays with their unmistakeably Keynesian taint. In a statement in 1942 before the House Ways and Means Committee, Friedman declared that 'inflation ... must be neutralised by measures that restrict consumer spending. Taxation is the most important of those measures'. Looking back he was shocked: "The most striking feature of this statement is how thoroughly Keynesian it is. I did not even mention 'money' or "monetary policy"! The only "methods of avoiding inflation" I mentioned in addition to taxation were "price control and rationing, control of consumers' credit, reduction in government and war bond campaigns". Until I reread my statement to Congress in preparing this account, I had completely forgotten how thoroughly Keynesian I was then. (Friedman quoted by Leeson (2003a: 7))

The need to clearly break away from all things Keynes[11] begins with a critical 1947 meeting in Switzerland and the subsequent founding of

---

[11] Milton Friedman and his close friend and ally George Stigler did not only want to refute the Keynesian contentions and policies. They wanted to obliterate and expunge all memory of his work. Of course, this was too much to hope for but they attempted to discredit his work as much as possible.

> I congratulate you on restraining yourself from including a picture of Keynes, and even more on not even having a mention of him in your index. (Milton Friedman to George Stigler, 16 December 1986 on the publication of Stigler's fourth edition of *The Theory of Price*.)

the Mt. Pelerin Society. For Friedman this would mark the time when it became clear who wore the white hats and who wore the threatening black ones. The importance of the battle at hand and what had to be done to conduct it first took shape at this Swiss resort. For Friedman there would clearly become a group of 'good eggs', those who were part of his band of brothers, and everyone else. Decisions would always be flavoured by questions of loyalty. This is not surprising since Milton Friedman quite rightly saw himself as a dedicated counter-revolutionary. The goal, as was true for his ghostly opponent with whom he continued to shadow box, was more than a question of theoretical economics. What was at stake was the future shape of society.

> Another strong characteristic is the unity of this group who properly felt that they were lone voices crying in the wilderness, that most of the profession was against them. They defended each other. Aaron Director, for example, would never have written a good letter of recommendation for somebody who wasn't a staunch conservative but neither would Milton. And I remember for years after I left the University of Chicago, when they were contemplating influential appointments they would ask me about the person, 'Is he really sound?' In fact, Milton once showed his naïveté to me, but it wasn't about appointments. He said, 'Tell me the truth, is Galbraith a Commie?' You know, the amount of naïveté that's in that. (Conversation with Paul Samuelson, October 1997)

2. Reshaping Economics

> The great virtue of a free market is that it enables people who hate each other, or who are from vastly different religious or ethnic backgrounds, to cooperate economically. Government intervention can't do that. Politics exacerbates and magnifies differences. (Friedman, 2006: 3)

Because only John Maynard Keynes ever rivalled Milton Friedman as a consummate polemicist, it is in practise difficult to separate his theoretical and empirical achievements from those with which he hoped to sway public debate[12]. Work ostensibly addressed to practitioners

[12] The one issue where Friedman and Stigler fundamentally disagreed was on the public role of an economist. Stigler was inward focused, concerned with changing the profession. Friedman, however, remained the quintessential public face of economics

within the economics discipline was also intended to foster the purposes of his broader counter-revolution. In a sense you can understand Friedman's professional work by pointing out its underlying contrariness. Whatever pronouncement Keynes or his followers had made, Friedman simply insisted on the direct opposite. Keynes backed a system of fixed exchange rates, Friedman pushed for floating rates. Keynesians saw a Phillips curve that allowed for a trade-off between inflation and unemployment, Friedman saw a natural rate of unemployment that allowed for no such thing. Keynes pointed out a decreased consumption rate with increased wealth and speculated whether it would lead to more unstable economies. Friedman explained why this apparent problem did not in fact insist. If Keynesians saw a demand for money function that responded to interest rates,

---

starting with being Goldwater's chief economic advisor during that ill fortuned presidential race. He advised both Nixon and Reagan (though informally) and travelled tirelessly through out the world preaching the virtues of the market place.

> He [George Stigler], on more than one occasion, asked me the question — he never gave the answer himself and I never knew how to answer the question myself — 'Did I think that Milton Friedman would be remembered most for his polemics on policy or his scientific work on things like the consumption function?' He never gave the answer himself and I didn't know what the answer to that question was. I still don't know what the answer to that question is, but he obviously thought about this issue. This was an issue in his view and I would have to infer from his own behavior that he was of the opinion regarding his good friend and respected colleague, that Milton's scientific work would be the hallmark by which he was most remembered. But that remains to be seen. The real issue, you know, is whether that's in fact going to be, whether that's going to hold up or not. On one other personal occasion I remember something related to this question coming up. I was at lunch with Milton Friedman and George Stigler at the Quadrangle Club in Chicago and I was then a very young man. And somehow the younger you are, the more evangelistic you are. And so I would debate and argue with people about policy issues and as I recall Milton asked me if I would be interested in going on a tour of some campuses, I think in the Southern United States, to talk on these policy issues. Milton said, 'What have you got to lose by doing this?' And George said at the table to me, 'Only your anonymity.' (Conversation with Harold Demsetz, October 1997).

Friedman could only find a function that was perfectly inelastic. Part of Friedman's strategy behind making such bold and contrary claims was to shock the profession out of its dogmatic sleep and force economists to engage him. For a true counter-revolutionary the very worse fate is to be completely ignored.

> The sterility of the early Walrasian system arose because it was ignored by most economists and adopted by a few but criticized by almost none. Milton Friedman's work is bound to be spread rapidly in the science and to achieve a wide scope and high rigor because of his wondrous gift of eliciting the probing attention of eminent contemporaries. (Stigler, 1982a: 111)

Nonetheless, for analytical reasons it is possible and useful to forget about the polemical purposes behind each area touched upon by Milton Friedman. Like all economists, much of his work has been superseded or pushed aside by subsequent work. What, however, is most important is that Friedman's work did influence and shape the terms of debate and the questions raised in each of these areas.

2.1. *Permanent income hypothesis*

Although more widely known as the father of monetarism, it could be argued that the one piece of empirical analysis that most nearly has survived the test of time has been his work on the consumption function (1957) that came hard on the heels of his revival of the quantity theory of money (1956). These could be seen as a proverbial one-two to the heart of Keynesian fiscal policy. Both focused on individual decisions, one on consumption/saving decisions and the other on choosing the composition of one's wealth portfolio. In each case, fiscal policy aimed at changing these choices would prove to be ineffectual. Logically, government intervention became self-defeating whatever its stated objectives might be.

It is also useful to point out another common theme underlying these landmark works which all too often is overlooked. The important characteristic that defines markets in the Chicago approach is their similarity. By focusing on what linked all markets together, the application of simple market theory could be extended far more widely then previously projected. The Chicago analysis, as developed in these post-war years, examined what appeared to be market failures and dispelled these misleading appearances. Cleverly, an argument could be woven and evidence produced which would demonstrate that all markets operated efficiently, at least where outside intervention was not the defining characteristic. Like an observant, orthodox Jew, Milton Friedman would prove to have no other God before him than price theory.

In his permanent income hypothesis, Friedman cut across the paradox that though average consumption spending did lower as incomes rose, over time, what an economy consumed out of income remains relatively constant. Friedman's resolution was that people spent not based on the income they currently enjoyed but the income enjoyed by removing temporary variations. This idea of permanent income wisely included flows generated from assets held as well as from earned income. The important implication is that any sudden increase in either wealth or income due to fiscal policy would only take effect over a number of years. These lags inevitably made fiscal policy aimed at the consumer ineffective since it was virtually impossible to match the fiscal instrument with the aimed for objective.

2.2. *Quantity theory of money*

One of Friedman's strengths as a would-be prophet was a rare talent (one also possessed by his compatriot, George Stigler) of asking the right question. This may be a more important and much rarer talent than an ability to actually grind out potential answers. Like any other economist, only some of Friedman's results have survived the test of time. However, what his finely tuned economic intuition recognised in those post-war years was the woeful underdevelopment of monetary theory (particularly in the case of demand for money functions). Keynes himself had at least implicitly recognised this deficiency in his post *General Theory* debates (conducted in the *Economic Journal*) with the Stockholm School (as represented by Bertil Ohlin). Ill health, the war and ultimately a relatively early death conspired to prevent a sequel to *The General Theory*. But this did by no means imply that he went silent on the matter of monetary theory. The explication of a 'finance motive' was one attempt to expand and deepen his liquidity preference model. However, with the death of Keynes in 1946 a dearth of research in monetary matters followed. Friedman in his usual elbows first way pushed the monetary question to the surface of economic debate, adopting a strategy that could brook no silence. In doing so, he was able to determine the terms of debate and essentially capture the high ground from the napping Keynesians at Harvard and elsewhere.

To capture the high ground meant framing the debate in a manner that would be sure to elicit a savage response from the profession. The target then could not be the correctness of Keynes's work, but rather its value. It is far more dismissive to argue that he had nothing new or important to say, than to attempt to prove that he was wrong or in error. To do the latter is to dignify an opponent's work with a sense of importance[13]. There is no evidence, despite some ill-tempered charges[14], that Milton Friedman conducted his attack on Keynes with

[13] Both Friedman and Stigler were accomplished stirrers. One can even characterize their behavior as engaging in adversarial debates not only as an effective strategy to achieve a given end but also for the sheer adrenaline charged joy of the combat itself.

> ... the later attacks by Friedman on Keynes for underplaying the influence of changes in the stock of money on economic activity called forth extensive defenses of Keynes by James Tobin, Franco Modigliani, and others. It is an achievement when others think that one's arguments are important enough to be denounced and demolished. Even to be demolished is better for one's self-esteem and reputation that to be ignored: It requires some ability to excite and especially to outrage one's fellow professionals. (Stigler, 1988: 213)

[14] The debate tended to heat up. Harry Johnson was never one to avoid blunt opinions though never in a one-sided fashion. If he was unsparing of the motives behind Friedman's counter-revolution, he was equally merciless toward the original Keynesian revolution.

> Nevertheless, one should not be too fastidious in condemnation of the techniques of scholarly chicanery used to promote a revolution or a counter-revolution in economic theory. The Keynesian revolution derived a large part of its intellectual appeal from the deliberate caricaturing and denigration of honest and humble scholars, whose only real crime was that they happened to exist and stand in the way of the success of the revolution. (Johnson, 2003: 179)

anything like malice aforethought. But like many others with the instinct of a polemicist, he was skilled at finding within a work exactly what he needed to see.

The first casualty of such an approach is inevitably any balanced or objective assessment of the perceived opposition. Caricature and ridicule become prime rhetorical weapons in unseating the status quo provided by mainstream theory. In other words, it simply is not enough to provide a solid and even superior alternative to existing theory. That reigning theory itself had to be denigrated. By doing this, entrepreneurial economists could manage to strategically shift the terms of debate towards more conducive territory. The entrenched mainstream had to be reduced to a form of repetitive idiocy. This could be done by transforming intellectual and economic history into a series of fractured fairy tales for well-behaved infants. The aim was to provoke the opposition into debating along pre-arranged terms. The worse response for any intellectual warrior of this type has always been silence. Deliberately generating outrage allowed the would-be revolutionary (or counter-revolutionary) to seize control of the debate. If confronted by overwhelming armies of fact or logic, a tactical retreat of one kind or another was always possible. But by that time the damage would have been done. The focus of the debate would have noticeably shifted.

Friedman's counter-revolution in essence wanted to fit the demand for money into a framework describing the demand for any other generic flow of services. Once done, this accomplishment would supposedly anchor monetary theory once more in the snug harbour of neoclassical thought. Individual portfolio adjustments leave little room for monetary policy to effect anything other that price levels in the long run. The result again is a minimal role for government intervention with rules (a given increase in the money supply) superseding the discretion of any central banker or politician. Unfortunately, the success of Friedman's counter-revolution against Keynesianism very soon undercut the ground from beneath his own monetary theory. In the rush to provide micro-foundations for macroeconomic theory, rational expectations soon replaced Friedman's vision of adaptive expectations. Further, the money supply data of the nineties seemed to require overly convoluted explanations if Friedman's theory of money demand was to be maintained.

> In fact, Lucas's rational expectations really stole the show from Friedman's monetarism. There's almost nobody left, including I think Milton quite quietly, who believes that there's a tight relationship between one of the M's and effective demand. (Conversation with Paul Samuelson, October 1997)

2.3. *Natural rate of unemployment*

Friedman finally buried old style Keynesianism with an impeccable display of timing. No one succeeds like a prophet redeemed by events and Friedman had the vindication of time and place working in concert to push forward his cause. Giving the Presidential Address at the 1967 meetings of the American Economic Association, Milton Friedman banished one of the bulwarks of the theory. The empirical Phillips Curve quite nicely plugged a gap in the generally accepted IS/LM framework by allowing price changes to be endogenously incorporated. This eliminated the need to treat prices exogenously, which had added an unwanted ad hoc element to the theory. It also undermined the danger of a Keynesian free lunch by assuring the profession that, as in any decision, there was an opportunity cost to be paid for employment growth. Though surely, a bit of inflation was well worth it. Besides, economists only needed to offer the menu to policy-makers who would have to then live with their subsequent choice. Perhaps the Phillips curve gained strength and was so heatedly defended because its ambiguity lent itself to multiple uses. In the marketplace of ideas it admirably met the existing demands of the profession.

The trade-off between unemployment and inflation depended on assuming reversibility as a defining characteristic of the Phillips curve. This is what Friedman (1968) and Phelps[15] (1967) successfully undermined.

> Now, Friedman and Phelps had no way of foreseeing the inflation of the 1970s, any more than did the rest of us, but the central forecast to which their reasoning led was a conditional one, to the effect that a high inflation decade should not have less unemployment on average than a low inflation decade. We got the high inflation decade, and with it as clear-cut an experimental discrimination as macroeconomics is ever likely to see, and Friedman and Phelps were right. (Lucas, 1981: 568)

The supposed trade-off then tended to be illusory. Once inflationary expectations adjusted properly, individual workers would no longer be fooled. Like any other market, labour markets cleared at an equilibrium range creating a natural rate of unemployment. Attempts to change choices made within such a market were apt to do more harm than good. However, it is questionable to what extent subsequent data has supported Friedman's stance.

2.4. *Positive economics*

Lastly, there is Milton Friedman's one and only one contribution to methodological discussions. His understanding of the nature of economic method is one that continues to define (some would say plague) the profession. That this approach became almost notorious within the profession is best symbolised by the classic 'assume a can opener' joke that quickly spread wherever economists gathered.

> From the start, of course, they [The Chicago School] didn't like the notion that if you were analysing imperfect competition, then you were analysing cases of market failure. They always played this down. The early

[15] Edmund Phelps would achieve recognition for his work with a 2006 Noble prize, three decades after Friedman. By the time that he did, the concept of a long-run vertical Phillips curve would have already become a matter of debate within the profession given the relevant data coming out of the eighties and afterwards. In any case, it is reasonable to wonder whether it was Friedman's marketing abilities that shifted the limelight away from Phelps.

> Stigler wasn't as strong on this as he was later on. But Friedman was from early on. And I think that part of the reason for it, was this development of his, was it 1953, his version of positivism? It's partly a licence for self-indulgence. You don't have to have a correspondence between a theory and the facts, or a close correspondence. In fact, the theory is all the better if it doesn't fit the facts, closely. And I think that there are some profound errors in that form of positivism, but it is there for a purpose. It serves a purpose. Do you think the cigarette industry with only four big producers in it is not competitive? Well, if one raises its price, another one will and so forth. That's the same paradigm of comparative statics that would happen under competition. So under the doctrine of 'as if', we can use the competitive theory? (Conversation with Paul Samuelson, October 1997)

Friedman put out his methodological manifesto not so much to advance a then vibrant methodological debate as to bury it[16]. Part of attacking Keynesianism was to destroy any potential microeconomic foundations that could serve to anchor it against all and any attacks. In fact, the failure of alternative micro approaches in the immediate post-war period would create something of an Achilles heel for the dominant Keynesian structure. Most of this work was spear headed by Friedman's ally, George Stigler, who beat back attempts to replace price adjusted equilibrium markets. In fact, Stigler's influence in the development of Friedman's positivism is often undervalued. Yet a rudimentary version was on display in Stigler's (1949) demolition of Monopolistic Competition in one of five lectures delivered in 1948 at the London School of Economics. Letters between the two leading up to these lectures makes it clear of the mutual collaboration that underlay this methodological approach.

MF: I had written the methodology paper, which was later formally published. This preceded, by three or four years, the earlier versions. And he refers in one of those lectures to the fact that we had been talking about it.

Yes. And how influential were you in each others thinking on this matter?

---

[16] Fifty years later, during the 2003 Allied Social Science Association meetings held in Washington, Milton Friedman, via phone hook-up, would affirm his unwavering belief in his original profession of faith.

> *MF: We were very influential. I think there's no doubt that my work would have been different if I hadn't been influenced by George and George's work would have been different if he hadn't been influenced by me.* (Conversation with Milton Friedman, August 1997)

Serving as a rationale to drive forward a counter-revolution in economics is unfortunately not equivalent to a serious consideration of the problem at hand. Friedman's own colleagues seem aware that this must be the case. As Coase notes,

> If choosing theories in accordance with Friedman's criteria is to be treated as a positive theory, economists would need to adopt a procedure somewhat similar to the following. When a new theory is advanced, economists would compare the accuracy of its predictions ... with that of the predictions of the existing theory and would choose that theory which gave the best predictions. ... If all economists followed Friedman's principles in choosing theories, no economist could be found who believed in a theory until it had been tested, which would have the paradoxical result that no tests would be carried out. This is what I meant when I said that acceptance of Friedman's methodology would result in the paralysis of scientific activity. Work could certainly continue, but no new theories would emerge. (Coase, 1994: 23)

Or looked at pragmatically by one of Friedman's former students,

> When I was a graduate student we were taught a paradigm of how you do research. I've got to tell you it's all wrong and it's not the way we operate. We don't sit up here and develop hypotheses and go out and test them, that's just not what we do. George taught me that. Milton taught me that. They're wrong! And I understand that. I'm older enough now to figure out that's not the way we do work. There's a lot of salesmanship, there's a lot of taking positions, defending them. The facts will win out. I'm not saying that we're not in that sense correct. The facts do win out. But the process by which that happens is not the clean one of scientific method rigorously applied all the time. (Conversation with Sam Peltzman, October 1997)

3. Death of a Salesman

> ... the categories of 'honest' and 'dishonest' are quite irrelevant. What is instead relevant is the far more subtle phenomenon involved in human failing (to which we are all subject) of sometimes suppressing that which it

would be more convenient for us not to note or remember — with reference to questions to which we are strongly involved." (Patinkin quoted in Leeson (2003b: 258)

Although frustrated opponents may have labelled Milton Friedman something of a charlatan[17], he never was deliberately fraudulent or driven to consciously deceive his professional or wider audience. His objectives, however, dominated all else he undertook. He unconsciously "let [policy] wag … theory." (Patinkin, 2003c: 126). This pattern flowed from a strong and unshakeable *a priori* faith in his own correctness. The only problem posed was to figure out how to convince others that this was the case. Playing to win then was the only available option given what was at stake. To paraphrase Ronald Reagan, Milton Friedman was a consummate freedom fighter. There was more to the battle than a mere theoretical issue. Friedman morally could not afford to lose. He, therefore, made himself an elusive target by constantly shifting the terms of professional debate on to more conducive territory. This might have enraged his academic opponents who naively believed that logic and evidence must always prevail. But it won him the high ground whenever and whatever he argued.

> He [Milton Friedman] was always patient, always polite, never got short tempered like I do in an argument, never got nasty. He was a horrible person to argue with, just a nightmare. My idea of a nightmare is to stand on a stage and debate with him in front of the public. I watched him debating at Cambridge with Joan Robinson on flexible exchange rates. Unbelievable! I mean, Joan Robinson was one of the world's most aggressive, hostile, debaters. He wiped her analytically, he wiped her rhetorically, and he had the entire audience eating out of his hand, after an hour, an hour and a half. An amazing, amazing guy, but a madman, a madman. One of the few people I could strangle with my bare hands. I feel I could actually do it. (Conversation with Mark Blaug, July 1998)

This need to triumph led to a curious relationship with empirical data. Facts have a story to tell but it is the analyst that gives mute data a

---

[17] There are reports that Harry Johnson characterized Milton Friedman as being something of the sort. Certainly, his 1970 Ely lecture pulled no punches in displaying an academic disdain for Friedman and his techniques.

voice. The tune this evidence ultimately sings is shaped by the researcher. The problem is that unacknowledged desires may shape the treacherous eyes of the ambitious scholar.

> [Friedman] has frequently trapped and sandbagged critics of reputation and integrity by the technique of under-disclosure of analysis and evidence and apparent overstatements of the strength of his results. (Johnson quoted in Leeson (2003a: 261)

Milton Friedman was ultimately a great strategist, one of the commanding generals in an epic and successful counter-revolution. The battle was not over the mere shape of economic theory but of society itself. There could be no retreat or compromise from the immutable goals driving Friedman and his band of brothers[18]. "I think Milton quietly changed, he just quietly dropped that [100% money a la Fisher]. He doesn't particularly announce changes in positions, but instead, lets them just decay away." (Conversation with Paul Samuelson, October 1997)

Though his very methodology demanded testable hypotheses, it is difficult to conceive of any evidence that would shake his fundamental belief in the primacy of free markets.

> It's hard to imagine an empirical observation that would convince most members of this department [University of Massachusetts] and the University of Chicago to change their minds. My personal view is that if someone holds a view it cannot be dislodged by any conceivable empirical data. Evidence from a data system doesn't convince them. These people have made their decisions already. They've become true believers and no

[18] There is a clear ferociousness common to much of the Chicago approach that has done much to advance the "winner-take-all" adversarial approach to economics.

> I think you're getting at something that is (a) the atmosphere at Chicago, and (b) intensified by Knight. That an academic is concerned not with being diplomatic, not with trying to avoid hurting people's feelings, but an academic is concerned with saying what's right. Telling the truth, or trying to get at it. And if you disagree with somebody you don't say, "Well, now there may be something in what you say, you may be right. You say, that's a bunch of nonsense. (Conversation with Milton Friedman, August 1997)

> amount of empirical evidence will ever convince them by definition. (Conversation with Jim Kindahl, October 1997)

Ultimately, Friedman's rhetorical brilliance would elevate salesmanship to an unwonted position, dominating too much of economic debate. One of Milton Friedman's most enduring contributions to his profession may be one of the least desirable, the economist as preacher.

> The degree of popularity of a preacher does not necessarily measure his influence as a preacher, let alone as a scholar. In fact one could perhaps argue that unpopular sermons are the more influential — certainly if the opposite is true, and preachers simply confirm their listeners' beliefs, pulpits should be at the rear of congregations, to make clearer who is leading. (Stigler, 1982b: 13)

4. Old Economists Never Die, They Only Slowly Fade Away

Why so many noted figures in the economics profession enjoy or endure such longevity of life is an as yet unexplored mystery. Curiously, there seems to be some sort of superficial correlation between conservative ideology and life expectancy. In any case, Milton Friedman in his last decade, released from making any fundamental theoretical contributions, was still a premier polemicist and never at a loss when it came to policy prescriptions and advice. The consistency, persistence and unwavering nature of his market vision eventually saw many of these suggestions adopted in one form or another. His career was a success by his own standards and those of the discipline he served.

Only the most narrow and mean minded within the profession would deny Milton Friedman's place in the pantheon of economic gods. If, for instance, Nobel prizes (at least of the ersatz variety) are to be awarded for economic achievement, who would have the temerity to overlook someone who reshaped his discipline. Like his close friend George Stigler, Milton Friedman had a knack for asking the right question and not accepting common wisdom at face value. For this, all economists owe him a large measure of gratitude. But there is also much to regret as well in his legacy. Letting the polemical tail wag the theoretical dog is never good practise no matter what one's goals or intentions might be. Transforming discussion into an adversarial debate of the zero sum variety lacks true, admirable qualities. This characterizes the enduring problem of the relation between means and ends. For Milton Friedman, ends were of such overwhelming importance that he sometimes failed to see how means could become so sadly neglected.

> I sometimes think some of the Chicago people are hopeless. Well, I wouldn't include Milton as among the hopeless because he was smart enough to punch his way out of a paper bag sometimes. But in the end he didn't want to do so. (Conversation with Paul Samuelson, October 1997)

References

Friedman, M (1953). The methodology of positive economics. In *Essays in Positive Economics*, pp. 3–43. Chicago: University of Chicago Press.

Friedman, M (1956). The quantity theory of money: A restatement. In *Studies in Quantity Theory*, M Friedman (ed.). Chicago: University of Chicago Press.

Friedman, M (1957). *A Theory of the Consumption Function*. Princeton, New Jersey: National Bureau of Economic Research.

Friedman, M (1968). The role of monetary policy. *The American Economic Review*, 58(1), 1–17.

Friedman, M (2003a/1967). The monetary theory and policy of Henry Simons. In *Keynes, Chicago and Friedman*, Vol. 1, R Leeson (ed.), pp. 53–68. London: Pickering & Chatto.

Friedman, M (2006). Free markets and the end of history. *New Perspectives Quarterly (NPQ)*, 23(1), 1–7 http://www.digitalnpq.org/archive/2006_winter/friedman.html, 14 February 2006.

Hammond, JD and CH Hammond (eds.) (2006). *Making Chicago Price Theory: Friedman-Stigler Correspondence 1945–1957*. London and New York: Routledge.

Goolsbee, A (2006). A charismatic economist who loved to argue (17 November). *The New York Times*, pp. 1–2, http://wwwnytimes.com/2006/11/17/business/17milton/html?

Johnson, H (2003/1971). The Keynesian revolution and the monetarist counter-revolution. In *Keynes, Chicago and Friedman*, Vol. 1, R Leeson (ed.), pp. 169–182. London: Pickering & Chatto.

Leeson, R (2003a). The initial controversy. In *Keynes, Chicago and Friedman*, Vol. 1, R Leeson (ed.), pp. 1–30. London: Pickering & Chatto.

Leeson, R (2003b). How unique was the Chicago tradition? In *Keynes, Chicago and Friedman*, Vol. 2, R Leeson (ed.), pp. 1–25. London: Pickering & Chatto.

Leeson, R (2003c/2000). Patinkin, Johnson, and the shadow of Friedman. In *Keynes, Chicago and Friedman*, Vol. 1, R Leeson (ed.), pp. 249–279. London: Pickering & Chatto.

Lucas, RE Jr (1981). Tobin and monetarism: A review article. *Journal of Economic Literature*, 29(2), 558–585.

Nobel, HB (2006). Milton Friedman, Free-market theorist, dies at 94 (17 November). *The New York Times*, pp. 1–8, http://wwwnytimes.com/2006/11/17/business/17friedman/html?

Patinkin, D (2003a/1969). The Chicago tradition, the quantity theory, and Friedman. In *Keynes, Chicago and Friedman*, Vol. 1, R Leeson (ed.), pp. 87–120. London: Pickering & Chatto.

Patinkin, D (2003b/1979). Keynes and Chicago. In *Keynes, Chicago and Friedman*, Vol. 2, R Leeson (ed.), pp. 373–392. London: Pickering & Chatto.

Patinkin, D (2003c/1974). Friedman on the quantity theory and Keynesian economics. In *Keynes, Chicago and Friedman*, Vol. 2, R Leeson (ed.), pp. 123–143. London: Pickering & Chatto.

Phelps, ES (1967). Phillips curves, expectations of inflation and optimal unemployment. *Economica*, 34(2), 254–281.

Reder, MW (1982). Chicago economics: Permanence and change. *Journal of Economic Literature*, 20(3), 1–38.

Rinfert, PA (2000). Milton Friedman: Conceited, lying, egotistical and disastrous. A lousy economist with dangerously simplistic vision and explanations of the economic world, 5 November, p. 1, http://www.parida.com/mf.html. 28 November 2006.

Stigler, GJ (1982a). Does economics have a useful past? In *The Economist as Preacher*, pp. 107–118. Chicago: University of Chicago Press.

Stigler, GJ (1982b). The economist as preacher? In *The Economist as Preacher*, pp. 1–13. Chicago: University of Chicago Press.

Stigler, GJ (1988). *Memoirs of an Unregulated Economist.* New York: Basic Books.

Summers, LH (2006). The great liberator (17 November). *The New York Times*, pp. 1–2, http://www.nytimes.com/2006/11/19/opinion/19summers.html?

Chapter 9

Entre Nous — A Review of the Friedman–Stigler Correspondence

Daniel Hammond, J and CH Hammond (2006). *Making Chicago Price Theory: Friedman–Stigler Correspondence 1945–1957*, xvii + 165 pp. $120 (hardcover), ISBN:0-415-70078-7. London and New York: Routledge.

> 'Indifferent! Oh no — I never conceived you could become indifferent. Letters are no matters of indifference; they are generally a very positive curse'.
>
> 'You are speaking of letters of business; mine are letters of friendship'.
>
> 'I have often thought them the worst of the two, replied he, coolly. 'Business you know, may bring money, but friendship hardly ever does'. (Jane Austen — *Emma*)

Reading this volume generates reflections which are more substantial than a mere nostalgic yearning for times past. Technology has condemned to the museum archives a means of personal and business communication which had outlasted the centuries. Letters not only were for most of history the only way accurately to convey thought, emotion and information over long distances, but a method that was remarkably cheap as well. In the 90s, the rise of e-mail has largely put paid to those fondly received missives. Today, I would be hard pressed to recall the last time I received an overseas letter, although in the late 80s and early 90s such occurrences were routine. What makes this more than just a yearning for familiar ways is that technology changes not only communication channels but the very content of that medium. The style, structure and thought behind a handwritten (and perhaps even a typed) letter is definably different from the modest e-mail which is more of an off-the-cuff note. Moreover, e-mail is ephemeral. Few people print out and store them as they might preserve letters. So the sad news when we read this wonderful collection is that future generations will turn to the equivalent of the Stigler or Friedman archive and find a bare cupboard instead of a treasure trove of material. Future biographers and historians of thought will come to mourn this loss. What is to be done? Nothing, except to enjoy those opportunities that we still have at hand.

Claire and Daniel Hammond (both at Wake Forest University) have performed a real service in making so many of the key exchanges between Milton Friedman and George Stigler available to the interested reader. Many economists today simply take for granted the wonders these two men performed in the post-war period. They set out to overturn the then prevailing orthodoxy and (for better or worse) largely succeeded. When economists today refer so blithely to the Chicago School, they are implicitly referring to the work, effort and campaign of these two long-time friends and colleagues. (Even today, Milton Friedman still mourns the loss of his remarkable compatriot.) Though most economists, let alone the general public, will associate Friedman with the Chicago School counter-revolution to overthrow the teaching of Keynes and other heretics, it is perhaps Stigler who had in his more quiet way the greater influence (at least academically). In any case, their spheres of operation were largely separable with Stigler focusing almost exclusively on microeconomic matters. What the two did have in common, besides their fierce dedication to market principles, was the ability to sell economic ideas in a rhetorical way that had a significant impact[1]. What the letters themselves show,

[1] "I've come to the conclusion that no economic theory is important unless one's contemporaries are persuaded to adopt it. If it meets this test it is important; if it does not, it is unimportant — no matter how correct or profound it may be." (George Stigler to Milton Friedman, March 1950: 112)

besides a mutual affection and respect, is the ways in which the ideas that formed the core of the Chicago School developed and the role which the two had in cross-pollinating each other's work. (This despite the fact that the only joint work they ever formally endeavoured was a paid for pamphlet brought out shortly after World War Two (*Roofs or Ceilings*) which examined ceilings on rental prices.)

By a stroke of luck, the two were forced apart in the immediate post-war period except for a brief year together in Minnesota (1945). Like some modern-day couple forced to pursue widely separated careers, Milton Friedman went off to Chicago (1946) and Stigler to Columbia (1947) after a short stop at Brown (1946). As a result, these two close colleagues and friends spent the years between 1946 and 1958 largely apart except for periodic visits. Their loss was our gain[2]. This enforced separation is the reason that we now have this fascinating correspondence which reflects the way in which the two attempted to transform economics. In particular, we can discern their attempts to reshape economic methodology as well as their changing views on such issues as equality and income distribution. As we read these letters, the outline of what would form the bedrock of the Chicago School, a distinctive take on price theory, becomes progressively clearer.

Friedman's counter-revolution against the prevailing dominance of post-war Keynesian theory is well known by most economists. Less appreciated is Stigler's role in defending traditional price theory against heretical challenges. At least in part through his efforts, Stigler maintained what would later be accepted as the microfoundations of economics, defending Marshallian partial equilibrium analysis (or at least the Friedman–Stigler version) against the seemingly invincible tide of Walrasian general equilibrium theory. What both of these lynchpins of the Chicago school held in common was an unshakeable belief in the efficiency of markets. They especially viewed this form of economic structure as a bulwark of individual choice and liberty against the omnipervasive depredations of the chronic economic planners.

[2] '... there is no one anywhere I would rather have as a colleague than you'. (George Stigler to Milton Friedman, 19 October 1954: 133)

There are notoriously few minor omissions or curious lacunae in this volume that I can point out, and only if strongly pressed. In the very useful introduction to this series of letters the Hammonds wonder why there is no mention made of Friedman's pioneering work on monetary theory. Friedman's quantity theory of money was, after all, at the heart of his counter-revolution. However, this is much like being puzzled by the lack of any direct references to the Napoleonic wars in Jane Austen's novels. The solution is simple. This bit of geopolitics failed to fall within the attention of Ms Austen's interests in writing her novels. She was not about to drag it into the picture by virtue of its sheer topicality. In a similar manner, George Stigler displayed only minimal interest in macroeconomic matters and claimed to possess no particular insights in this area. Instead he tended to defer to Milton Friedman's expertise (though Stigler does provide useful comments on Friedman's seminal work dealing with the Consumption Theory).

There is also a strange lapse in what otherwise amounts to a comprehensive set of endnotes attached to these letters. Two items transmitted by Stigler to Friedman would later appear in an idiosyncratic collection entitled '*The Intellectual And The Market Place And Other Essays by George Stigler*' ('Stigler's Law' and 'On Scientific Writing'). True, the publication date (1963) puts it outside the boundaries set by the editors. But it is still a useful bit of information to provide to interested readers.

Lastly, the Hammonds claim that the close bond between George Stigler and Milton Friedman only commenced with their mutual employment by the Statistical Research Group during the war (1943–1945). It can be easily argued that they were already close from their days as graduate students in Chicago. Though, it does seem clear that Stigler was initially closer to Allen Wallis[3]. (It was in fact Wallis as director of the Statistical Research Group who reunited

---

[3] I base my alternative view on the recollections of Rose and Milton Friedman as well as Paul Samuelson who knew them while enrolled as an undergraduate at Chicago. Additional insights on this matter may be gained in Stigler's own autobiography (1988).

the two.) This issue is however more a question of nuance and interpretation than any clear disagreement.

The very low level of my nitpicking is perhaps the best indication of my admiration for what the two editors have achieved in selecting these letters for publication. It is a work that can be enjoyed on several levels. It displays economists in their most human mode. Here we see two relatively young academics advancing their careers, discussing economics, worrying about their families, gossiping and making withering remarks about colleagues and competitors. 'It may merely be prejudice, but I'm inclined to write him [Samuelson] off as an economist'. (Stigler to Friedman: 97). 'Of the many speakers only one was terrible — shallow and pretentious, Joe Schumpeter'. (Stigler to Friedman: 96)

Let me add a minor final note which may only display a creeping onset of curmudgeonly attitude rather than anything resembling good judgement on my part. The publisher, Routledge, seems determined to prove that you cannot tell a book by its cover. In fact, you can not determine anything about a Routledge book by its cover. The firm seems unshakeable in its belief that the more that cover is dull and indistinguishable, the more scholarly is the work. Potential readers of excellent volumes, like the one under review, are actively discouraged from opening the work rather than enticed. It would be kind to think that Routledge is taking some principled, if obscure, stand by its choices in artwork. But, the more likely explanation is that it is simply succumbing to the rather lazy option of not trying. By doing so, Routledge fails to do justice to the volumes it publishes.

Craig Freedman
Macquarie University

References

Stigler, GJ (1963). *The Intellectual and the Market Place And Other Essays by George Stigler*. Glencoe, Illinois: The Free Press.

Stigler, GJ (1988). *Memoirs of an Unregulated Economist*. New York: Basic Books.

Chapter 10

Not for Love Nor Money: Milton Friedman's Counter-Revolution

Craig Freedman

Macquarie University
craig.freedman@efs.mq.edu.au

A Review Essay of Leeson, R (ed.), (2001). *Keynes, Chicago and Friedman*, vol. 1 (i–x), 1–381; vol. 2 (i–vi), 1–534, ISBN 1851967672. London: Pickering & Chatto.

> I was baffled at the time, and have been ever since, at what all the fuss was about. So far as I could see, very little was at stake. ... I am impressed — or perhaps, depressed might be better — by the amount of subtle scholarship and hard research the articles embody. (Friedman, 2003a: x)

In his monumental and seemingly endless work, *Summa Theologica*, Thomas Aquinas notes that argument according to authority is of the weakest sort[1]. Yet, economists, even those tending to an extreme

[1] The force of this statement is immediately undercut by attributing this claim to another theologian. This seems more of a moment of unintentional irony than an intentional departure from Thomas' uniformly sombre presentation. (We all still await publication of a volume detailing scholastic humour.) Those interested in the exact reference for this quote are encouraged to fossick through all of the interminable volumes. Otherwise, those lacking a theological bent may save time by trusting to my memory.

mathematical persuasion, feel obliged to buttress their arguments by forcibly dragging onto the stage of their presentations other significant economists both old and new. In some sense this obeisance to authority serves no discernible purpose. An argument needs to stand on its own merits and receives no serious bolstering by finding support in some previous volume of work. What then is the purpose behind this obligatory name dropping? In part it is traditional. Those who continue to worship, as demanded by the conventions of professional courtesy, need only go through the form rather than be filled with the spirit of such practise. It is these days more of a signal to convey the fact that the writer should be accorded some respect since he or she intimately knows, and may possibly even have read, the relevant professional literature. However, this simple act of obeisance in this era of time constraints has seen its requirements drastically abridged. The current rule of thumb is that anything extending back beyond five, or perhaps ten, years bears no real significance to ongoing research, at least to anything outside the backwaters of the profession. Following this train of thought, we then would be forced to entertain the possibility that at its core, History of Thought, in this age of the specialist, is best left to those whose competence is suspect. Any respectable economist who fritters away valuable space by dropping the name of a long dead economist into the middle of a serious paper can have no other discernable objective than self-display. Most referees would be forced to dismiss such habits as unnecessary vanity, of the same type that led 19th century English gentlemen to employ Latin tags.

Adopting this standpoint constrains the intellectual contribution of these two lengthy volumes (of more than 900 pages) to territory once inhabited by the long-running sitcom *Seinfeld*. Both of these two time-consuming efforts realistically can be dismissed as endless dissertations about nothing at all. In other words, it is quite possible, entertaining and even at times fascinating to discuss and debate trivia, but to do so, ranks as a past-time rather than as a serious endeavour. This seems to be the dismissive import of Milton Friedman's retrospective evaluation of a debate he touched off in 1956 and which ran over into the new century. The debate ranged over some of the most respected journals in the profession and swept in a number of well-known economists. (The list of suspects included not only Friedman, Patinkin and Johnson but also Laidler, Parkin, Tobin and others.)

But I am afraid that Friedman may be taking a deliberately ingenuous stance when posing as baffled by all the subsequent fuss.

> So far as I could see, very little was at stake. What seemed to me important was the validity and usefulness of the theory that I sketched in my essay. Suppose I was wrong in asserting that that theory conveyed 'the flavor of the oral tradition that nurtured the remaining essays in this volume.' That would simply mean that I was confused about the origin of the ideas I was presenting but it would not affect by an iota the validity or usefulness of those ideas. (Friedman, 2003a: x)

Friedman appears to be intentionally ignoring the real issue lurking throughout these many pages. It was, after all, not some obscure history of thought dispute that ignited Patinkin's fury and shaped Johnson's 1970 *Ely Lecture*. Much of what Friedman claims in retrospect is undoubtedly true. The validity, or lack of validity, of Friedman's monetary theory does not depend in any way on what the oral tradition in Chicago during the thirties might have been. This 'issue is entirely about the origin of ideas, not about the validity of content'. (Friedman 2003a, vol. 1: x). It is in fact possible to confine this long-running debate to the scrutiny of those specialists interested in this rather narrow arena. But in that case, the unintended consequences of this tedious controversy would be limited to an expansion of our historical knowledge of monetary theory. This is in fact the cautious path pursued by the volumes' editor, Robert Leeson.

Leeson's insight unfortunately grasps only the tail of the elephant by dismissing all these written words as no more than a squabble over the origin of ideas. By focusing on this tail alone, the significance of the elephant is ignored. We need to go directly to the heart of the matter. The question lurking not far from the historical surface remains Friedman's purpose or objective in including those controversial paragraphs at the beginning of his acclaimed 1956 work on monetary theory (*The Quantity Theory of Money — A Restatement*).

Since these are the phrases that launched a thousand articles, let me quote Milton Friedman at length.

> The present volume is partly a symptom of this re-emergence and partly a continuance of an aberrant tradition. Chicago was one of the few academic centers at which the quantity theory continued to be a central and vigorous part of the oral tradition throughout the 1930s and 1940s, where students continued to study monetary theory and to write theses on monetary problems. The quantity theory that retained this role differed sharply from the atrophied and rigid caricature that is so frequently described by the proponents of the new income-expenditure approach — and with some justice, to judge by much of the literature on policy that was spawned by quantity theorists. At Chicago, Henry Simons and Lloyd Mints directly, Frank Knight and Jacob Viner at one remove, taught and developed a more subtle and relevant version, one in which the quantity theory was connected and integrated with general price theory and became a flexible and sensitive tool for interpreting movement in aggregate economic activity and for developing relevant policy prescriptions.
>
> To the best of my knowledge, no systematic statement of this theory as developed at Chicago exists, though much can be read between the lines of Simons' and Mints's writings. And this is as it should be, for the Chicago tradition was not a rigid system, an unchangeable orthodoxy, but a way of looking at things. It was a theoretical approach that insisted that money does matter — that any interpretation of short-term movements in economic activity is likely to be seriously at fault if it neglects monetary changes and repercussions and if it leaves unexplained why people are willing to hold the particular nominal quantity of money in existence.
>
> The purpose of this introduction is not to enshrine — or, should I say, inter — a definitive version of the Chicago tradition. To suppose that one could do so would be inconsistent with that tradition itself. The purpose is rather to set down a particular 'model' of a quantity theory in an attempt to convey the flavor of the oral tradition which nurtured the remaining essays in this volume. In consonance with this purpose, I shall not attempt to be exhaustive or to give a full justification for every assertion. (Friedman, 2003b: 33–34)

Milton Friedman was too good a strategic rhetorician and outright polemist to preface his argument with such a deliberate grounding if merely following some stylistic convention of the time was his paramount consideration. The reference had to be deliberate, constructed with a very specific objective in mind. What this objective seems to have been is made clearer retrospectively by two of Friedman's additional pieces on monetary theory, also reproduced in this edition[2]. It is likely that these articles served to bring a long simmering debate to a boil.

Patinkin clearly recognised Friedman's tactics early on. Friedman was attempting to marginalise Keynes' economic contribution by presenting his own demand for money model as completely bypassing Keynes' monetary contribution (his liquidity preference approach).

> As an aside, I might add that my only other objection to your [1956] essay is its refusal to recognise the strongly Keynesian flavour of the analysis it presents ... an exposition with the contents and spirit of yours could not have been written (and was not written) before Keynes. I find it particularly difficult to accept your implication that your essay represents the kind of thing that was taught at Chicago by Knight, Viner, Simons and Mints. My own recollections are different. (1959 letter, Patinkin to Friedman, quoted in Leeson, 2003a: 8)

In contrast, Friedman's stated position implied that if he seemed to owe anything to Keynes, that was simply because Keynes' own monetary theory was a derivative of the quantity theory approach, advancing that theory in a relatively minor rather than revolutionarily major way[3]. The essential difference between Friedman's teacher Simons

---

[2] The two articles were 'The Monetary Theory and Policy of Henry Simons' and 'The Quantity Theory of Money' both reproduced in the first volume of this work.

[3] Friedman insists that except for the idea of Keynes' liquidity trap, Keynes is doing nothing that radically departs from the ideas advanced by Fisher.

> Except for somewhat different language, the analysis up to this point [in *The General Theory*] differs from that of earlier quantity theorists, such as Fisher, only by its subtle analysis of the role of expectations about future interest rates and its greater emphasis on current interest rates and by restricting more narrowly the variables explicitly considered as affecting the amount of money demanded.
>
> Keynes's special twist concerned the empirical form of the liquidity-preference function at the low interest rates that he believed would prevail under conditions of underemployment equilibrium. Let the interest rate fall sufficiently low, he argued, and money and bonds would become perfect substitutes for one another, liquidity preference, as he put it, would become absolute. (Friedman, 2003d, vol. 1: 76)

and Keynes was not therefore a theoretical difference but one of the policies based on differing ideological beliefs.

> As we shall see later, though some of his (Keynes) policy recommendations parallel Simons', in other respects they differ drastically. But they differ not because of a difference in monetary theory or a different interpretation of 1929–1933 but because of a different basic attitude toward social policy — Keynes was a reformer, Simons, a radical. (Friedman, 2003c: 58)

To label someone as highly derivative is to rhetorically dismiss him or her as being inconsequential. In this way Keynes becomes a minor quantity theorist, allowing Friedman to characterise his major contribution to monetary theory as being based on a longstanding, and thus much older, tradition derived from the work of quantity theorists[4]. By dressing up traditional theory in new terminology, Keynes is accused of providing the economics profession with an excuse for ignoring the importance of money while adding little of importance to the received standard theory.

What was at stake, when viewed from a rhetorical standpoint, was Milton Friedman's counter-revolution, which sought to supplant the reigning Keynesian approach with his own brand of monetarism. As always with Friedman the contest was not restricted to the theoretical realm. Policy issues were clearly at stake. As early as 1946 the lines were starkly drawn.

> Howard Ellis saw the dispute as a confrontation between 'a political wing favoring a very large amount of government activity, and another wing which, mistrustful of the concentrated power which the bureaucracy would possess under these circumstances, would reduce it to a minimum. (Leeson, 2003a: 17)

---

[4] Earlier, Samuelson used the same type of approach to dismiss Marx's contribution to economic theory. In Samuelson's analysis Marx becomes a minor Ricardian and autodidact. This deliberate relegation of an economist and his or her theoretical work to the minor leagues is more damning (from a rhetorical standpoint) than any other detailed refutation could possibly be.

> A minor Post-Ricardian, Marx was an autodidact cut off in his lifetime from competent criticism and stimulus. (Samuelson, 1957: 911)

Behind this was a clash of ideologies. For conservatives 'Keynesianism' was a code word for economic planning, inevitably shifting countries towards totalitarianism[5]. Right wing intellectuals judged that individual liberty and freedom were at stake, as well as the right of the individual to choose and bear full responsibility for those choices. Planning institutionalised power while competitive markets rendered power meaningless. Not coincidentally, Friedman dedicated a major polemical piece, *Capitalism and Freedom* (1962), 'to his two children "and their contemporaries who must carry the torch of liberty on its next lap"'. (Leeson, 2003a: 9)

While it is feasible that at one level the crux of the matter was simply an argument over the origin of ideas, that such incendiary remarks should just happen to appear in this manifesto of the monetarist counter-revolution seems unlikely. Not only did Friedman propose to offer a better account of monetary demand but he also intended to pull the theoretical rug from beneath Keynesian analysis by denigrating its originality.

Curiously, Keynes himself had used similar rhetorical devices when launching his own revolution against mainstream theory. For these

---

[5] Except for the professionally naïve, there should be little doubt that Friedman was deliberately trying to minimise Keynes' contribution. In this, Patinkin was quite accurate.

> The exaggerated claims for the quantity theory have expressed themselves in the attempt (especially by Milton Friedman) to present Keynes's monetary theory not as a new theory, but as a variation on the Cambridge cash-balance theory. (Patinkin, 2003, vol. 2: 317)

It is then a reach to claim that undermining Keynes' reputation had no relation to the polemical wars breaking out in the immediate post-war period (not coincidentally mirroring the growing polemics of the Cold War).

> According to his disciples, Keynes trusted to human intelligence. He hated enslavement by rules. He wanted governments to have discretion and he wanted economists to come to their assistance in the exercise of that discretion. In Aaron Director's [Milton Friedman's brother-in-law] judgement, Keynes work provided the foundations for 'collectivism' while Simons' work provided the foundation for 'freedom and equality'. (Leeson, 2003, vol. 2: 308)

progenitors of the economic reformation and counter-reformation of the 20th century, history of thought and economic history were rhetorical devices to be used to achieve strategic positions. The two were both expert popularisers and polemists. Policy objectives rather than objective analysis remained the guiding stars for Keynes as well as for his latter day nemesis Friedman. Strict accuracy was only for the overly fastidious, those professional and tedious scholastics, rather than for the truly committed.

1. The Economist as Polemist — Using an Unpredictable Past

> War is nothing but a continuation of politics with the admixture of other means. (Clausewitz, 1832, Bk. 8, Ch. 6, Sec. B)

Deirdre McCloskey created something of a cottage industry by pointing out the obvious[6]. (Though like all academics, economists have sometimes proven themselves immune to accepting the undeniable.) Even economists are in the persuasion business and use rhetorical strategies to try to win over members of their professional circle as well as those outside the pale of erudition. Simply put, economists write in order to persuade. Unfortunately, in the case of economic theories, unlike the fable of the better mousetrap, academics tend not to beat a path to the originator's office door. It can easily be argued that part of the post-war success of Chicago economists, in their roles as counter-revolutionaries, was their great skill in marketing.

> Part of it is the persuasion. There's no question. I mean George Stigler, I remember when I was a young person, wired and said 'Selling is very important in your research. So write better. Work on writing because that is important. You've got to sell what you are doing. I think he's exactly right. You've got to sell what you are doing. It may be that in the long run good ideas do surface but they surface faster, if written in a persuasive fashion. (Conversation with Gary Becker, October 1997)

---

[6] In her previous Donald incarnation, McCloskey started the discussion with the very well-known article appearing in the *Journal of Economic Literature* (1983) and later stretched into a book (1985).

An economist tries to sell his or her theory as being congruent with the pre-existing preferences of the majority of the profession. This resembles the same way in which commercial marketing involves convincing the potential customer that a product generates the flows of services, which satisfy the consumer's underlying desires. In this sense, it is not enough to come up with the superior mousetrap. It is at least as important to convince customers of the superiority of that mousetrap by demonstrating that this (but not that) will deliver satisfaction. In simple terms, an economist is always constrained by the fact that he or she needs to give the profession what it wants to hear. This does not equate to an obvious pandering to prejudices. But the rules of the market hold here as they do in any other exchange. If you are going to successfully pitch an idea you have to be aware of the flows of services delivered to your target audience as well as of the associated user costs in gaining those service flows. This says nothing about the actual accuracy or truthfulness of any theory. Marketing is simply meeting market demand better than some competing theory.

> Moreover, bad ideas may be put persuasively. And they may gain the necessary threshold. However, taking that same analogy in competition among ideas, there is a presumption, although not a certainty, that in the longer run, the good ideas are going to compete out the bad ideas. But that may take a long time and may not even always operate. There's nothing necessary about that. Nothing guaranteed about that. (Conversation with Gary Becker, October 1997)

Though Pigou might have disparaged the rough elbow approach taken by Keynes in pursuing these methods, in fact economists have never been gentle in pushing their ideas and policies. However, Pigou may have had a point in decrying (and unintentionally foreseeing) the rise of marketing in what are notionally academic debates. It is far from clear that moving from the positive-sum game of the Senior Common Room to the zero-sum game that describes the adversarial approach most commonly displayed in the courtroom proceedings, represents progress.

> Controversy for its own sake is a prodigious waste of time ... Are we, in our secret hearts, wholly satisfied with the manner, or manners, in which some

> of our controversies are carried on? A year or more ago, after the publication of an important book, there appeared an elaborate and careful critique of a number of particular passages in it. The author's answer was, not to rebut the criticisms, but to attack with violence another book, which the critic had himself written several years before! Body line bowling! The method of the duello! That kind of thing is surely a mistake. It is a mistake, not merely in general and in the abstract, but also for solid reasons of State. Economists in this country lack influence which — in their own opinion — they ought to have, largely because the public believe that on all topics they are hopelessly divided. Controversies conducted in the manner of Kilkenny cats do not help to dissipate this opinion. (Pigou quoted in Leeson 2003d: 302)

1.1. *John Maynard Keynes — economist as provocateur*

> As a historian of thought in areas in which he was emotionally involved as a protagonist and prophet, Keynes seemed to me to be seriously lacking in the unexciting but essential qualities for the intellectual historian of objectivity and of judiciousness. Even when he was engaged in selecting those upon whom to bestow laurels for having in some degree anticipated his discoveries, his selection seemed to me then, and still seems to me now that I have acquired more knowledge of the older literature, often to have been random when not eccentric. (Viner, 2003: 418)

For Keynes, economics was above all an applied discipline, an approach he would have imbibed from his teacher, Alfred Marshall. Theory was interesting not so much in and of itself but for the policy guidelines provided by such models. In his innermost heart he was above all the pamphleteer who urged economists to "eschew the Treatise, pluck the day, fling pamphlets to the wind". (Keynes, 1972: 199) He initially came to public notice with his first popular work, *The Economic Consequences of the War.* This was a work that prefigured aspects of his future writing. It was a book strong on rhetoric and convincing in its arguments, but sporadically forgetful in its economic history[7].

[7] The English Historian AJP Taylor (1962) claims, with some justice, that by painting Germany as the victim of a rapacious coalition of victors, Keynes helped to create a too understanding and too sympathetic mindset amongst the political and intellectual class in England during the interwar years. He takes clear issue with Keynes' assertion that reparation demands on Germany were overly onerous.

As Patinkin remarks, Keynes' first major work in monetary theory, *A Tract on Monetary Reform* was 'not really a book, but a short and somewhat unsystematic revision and elaboration of the series of articles on post-war economic policy that Keynes first published in 1922 in the "Reconstruction Supplements" of the *Manchester Guardian Commercial*'. (Patinkin, 2003b: 351–352) These essays, like others, initially written for the press and later collected (as in the aptly named *Essays in Persuasion*), all allowed Keynes to 'give full expression to his brilliant publicist style'. (Patinkin, 2003b: 365)

No matter what style he ultimately chose, what was almost always uppermost in Keynes' writing was the need to convince his readers. *The Treatise on Money* (1930) is perhaps his least successful of his economic works because 'it represents a Keynes out of character: a Keynes attempting to act the role of a Professor, and a Germanic one at that'. (Patinkin, 2003b: 365). The work commits the cardinal sin of being unable to sway the majority of its readership.

Perhaps, this leads him in *The General Theory* (1936) back to using a rhetorical strategy with which he was always, ultimately, more comfortable. Unlike his newspaper articles he addressed this work (as he did with *The Treatise* (1930)) chiefly to his fellow economists. Where then lies the difference? There would be no more Germanic professors on stage this time. Instead, the volume would resemble a testimony to sustained battles with his inner intellectual demons while journeying toward a more rational and general understanding of economic issues. What Keynes claims to have done in *The General Theory* is to write down the fruit of his "struggle of escape from habitual modes of thought and expression". (1936: viii). He indicates clearly in the preface what this rhetorical strategy would be.

> The ideas which are here expressed so laboriously are ideas which are extremely simple and should be obvious. The difficulty lies, not in the new ideas, but in escaping from the old ones, which ramify, for those brought up as most of us have been, into every corner of our minds. (Keynes, 1936: viii)

Keynes realises that he will have to induce economists to make a similar journey. His fellow economists must be made to feel that sticking with the *status quo* offers only a dead end. He must manage to tie in their own self-interest (their hopes for advancement and professional recognition) with a belief that at this time of economic crisis they are being provided with a road map out of a theoretical morass. Keynes offered not so much policy prescriptions (others, including those economists at Chicago offered similar programs), as a sound theoretical basis for doing so. He offered an approach that was applicable, not on an *ad hoc* basis, but as part of a convincing explanation of how the economy worked. To do this, Keynes used whatever material happened to come to hand. As a recognised word wizard, it mattered not whether this involved the strategic use of data, conveniently outreaching himself on historical precedents[8], or the opportunity to create a variety of strawman opponents, all of whom provided easy targets for Keynes' brand of exquisite ridicule.

> In the *General Theory* we once again find the true Keynes. Here (as in so many of Keynes's writings) is the stirring voice of a prophet who has seen a new truth, and who is convinced that it — and only it — can save a world deep in the throes of crisis. It is a sharp, polemical voice directed at converting economists all over the world to the new dispensation — and combating the false prophets among them who perversely continue with the erroneous teachings of the earlier gods whom Keynes had already abandoned. (Patinkin, 2003b: 365)

---

[8] To turn the medieval scholastics into a gaggle of proto-economists focused on the problems of dealing with insufficient aggregate demand is a testament to faith that Thomas Aquinas himself might have honoured.

> I was brought up to believe that the attitude of the Medieval Church to the rate of interest was inherently absurd, and the subtle discussions aimed at distinguishing the return on money-loans from the return to active investment were merely Jesuitical attempts to find a practical escape from foolish theory. But I now read these discussions as an honest intellectual effort to keep separate what the classical theory has inextricably confused together, namely, the rate of interest and the marginal efficiency of capital. For it now seems clear that the disquisitions of the schoolmen were directed towards the elucidation of a formula which should allow the schedule of the marginal efficiency of capital to be high, whilst using rule and custom and the moral law to keep down the rate of interest. (Keynes, 1964: 351–352)

Keynes, who often had a sense of what his audience wanted to hear, used his rhetorical skills, honed over many decades, to provide an illusion of hope for the economic profession, especially the younger generation of the breed. Such rhetoric appeals especially to the young, who have less at stake in maintaining the existing wisdom of their elders and more to gain in providing a viable alternative.

> Keynes's analysis was adopted in the main because it seemed to make more sense to most economists. Or, as I put it earlier, it provided a better base for thinking about the problems of the working of the economic system as a whole. And to those economists who were less concerned about the niceties of the analysis, Keynes' policy recommendations undoubtedly provided a sufficient reason for many of them to adopt his theory and to reject that of Hayek. (Coase, 1994b: 21–22)

1.2. *Milton Friedman — The silence of the lambs*

> I congratulate you on restraining yourself from including a picture of Keynes, and even more on not even having a mention of him in your index. (Milton Friedman to George Stigler, 16 December 1986 on the publication of Stigler's fourth edition of *The Theory of Price*)

As already noted, Milton Friedman steadfastly refused to grant any significant degree of originality to Keynes and especially to his most influential work, *The General Theory*. Like Keynes, he was willing to take whatever material came to his hand, stretching and moulding them into effective weapons to undercut Keynes' credibility. In this he was very much like the economist he sought to annihilate. In Friedman's estimation, Keynes had provided a false trail that had been pursued in a mindless manner by the majority of the economics profession. Friedman took it as an obligation to redirect the train of economic thought back down the correct track, but more than theory or even policy stood at stake. As mentioned, Friedman's counter-revolution is framed during a growing Cold War period[9]. For Friedman, one can

[9] Remember that Friedman was an active member of the intellectual counter-revolution represented by the Mt Pelerin Society. Combating totalitarian communism was more important than any minor niceties.

say without blushing, that the battle was over maintaining freedom, choice and individual responsibilities.

In many ways (a comparison that might be all too unflattering to both) Friedman was Keynes' rhetorical doppelganger. They were supremely gifted polemists who could argue a position and drive an opponent relentlessly into the ground[10]. In a manner of speaking, Milton Friedman in battling against the ghost of John Maynard Keynes was in fact shadowboxing with himself. Patinkin's quote (above) essentially describes Keynes as a gifted polemist. However, with only minor alterations, even a somewhat meticulous reader would assume that Patinkin is characterising Friedman.

> In the *Quantity Theory* we once again find the true Friedman. Here (as in so many of Friedman's writings) is the stirring voice of a prophet who has seen a new truth, and who is convinced that it — and only it — can save a world deep in the throes of crisis. It is a sharp, polemical voice directed at converting economists all over the world to the new dispensation — and combating the false prophets among them who perversely continue with the erroneous teachings of the earlier gods whom Friedman had already abandoned.

---

[10] With the possible exception of his close friend George Stigler, Milton Friedman was basically unbeatable in a one on one debate. (Unfortunately Stigler and Friedman were never known to take opposing views on any key economic issue.) He would literally wear down an opponent whatever his actual knowledge on a given subject might be.

> He [Milton Friedman] was always patient, always polite, never got short tempered like I do in an argument, never got nasty. He was a horrible person to argue with, just a nightmare. My idea of a nightmare is to stand on a stage and debate with him in front of the public. I watched him debating at Cambridge with Joan Robinson on flexible exchange rates. Unbelievable! I mean, Joan Robinson was one of the world's most aggressive, hostile, debaters. He wiped her analytically, he wiped her rhetorically, and he had the entire audience eating out of his hand, after an hour, an hour and a half. An amazing, amazing guy, but a madman, a madman. One of the few people I could strangle with my bare hands. I feel I could actually do it. (Conversation with Marc Blaug, July 1998)

One of Friedman's strengths as a would-be prophet was a rare talent (one also possessed by his compatriot, George Stigler) of asking the right question. This might be a more important and much rarer talent than an ability to actually grind out potential answers. Like that of any other economist, only some of Friedman's results have survived the test of time. However, what his finely tuned economic intuition recognised in those post-war years was the woeful underdevelopment of monetary theory (particularly in the case of demand for money functions). Keynes himself had at least implicitly recognised this deficiency in his post *General Theory* debates (conducted in the *Economic Journal*) with the Stockholm School (as represented by Bertil Ohlin)[11]. Ill health, the war, and ultimately a relatively early death conspired to prevent a follow-up book to *The General Theory*. But this did by no means imply that he went silent on the matter of monetary theory. The explication of a 'finance motive' was one attempt to expand and deepen his liquidity preference model. However, with the death of Keynes in 1946 a dearth of research in monetary matters followed. Friedman in his usual elbows first way-pushed the monetary question to the surface of economic debate, adopting a manner that could brook no silence. In doing so, he was able to determine the terms of debate and essentially capture the high ground from the napping Keynesians at Harvard and elsewhere.

To capture the high ground meant framing the debate in a manner that would be sure to elicit a savage response from the profession. The target then could not be the correctness of Keynes' work, but rather its value. To deny Keynes his place in the economic sun ultimately required misinterpreting him. But there existed a clear compulsion to do so. It is far more dismissive to argue that he had nothing new or important to say, than to attempt to prove that he was wrong or in error. To do the latter is to dignify an opponent's work with a

[11] The debate scrupulously covered in these two volumes makes it clear that none of the combatants mentioned Keynes' own quandaries after publishing *The General Theory*. As far as these debates are concerned, Keynes' thoughts on monetary theory largely came to an end with *The General Theory*.

sense of importance. There is no evidence, despite some ill-tempered charges[12], that Milton Friedman conducted his attack on Keynes with anything like malice aforethought. But like many others with the instinct of a polemist, he was skilled at finding within a work exactly what he needed to see[13]. Unfortunately, the structure of *The General Theory* makes it far too easy to misunderstand and even to distort Keynes' purpose[14].

---

[12] The debate tended to heat up. Harry Johnson was never one to avoid blunt opinions though never in a one-sided fashion. If he was unsparing of the motives behind Friedman's counter-revolution, he was equally merciless towards the original Keynesian revolution.

> Nevertheless, one should not be too fastidious in condemnation of the techniques of scholarly chicanery used to promote a revolution or a counter-revolution in economic theory. The Keynesian revolution derived a large part of its intellectual appeal from the deliberate caricaturing and denigration of honest and humble scholars, whose only real crime was that they happened to exist and stand in the way of the success of the revolution. (Johnson, 2003: 179)

[13] Friedman's position on Keynes changed very little. In 1971 he would still give Keynes almost no credit by asserting that Keynes in *The General Theory* deviated little from his ideas in the *Tract*. The latter, as Keynes himself acknowledged, was very much in the Cambridge Quantity Theory tradition. Friedman is implicitly asserting that Keynes' 'struggle of escape from habitual modes of thought and expression,' (Keynes, 1964: viii) was either a case of self-delusion or an instance of deliberate fraud.

> The major points which Milton made is that there is nothing particularly Keynesian about the liquidity preference function, and that the demand for money sections of the *General Theory* are simply a slightly inferior version of Keynes' views in the *Tract*. (Stanley Fisher quoted in Leeson, 2003e: 513)

[14] Too many economists (Friedman being no exception) seem to have skimmed over most of the later chapters of *The General Theory*. Instead they focus only on an almost textbook-type version of the more familiar bits. This belies an inability, or unwillingness, to read a text in any way other than in a linear fashion, as though dutiful students attending a typical lecture. Keynes does not opt to follow such a mundane structural form favoured by the profession. (Perhaps this is why *The Treatise* found more favour amongst his Chicago readers as well as others of that period). Keynes

The ever-garrulous Mark Twain is reputed to have remarked 'Everyone talks about the weather but no one does anything about it'. After trudging my way through endless pages in this two-volume edited collection, a number of which purport to discuss and make assertions about *The General Theory* (including Keynes' presentation of monetary theory), it seems fair to conclude that everyone talks about *The General Theory*, but no one appears to have read it. Economists seem to single out a few convenient paragraphs, or even lines, as though Keynes had simply amassed a collection of unrelated topics and jammed the result into a single volume. It has become something of a universal truth that most economists find it extremely difficult to approach a work having first jettisoned all of their more regrettable preconceptions. Consequently, many let those same preconceptions overrule their comprehension. Once again, to paraphrase Mark Twain, 'Reports of *The General Theory* have been greatly exaggerated'.

The first casualty of such an approach is inevitably any balanced or objective assessment of the perceived opposition. Caricature and ridicule become prime rhetorical weapons in unseating the *status quo* provided by mainstream theory. In other words, it simply is not enough to provide a solid and even superior alternative to the existing theory. That reigning theory itself had to be denigrated. By doing this, entrepreneurial economists could manage to strategically shift the terms of debate towards more conducive territory. The entrenched mainstream had to be reduced to a form of repetitive idiocy. This could be done by transforming intellectual and economic history into a series of fractured fairy tales for well-behaved infants. The aim was to provoke the opposition into debating along prearranged terms. The worst response for any intellectual warrior of this

---

takes a literary approach, combining circularity with more linear exposition. The entire book lies within the first three chapters with the remaining ones circling back to deepen and make more explicit the bones of the framework glimpsed at the beginning. In a sense these are circular blocks of exposition written within ever larger circular blocks. Those readers with a few months to spare might do well to invest in an intensive reading of Proust's epic work *Remembrances of Times Past* for a precise example of how such a narrative structure works in the field of literature.

type has always been silence. Deliberately generating outrage allowed the would-be revolutionary (or counter-revolutionary) to seize control of the debate. If confronted by overwhelming armies of fact or logic, a tactical retreat of one kind or another was always possible. But by that time the damage would have been done. The focus of debate would have noticeably shifted.

> I think Milton quietly changed, he just quietly dropped that [100% reserve ratio in banking]. He doesn't particularly announce changes in positions, but instead, lets them just decay away. (Conversation with Paul Samuelson, November 1997)

The bare bones of Keynes' monetary theory, as presented in *The General Theory*, are fairly straightforward. For Keynes, interest rates equilibrate the supply and demand for money. But it does so through basic stock adjustments between those wishing to hold money assets and those preferring non-money assets (or bonds in the short hand adopted by Keynes). Money mattered, but only indirectly by affecting the nominal rate of interest[15]. This in turn when placed in combination with the marginal efficiency of capital determined investment. Thus, money could change the real economy by helping to alter a component of aggregate demand. However, interest rates tended to be sticky downwards, because attached to the loan process itself are ineradicable transaction costs, the expectations of both lenders and borrowers can over (or under) estimate prevailing risk and the expectations of speculators largely depend on the past behaviour of these same rates. This leads them to adopt what Keynes calls a conventional view of current and future rates when making monetary decisions.

> It might be more accurate, perhaps, to say that the rate of interest is a highly conventional, rather than a highly psychological, phenomenon. For its value

[15] Not in any simple monotonic function since investors could see a drop in nominal interest rates as signalling an expectation of lower aggregate demand. Such expectations would lead to a drop in the marginal efficiency of capital schedule. Depending on the size of the drop in the marginal efficiency of capital relative to the nominal interest rate, investment might increase (though the amount would be relatively diminished), remain unchanged or shrink.

> is largely governed by the prevailing view as to what its value is expected to be. *Any* level of interest which is accepted with sufficient conviction as likely to be durable will be durable; subject, of course, in a changing society to fluctuations for all kinds of reasons round the expected normal. (Keynes, 1964: 203)

The profession's obsession with the idea of a liquidity trap, where the demand for money becomes perfectly elastic, is only of theoretical (and thus minor) importance for the practical-minded Keynes. Observation led him to believe that interest rates had not been (and would not be) pushed so low as ever to test the seriousness of such a hypothetical problem. The effectiveness of monetary policy is almost inevitably limited in a depression since it will prove impossible to push the nominal interest rate sufficiently low to induce an adequate increase in investment.

> But the most stable, and the least easily shifted, element in our contemporary economy has been hitherto, and may prove to be in future, the minimum rate of interest acceptable to the generality of wealth-owners. (Keynes, 1964: 309)

Agree with Keynes or not, it is an unwarranted leap to identify Keynes' monetary analysis with that of the quantity theory.

> ... the term 'income-velocity of money' carries with it the misleading suggestion of a presumption in favour of the demand for money as a whole being proportional, or having some determinate relation, to income, whereas this presumption should apply, as we shall see, only to a *portion* of the public's cash holdings; with the result that it overlooks the part played by the rate of interest. (Keynes, 1964: 194)

Yet Friedman insists that Keynes is a quantity theorist. As he states 'if Keynes were alive today he would no doubt be at the forefront of the counter-revolution. You must never judge a master by his disciples'. (Friedman quoted in Leeson 2003e: 263). Ultimately, to understand Friedman's audacious claim we need to analyse his interpretation of *The General Theory*.

Friedman's grasp of *The General Theory* is best understood in his one attempt to confront his critics or to be more specific, to annihilate

Patinkin. In a typical adversarial style, Friedman is not content to indicate where their differences lie, or where Patinkin has misunderstood the existing evidence, but to utterly destroy Patinkin's arguments so that Friedman may then ceremoniously piss on their smouldering ashes. One of the ways of doing so is to dismiss Patinkin's understanding of Keynes' *The General Theory.* But equally important, Friedman aims to reinforce his previous claim that Keynes contributed nothing new when laying out his liquidity preference framework. Friedman concedes to Keynes only one innovation in *The General Theory* that distinguishes it from the much earlier *Tract on Monetary Reform*, a work Keynes clearly acknowledged as being in the tradition of the Quantity Theory.

> There is one respect — and I believe only one — in which the discussion of the demand curve for money in the *General Theory* is distinctively Keynesian and that is the importance attached to 'absolute liquidity preference' or a high-interest elasticity of the demand for money. This element is distinctively Keynesian in the double sense that it is, so far as I know, introduced for the first time in the *General Theory*. (Friedman, 2003e: 157)

As previously discussed, the idea of a potential liquidity trap, despite the endless discussion by Keynesian and non-Keynesian economists alike, is far from the key focus of Keynes' analysis of the role and effectiveness of monetary policy. The major, though brief, discussion of the problem is on p. 202 where at low rates, the probability of a capital loss from rising rates is greater than the loss of a small yield from remaining liquid.

> ... a long-term rate of interest of (say) 2 per cent, leaves more to fear than to hope, and offers, at the same time, a running yield which is only sufficient to offset a very small measure of fear. (Keynes, 1936: 202)

Friedman realises that if he can convince economists that Keynes had nothing to offer but the liquidity trap, he can trivialise Keynes' contribution, dismiss Patinkin's criticism and also undercut Patinkin's own work which was an attempt to transform Keynes' work into a more rigorous analytic model. Whether Friedman could feasibly accomplish this should depend on what actually is written in *The General*

Theory. It is essentially an empirical question. Friedman does seem to treat it this way, but in fact simply reads into Keynes' work the meaning he needs to find there. Friedman states:

> Patinkin objects to my treating 'the case of "absolute liquidity preference" — as part of "Keynes's basic challenge to the reigning theory".' He cites as counterevidence Keynes's own statement ... that 'whilst this limiting case might become practically important in the future' he knew 'of no example of it hitherto'. ... More important, Patinkin does not quote the sentence immediately following Keynes's disclaimer, to wit, 'indeed, owing to the unwillingness of most monetary authorities to deal boldly in debts of long term, there has not been much of an opportunity for a test'. (Friedman, 2003e: 157–158)

This statement, from page 207 of *The General Theory*, also quoted in the appendix of Friedman's Absolute Liquidity Preference statements (2003e: 161–162), is beset with two problems. First, while accusing Patinkin of not quoting the next line, Friedman is also guilty of not quoting the line that then follows, 'Moreover, if such a situation were to arise, it would mean that the public authority itself could borrow through the banking system on an unlimited scale at a nominal rate of interest'. (Keynes, 1936: 207) Friedman also conveniently overlooks the fact that throughout the book, Keynes is more interested in what he has observed happening than he was in theoretical possibilities. The other reasons he provides for concluding that interest rates are sticky downwards are all empirically observed and are sufficient to account for the current and future situations.

Friedman then attempts to bury Patinkin's observation concerning Absolute Liquidity Preference by baldly stating

> Neither does Patinkin note that, so far as I can discover, this is the only disclaimer in the *General Theory*: while there are repeated statements in the opposite direction, such as, to pick only one, 'The most stable, and least easily shifted element in our contemporary economy has been hitherto, and may prove to be in the future, the minimum rate of interest acceptable to the generality of wealth-owners'. (Friedman, 2003e: 158)

Again, Friedman succumbs here to the temptation of stopping a quotation at a strategically advantageous point, rather than where Keynes' full meaning becomes clear. If we carry on with Friedman's quotation we find that Keynes is not obsessed by absolute liquidity preference in the sense that Friedman means.

> If a tolerable level of employment requires a rate of interest much below the average rates which ruled in the nineteenth century, it is most doubtful whether it can be achieved merely by manipulating the quantity of money. From the percentage gain, which the schedule of marginal efficiency of capital allows the borrower to expect to earn, there has to be deducted (1) the cost of bringing borrowers and lenders together, (2) income and sur-taxes and (3) the allowance which the lender requires to cover his risk and uncertainty, before we arrive at the net yield available to tempt the wealth-owner to sacrifice his liquidity. If, in conditions of tolerable average employment, this net yield turns out to be infinitesimal, time-honoured methods may prove unavailing. (Keynes, 1936: 309)

Friedman, however, perhaps because it is in his own interest, manages to convince himself that he sees what is in fact not apparent in Keynes' work. He somehow dismisses mentally everything else relevant to the interest rates and monetary policy except for one single aspect. Though there is no evidence that Friedman does this consciously or even cynically, his analysis remains without sufficient textual support.

> One consequence of my rereading large parts of the *General Theory* in the course of writing this reply has been to reinforce my view that absolute liquidity preference plays a key role. Time and again when Keynes must face up to precisely what it is that prevents a full-employment equilibrium, his final line of defense is absolute liquidity preference. To document this point, I have assembled the relevant quotations in Appendix 1. ... I do not see how anyone can read through these quotations and come to any other conclusion than that his 'special twist' was highly elastic liquidity preference and that this 'was a key element in Keynes's proposition' about the possibility that there might not be a full-employment equilibrium even with flexible prices. Patinkin sees the fly on the barn door but not the door! (Friedman, 2003e: 158–159)

Friedman unfortunately seems prone to confuse the fly with the barn door. Since Keynes' contribution must be trivialised to strategically forward his own counter-revolution, Friedman turns Keynes into a quantity theorist (much to Keynes' own surprise were he still alive). To further this aim, Friedman lists what he characterises as 13 relevant quotes. Unfortunately, some of them have nothing to do with the idea of absolute liquidity preference while others are taken out of context. It is sufficient to state two clear examples.

> Circumstances can develop in which even a large increase in the quantity of money may exert a comparatively small influence on the rate of interest. (Keynes, 1936: 172)

If Friedman had bothered to trudge further along the paragraph, he would have discovered that the quote clearly reflects the role played by expectations and uncertainty rather than absolute liquidity preference. Such circumstances are not restricted to very low interest rate levels. The actual quote continues:

> For a large increase in the quantity of money may cause so much uncertainty about the future that liquidity-preferences due to the security-motive may be strengthened; whilst opinion about the future of the rate of interest may be so unanimous that a small change in present rates may cause a mass movement into cash. It is interesting that the stability of the system and its sensitiveness to changes in the quantity of money should be so dependent on the existence of a *variety* of opinion about what is uncertain. (Keynes, 1936: 172)

This may be what Friedman wants to denote as absolute liquidity preference but Keynes reserves this terminology for a special case dependant on very low interest rates. Nor is Friedman correct in insisting that the following quote also demonstrates Keynes' fixation with absolute liquidity preference. It is Friedman who finds liquidity traps embedded within each and every paragraph dealing with monetary issues. These discoveries remain largely fictitious.

> ... the position of equilibrium, under conditions of *laissez faire*, will be one in which employment is low enough and standard of life sufficiently miserable to bring savings to zero. (Keynes, 1936: 217–218)

Even the idly curious might wonder what the connection is between such a mystifying statement and any idea (no matter how strained) of absolute liquidity preference. The concise answer is that the connection is largely, if not entirely, absent. The quote is found in a chapter entitled,

'Observations on the Nature of Capital'. It deals with a hypothetical situation in which capital has accumulated to the level where its marginal efficiency is zero. The problem is to continue to generate additional investment even under such a situation, especially given the fact that nominal interest rates are sticky downwards. Keynes might have focused on absolute liquidity preference here, but clearly chooses not to. This indicates the relevant weight Keynes attached to such a concept.

> We have seen that capital has to be kept scarce enough in the long-period to have a marginal efficiency which is at least equal to the rate of interest for a period equal to the life of the capital, as determined by psychological and institutional conditions. What would this involve for a society which finds itself so well equipped with capital that its marginal efficiency is zero and would be negative with any additional investment; yet possessing a monetary system, such that money will 'keep' and involves negligible costs of storage and safe custody, with the result that in practice interest cannot be negative; and, in conditions of full employment, disposed to save? (Keynes, 1936: 162)

Friedman, like Keynes, displayed a similar rhetorical strategy. Both can be viewed as accomplished polemists focused on policy matters. Both clearly are ideologically driven. Intellectual history, economic history and even data are so much grist for their strategic mills. They do not knowingly bend facts, but see them in such a way that what comes to hand seems to fortuitously conform to prior requirements. Thus, as can be determined in Sec. 2, Patinkin could marshal his arguments and facts in a more objective fashion than Friedman. Johnson could deftly expose Friedman's motivations. Yet, Friedman could end up trumping both his former colleagues. Marketing, knowing how to anticipate the demands of the profession, is at least as important as the content of the theories presented.

2. Knocking on Heaven's Door — Loyalties, Betrayals and Obfuscation

> I turned on the radio. G. Gordon Liddy was answering a caller's question about morality and loyalty. G. Gordon said he had gone to jail in the Watergate case because he refused to lie under oath ...You give your loyalty to someone and you don't betray it even if the person you've given it to abandons you. (Kaminsky, 1999: 230)

There is more than a stale whiff of Alain Resnais classic film, *La Guerre est Finie* lingering around the pages of these two bulky volumes. That movie, as older cineastes may recall, depicts the almost forgotten struggle of a group of anti-Franco partisans sometime in the 1960s. What compels them to continue is not so much their stated objective as the ongoing process, the sense of belonging. Achieving their aims is subordinate to the bonds formed between members and the unquestioning mutual acceptance that defines fighting either in a revolutionary or counter-revolutionary struggle.

It would be reaching too far to claim that Milton Friedman and his loyal band of allies were less than interested in overturning the despotism of the Keynesian revolution. Like any dedicated counter-revolutionary, Friedman's strong ideological grounding insured that policy objectives were always uppermost in his mind. It is fair to say that loyalty to those in the group was almost indistinguishable from loyalty to the ideology that defined the group. There is certainly a strong sense of *Henry V* about his project[16], in the strategies adopted and the tactics devised to win battles. Chicago, under the very active

[16] Think of his band of brothers' speech at Agincourt (St Crispian's day) to gain the parallel here. As a colleague who was unwilling to be quoted ('I have to work with these people.') summarised, 'If you were not one of their group you were scorned'.

> Now, what you have to understand with somebody like Alan Wallis, and so to a degree those people [like Milton Friedman and George Stigler] who were in his circle, is that Alan Wallis had the sharpest priors — I'm using the language of Bayesian probability — of anybody I ever knew. Almost no new data could change his view for this reason. On the other hand, if he thought of somebody as a dangerous, or an incompetent thinker, but Jimmy Savage assured him that the man was very smart and had good judgment that carried more weight with Alan Wallis than a two-year study of the person's vitae and an audit of his writings. There's an in-group of the good guys and the much larger out-group. George Stigler, who was very critical of people, was almost worshipful of Milton Friedman. And I remember that one of his dicta was that a Milton Friedman theorem was more credible than any other theorem, because everybody picks on Milton. It's an unfair world and so forth which means that he gets a more rigorous testing than anyone else. (Conversation with Paul Samuelson, November 1997)

generalship of Friedman and Stigler, expected and rewarded loyalty[17]. (Those loyal to them happened to turn out work that won their strong approval and vice versa.) Suspected apostates on the order of Don Patinkin and Harry Johnson could expect little mercy if seen to pose something of a palpable threat[18].

In essence, these two volumes deliver what is almost a morality play focused on divided loyalties. The admixture of polemical opponents, ideological foes, along with the human sentiment of frustration and envy succeeded in driving this inexorable and entrenched debate for some 35 years. A mere tiff over a minor point concerning the origin of ideas could never sustain an argument that dominated so many pages in the journals of their time. From any objective standpoint, the surface crux of the argument was an interesting, but hardly earth-shattering issue for historians of thought.

Why should such a relatively minor issue have ignited an increasingly rancorous debate? In essence there are interlinked regions within this debate that are broadly covered by this large collection of articles. Most narrowly there are the pure intellectual history issues, which, at least some of the disputants maintain, comprehend the

---

[17] What was labelled the Chicago School operated as a very close-knit community with a common ideology and a sense of a shared and vital project. (What could matter more than shoving the profession back on the right track after having been diverted down a spur line by the Keynesian revolution and attempts to undermine the core paradigm of perfect competition?) Like any other 'band of brothers', perceived disloyalty, because it so often ideologically based, is viewed as something akin to betrayal that must necessary meet with severe punishment.

> One Senior Fellow [at the Hoover Institute] expressed his admiration for both Friedman and Stigler but was surprised when they both walked out of a seminar given by a newly recruited junior economist who had expressed support for some aspects of Galbriath's work. The junior economist was promptly removed from the Hoover Institution. (Leeson, 1997: 34)

[18] We could see this as the archetypal Western, a modern day version of 'Pat Garrett and Billy the Kid'. Patinkin naturally plays the conscience-stricken Marshall appalled at the increasing notoriety gained by the stop at nothing gunslinger, Milton Friedman. If we then add in Harry Johnson as the typical hard-drinking, cynical journalist from back East, the drama is set with the players ready to act out their roles.

entirety of the issues, at hand. From this simplified standpoint, the only question of interest concerns Friedman's accuracy. This is an entirely factual issue, though the ever-present need for interpreting those rather slippery facts means that the available evidence can sometimes fail to speak for itself. However, if what was involved was purely a factual history of thought question, it would have hardly received such extensive (and intensive) attention.

The more compelling issue (and that which reflects on larger economic areas) remains, as previously stated, ferreting out Friedman's overarching reason for such a statement at all. The last, and more general, problem underlying this long-running debate deals with Monetarist versus Keynesian positions and the policy questions associated with them. Today, that particular controversy has largely receded safely into the mists of History of Thought. Yet, in many ways, the same issues are very much alive between the descendants of these associated theoretical and policy-oriented stances. Clearly, the first and last questions are to a large extent shaped and driven by the middle issue.

On the face of it then, the Patinkin/Friedman quarrel was essentially an absurd feud. No one should have rightfully cared except those intrigued by doctrinal positions. But in the perverse manner that these contests occasionally can unfold, Friedman's claim provided his opponents with an opening through which a counter-attack could be launched. Ironically, Friedman's rhetorical attempt to discredit Keynes would be used as a leverage point to undermine Friedman's own credibility. Patinkin and Johnson glimpsed the possibility of taking away Friedman's ability to define the terms of debate. In the grand tradition of von Clausewitz, Friedman always attempted to capture ruthlessly the high ground in any extended campaign. In fact, it was Friedman's consistent ability to determine the terrain for debate and its associated rules that seemed, in part, to insure the predictability of his growing and continuing great success.

> [Friedman] has frequently trapped and sandbagged critics of reputation and integrity by the technique of under-disclosure of analysis and evidence and apparent overstatements of the strength of his results. (Johnson quoted in Leeson, 2003: 261)

As stated, this fiercely fought controversy had its roots entangled in unresolved issues dealing with conflicting loyalties. The underlying loyalties that helped fuel the conflict trace back to Friedman and Stigler's Chicago days as graduate students during the early thirties. Like others of that era, they were both very much dazzled by Frank Knight.

> Knight had a very strong influence on George Stigler and all the graduate students. ... At that stage he was, as many people were at the University of Chicago, quite besotted with Frank Knight. ... Frank Knight's influence on the student body was profound and not, I say in retrospect, a hundred per cent positively constructive. ... In fact, Knight's major influence at that time resulted in the view that Knight had done everything and there was nothing left to do. (Conversation with Paul Samuelson, October 1997)

Knight however was not impressed by Keynes. The feeling might have been mutual. In the *General Theory* (1964), Keynes makes little or no reference to Knight's theory of risk and uncertainty despite the key role that uncertainty plays in Keynes' model of the economy. The one reference is a footnote (1964: 176n.2) that mentions Knight's observation regarding the nature of capital. Whether from personal antipathy, wounded self-pride or irreconcilable theoretical differences, Knight's reaction to Keynes' work in *The General Theory* (1964) was starkly virulent[19]. He correctly recognised Keynes as a polemist, which was not in his vocabulary as a term of endearment.

> In his review of the *General Theory*, Knight ... complained that Keynes' references to 'classical economists' were 'the sort of caricatures which are typically set up as straw men for purposes of attack in controversial writing'. He sought to defend his own Chicago teaching from Keynes' influence: 'In the great majority of cases the doctrines so labelled [as classical]

---

[19] Keynes was presented with the opportunity by the editor of the *Canadian Journal* to reply to Knight's strongly worded review.

> ... Keynes declined, saying that 'with Professor Knight two main conclusions, namely, that my book caused him intense irritation, and that he had had great difficulty in understanding it, I am in agreement. So perhaps you will excuse me if I leave the article alone'. (Patinkin, 2003d: 384)

> seem to me to be quite at variance with, and often contradictory to anything I was ever taught as academic doctrine in any modern sense … and they are certainly alien to anything I have ever taught as such, and I have been rated, and have supposed myself an adherent of the general type of position referred to by the term. On the other hand, many of Mr Keynes' own doctrines are, as he would proudly admit, among the notorious fallacies to combat which have been considered a main function of the teaching of economics'. Knight noted that 'where once it was necessary in writing to pose as merely restating and interpreting doctrine handed down from the Fathers, the surest way to public interest and acclaim now lies through pulling down and overturning everything established or accepted'. (Leeson, 2003e: 17)

Knight always made his animosity to Keynes' economic contribution apparent. This flared into full-hearted contempt when in 1940 Jacob Viner proposed awarding Keynes an honorary doctorate during Chicago's 50th anniversary celebrations. To say the least, Knight found the idea offensive.

> Knight grumbled that Keynes' work, and the enthusiasm with which it had been greeted by academics and policymakers, had created 'one of my most important … sources of difficulty in recent years'. After crediting Keynes with 'a very unusual intelligence, in the sense of ingenuity and dialectical skill', he went on to complain: 'I have come to consider such capacities, directed to false and subversive ends, as one of the most serious dangers in the whole project of education … I regard Mr. Keynes's [views] with respect to money and monetary theory in particular … as, figuratively speaking, passing the keys of the citadel out of the window to the Philistines hammering at the gates'. (Bernstein, 1999: 222)[20]

[20] Knight went on to make his contempt for Keynes' monetary theory even more explicit.

> I regard Mr. Keynes' neo-mercantilistic position in economics in general, and with respect to money and monetary theory in particular, as essentially taking the side of the man-in-the-street, against the effort of the economic thinker and analyst to get beyond and to dispel the short-sighted views and prejudices of the former … His work and influence seem to me supremely 'anti-intellectual', in the only meaning of intellectual life which is worthy of approval or support. (Knight quoted in Patinkin, 2003e: 385)

Given the respect (and awe) in which Friedman and Stigler both regarded Knight (especially in those early years) it is hard to believe that either one would have been highly receptive to Keynes' views, especially those focused on monetary theory. This vestigial loyalty could only reinforce the desire, as witnessed in the counter-revolution, to dethrone those views.

With Knight as such a common pivotal figure, the break between Friedman and Patinkin should have never started, let alone evolved to such an intense level. Superficially, the two had much in common. Patinkin came to Chicago less than a decade after Friedman first entered. They shared and respected a number of the same teachers including Knight (who Patinkin also greatly admired) and Mints who taught both of them monetary theory. However, in key respects their approaches differed fundamentally. In the field of monetary theory their projects clashed dramatically. While Friedman sought to hack away at the essential structural support of the Keynesian revolution, Patinkin attempted to develop a more rigorous structure for what he defined as the Keynesian model. Patinkin viewed himself as completing the revolution that Keynes began. Friedman's counter-revolution in essence wanted to fit a demand for money model into a generalised framework that described the demand for any other generic flow of services. Once done, this accomplishment would supposedly anchor monetary theory once more in the snug harbour of neoclassical thought. To achieve this objective, Keynes' monetary theory would need to be transformed into a mere incremental addition to this mainstream tradition. It is in part Patinkin's perception of this aim that helped to fuel their quarrel. Patinkin, not without justification, saw Friedman as operating within the tradition of Keynes, benefiting from the pioneering departures that Keynes took from traditional theory, but lacking the integrity to acknowledge his debt.

> Thus the picture which Friedman attempts to create is clear: namely, the conceptual framework he uses for monetary analysis is that of the quantity theory; its basic differences from the Keynesian theory lies in the fact that the latter assumed the demand function for money to become highly (infinitely) interest elastic. As against this picture, I would like to present the following one: the conceptual framework which Friedman uses to analyze the

demand for money is that of the Keynesian theory of liquidity preference — with Friedman's addendum that empirically this demand does not become highly (infinitely elastic), and is indeed relatively inelastic. And, as important as are the policy implications of this addendum, we should not let it wag the theory. (Patinkin, 2003c: 125–126)

While both were very much concerned with policy applications (Patinkin during his many years in Israel made such interests clear), the ideological imperative of Friedman's work might have started to grate. 'In a posthumously published essay, Patinkin stated that in his judgement, Friedman returned to Chicago in 1946 "to continue the school's fundamental ideological advocacy of free-market economic liberalism".' (Leeson, 2003: 2)[21]. That the ideological fervour had increased given the efforts of Friedman after 1946 seems clear; at least this was the impression of a particularly appropriate eyewitness.

It was not until after I left Chicago in 1946 that I began to hear rumors about a 'Chicago School' which was engaged in *organized* battle for *laissez faire* and 'quantity theory of money' against 'imperfect competition' theorizing and 'Keynesianism'. I remained sceptical about this until I attended a conference sponsored by University of Chicago professors in 1951. The invited participants were a varied lot of academics, bureaucrats, businessmen, etc, but the program for discussion, the selection of chairmen, and everything about the participants were so patently rigidly structured, so loaded, that I got more amusement from the conference than from any other I ever attended. Even the source of the financing of the Conference, as I found out later, was ideologically loaded. (Jacob Viner quoted in Patinkin, 2003e: 112)

Patinkin and Friedman also clearly differed on their use of available evidence. Despite Friedman's frequent use of data and his considerable

---

[21] In many ways, 1946 marks the opening bell of the counter-revolution staged by the right-wing intellectuals. The beginning of that year is signalled by Hayak's call to arms at the first Mt Pelerin meeting. This fight against the planned, totalitarian agenda of the left would need to be taken to the campuses, which, as far as Friedman was concerned, were overwhelmingly filled with communist sympathisers.

Friedman calculated that by 1934 'close to a majority' of faculty and students within the social sciences at the University of Chicago were 'either members of the Communist party or very close to it'. (Leeson, 2003g: 288)

empirical work, evidence, whether statistical in nature or historical, was a factor to be managed in order to advance the given objectives rather than a decisive element in resolving disputed claims[22]. In this he displayed a distinct loyalty to approaches taken by the first Chicago

---

[22] Friedman (2003c: 58) makes the clear claim that both Simons and Keynes erred by basing policy recommendations on a misunderstanding of the events that occurred between 1929 and 1933. Had they had the relevant data available that featured in the work that he jointly did with Anna Schwartz (1963), such a mistake would not have been possible.

> The keystone of Simons' interpretation of 1929–1933 was that the trouble originated with business earnings and the shock to business confidence, documented or perhaps initiated by the stock-market crash. The subsequent widespread pressure for liquidation, on his interpretation, left the monetary authorities, narrowly defined, largely powerless. Once the scramble for liquidity was on, there was no way they could prevent a decline in the value of private claims and debts, which in turn rendered banks insolvent, and induced their depositors to try to withdraw deposits. We now know that the critical relations ran precisely the other way. (Friedman, 2003c: 63)

This is a lovely bedtime story resembling those that Keynes also favoured. However, we now know that both Simons and Keynes had access to the same type of monetary data that allowed Friedman to draw contrary conclusions. Laughlin Currie had published the relevant money supply figures in a book (*The Supply and Control of Money in the United States*) published in 1934 and reviewed by Simons in *The Journal of Political Economy.* In that work, Currie attacked Federal Reserve policies as being the root cause of the economic depression.

> Even more relevant to the question at issue … is the fact that in November 1933 Laughlin Currie published an article in the *Quarterly Journal of Economics* in which he provided annual estimates of the money supply for 1921–1932 whose year-to-year percentage changes during the Great Depression are also similar to those described by Friedman and Schwartz. And in April 1934 Currie used this series as the basis of an article which he published in the *Journal of Political Economy* on 'The Failure of Monetary Policy to Prevent the Depression of 1929–1932'. Indeed the major conclusion of this article was that 'The [Federal Reserve] policy followed throughout 1929, so far from tending to prevent the depression, actually operated, in the view of this paper, to bring it on …' Later in that year, Currie published a book on *The Supply and Control of Money in the United State* in which he reproduced the monetary data of his 1933 article. (Patinkin, 2003d: 381)

school where for Knight and his protégé Simons it was *a priori* reasoning, not data, that was ultimately conclusive. It was almost as though their response to contrary evidence would be to question and possibly dismiss data that disagreed with what they knew to be true[23].

> For critical students, however, Dr. Currie's inductive verifications will be largely gratuitous ... In general, the author's fundamental insights are so sound that failure of statistical confirmation would only indicate error or inadequacy in the statistics. (Simons, 2003: 370)

Friedman seemed willing at times to overlook or even ignore evidence that was inconsistent with his *a priori* objectives. '... the categories of "honest" and "dishonest" are quite irrelevant. What is instead relevant is the far more subtle phenomenon involved in human failing (to which we are all subject) of sometimes suppressing that which it

---

[23] For all his empirical work, it is difficult to argue that Friedman used it as anything more than a rhetorical tool. Like his teacher Henry Simons, he did not need data to generate conviction. It is almost a hallmark of Friedman and his loyalists that they are almost immune to empirical evidence.

> It's hard to imagine an empirical observation that would convince most members of this department and the University of Chicago to change their minds. My personal view is that if someone holds a view it cannot be dislodged by any conceivable empirical data. Evidence from a data system doesn't convince them. These people have made their decisions already. They've become true believers and no amount of empirical evidence will ever convince them by definition. (Conversation with Jim Kindahl, October 1997)

It is then ironic that in later years, both Stigler and Friedman came to view Knight as unwilling to accept the empirical evidence that contradicted his *a priori* truths.

> Knight would not look at any data. In fact, Frank could hardly be convinced by any data. Like inequality. Knight always thought inequality was growing in the United States while all the evidence up until 1970 said it was falling. And Stigler and Friedman and others would point this out to Knight, and George told me this, Knight would say 'yes, yes' but next time he'd say the same thing. So, I guess, he differed with Knight in this regard but that was not unusual, he began to differ with Knight in a lot of respects. (Conversation with Gary Becker, October 1997)

would be more convenient for us not to note or remember — with reference to questions to which we are strongly involved'. (Patinkin quoted in Leeson, 2003b: 258). In this way Friedman could deftly ignore the work of someone like Laughlin Currie both because it undercut some of the initial claims he had made regarding the history of monetary theory, and perhaps more importantly, because he considered Currie himself, a communist sympathiser like Harry Dexter White, as disloyal to the United States.

> In 1966, as Brunner [Karl Brunner] was preparing the reprint [of Currie's *Supply and Control of Money in the United States*], Friedman informed him that 'Currie is a fugitive from justice somewhere in South America. ... Friedman did not initially acknowledge Currie's contribution'. (Leeson, 2003g: 289)

Even worse for Patinkin, Friedman seemed to be quite happy to 'let [policy] wag ... theory'. (Patinkin, 2003c: 126). In his discussions about the Chicago Oral tradition, Friedman impressively muddled policy issues with theoretical matters. It is quite true that the policy recommendations put forth by Keynes differed little from those supported by many Chicago economists in the 30s. Though both however might have suggested running budget deficits, the mechanisms through which such a policy might be effective in reviving the economy necessarily differed. In a similar manner, while for someone like Simons this is a short run policy due to exceptional circumstances, Keynes saw the need for government intervention in economic cycles as inevitable, given the nature of the investment function. In contrast to Friedman's deliberate muddle, Patinkin's intention was not to delve into matters concerning policy, but to focus purely on theoretical concerns.

> ... what interests me now is monetary theory, not monetary policy. These represent two different spheres of discourse. And whatever the relationship between the two, it is clearly not a one-to-one correspondence: different policy recommendations can emanate from the same conceptual theoretical framework; and different frameworks can lead to the same policy recommendation. (Patinkin, 2003a: 319)

It is Friedman's willingness to blur these distinguishable areas that created an opportunity for the Patinkin/Friedman debate. Given Friedman's clear policy objectives and ideological stance, it is difficult to believe that Friedman was entirely unaware that he was trying to achieve a policy objective via a theoretical debate. In the same way, Don Patinkin (and soon after Harry Johnson) used Friedman's rhetorical strategy as an opening to attack Friedman's creditability. They tried to neutralise Friedman's ability to determine the terms of debate. What seems clear is that despite Patinkin's and Johnson's evident frustration with Friedman, which led to some of their more extreme comments, Friedman himself did not stoop to dishonesty. However, he remained at heart something of a guerrilla commando, a tough fighter leading a counter-revolution against what he viewed as a dangerous heresy where battles were conducted according to the sharp elbowed rules of war. He did not let niceties of conduct deflect him from his all-important objectives, nor did he neglect building up the loyal support of his fellow counter-revolutionaries. Nonetheless, shorn of policy issues and distractions (a veritable fog of war), Patinkin did have a strong case to make on purely theoretical grounds. This is one of the rewards to be garnered from a detailed reading of the evidence provided in these two volumes.

> In any event, the examples of Simons, Pigou, and others have led me to suspect that the real Keynesian Revolution took place not in the sphere of economic policy where change were already occurring in the early 1930s), but in that of economic theory. I suspect that the real change wrought by Keynes's *General Theory* was in the conceptual framework from which we viewed the problems of employment, interest and money. (Patinkin, 2003a: 321)

What seems correct is that Milton Friedman on his return to Chicago (1946) brought with him the seeds of a crusade, snugly secured in his ideological knapsack. He entrenched himself there despite being granted relatively low pay at an associate professor's rank. He endured the indignity of only being offered the position after the department's first choice (George Stigler) was overruled by the then University

President[24]. Moreover, Friedman faced a department where the traditional liberalism espoused by Knight and Simons was under attack. Friedman's efforts did see the Cowles Commission (producing highly theoretical and econometric work which lacked appeal for Friedman as did their research work conducted in the Keynesian tradition) move from Chicago to its current base at Yale University. In contrast, Patinkin from an early age worked closely with the Cowles people. Ultimately, though Patinkin deferred to Friedman in his younger years, their ultimate loyalties differed. As is also natural with two very ambitious economists, at different times in their careers, each tended to feel jealous of the recognition accorded to the other.

> As a twenty-four year old, Patinkin was moving in some high-powered circles at Cowles and Chicago: Klein, Hurwicz, Jacob Marchak, Tjalling Koopmans, Trygve Haavelmo and Ragnar Frisch attended the staff seminar on his essay on 'Unemployment in Keynesian Economics' (February 1947). In his early thirties, Patinkin was a valued adviser to David Ben-Gurion ... At this age, he was more influential than Friedman was at a comparable age. In the same year as Friedman's (1956) revival of the quantity theory ... Patinkin ... attempted to consolidate that consensus (the post-war economic consensus) by integrating monetary and value theory ... . (Leeson, 2003f: 234)

As noted earlier, the debate should have run its course soon after it started. Friedman uncharacteristically acknowledged Patinkin's key points. First, Friedman granted Keynes a more significant contribution to monetary theory in his entry on the Quantity Theory to the *International Encyclopedia of the Social Sciences* (1968/2003f).

> Friedman complained that he had revised the entry as Patinkin suggested and had included a reference to Knut Wicksell and made a greater acknowledgment of Keynes' influence. (Leeson, 2003c: 257)

---

[24] Milton Friedman was hired only as an associate professor. A year after he was hired he questioned in a letter to George Stigler whether he should remain at Chicago given that he faced an offer from John Hopkins (through the offices of Fritz Machlup) which provided a noticeably higher salary (an increase of more than 20%). Loyalty to Knight, the department and the University of Chicago prevailed.

Friedman in a letter to Patinkin in 1968 seemed to have completely yielded on the issue of the Chicago oral tradition. In this case, the possible harm incurred by a strategic retreat could be minimised. Friedman had tried a rhetorical ploy. After some critical delay, his bluff had been called. But, as Friedman well knew, such ploys could be jettisoned without touching the core of his theoretical work.

> I find your description of the oral tradition entirely acceptable and much better and more acceptable than mine. In extenuation, I can only say that the 1956 essay did not set out to be an essay in the history of thought but an introduction to a collection of studies. (Friedman quoted in Leeson, 2003c: 257)

What remained, after sweeping away most of this superficial and distracting dust, were the core differences that formed an unbridgeable gulf between the two major combatants. Patinkin and Friedman had developed theoretical projects characterised by their conflicting and opposing natures. This is most clearly demonstrated when comparing their very different evaluations of Keynes. This clash, however, belonged firmly to the then ongoing Monetarist/Keynesian debate. Issues surrounding monetary theory in the 30s were a sideshow, rather than an intrinsic or clarifying component. There was really nothing more to discuss about some mythical oral tradition based in Chicago. The modest tempest should have staged a quiet retreat back into the teapot from whence it arose. But both sides remained inflexible. Neither one wanted to yield any potentially strategic territory.

> I continue to regard what I wrote as a reformulation of the quantity theory of money, just as I continue to regard Keynes' Monetary Reform, and large parts of his Treatise, and some parts of his Gen. Theory, as the writings of a quantity theorist. I have increasingly become persuaded that the really Keynesian element ... in the Gen. Theory is the treatment of prices as institutional datum. (Friedman quoted in Leeson, 2003c: 257)

Perhaps, ultimately, time would have buried this particular extended tiff. Unfortunately, an idiosyncratic squabble was provided with a second life through the mischievous intervention of James Tobin. Quite opportunistically, he saw this debate as a tempting chance to score points against the growing power of monetarism. Friedman's star had risen alarmingly following his 1968 AEA presidential speech and later with the fortuitous rise of stagflation in the US economy. As a president of the American Economic Association that year, Tobin would have had the prerogative to determine the programme for that year's meeting. While his own 1970 presidential speech would take the high road by responding indirectly to Friedman through his theoretical take on inflation, he would delegate the trench warfare to Harry Johnson, who, like his colleague Milton Friedman, had a 'no quarter given or asked for' approach to economics.

In many ways, Johnson's dissection of Friedman's motives serves as a warm up for his later deconstruction of Keynes accomplished in partnership with his wife Elisabeth. Johnson simply uses standard economic tools to establish Friedman's objectives and the methods he used to accomplish them. In doing so, Johnson was highly successful, although his portrait would not endear itself to either the subject of such a merciless analysis or those closely associated with him or with his counter-revolution. This is a clear case of self-interest creating strong bonds of loyalty.

> My concern, specifically, is with the reasons for the speed of propagation of the monetarist counter-revolution; but I cannot approach this subject without reference to the reasons for the speed of propagation of the Keynesian revolution, since the two are interrelated. Indeed, I find it useful in posing and treating the problem to adopt the 'as if' approach of positive economics, as expounded by the chief protagonist of the monetarist counter-revolution, Milton Friedman, and to ask: suppose I wished to start a counter-revolution against the Keynesian revolution in monetary theory, how would I go about it — and specifically what could I learn about the technique from the revolution itself? (Johnson, 2003: 171)

Clearly Johnson is hoisting Friedman by his own peculiar petard of positivism. But Johnson is particularly insightful in establishing the hows and the whys of creating both successful revolutions and counter-revolutions in academic endeavours. Johnson makes the compelling point that monetarism, if it was to provide a successful staging ground for a counter-revolution, could not be content in presenting itself as some mere generalisation of Keynesian liquidity preference. Wiser tactics must insist on a complete divorce from its rival by claiming descent from an older tradition. This approach, while convenient, was not unfortunately free from difficulty.

> A counter-revolution, however, has to cope somehow with a problem that a revolution by definition can ignore ... the problem of establishing some sort of continuity with the orthodoxy of the past. Specifically, the monetarist counter-revolutionaries were burdened with the task of somehow escaping from the valid criticisms of the traditional quantity theory, which the Keynesian revolution had elevated into articles of dogma and self-justification. (Johnson, 2003: 178)

Specifically, monetarists tried to ease their way through this difficulty by making two counter-contentions. The question of the degree to which an economy responds to monetary changes through output or price level displacements could be set aside as simply as an empirical issue. The issue of whether velocity in a demand for money model was stable could be transformed into the more reasonable and tractable question asking if there is a stable functional dependence of velocity on a limited number of variables. (Johnson, 2003: 178)

> The problem in the case of both counter-contentions was to establish a plausible linkage with pre-Keynesian orthodoxy. The solution to this problem was found along two lines. The first was the invention of a University of Chicago oral tradition that was alleged to have preserved understanding of the fundamental truth among a small band of the initiated through the dark years of the Keynesian despotism. The second was a careful combing of the *obiter dicta* of the great neo-classical quantity theorists for any bits of evidence that showed recognition (or could be interpreted to show recognition) of the fact that the decision to hold money involves a choice between holding money and holding wealth in other forms, and is conditioned by the rates of return available on other assets. (Johnson, 2003: 170)

Far more wounding is Johnson's cynical absolution of any academic crime or misbehaviour by Friedman. Almost patronisingly, Johnson caustically defers to Friedman's polemical ends. The cruelty lies in the accuracy of such a comment.

> Nevertheless, one should not be too fastidious in condemnation of the techniques of scholarly chicanery used to promote a revolution or a counter-revolution in economic theory. The Keynesian revolution derived a large part of its intellectual appeal from the deliberate caricaturing and denigration of honest and humble scholars, whose only real crime was that they happened to exist and stand in the way of the success of the revolution. The counter-revolution had to endow these scholars, or at least their intellectual successors, with a wisdom vastly superior to what their opponents had credited them with. *Obiter dicta* and an oral tradition are at least semi-legitimate scholarly means to this polemical end. (Johnson, 2003: 179)

It is fair to say that the disillusionment of both Patinkin and Johnson in Milton Friedman displayed the natural disappointment of two very ambitious and highly intelligent economists. The intensity of their criticism rose with Friedman's overwhelming success and the corresponding relative neglect of Patinkin and Johnson. Perhaps they felt wrongly usurped by him in the same way that Schumpeter had fumed in the shadow of Keynes decades before. Certainly they would have felt their own work to be equal if not superior to that of Friedman. Yet, Friedman received the disproportionate share of attention. However, what might have driven this pair or subsequent opponents, though interesting, is largely irrelevant. Bitterness is not automatically correlated to distortion and inaccuracy. In the case of Patinkin and Johnson, no matter what sense of resentment, bitterness or envy they might continue to harbour, each one tended to fabricate stronger arguments and provide better evidence than the opposing loyalists.

Perhaps, the subsequent vehemence of the response was due to the accuracy of Johnson's attack. Patinkin had inflicted a grievous wound on Friedman's rhetorical strategy but Johnson was worse. He showed how the wizard behind the curtain was manipulating the various levers to produce a desired result. He moreover was rash enough to openly and clearly identify Friedman's polemical objectives. This served as a virtual call to arms for the Friedmanites. The following small example of how skirmishes were conducted demonstrates the overriding value accorded to loyalty within the troops when trying to sweep the field of opposing views.

George Stigler had little interest in macroeconomic matters yet complete confidence in the views of Milton Friedman. If anything, Stigler was a loyalist not only to his friends, but to institutions and ideas as well. It should not then come as a surprise that when presented with the opportunity to damage the perceived opposition, Stigler would display no qualms in seizing it. That opportunity came in the form of a note submitted by Frank Steindl (2003) to *The Journal of Political Economy.* The note purported to discuss the oral tradition of Chicago in the 30s. 'Patinkin believed that Stigler was attempting to ensure that Friedman got the last laugh with respect to the Chicago monetary tradition'. (Leeson, 2003g: 294) Patinkin had every reason to believe this to be the case. The note was accepted without going through the normal refereeing process. A short reply by Patinkin was rejected by Stigler in his role as editor. Patinkin was duly outraged while in contrast, Friedman, as might be expected was quite appreciative of the Steindl piece (Leeson, 2003g: 294). Patinkin's anger was in this case quite justified. Steindl gets the argument wrong. 'For that disagreement was not (as Steindl presents it) about whether or not there was such an oral tradition, but what the nature of that tradition was'. (Patinkin, 2003f: 381) Two years earlier, Stigler had the presumption of using his autobiography (1988: 152–154) to misrepresent Patinkin's views in a similar manner:

> He [Patinkin] informed Laidler ... that Friedman's attempt to defend himself against the criticisms contained in the original *JMCB* essay 'by expounding at length on the Chicago advocacy in the 1930s of an activist monetary and [sic] policy' was irrelevant because the point was 'never in question'. Patinkin continued: 'Unfortunately — for we would expect that a leading historian of thought would base his views on a careful reading of texts' — Stigler in his autobiography attempts to defend Friedman with the same irrelevant argument. (Patinkin quoted in Leeson, 2003g: 296–297)

Unfortunately, partisanship led to a continuation of this debate for another three decades. It is then safe to say that at some stage the initial incentives faded and the debate did dwindle into a squabble over who said what and when it was said. Thus, it sputtered to an inglorious close propelled by some sort of an inertial drift. None of the remaining participants had the good grace to leave the field of battle first.

Loyalty, whether to colleagues, institutions or objectives, is not good in and of itself. Misplaced loyalty clouds judgement and makes loyalists reluctant to listen to anything that runs counter to their pre-existing positions. In academic endeavours this refusal to seriously entertain diametrically opposed arguments (markets are not efficient) can prove fatal. Exchanges become exercises in defending a pre-existing position rather than a search for true understanding. Economics descends into the nether world of adversarial proceedings where winning is not the most important thing, it is the only thing[25].

3. The Editor Edited

> Your manuscript is both good and original: but the part that is good is not original, and the part that is original is not good. (Samuel Johnson quoted in Bernard, 1990: 75)

Towards the end of an article, any reviewer who has put in the hard time required to conscientiously plod through all the material on offer has won the right to state at least a few quibbles with the way in which the book has been put together and the choices the editor has

[25] The quote is attributed to a famed US football coach Vince Lombardi who is also reputed to have said that a tie is like kissing your sister. The clear consequence of taking this position is that if you disagree with a viewpoint, especially if it is contrary to one's ideological leanings, then there must be nothing of value worth considering in the opposing idea.

> I think you're getting something that is (a) the atmosphere at Chicago, and (b) intensified by Knight. That an academic is concerned not with being diplomatic, not with trying to avoid hurting people's feelings, but an academic is concerned with saying what's right. Telling the truth, or trying to get at it. And if you disagree with somebody you don't say, 'Well, now there may be something in what you say, you may be right. You say, that's a bunch of nonsense'. (Conversation with Milton Friedman, August 1997)

made. To a casual reader, such whining might appear unnecessarily small-minded. But matters that in isolation might seem to be of small import manage to gain importance when accumulated over the seemingly endless expanse of more than 900 pages.

Clearly this is meant to be a reference book. Except for a small group of luckless reviewers, no one else would be likely to plough through so many pages. Because of the essential nature of these edited volumes there remains the whiff of the kitchen sink about a number of its editorial decisions. Too much is included without sufficient evidence that a full weighting of the marginal contribution of each additional article was ever attempted. George Tavlas, for instance, rapidly wears out his welcome by repetitious variations of a single argument without showing any willingness to consider and fully evaluate opposing analysis and evidence. It is as though sheer repetition alone is sufficient to wear down and defeat alternative views. Though this approach might have gained Tavlas a number of publications, the wisdom of reproducing so many is not apparent.

There is also a glaring omission, which is perhaps even more noticeable given the abundance of other material. Like a ghost, Keynes lurks behind much of the issues and debates documented in many articles. A relevant chapter or two from *The General Theory* would not have gone amiss. Readers can always go back to the original to check whether an author is doing Keynes justice. But except for the compulsive or inherently sceptical reviewer, many readers will never get around to doing this. It would be much more convenient if some of this material was at hand. Admittedly, choices would have to be made. The conscientious reader would be better off scrupulously reviewing all the three books in what Patinkin denotes as Keynes' trilogy on monetary theory (*The Tract on Monetary Reform, The Treatise and The General Theory*). Realising however that such readers are unlikely to exist, some assistance from the editor would not go amiss.

The actual order of the articles is often curious. For instance, an article by Patinkin in response to Friedman's attempt to slay his critics comes before the Friedman paper. Again, this is often a matter of judgement, but my curiosity was raised on more than one occasion with regard to this issue. There are also some bits of carelessness.

The references are not provided at the back of a few articles. This most likely occurs because they were part of an edited volume with such references done centrally. Still, it is annoying to have a citation of a work within an article without the full reference available.

The quality of reproduction also varies unnecessarily. A type of camera-ready process must have been used since some included articles are blurry or employ faint type. Also, placing all material included in this work in sufficiently large fonts would have been a mercy for older eyes. And it is safe to conclude that many of the potential readers of these volumes are in that unenviable age group.

As an editor, Leeson has allowed himself the prerogative to include a number of his own contributions. Some critics might claim that Leeson as an editor has been far too indulgent to Leeson the author. This however would be a remark characterised more by its maliciousness than by its accuracy. Leeson provides much that is useful in the way of information and also critical insights in these authored pieces. However, it is not the number of pages he has written, but the very last article in the edited collection that poses real problems. It is meant to sum up and resolve many of the issues that arise over the numerous pages of these volumes. Instead, Leeson pulls his punches in this concluding piece (though this is not usually the case in his contributions to these two volumes). His summation sounds suspiciously similar to what Friedman claims in this preface. In other words, Leeson sticks safely to the surface issues.

> However, Patinkin performed a great service by undertaking such a one-sided historical examination. Had he been more dispassionate, and not played the role of 'economist-as-matador' the dispute may never have taken place and we would presumably know a lot less about the evolution of monetary thought than we do today. Hence the dispute over the oral tradition illustrates the pervasiveness of the principle of unintended consequences. Patinkin, like Friedman, was 'led by an invisible hand to promote an end that was no part of his intention'. (Leeson, 2003e: 515)

To conclude that this was simply an issue involving the history of ideas and that the result was greater enlightenment concerning the history of monetary policy is to largely miss the context of this debate. Intentions are always difficult to fathom without a questionable psychic ability. But it is safe to say that more was at stake than simply pinning down who said what at what date or when certain views were held. Furthermore, the conclusion is curious because the weight of evidence does seem to lie with the Patinkin camp[26].

> Clearly, questions about the history of economic doctrine are empirical questions which can be answered only on the basis of evidence cited from the relevant literature. ... My criticism of Friedman is, accordingly, that on many occasions he has not provided such evidence; that, indeed, on some occasions he has ignored the detailed evidence which has been adduced against the views he expresses; and that on still other occasions he has indulged in casual empiricism in the attempt to support his doctrinal interpretations. (Patinkin, 2003c: 123–124)

As Friedman admits in the preface to this lengthy two-volume set, '... this evidence convinces me that I gave Chicago more credit for uniqueness than was justified'. (Friedman, 2003a: x). But it seems equally clear that whatever the oral tradition might have been in the 30s and 40s, that Chicago brand of monetary analysis did not focus

---

[26] Patinkin does display a certain frustration at times. Perhaps this is what Leeson means by playing 'economist-as-matador'. (Leeson, 2003e: 515). But it is entirely understandable given that Patinkin's opponents do not really respond to his clearly articulated arguments or seem to wilfully misinterpret them. It is unsurprising that Patinkin starts his response to one of Milton Friedman's replies with the well-known quote from Lewis Carroll's *Through the Looking Glass.* In some ways Humpty Dumpty can be seen as a forerunner to Milton Friedman both in looks and debating techniques.

> 'When *I* use a word', Humpty Dumpty said, in a rather scornful tone, 'it means just what I choose it to mean — neither more nor less'.
> 'The question is', said Alice, 'whether you *can* make words mean so many different things'.
> 'The question is', said Humpty Dumpty, 'which is to be master — that's all'.
>
> (Carroll quoted in Patinkin, 2003c: 123)

on constructing a theory detailing the demand for money[27]. Friedman and his loyalists are simply unconvincing in initially claiming that he (Friedman) was untouched by Keynes' formulation of liquidity preference. Nor is the argument any more convincing when Friedman backtracks by claiming that he was influenced by the monetary ideas within the *General Theory* (1964), but those ideas were largely derivative of the Cambridge tradition of the quantity theory. Friedman then is basically claiming that either his theory owed no debt to Keynes or that any notional debt was irrelevant since Keynes himself had contributed little to the advancement of monetary theory. Despite all of the trees sacrificed for the purpose, Friedman's claims are largely unconvincing since his aims in bringing to light this issue are purely ideological and rhetorical. He is not driven by any desire to contribute to an understanding of the history of economic thought. Moreover, as previously discussed, Friedman's overriding interest lay with policy issues rather than strictly theoretical matters. He was however quite willing to muddle the delineable differences between theoretical and policy aspects when discussing the Chicago tradition. Patinkin in contrast kept the distinction much sharper, concentrating his fire on theoretical concerns and differences.

To return to the main issue, despite being quite personalised at times, the battle waged was over dominance. What was at stake was that Friedman's counter-revolution squarely pitted itself against the then Keynesian orthodoxy. At least that is the core issue that

---

[27] This is the theoretical link that Friedman claims, yet neither he nor his supporters are able to demonstrate that Chicago in that interwar period was much concerned with the demand for money or the role interest rates played within such a theory.

> Using Friedman's … widely imitated methodological distinction, Laidler … found the 'positive' theoretical content of the Chicago tradition to be essentially indistinguishable from this Harvard-Hawtry tradition; whereas the 'distinctive feature of Chicagoan analysis was normative, namely to forge a link between a monetary explanation of the cycle and a liberal political agenda'. Laidler provided support for Patinkin's conclusion: in interwar Chicago in the 1930s and 1940s the quantity theory was not 'first and foremost' a theory of the demand for money. (Leeson, 2003e: 6)

initially propelled the controversy. Perhaps in later years the debate did seem to settle more comfortably into something that resembled the standard characteristics of a history of economic thought fracas. Yet even here an unusual amount of contentiousness and obduracy adhered to the exchanges, perhaps an inheritance of the roots of this argument. What is finally more curious is Leeson's lapse in forgetting the earlier Leeson. In a 1997 draft article on 'The Chicago counter-revolution and the sociology of economic knowledge', Leeson clearly depicts the aims and strategies of Friedman and Stigler. 'Stigler and Friedman also sought influence and control over economists' research agenda'. (Leeson, 1997: 32) It remains inexplicable then why this aspect of the debate is muted in Leeson's final summing up. This is the time and place for Leeson to post his valedictory of a long and often confusing journey. It is Leeson's best opportunity to lodge a final idea into the tired mind of the reader. Without the ideological impetus, it is doubtful that Friedman would have had the inclination to make his original remarks and Patinkin in turn would have lacked the occasion of making his scathing rejoinder. For some reason, in this final chapter Leeson wishes to play down the ideological aspects of both the Keynesian revolution and Chicago School counter-revolution. Leeson does this despite the fact that both Keynes and Friedman were ideologues and polemists. They both chose to subjugate economic history, history of ideas and empirical evidence to other (higher) objectives.

In contrast, Stigler, an expert in such commando operations, easily recognised a fellow practitioner of the persuasive art. Thus, he quickly spots that Keynes is being deliberately ingenuous when in his *Essays in Persuasion* (1963) he suggests that economists should aim to provide useful services to the society much like the friendly neighbourhood dentist. Perhaps, that might be an acceptable aspiration for run of the mill economists, but certainly not how Keynes viewed himself. 'He [Stigler] concluded that Keynes sought to be, not a dentist, but "a brain surgeon who operated on ideologies"; and this analogy can be applied to Stigler and Friedman who sought to influence the process of knowledge construction and destruction'. (Leeson, 1997: 6)

References

Bernard, A (ed.) (1990). *Rotten Rejections.* Wainscott, New York: Pushcart Press.

Bernstein, PL (1999). *Against the Gods — The Remarkable Story of Risk.* New York: John Wiley Sons.

Clausewitz, KV (1984/1832). *Vom Krige* [On War]. Princeton: Princeton University Press.

Coase, RH (1994). The Appointment of Pigou as Marshall's Successor. In *Essays on Economics and Economists.* Chicago: University of Chicago Press. pp. 151–166.

Friedman, M (2003a). Preface. In *Keynes, Chicago and Friedman*, R Leeson (ed.), Vol. 1, pp. ix–x. London: Pickering & Chatto.

Friedman, M (2003b/1956). The quantity theory of money — a restatement. In *Keynes, Chicago and Friedman*, R Leeson (ed.), Vol. 1, pp. 31–52. London: Pickering & Chatto.

Friedman, M (2003c/1967). The monetary theory and policy of Henry Simons. In *Keynes, Chicago and Friedman*, R Leeson (ed.), Vol. 1, pp. 53–68. London: Pickering & Chatto.

Friedman, M (2003d/1968). The quantity theory of money. In *Keynes, Chicago and Friedman*, R Leeson (ed.), Vol. 1, pp. 69–84. London: Pickering & Chatto.

Friedman, M (2003e/1972). Comments on the critics: Patinkin. In *Keynes, Chicago and Friedman*, R Leeson (ed.), Vol. 1, pp. 145–166. London: Pickering & Chatto.

Friedman, M (2003f/1968). The quantity theory of money. In *Keynes, Chicago and Friedman*, R Leeson (ed.), Vol. 1, pp. 71–84. London: Pickering & Chatto.

Friedman, M (1962). *Capitalism and Freedom.* Chicago: University of Chicago Press.

Friedman, M and R Friedman (1998). *Two Lucky People: Memoirs.* Chicago: Chicago University Press.

Friedman, M and A Schwartz (1963). *A Monetary History of the United States, 1867–1960.* Princeton: Princeton University Press.

Kaminsky, SM (1999). *Vengeance.* New York: Forge Publishing.

Keynes, JM (1972/1923). *The Collected Writings*, Vol. X. London: Macmillan.

Keynes, JM (1964). *The General Theory of Employment, Interest, and Money.* New York: Harcourt, Brace, Jovanovich.

Keynes, JM (1963). *Essays in Persuasion.* New York: W.W. Norton & Company.

Johnson, E and H Johnson (1978). *The Shadow of Keynes.* Oxford: Basil Blackwell.

Johnson, H (2003/1971). The Keynesian revolution and the monetarist counter-revolution. In *Keynes, Chicago and Friedman*, R Leeson (ed.), Vol. 1, pp. 169–182. London: Pickering & Chatto.

Leeson, R (1997). The Chicago counter-revolution and the sociology of economic knowledge. Mimeo. pp. 1–43.

Leeson, R (2003a). The initial controversy. In *Keynes, Chicago and Friedman*, R Leeson (ed.), Vol. 1, pp. 1–30. London: Pickering & Chatto.

Leeson, R (2003b/2000). Patinkin, Johnson, and the shadow of Friedman. In *Keynes, Chicago and Friedman*, R Leeson (ed.), Vol. 1, pp. 249–279. London: Pickering & Chatto.

Leeson, R (2003c). Introduction. In *Keynes, Chicago and Friedman*, R Leeson (ed.), Vol. 2, pp. 1–27. London: Pickering & Chatto.

Leeson, R (2003d). Towards a resolution of the dispute. In *Keynes, Chicago and Friedman*, R Leeson (ed.), Vol. 2, pp. 293–314. London: Pickering & Chatto.

Leeson, R (2003e). How unique was the Chicago tradition? In *Keynes, Chicago and Friedman*, R Leeson (ed.), Vol. 2, pp. 1–25. London: Pickering & Chatto.

Leeson, R (2003f/1998). Early Patinkin — Friedman correspondence. In *Keynes, Chicago and Friedman*, R Leeson (ed.), Vol. 1, pp. 231–246. London: Pickering & Chatto.

Leeson, R (2003g). The Debate Widens. In *Keynes, Chicago and Friedman*, R Leeson (ed.), Vol. 1, pp. 283–309. London: Pickering & Chatto.

McCloskey, D (1983). The rhetoric of economics. *Journal of Economic Literature*, 21(2): 481–517.

McCloskey, D (1985). *The Rhetoric of Economics.* Madison: The University of Wisconsin Press.

Patinkin, D (2003a/1974). Keynesian monetary theory and the Cambridge School. In *Keynes, Chicago and Friedman*, R Leeson (ed.), Vol. 2, pp. 315–344. London: Pickering & Chatto.

Patinkin, D (2003b/1975). The collected writings of John Maynard Keynes: From the *Tract to The General Theory.* In *Keynes, Chicago and Friedman*, R Leeson (ed.), Vol. 2, pp. 347–369. London: Pickering & Chatto.

Patinkin, D (2003c/1974). Friedman on the quantity theory and Keynesian economics. In *Keynes, Chicago and Friedman*, R Leeson (ed.), Vol. 2, pp. 123–143. London: Pickering & Chatto.

Patinkin, D (2003d/1979). Keynes and Chicago. In *Keynes, Chicago and Friedman*, R Leeson (ed.), Vol. 2, pp. 373–392. London: Pickering & Chatto.

Patinkin, D (2003e/1969). The Chicago tradition, the quantity theory, and Friedman. In *Keynes, Chicago and Friedman*, R Leeson (ed.), Vol. 1, pp. 87–120. London: Pickering & Chatto.

Patinkin, D (2003f). The Chicago tradition: A comment. In *Keynes, Chicago and Friedman*, R Leeson (ed.), Vol. 1, p. 381. London: Pickering & Chatto.

Samuelson, PA (1957). Wages and Interest: A modern dissection of Marxian economic models. *The American Economic Review*, 47(6): 884–912.

Simons, H (2003/1935). Review of Currie's *Supply and Control of Money in the United States.* In *Keynes, Chicago and Friedman*, R Leeson (ed.), Vol. 1, pp. 367–372. London: Pickering & Chatto.

Steindl, F (2003/1990). The 'Oral Tradition' at Chicago in the 1930s. In *Keynes, Chicago and Friedman*, R Leeson (ed.), Vol. 1, pp. 375–377. London: Pickering & Chatto.

Stigler, GJ (1988). *Memoirs of an Unregulated Economist.* New York: Basic Books.

Taylor, AJP (1962). *The Origins of the Second World War.* New York: Antheneum.

Viner, J (2003/1963). Comment on My 1936 Review of Keynes' *General Theory.* In *Keynes, Chicago and Friedman*, R Leeson (ed.), Vol. 2, pp. 417–430. London: Pickering & Chatto.

Part II

Method or Madness — Why Methodology Matters

I am but mad north-north-west; when the wind is southerly,
I know a hawk from a handsaw (Hamlet, act 2, scene 2: 1)

Chapter 11

Why Economists Can't Read

I'd write my Congersman if he could read, if I could write. (Walt Kelly)

It is not as if we have not been warned in the past. John Stuart Mill tried to, but his pointed remarks about the strength of cultural inertia have been largely forgotten, buried as they are beneath a welter of Victorian prose[1]. Thorstein Veblen emphatically delineated the power of habits of wont and usage[2], but economists seemed more intrigued by his sexual forays than his institutional investigations. Of course, both were analysing general economic relations rather than turning the searchlight in upon the economics profession. But cultural inertia leaves just as distinctive an imprint in this area as in those less-restricted domains. In all endeavours, there is an inevitable resistance to change.

[1] 'Political economists generally and English political economists above others, have been accustomed to lay almost exclusive stress upon the first of these agencies, to exaggerate the effect of competition, and to take into little account the other and conflicting principle (custom). They are apt to express themselves as if they thought that competition actually does, in all cases, whatever it can be shown to be the tendency of competition to do'. (Mill, 1965: 242)

[2] '... so that the German people have been enabled to take up the technological heritage of the English without having paid for it in the habits of thought, the use and wont induced in the English community by the experience involved in achieving it'. (Veblen, 1976: 364)

Once a convention becomes established, changing it involves significant costs. This can be all to the good, since using such conventions or standard procedures reduces the transaction costs associated with economic activity. But as in those broader economic realms, so it is in the economics profession itself. This tendency to protect the *status quo* also helps to perpetuate bad habits.

When examined at a distance, the average journal article comes to epitomise such bad habits[3]. As Donald McCloskey has so cheerfully pointed out[4], the development of economic rhetoric has gone badly astray. The question for those who still nurture a bit of intellectual curiosity is why this should be the case.

McCloskey has done yeoman-like work in detailing what might be called the supply-side determinants of this issue. But in doing so he has not sufficiently emphasised the archetypal story economists like to tell each other, *going to market*. Economists are not an exception to their own rules. In this way, they are no different than butchers, bakers or candlestick-makers. Economists carry other goods to market, also in hope of a sale. Therefore, their motley output of tall tales, romances and epic poems must be constructed with an audience in mind. It takes two to communicate, or if we were dull economists, and in fact we all are, we would say there has to be both a demand for and a supply of information. If we find fault with the aesthetic quality of that output, we cannot at the same time absolve that readership of all blame. In the absence of a regime of imposed central planning, markets are supposed to provide people with what they want, possibly even what they deserve. If the profession is cursed with lame rhetoric, we can only conclude that this is what economists want and what they are capable

---

[3] Throughout the article, I accept Donald McCloskey's concerns about the current state of economic literature. By spurning the value of rhetoric, economists have developed a predilection for unnecessarily turgid prose. The issue I concentrate on is why such writing exists and seems likely to persist. These are the bad habits, which far too few in the profession seem eager to shake.

[4] McCloskey has been making this point with increasing fervour at least since his 1983 *Journal of Economic Literature* article. This has occasioned some debate but no noticeable results. Those interested should look at such efforts in his book, *The Rhetoric of Economics* (1985) or a latter elucidation, *If You're So Smart* (1990).

of digesting. Or, to get more to the heart of the matter, economists cannot write because economists have never learned how to read.

This is a particularly dismal conclusion since it minimises the chance for any constructive change. With the market delivering the articles that the profession demands, it is hard to envisage from whence reform of the sort that McCloskey champions can originate.

Here, as in so much of life, we find that standards once formed acquire an inertial endurance. Other alternative formats become more difficult for readers to comprehend and thus less acceptable. Moreover, the constraint of needing to publish in a limited number of dominant economic journals, all of which subscribe to a fairly rigid format, perpetuates a nearly ubiquitous writing style. Strangely enough, the durability of this chosen style is strengthened by its lack of flexibility. By clearly distinguishing those failing to conform, it forms an effective and easily recognisable entry barrier to these key journals. Trends in journals are strengthened and fads perpetuated as hopefuls imitate already published articles. Faced with this flood of uniformity, an editor becomes a virtual prisoner of submitted material.[5] Thus, a revolt against these standards is unlikely unless the journals themselves should opt, or be forced, to change. Economists cannot read because they have no incentive to learn how to read. While that incentive continues to absent itself, no improvement in the standard of writing can realistically be expected to appear. When the spirit is not willing, the flesh will necessarily be weak.

1. The Tailors of Laputa — Journals and the Canonical Form

> Those to whom the King had entrusted me, observing how ill I was clad, ordered a Taylor to come next morning, and take my Measure for a Suit of

[5] 'Yet even here, an editor is to some extent a captive, a passive recipient of material sent to him unsolicited; and as authors send articles to journals which they hope will publish them any editor tends to get more of the same i.e. having printed material of a certain type or on a specific topic prospective authors will expect him to more or less continue in the same vein. This practice may well restrict the range of his choice'. (Coats, 1991: 105–106)

> Cloths. This Operater did his Office after a different Manner from those of his Trade in Europe. He first took my Altitude by a Quadrant, and then with Rule and Compasses described the Dimensions and Out-Lines of my whole Body; all which he entered upon Paper. And in six Days brought my Cloths very ill made and quite out of Shape, by happening to mistake a Figure in the Calculations. (Swift, 1958: 126–127)

It should come as no surprise that the slow ascent of the journals to a position where they became the makers and breakers of reputation, the arbiters of taste and breeding, began the year after Marshall took up his chair at Cambridge, 1885. Marshall would have as his central goal, if not obsession, the professionalisation of economics as a discipline[6]. This campaign is best represented by his successful struggle *to establish economics as a science independent of the Cambridge Moral Sciences Tripos* (Coats, 1991: 94). Three of the journals that are still essential to an ambitious economist, *The Quarterly Journal of Economics* (1886), *The Economic Journal* (1891) and *The Journal of Political Economy* (1892) followed in quick succession[7]. Hitherto, writers of economics had no officially sanctioned venue in which to publish, one that was universally recognised as such. With their establishment, these journals eventually became the professional bouncers of the trade, defining what was and was not to be considered as a contribution to the field of economics.

> Increasing numbers of researchers, as well as their growing dispersion, encouraged further formalisation and standardisation of the communication system which in turn affected the standardisation of work practices and ways of reporting results. The importance of this system for gaining reputations,

---

[6] A fairly comprehensive look at Marshall's role in this process can he gained by reading Mahoney (1985).

[7] Not coincidentally, each of these journals was associated with a leading University, giving these institutions an ever-increasing power to exclude. The QJE was an offspring of Harvard, the JPE of Chicago and the EJ, though officially a product of the newly formed British Economic Association, of Cambridge. In particular, Chicago founded the journal in hopes of enhancing its newly formed Department of Economics. Although Marshall himself was not initially a moving force behind the birth and subsequent status of any of these journals, it is hard to see how his professionalisation process could entirely have succeeded without them.

> and hence rewards, means that its organisation and control are closely linked to the authority structures of different fields, both intellectual and organisational, and it is important to recognise that scientific communication systems are both functional and authoritative (Whitely, 1991: 11).

With the advent of the journals, economics took the first step towards standardisation. In the long run, non-professionals would be excluded. The gifted amateur without the proper university credentials would be forced into perpetual obscurity. Recognition of such work would be forever withheld. The desire, welling within self-anointed professionals like Marshall, was to reduce future Henry Georges to the rank of mere scribblers[8]. Journal articles, not books, would hold the key to advancement. The journals themselves would be monopolised entirely by the credentialed academic community. In much the same way that the then contemporary medical profession waged war on unlicensed quacks, so did economic orthodoxy root out and destroy unqualified economic theorists.

The process of standardisation has succeeded to an almost mind-numbing degree. Today the journal article has an almost generic feel to it. Given the minute variability in form between offerings, one would be willing to guess that there is at least an implicitly acknowledged format which exists as a core requirement for publication. This format has become a sort of synthetic stretch garment capable of adjusting to any conceivable content.

My interest lies with the way economists choose to convey their analysis. My contention is that this form is not accidental, but the product of meeting the type of demand set by the consumers of these articles. To reiterate, economists are trying to sell their output to the leading journals and thus to the editors and reviewers involved in the publication process. They adopt the structure and writing style which is most

[8] In 1883 Alfred Marshall presented three public lectures in an attempt to refute the claims made by Henry George in *Progress and Poverty* (1958). This book 'circulated in Great Britain as no economic work had ever circulated before' (Stigler, 1963: 181 n. 2) This was an early but singular attempt by Marshall to define a new science of economics. He would later be instrumental in marginalising most of the work produced by J. A. Hobson.

pleasing to these potential consumers, in which case, the predominant style of writing need not be solely a reflection of the nature of its content. Instead, it is the end result of an evolutionary process in which the nature of demand has also evolved over the decades.

We can start to understand what sort of commodity is demanded by searching for a structure common to those articles usually published in the leading journals. Instead of presupposing what that ruling standard might be, only those articles recently appearing in the two most influential journals were chosen for examination. The year selected was merely the result of a random decision[9].

In 1991, *The Journal of Political Economy* (JPE) published 42 articles (excluding notes and comments) in five volumes. Thirty-six of them had absolutely identical formats. The other six varied in very trivial ways. An article by someone at the Harvard Law School displayed the greatest deviation. We can suppose that he was to some degree ignorant of how strict the standard format has become.

Everyone in the profession is well aware of what this singular structure is, at least at some semi-conscious level. The introduction extends to approximately a page. Most authors feel obliged to formally label the introduction as 'introduction'. A minority is willing to risk the obvious. An author explains exactly what he or she plans to do and how he or she will carry out this plan. The specifics of this exposition make it more than a general run-through. Each section of the paper is described in turn. For each section, the reader is made aware of exactly what service these individual sections will perform relative to the whole. The introduction also includes a review of literature which places the article in its proper relation to previous work. This allows the author to describe how his or her article makes a departure, contribution, etc., to this ongoing debate. The individual sections themselves manage to repeat much of this information when

[9] According to a recent article (Ellis and Durdeen, 1991) the two most respected economic journals are *The American Economic Review* (AER) and *The Journal of Political Economy* (JPE). I chose the year 1991 by shutting my eyes selecting a copy of the JPE at random from a shelf containing the last six years of the journal. I then used the same year to compare the AER. These results cannot be conclusive. But I do think they are indicative. Such clear patterns are unlikely to be a pure fluke.

they are centre stage. The final section is most often labelled 'Conclusion'[10]. In the way of a farewell, the solicitous author reminds the ever-forgetful reader of what the article has just revealed. In short hand the entire process: (a) tells the readers what you will do; (b) tells the readers what you are doing; (c) tells the reader what you have done. We have all heard this formula for writing an article satirised. But the reality serves as proof against the power of ridicule.

In 1991, the *American Economic Review* (AER) ran 46 articles spread out over four volumes (excluding the volume of papers and proceedings). The articles in the AER are more likely to diverge from the strict canonical form. Nineteen show at least some variations[11]. On the whole, articles have greater variation as to the length of introduction, the detailing of sections and the labelling of the concluding section. One article even starts off with a quote from Garrison Keilor. The formatting strait-jacket is relaxed a notch or two, though the end results are immediately recognisable as close cousins to the acknowledged standard. The two articles which demonstrate the greatest departure from this norm are not surprisingly from economists who already have an unassailable reputation, Debreu[12] as well as co-authors Friedman and Schwartz.

---

[10] Though 'Conclusion' is the most common label, this can vary. Sometimes of course it is 'Conclusions' or 'Summary and Conclusion'. Also seen are: Remarks, Concluding Policy Implications, Extensions and Concluding Comments. There are definite differences in these choices. For the most part they are chosen to be appropriate to the material in that concluding statement. But they all share the common characteristic of letting the reader know that the author is about to confess to what has been done throughout the article and why it was done. Though one wonders why readers cannot discern for themselves that they are looking at the conclusion to the article.

[11] This includes the article with the intriguing title, 'Sorority Rush as a Two Sided Matching Mechanism' (Mongell and Roth, 1991). It lacks a literature review. Since 11 out of the 19 references cited are by the author or authors, one suspects that this deviation from form was not entirely intentional but driven by necessity.

[12] Debreu's article is based on his presidential address at the ASSA convention. As in the case where the Nobel Prize winner's address is reproduced, one can expect some variation from the canonical form. Economists have not yet reached the point where they speak in the exact same way that they write.

These journals serve to grant reputation and thus academic awards to aspiring economists. This internal route is currently the only way for an ambitious economist to achieve success. The journals have increased the need to conform to gain this precious recognition. The unacknowledged but omnipresent fear must be that any deviation from this norm will increase the risk of rejection. Increasing standardisation becomes an effective screening device given the space constraints these journals face.

Even with the best of motives, the young economist must be expedient to be effective. No one will read his or her work if it does not get published in a widely read and esteemed journal. The aspiring economist can not publish unless he or she accepts the canonical rhetorical form. Or to be a bit more accurate, publishing becomes increasingly more difficult, especially publishing in one of the more prominent journals. An economist must be able to appeal to the potential reviewers employed by the journal to succeed. Decades of marketing have succeeded admirably. Professional consumers will accept no substitutes.

Thus, these articles are demand-driven except in the case where the author's reputation precedes him or her. A sufficient reputation creates a Say's Law type of effect. Supply does seem to create its own demand. Once one has a sufficient reputation, it becomes safe to assume that what one writes will be widely read. In a sense, demand for the content is largely guaranteed. One sometimes wonders whether a journal would be equally likely to publish the same submitted article if it bore an unknown name[13].

Journals grant this license to deviate more readily to those who have already been recognised as masters of the reigning form. Contemplative essays are widely seen as an outlet for well-known economists nearing retirement, a sort of indulgence granted to the elders of the profession.

---

[13] Many economic journals, more than half of the top 40, use a single blind reviewing system. Thus the reviewer is aware of the author of the article and the institution where he/she is based. See Rebecca Blank's article (1991) for additional insights into this process.

Only those economists who are clearly acknowledged masters of the prevailing form are granted such latitude. It is as if Monet would first have had to paint like Ingrés before anyone would deign to take him seriously. Or, as if literary critics had decreed the detective novel to be the one legitimate genre. Only by utilising that format could a writer gain an audience for his or her ideas. Once a reputation was secured, other forms could be ventured. But such alternative approaches could never gain widespread approbation. The established writer's reputation would not be critically impaired. However, only those works cast in the conventional mode would continue to be taken seriously by these critics.

Journal articles were not always so narrowly defined. I need not remark, as many have before, on the change in the subject matter of the journals and of the techniques displayed there. The surprising discovery to be made lies in the extent to which the actual structure has changed. There is no need to go back a hundred years to when Veblen was writing on the price of wheat for the JPE to discover this difference. In 1951 the JPE published 37 articles spread over six different issues. Almost none of those papers followed what would become the canonical form for this literature. The only exceptions came in two papers published by a pair of rising young economists, George Stigler and Milton Friedman. It may be indicative that these two economists who would, along with a few others, come to dominate the discipline were already perfecting the future ubiquitous form. We might tentatively posit that the campaign to capture the high ground of economics in the form of control over the leading journals was already underway[14].

There are also in these issues of the JPE an additional eight articles that resemble to varying degrees what I have labelled the canonical form. But, there is altogether more variance in presentation regardless of the content of the piece. This holds true whether the article is largely

[14] It is important to point out here that I am not automatically identifying this standard form with poor or lackluster writing. Even the most pedestrian of formats is capable of yielding an outstanding result. Both pieces by Stigler and Friedman are clearly written and lively in style. The focus of this article is on the effect of universalising one particular format.

discursive, empirical or contains some mathematical formalisation. There seems amongst the authors no awareness or recognition that one form alone should have any innate greater suitability. The same sort of comments could be made if one looks at the 29 articles printed in the 1951 volume of the AER. There was still room in 1951 for Frank Knight to go on for 29 undivided pages without making one single cited reference. In all, the now obligatory review of literature appeared to be optional, instead of serving as a required litany. It was provided only if the author felt it to be necessary. Nor was there an obligation for such a review to be particularly extensive. Overall, these articles were written for a mature audience, one that could be depended upon to grasp the obvious.

Change begins with the late fifties and early sixties[15]. By 1963, all the articles in the JPE bear at least a close resemblance to this standard form, while 25% are identical to it. In the AER the variance in articles has also narrowed with 50% of them adopting the now familiar format.

It is also true that the intervening years had seen the increasing mathematical formalisation of economics. But it is far from obvious that such formalisation, whether appropriate or not in all instances, also demanded a standardised form. An alternative explanation is that both are the result of a common agenda successfully accomplished by a core group of economists who were able to rather narrowly define what doing economics involved.

Today, the intelligent lay reader of an economics article might conclude that economists were an unusually inattentive bunch. In reading an article an economist is first prepared for what he or she is about to read. Not only its content but the method of presentation is gone over in some detail as though all economists have dicky hearts incapable of withstanding even the slightest shock. By constantly preparing the reader for what is about to transpire, describing what

[15] One curious change was the addition of a mandatory list of references at the end of an article. This first became noticeable in the AER during the 1957–1958 period. By 1959 it was nearly universal. On the other hand, though first appearing in the JPE in 1961, it did not become general practice in that journal until 1967. I have no explanation for the delay in adopting what seems to me to be a very useful practice.

point is being made as it occurs, and then reminding the feckless reader of what has happened, economists have taken the path blazed by the typical television drama. There, characters alternate in recapping the plot every 10–15 min. In that way viewers who tune in late or who are given to taking short naps are not placed at a disadvantage. Do economists like TV viewers suffer from ever-shortening attention spans? Economists seem incapable of following a sustained argument or grasping the point of an article without having their collective noses rubbed in it several times.

The time has long passed when we could say with any honesty that we are all now Keynesians. But surely we do not want to replace that unanimity by admitting that we are now no more than Sesame Street dropouts. One is loathe to label the average economist with that tag. The question must then become one of finding out why a standard form has been so universally adopted. Surely, such ubiquity does not flow out of any self-evident merit. The best that can be said about the intrinsic value of the form is that it is utilitarian if rather uninspiring. At worst, it is unimaginative and undemanding of any obvious skill on the part of the writer. The pronounced use of stock formulas can gradually destroy the ability of an author to write in a commanding manner.

The mysterious charm of this universal format will remain a puzzle until we come to understand why economists cannot read. Accepting that this style is a demand-motivated response, we need to discover why there is no pay-off for displaying an ability to read critically, why no audience exists for papers which demand such skills. It is this inability of economists to read that is reflected in the standard style of an article. We need to turn now to an examination of what is involved in critical reading and why economists regard this skill as largely irrelevant.

2. Ariadne's Thread — Journal Articles as the Source of Reputation

> Now, before Daedalus left Crete, he had given Ariadne a magic ball of thread, and instructed her how to enter and leave the labyrinth. (Graves, 1955: 339)

To make more explicit what is already apparent in McCloskey, economists write for a particular audience. They must be assumed to be successful at this task unless we want to entertain the possibility that an irremediable distortion in the market process exists. In any case, why economists want the sort of writing that they demand still remains the question. My answer would be that they have never learned to read, but more importantly that they fail to see this as an oversight to be corrected.

Many economists might be tempted to see this increased standardisation of writing as the result of the concurrent increase in mathematical formalisation in economics. Together they would encompass a drive for greater precision, for becoming more scientific in the never-ending task of exploring what are very complex problems[16]. In this vision, the current existing form, as well as the predominance of mathematical formalisation, reflects a Darwinian process of evolution. Not only is the dominant form the result of a demand-driven process but also one that leads to greater clarity and light.

> Survival in the literature is a test of fitness, if an imperfect one. If mathematical techniques continue to produce good economics then, still as a Darwinian, I predict that long before the appendix has disappeared from the human digestive tract most people interested in economic theory will as a matter of course learn some mathematics. (Solow quoted in Caldwell, 1991: 27–28)

Solow is not alone among economists who seem to have trouble distinguishing Charles Darwin from Herbert Spencer when they reach for stock evolutionary metaphors. They muddle an idea of natural

---

[16] 'First, the scientific paper in economics has an implied reader it shares with other self-consciously scientific productions of the culture. The implied reader has some features that are unattractive: he is cold-blooded, desiccated, uninvolved. The case of Isaac Newton and his invention, the scientific paper, is the model'. (McCloskey, 1990: 138)

selection with a specific survival of the fittest scenario[17]. These are far from identical ideas[18].

Darwinian struggle is far removed from the historical rise to predominance of a particular form of economic writing that Solow wants to describe. It is not some impersonal match between environment and species. Economists consciously tried to shape the academic environment in which they operated to reflect their own personal goals. The perpetuation of dubious writing styles is not sustained by chance. The rather visible hand of the profession intervenes to insure a particular result.

Nor, will critical reading[19] eventuate as some fortunate happenstance of an unforeseen process. It takes the sort of deliberate training that is disregarded if not shunned by each generation of

---

[17] By confusing these two, the defining characteristics of evolution receive a moral uplift which they neither need nor desire. Biology provides no obvious or implicit ladder waiting to be scaled over the course of history. Only varying species and changing environments exist. Predetermined purposes have a hard time loitering around such premises. Selection, in this context, serves only to confuse since Darwin does not use the term quite so literally. No one selects. A multitude of random variants operate in a time-specific environment. Those that make an appropriate match flourish. This is not a matter of superior planning, but of chance. Strictly speaking, there are no edifying lessons to be drawn, no superior claims for one species over another. 'Darwin's "law of the survival of the finest" is often misunderstood; Nature being supposed to secure, through competition, that those shall survive who are fittest to benefit the world. But the law really is that the races are most likely to survive who are best fitted to thrive in their environment: that is to turn to their own account those opportunities which the world offers to them'. (Marshall, 1923: 175)

[18] The traditional misuse of evolutionary metaphors is symptomatic of the failure of economists to actually read critically. Few seem to have actually read Darwin or other works on evolution. Instead they accept an oral tradition that allows economists to ignore the original work while still citing it as an authority. The consequence of this form of intellectual laziness will be explored further in the following section.

[19] The basis for critical reading will be discussed later. Among other things, it involves looking for a comprehensive and consistent interpretation of an article as well as adopting a generous attitude to an author. This means trying to understand what an author is trying to do before focusing on where he or she has gone wrong. Particularly, the latter objective should not inform the former.

entrenched economists. Graduate students who write in veins varying from the expected format soon find the cost of such deviation too heavy to bear. Without a potential audience that reads critically, experimenting with different writing formats is left to those who have already succeeded in the profession and are thus granted greater leeway in their projects. This then is as much a triumph of one set of vested interests over less powerful contenders as it is an intellectual triumph of superior over inferior presentations.

There are more compelling arguments which can explain the increasing standardisation and formalisation of journal articles. Economists tend to deny their own rhetoric, preferring to believe that facts speak for themselves. As a consequence, the deliberate and conscious use of rhetoric must be unscientific. By thinking in this manner, they are sadly in the position of those young Victorian ladies who saw sex as a short but squalid prelude to child rearing. Might it be true, that when economists sit down to write, they close their eyes and think of Science[20]?

This veil of science allows economists to excuse themselves from analysing the advantages that might lie behind one form of writing as opposed to available alternatives. Given only a single orthodoxy, such a problem refuses to intrude. Unfortunately, the prevalence of this rather pedestrian style is more than a simple nostalgia for the absolute. It reflects the defensive style that is now inextricably linked to economic debate. Because so much reading of economic articles is done as a probing action, seeking out points of weakness and possible errors, authors are forced to defend themselves by overstating and reiterating. They cannot assume that their audience will read with care and consideration. Economists grow to resemble the modern medical profession which is notorious for ordering extra and extraneous tests to protect themselves from possible legal action. The pretence of thoroughness is their shield. The result of this in economics is an

---

[20] 'One cause of disagreement is an oversimplified theory of reading. The theory of reading adopted officially by economists and other scientists is that scientific texts are transparent, a matter of "mere communication", "just style", simply "writing up" the "theoretical results" and "empirical findings"'. (McCloskey, 1990: 37–38).

overemphasis on defining terms to endless lengths and clarifying obvious points. Just as in defensive medicine, this process is costly in terms of the benefits it provides.

The mistake is to take reading for granted as though anyone can do it. Insightful reading is a learned skill not an intuitive one. Without being trained in critical reading, ambiguities become anathemas. Economists suffer from the idea that it is possible for writing to convey only one objective meaning[21]. In that case, interpretation ceases to be an intrinsic part of reading. Economists instead connect rhetoric with the decorative arts, with the unnecessary constructions of needlepoint embroidery, a type of tatting for the timid. Like Sergeant Friday, they profess to want just the facts, the unmediated facts.

Therefore, the belief arises that mathematics is more precise, less ambiguous and thus preferable to discursive explanation. Economists like to praise the preciseness of mathematical models. They should give more thought to their appropriateness[22]. Economists in their defence of mathematics seem to muddle the need for precision with the need for appropriate language. Precision implies neither accuracy nor appropriateness. But it does lessen the problem of interpretation. Faced with poor readers, no effort to alleviate confusion

---

[21] 'We cannot succeed in making even a single sentence mean one and only one thing; we can only increase the odds that a large majority of readers will tend to interpret our discourse according to our intentions'. (Gopen and Swan, 1990: 557)

[22] 'Clearly the existence of established standards provides a powerful rationalization for the continued use of formalisation. I maintain that formalisation for the sake of formalisation alone has never been, and will never be knowingly acceptable or confessed to by most economists'. (Katzner, 1991: 23) At least subconsciously, many economists identify a good paper as synonymous with the one which is highly formalised. Wishing to be published, an aspiring economist will not question whether in a particular case formalising is justified. That is simply what the market demands. Though, it would be the height of naivety for anyone, even an economist, to admit that he or she were presenting mathematical formalisation merely for the sake of formalising; that he or she were in effect opening a latch gate with a rocket launcher merely in order to get an article published. Such an innocent, candide-like character is hard to imagine. A wise economist knows his or her audience. How many economists when handed the work of a colleague simply respond only partially in jest 'Just show me the equations'. On such an audience, anything but the most rudimentary rhetorical style would be wasted.

is avoided. To justify this position, we have convinced ourselves that we maintain a scientific level of writing, that to violate the canonical form of economic writing is to slip from objective to interpretative prose.

The prevalence of *a priori* reasoning is similarly demand-driven, stemming from a flight from a seemingly ubiquitous and ever-threatening ambiguity. *A priori* formalisation does not require specific knowledge. Insights into abstract market processes relieve economists of any such responsibility. They can feel confident in extending their reach unhindered by having to scale any walls of concrete details. Articles that ignore this widespread predilection for *a priori* constructs, seeking instead to substitute a diet of nuggetty information, will find themselves serving up an uncongenial goulash to the limited palates of their audience[23].

The standard article is also structured to pander to the potential reader in a roundabout fashion. Economists choose a style that is deliberately reader-unfriendly. This tacitly invokes the self-importance of its potential audience. The obscurity of the presentation proclaims, 'This is a serious article not open to the casual reader. I, the author, do not pander to the masses". Simultaneously, the author encourages potential readers to browse through the article based on the provided menu (grazing not reading). The author clearly acknowledges how busy the reader is and that he or she must usually read selectively. The gentle reader is flattered as being technically advanced as well as faced with extreme demands on his or her limited time. Such flattery serves as an effective device with which to ensnare the prospective reader. Part of the charm of a rational expectation model is that it is abstruse enough to require a very concentrated reading. This forces the reader to approach the model seriously, since it takes such an expenditure of time to make it comprehensible. A more descriptive style would appear to be too simplistic and self-evident. A conspiracy of convenience

[23] Notice the parallel here with management theory of the post-war era. Leading business schools cultivated a dominant belief that one abstract model was capable of encompassing all situations. Lately, given the fiascos of the eighties, more emphasis is being given to the specifics of production.

ensnares both the author and reader. The specific readers these articles address are the discipline's gatekeepers, an amorphous group of unseen referees who feel obligated to maintain the assumed standards of the profession. At times, it seems as if writers expect no one but these potential reviewers to actually read their articles with any care. Instead, they provide quick previews for idle skimmers, like so many trailers for the forthcoming movies. The aim is to entice browsers into giving the article a look. It does seem rather a waste of paper to print more than the introduction and conclusions of such articles. The relatively few, dogged readers could apply to the author for additional details or, they could possibly look forward to the establishment of a new publication, *The Journal of Excluded Middles.* The suspicion lingers, that for many articles, only the reviewers ever read the whole piece thoroughly.

Thus there is something not entirely innocent about the rhetoric of the standard journal article. Though previewing the topic is of use given the limited time of most prospective readers, a good abstract accomplishes the same goal. Instead of purely utilitarian, objective prose, there is a subtext of flattery and enticement of the reader. The prickly exterior of non-indulgence, of making the reader struggle to reach the intellectual attainments of the author, has within it a soft core of addressing that same reader's self-importance. Anything too simple is considered as pandering to the masses. The reader is seen as someone to be challenged if not defied. Authors use masses of mathematics to cow all but the most determined reader into submission. This strategy of making a reader work unnecessarily hard can prove highly successful. It is unlikely that an economist will entirely dismiss something that has already absorbed so much time and effort, sunk costs notwithstanding. While ostensibly aimed at precision, the standardised and formalised article both protects the writer from attack and indirectly woos the reader with a potent form of flattery.

This idea of an unacknowledged subtext also shows up in the mandatory and standardised way in which a literature review appears in all introductions. Again there is an impeccable, scholarly justification for its presence, as well as hidden persuaders which lie beneath the surface. Arguments need to be placed within the discourse of any discipline. Given the necessary space limitations of a journal and the limited time of a potential reader, such a practice serves as a shorthand to place an article within the appropriate context. It also allows those not immediately familiar with the literature in that particular context to gain additional information if necessary.

This is the shiny side of the coin. Even here, the more cynical may sometimes wonder if, in the case of those papers most frequently cited, the author has actually bothered to read them. This is particularly true when there is a long-standing consensus on what such papers say and what they demonstrate. Ostensibly then, this required exercise in name-dropping is done to allow serious readers to explore the topic at greater depth as well as to place the argument within the ongoing economic debate. I would not deny these functions. But there is another implicit demand to which the authors cater (the subtext). Readers are unwilling to accept an argument on its own merits alone. Arguments made without such backup authority are disregarded. They are more receptive when convinced that other highly reputable individuals have held similar views or at least have considered the issue to be important, an academic equivalent of the celebrity endorsement, or the wall full of diplomas on a doctor's wall. The reader is reassured of the relevance of the work. Work of this type cannot then be carelessly disregarded.

The logic of this is curious. As Thomas Aquinas (1964) states in his *Summa Theologiae*, 'Arguments according to authority are of the weakest sort'[24]. Why is an economic model any more legitimate because Milton Friedman believes it or other noted economists have found an issue interesting? Does a breakfast cereal become more palatable simply because some Olympic Gold Medallist endorses it? A literature review and an incessant citing of sources not only serve the purpose of putting the work in context but also serve as a bit of protective colouration. Thus, the subtext which explains the format

[24] You will have to trust me on this one. I know it is in there but I am not prepared to dig through those two huge volumes just to silence the unbelievers.

of the article is twofold, a desire to cater to the taste of the consuming public and a need for self-protection.

For these reasons, the current rhetoric which is so predominantly deployed in economics is not found wanting by its users. This is hardly surprising since it has been tailored to suit prevailing tastes. Perhaps writers like Bronfenbrenner (1991) are correct. The nature of economics students changed in the post-war period. Without any training in critical reading they fell back on rhetorical styles most familiar to them. Unfortunately, once they gained the commanding heights of the profession, they took no prisoners. All other contending rhetorical styles fell like wheat before a thresher. Those occupying the heights of economics refused to read anything not written in the one style they approved.

Educating a budding economist is very much a guild system where the aspirant works his or her way up the ladder from graduate student, to tenure track lecturer, to tenured professor by replicating the techniques of the masters of the trade. Thus there is a conservative *status quo* to the process. Wagner's *Die Meistersinger* can be consulted as a treatise of the retribution that awaits those that show a rebellious inclination. The end result is that though the founders of the canonical format may have consciously chosen to pursue a set of these specific aims, their followers are likely to be narrower technicians unaware of the alternatives that exist and disdainful of any variation. These readers will find a non-standard prose style too demanding, too rich for their professional stomachs. For digestion to take place, only the thinnest of rhetorical gruels will serve[25].

Economists then have become suspicious of polished writing as though it was a piquant sauce covering up some suspicious meat, as though it was a siren's song lulling their critical faculties[26].

---

[25] Klamer and Colander (1990) have looked in some detail at the topic of professional education and the type of economists it tends to produce.

[26] John Kenneth Galbraith's efforts have long been dismissed as mere journalism, or the work of a novelist. The economics profession has somehow managed to causally link what commonly is termed 'good writing' with superficiality of treatment. Only the most stridently inoffensive, if not turgid, prose is deemed to be serious.

But if rhetoric is all pervasive and thus only effective or ineffective, any rhetorical device can be confronted without fear of being duped.

The way economists seem to react either with disdain or fright to any but the blandest of writing styles should reinforce the point just made. After a diet of white bread any pointed remarks or rhetorical flourishes become indigestible. Writing that tries to convince is rejected as biased and unscientific. This misses the object of any article. Why write if not to convince the reader? Spirited writing is not pandering to an audience. Somehow, a convention of disdain has grown up among economists. It is up to the poor downtrodden reader to hack through masses of impenetrable prose and mathematical formulation in order to reach the jewel of an idea hidden in that thicket.

Thus, Phillip Mirowski's recent book, *More Heat Than Light* (1989), on the mathematical metaphor that 19th century economists chose to represent human optimisation, attracted pointed reviews not only for the controversial thesis put forward, but also for the rhetorical style he chose to use.

The piece is meant to provoke in the same sense that Keynes put his case strongly, perhaps at times too strongly, in order to stir the pot. The aim is to occasion debate by causing economists to re-examine and defend their positions. Thus even the most extreme stories have their use in combating the stultifying effects of dogmatism. Like the intergenerational battle depicted in Turgenev's (1950) *Fathers and Sons*, conflict can clarify issues by forcing dogmatic beliefs out into the open, paving the way for compromise.

Unfortunately, a pronounced style like Mirowski's serves only as an irritant to the profession at large. Hal Varian (*Journal of Economic Literature*, 1990) not hitherto known for any remarkable dexterity with the English language can use the description 'well written' as the ultimate backhanded compliment. The impression conveyed is that good writing is used to cover up weak arguments. Varian stops short of accusing Mirowski of being a foot fetishist but seems as unconvinced by the way he argues as what he argues. In a similar vein, Kevin Hoover (*Methodus*, 1991) seems to have been provoked to the same sort of intemperate fulminations that he finds intolerable in Mirowski.

One wonders whether a blander, more standard format would have occasioned such heated ripostes[27].

This though is not a mere matter of taste. The prevalent inability or deliberate refusal to read in a critical fashion creates much unnecessary confusion. Communication begins to flow through fewer channels. If only in self-defence, the prevailing rhetoric becomes narrower and more proscribed.

3. The Beat of a Butterfly's Wings: The Importance of Critical Reading

> ... this translates into what is only half-jokingly known as the Butterfly Effect — the notion that a butterfly stirring the air today in Peking can transform storm systems next month in New York. (Gleick, 1987: 8)

3.1. *Friends and foes*

In any act of communication, misunderstanding has such a high probability of developing that only a considerable degree of goodwill

---

[27] Hoover's review is deliberately intemperate, matching Mirowski's confrontational style with spleen.

> Yet, reading this book gave me a slowly, rising feeling of outrage. Taken as a whole, it is an outrageous book: neither the history nor the methodology is persuasive; the scholarship is often slapdash; the tone is intemperate; and the style is often obnoxious. Mirowski's hatred of neoclassical economics borders on the pathological: one sometimes wonders if his mother didn't run off with a neoclassical economist, leaving little Phil bereft in the cradle. (Hoover, 1991: 9, 139)

Hoover's review is thus an attempt at demolition rather than any sort of critical analysis. If indeed he finds the rhetorical style so bereft of redeeming value, it is curious that he should take to imitating it in his review. As such he is guilty of much that he finds objectionable about Mirowski's approach. He should rather explain why the style is inappropriate and then like Varian point out the weaknesses in Mirowski's case. Using ridicule to plead a position is a legitimate choice. It simply does not seem to be an appropriate one for Hoover to use despite his protestations. 'Some may believe that my taking such great exception to Mirowski's style is part of an overly refined sense of academic decorum. I do not think so. Some styles of argument are calculated to shut off reasonable discussion. At that I feel bound to protest'. (Hoover, 1991: 145).

allows the process to continue. This was pointed out by Keynes, perhaps filled with some prescient dread of how his own works would be misinterpreted by less than generous readers.

> This means, on the one hand, that an economic writer requires from his reader much goodwill and intelligence and a large measure of cooperation; and, on the other hand, that there are a thousand futile, yet verbally legitimate, objections which an objector can raise. In economics you cannot *convict* your opponent of error; you can only *convince* him of it. And, even if you are right, you cannot convince him, if there is a defect in your own powers of persuasion and exposition or if his head is already so filled with contrary notions that he cannot catch the clues to your thought which you are trying to throw to him. (Keynes, 1973: 470)

Economists have largely cribbed their style from what they believe is a standard scientific format. But writers in the natural sciences also unnecessarily ignore their readers, seeming more eager to simply get their data and observations down on paper than worrying if they can be easily understood. This though displays a fundamental misunderstanding of the purpose of writing.

> The fundamental purpose of scientific discourse is not the mere presentation of information and thought but rather the actual communication. It does not matter how pleased an author might be to have converted all the right data into sentences and paragraphs; it matters only whether a large majority of the reading audience accurately perceives what the author had in mind. (Gopen and Swan, 1990: 550)

As previously stated, communication does not simply take care of itself any more than good teaching is realised by merely picking up a piece of chalk. Reading and writing are two halves of the same Aristophanean egg. Good writing is not an afterthought but rather something that improves the quality of thought. Complex ideas do not demand obscurity of presentation but rather need the preciseness of an appropriate presentation[28]. This is not automatically

[28] An appropriate presentation is one that conveys the author's intended meaning in the simplest and most accessible manner possible. This does not mean simplified to the lowest possible denominator. Instead, one needs to ask, 'How does this presentation convey the intended meaning of the piece more accurately than some feasible alternative? Is this bit of prose, poetry, or mathematical formalisation really necessary to further the aim of this article'?

accomplished by shoving ideas onto the Procrustean bed of formal mathematics.

Critical reading means looking for a comprehensive and consistent explanation of an author's work. We first have to labor to understand what he or she actually intends to say. The author needs to be given the benefit of the doubt. Ideally it is only when we find ourselves unable to rescue a work that we can fairly conclude that it is flawed. At that time we must take upon ourselves the sad task of pointing out the source of the error or the unexplained links in the logic. Readers need to be taught how to do this, but they are also more likely not to take a hostile stance if it is clear that the author has tried to reach out to the reader. Instead of pandering to the presumed reader in the indirect manner already described, an open-ended format would allow for a more direct type of appeal.

This flight from words into the supposed precision, the harder currency of mathematical formalisation, becomes more understandable if we consider how a failure to read properly has shifted the terms of economic debate in the past and occasioned endless bouts of wrangling.

3.2. *Textual analysis*

> Ancient and rooted prejudices do often pass into principles; and those propositions which once obtain the force and credit of a principle, are not only themselves, but likewise whatever is deductible from them, thought privileged from all examination. (Bishop Berkeley quoted in Kline, 1980: 160)

An inability to master textual analysis has produced the sort of aliterate form of writing that predominates in today's leading journals. Given the opportunity, economists have been adept at misinterpreting what they read. For simplicity, let us look at four reasons that can lead down this road.

3.2.1. *The ability to follow only certain lines of reasoning*

The narrowly trained mind often operates as if it were an unreconstructed Kantian tied to *a priori* categories. Faced with any deviation from these few, well-travelled paths, they resolve this potential dissonance by reshaping alien ideas to fit a more familiar outline.

Jensen and Meckling (1976) find themselves unable to assimilate Herbert Simon's assumption of bounded rationality. They are obviously incapable of making sense of a statement outside of the standard economising structure of their analysis. Since they have no intention of being cruel to Simon by casually dismissing his work, and since he is a recognised and reputable economist, they can only make sense of his work by ignoring its stated meaning. That there is no basis for their interpretation seems not to worry them. Either Simon must mean this or he is talking rubbish. Generosity on their part wins out. The naivety of one particular footnote is revealing.

> Simon developed a model of human choice incorporating information (search) and computational costs which also has important implications for the behavior of managers. Unfortunately, Simon's work has often been misinterpreted as a denial of maximizing behavior, and misused, especially in the marketing and behavioral science literature. His later use of the term "satisficing" has undoubtedly contributed to this confusion because it suggests rejection of maximizing behavior rather than maximization subject to costs of information and of decision making. (Jensen and Meckling, 1976: 306n)

Maximising behavior is however just what Simon has long sought to reject.

> But utility maximization, as I showed, was not essential to the search scheme ... As an alternative, one could postulate that the decision maker had formed some *aspiration* as to how good an alternative he should find. As soon as he discovered an alternative for choice meeting his level of aspiration, he would terminate the search and choose that alternative. I called this mode of selection *satisficing*. It had its roots in the empirically based psychological theories, due to Lewin and others, of aspiration levels. (Simon, 1979: 503)

Being unable to conceive that reputable economists may take an alternative approach is hardly a problem of recent vintage. Marshall felt that he had to rescue Ricardo from the grasp of those Marxists and Socialists who claimed that Ricardo depended upon a labor theory of value rather than the sort of cost of production theory with which Marshall felt more at home.

> And yet Rodbertus and Karl Marx claim Ricardo's authority for the statement that the natural value of things consists solely of the labor spent on them; and even those German economists who most strenuously combat the conclusions of these writers, are often found to admit that they have interpreted Ricardo rightly, and that their conclusions follow logically from his. (Marshall, 1920: 672)

The reason for this claim, which Marshall strives mightily to deny, is that Ricardo said as much in as straightforward a way as possible.

> We have seen that the price[29] of corn is regulated by the quantity of labor necessary to produce it, with that portion of capital which pays no rent. We have seen, too, that all manufactured commodities rise and fall in price, in proportion as more or less labor becomes necessary to their production. Neither the farmer who cultivates that quantity of land, which regulates price, nor the manufacturer, who manufactures goods, sacrifice any portion of the produce for rent. The whole value of their commodities is divided into two portions only: one constitutes the profits of stock, the other the wages of labor. (Ricardo, 1886: 60)

Instead, Marshall concentrates on Ricardo's shortcomings as a writer. This becomes a common refrain. It cannot be the readers who are at fault, but rather the poor, inadequate writer. The victim of sloppy reading is blamed, the perpetrators spared. The profession, as a result, is quite rightfully distinguished by a fear of prose, which can be so capriciously misread.

---

[29] Ricardo is using price here to refer to exchange value as he explains in a note. 'The reader is desired to bear in mind, that for the purposes of making the subject more clear, I consider money to be invariable in value, and therefore every variation of price to be referable to an alteration in the value of the commodity'. (Ricardo, 1886: 60n)

3.2.2. *Reading with prior expectations*

How strongly resistant we are to seeing the obvious when it does not accord with our own preconceptions and desires. Initially, economic education comes largely from textbooks and lectures. Later on, we may extend our knowledge of earlier work by reading more recent journal articles. Seldom do we make the time-consuming attempt to evaluate these interpretations[30]. We seem incapable of recognising them as only interpretations, rather than choosing to accept them as summarising indisputable conclusions. Thus those who finally journey back to the source are incapable of approaching a well-known work with open eyes. Starting with preconceived ideas, we find in a work what we expect to find. Our prejudices are conveniently confirmed.

An oral tradition allows economists, if they choose, to largely ignore the original work. If everyone already knows what it says, why bother reading it. The force of widely held opinion assures that a mistaken reading can be virtually unassailable.

Generations of economists, both left and right in their political persuasion, have done just this. Such is the power of received habits over men's minds that a tradition that insists on reading Marx as though he were an English classical economist has been sustained over the years. It then ceases to matter how carefully these myths are debunked or even the reputation of the debunker. The oral tradition rolls on impervious to such attacks.

Even careful attempts from the mainstream of the profession will fail. Baumol's (1979) bid to dismiss the idea of subsistence wages (the iron law of wages) from the canon of Marxian folklore fails, just as an earlier attempt by Sowell (1960) at refuting '*the increasing misery of the proletariat*' as a tenet propounded by Marx also accomplished nothing. Vested interests on the right and the left hold on to their cherished myths as they have held onto other common Marxian aphorisms that have no foundation in Marx's work. There is startling little evidence

[30] The lowly status accorded to the history of economic thought reflects the lack of regard the profession has for such work. This is not regarded as serious research but rather as a hobby capable of amusing economists in their declining years.

that self-styled followers and promoters of various dead economists have ever read these authorities to any advantage. Would their icons feel comfortable at a meeting of their acolytes, or would they be forced to follow Marx in declaring, 'Je ne suis pas une Marxiste'?

The myth-making activity of economics is even stronger in the case of Keynes where both the origin of and the force of those myths are evident in every textbook we open. Economists reading Keynes' *General Theory* crave the familiar. They reject the revolutionary content of his book for the more comforting stories of the profession. In doing so, *The General Theory* loses its generality as minor points are elevated to keystone concepts.

One can argue that by focusing on wage rigidity and the liquidity trap, Keynes' system could be domesticated to fit into the standard general equilibrium frameworks then gaining popularity. In journal articles consumer sovereignty reigns, the consumers being restricted to the class of professional economists.

Thus, the more mechanical explanations, those that involved endogenous, equilibrating prices triumphed over those that seemed to rest on exogenous psychological forces. The liquidity trap (not so named by Keynes) is presented as a theoretical possibility only[31] rather than a serious impediment in pushing interest rates low enough to generate additional investment. Rather it is those issues which we might lump together as transaction costs[32] which keep rates measurably above zero.

> There is, finally, the difficulty discussed in section IV of Chapter 11 p. 144, in the way of bringing the effective rate of interest below a certain figure, which may prove important in an era of low interest rates; namely the intermediate

---

[31] 'But whilst this limiting case might become practically important in future, I know of no example of it hitherto. Indeed, owing to the unwillingness of most monetary authorities to deal boldly in debts of long term, there has not been much opportunity for a test. Moreover, if such a situation were to arise, it would mean that the public authority itself could borrow through the banking system on an unlimited scale at a nominal rate of interest'. (Keynes, 1936: 107)

[32] Curiously enough, Coase's (1937) simultaneous foray into the issue of transaction costs would also be largely ignored. Perhaps it just was not obvious how to incorporate either insight.

> costs of bringing the borrower and the ultimate lender together, and the allowance for risk, especially for moral risk, which the lender requires over and above the pure rate of interest. (Keynes, 1936: 208)

In a similar manner, clinging to the key role played by rigid wages allowed policy debate to be shifted onto more barren ground. Rigid money wages became the institutional friction preventing the perfect spinning of the wheels of the economy. Once this is seen as the crucial analytical assumption, economists can, with good conscience, retreat to telling each other the cosy myths that they find agreeable.

Keynes however wished to make the point that completely flexible wages would not improve the situation but, due to increased price instability would only make matters worse. Not only would not wage cuts lead necessarily to higher employment but they could create even greater uncertainty[33].

> In the light of these considerations I am now of the opinion that the maintenance of a stable general level of money-wages is, on a balance of considerations, the most advisable policy for a closed system; whilst the same conclusion will hold good for an open system, provided that equilibrium with the rest of the world can be secured by means of fluctuating exchanges. (Keynes, 1936: 270)

As readers, economists generally find in an article what they expect to find. They seem incapable of looking at an article with fresh eyes. Perhaps they do not even realise it as a necessary precondition for critical reading. Thus, even when economists reject the established myths of the trade, they simply attempt to substitute a new myth for an old one. Keynes is again a fruitful source of this breakdown in reading.

3.2.3. *Deliberate misreading for rhetorical ends*

> Is it possible that Homer meant to say all they make him say, and that he lent himself to so many and such different interpretations that the theologians,

---

[33] Many articles have tried to dislodge this myth from the collective memory of the profession, all to no avail. One good attempt is made by Applebaum (1979).

> legislators, captains, philosophers, every sort of people who treat of sciences, however differently and contradictorily, lean on him and refer to him: the general master for all offices, works, and artisan, the general counsellor for all enterprises? Whoever has needed oracles and predictions has found in him enough for his purpose. It is a marvel what wonderful correspondences a learned man, and a friend of mine, draws out of him in support of our religion; and he cannot easily let go of this opinion that this was Homer's purpose (yet he is as well acquainted with this poet as any man of our century). And what he finds in favor of ours, many of old had found in favor of theirs. (Montaigne, 1965: 442–443)

The flurry to discover the real Keynes, which would grow into a small cottage industry, began sometime in the sixties with two key publications. Clower (1965) posited a world of producers and consumers not necessarily inconsistent with Keynes' analysis but hardly representative of it. Leijonhufvud (1968) was so insistent in showing that money does play an essential role for Keynes that he practically transforms the idea that money does matter into a monetarist formulation that only money matters.

Each one starts with a quite legitimate critique of the received wisdom concerning Keynes. Each one then substitutes his own personal hobbyhorse for the discredited notion. They are trying, whether entirely deliberately, or not, to use Keynes to provide an imprimatur for their own ideas. Or to be generous, we might conclude that they simply do not know enough to shed their previous economic baggage before trying to reinterpret an overly interpreted work. It is difficult to know whether they are being dishonest when they quote out of context or use edited quotes to support their cases. Perhaps they don't even realise the partisan nature of their reading.

Allan Meltzer (1981) follows this route in his attempt to come up with a re-statement of Keynes that is consistent with Keynes' work. The confusion enters when in practice Meltzer equates this as meaning consistent with Meltzer's own work. Meltzer has long focused on rules versus discretion in policy measures as well as on the underlying basis for stable economic systems. Unfortunately, it is hard to credit Keynes with similar inclinations unless we use the terms in a very broad sense. Keynes argues that because investment is inherently unstable, a market economy is unlikely to be able to sustain a full employment level of activity. As Meltzer points out, this led Keynes to call for the socialisation of investment in order to gain this goal and at the same time avoid the worst of the fluctuations such economics are heir to. Sometimes, Meltzer seems to forget the boosting investment part, concentrating instead on the stabilising goal.

Unfortunately it is far from obvious that Keynes has the same sort of stability in mind that Meltzer has. In Chapter 18, which Meltzer quotes from at length, Keynes tries to explain why, despite the inherent instabilities within the capitalist system, the whole structure is unlikely to collapse. The logic of his presentation allows this to be a not inconsiderable possibility. By adding certain psychological propensities and conventions the likelihood of such an occurrence is reduced.

> In particular, it is an outstanding characteristic of the economic system in which we live that, whilst it is subject to severe fluctuations in respect of output and employment, it is not violently unstable. Indeed it seems capable of remaining in a chronic condition of sub-normal activity for a considerable period without any marked tendency either towards recovery or towards complete collapse. (Keynes, 1936: 249)

This is indeed a strange sort of stability. Under such a broad umbrella, any system avoiding the extremes of blood on the streets or full employment would qualify. Meltzer's defence is that the fluctuations are around an intermediate mean. If, though, we accept Meltzer's version of the equilibrium position adapted by Keynes we allow a perfect classical dichotomy between the short run and the long run. This is what Meltzer cannot legitimately squeeze out of Keynes. Conventions, as Keynes points out (1936: 204), do not themselves rest upon secure knowledge and are liable to change. Is it then not logical to think that those very same fluctuations that Meltzer would like to dismiss could change one or more of the stabilising conditions? In other words the intermediate position around which the economy circles may in fact also be given to change due to short-run variations.

Innocence of intentions may inform and partially excuse such re-interpretations. No absolution should be extended when distortions are not the result of errors but rather an indication of malice afore-thought. Such instances help to explain the previously discussed trend towards defensive writing in economics.

3.2.4. *Reading with the intent to destroy*

Economists can so dislike the conclusions of an article, or what they perceive to be the conclusions, that they comb through the article with the sole hope of refuting its logic. If these ungentle readers are determined enough, they generally succeed. If need be, they take an intentionally obtuse position, refusing to admit anything that is not pointed out in lavish detail.

When attacking a theory it is perhaps advantageous to present that theory in a somewhat simplified version. At least initially a too nuanced presentation tends to muddle the critique, making it difficult to comprehend. The temptation is to simplify a theory not only for clarification purposes but to further one's own argument against it. When the simplification comes to light, we see a version of the theory constructed to be vulnerable to a specific attack. Equipped with a providentially tailored Achilles heel, critical arrows easily find their mark. A towering theory seems to collapse from its own inherent weakness rather than from the critic's cleverly applied prosthetic device. If presented forcefully enough, future debate focuses on this hot house theoretic version rather than the sturdier and more complex original[34]. With the passage of time too many academics gain stakes in keeping the lame version afoot. Their arguments and counter-arguments have been honed to the peculiar requirements of the constructed theory. At the moment when the simplification supplants the original, a tradition, a bit of folklore, becomes firmly implanted in the daily discourse of the discipline and nearly impossible to uproot.

---

[34] This is strangely equivalent to literary critics relying on the movie version of James Joyce's work as the basis of their analysis.

George Stigler, well known for his slash-and-burn rhetoric, recasts all arguments by thrusting them onto the rack of his own analysis. By assuming that critical reading is a combat sport, he approaches an article like a wrestler facing a deadly foe. Given the set up of his target, it is no great trick to successfully conduct an autopsy into the causes of its death. Most textbooks have taken Stigler's version (1947) of Sweezy's (1939) kinked demand curve as an accurate representation. Other commentators have gone so far as to reproduce his sardonic humour by using Stigler's ambiguous re-labelling of kinky for kinked demand curve.

Sweezy's (1939) article is too short and straightforward to make Stigler's reconstruction of it anything but deliberate. What has entered the textbooks is a model manufactured in order to self-destruct in a convincing manner. Stigler does not try to test Sweezy's suppositions but an easily dismissed concoction of his own. What he shoots down is Stigler's version of rigid prices. He does this by drawing conclusions, which do not necessarily follow from Sweezy's original model.

Sweezy starts by constructing a model where prices fail to respond automatically to changes in costs. This analysis is done holding demand constant. He not only presents the familiar kinked curve but the less familiar inversely kinked curve, which allows for price leadership and secret discounting from listed prices. Once the model is established, he allows for changes in demand, this being his real goal. His purpose is not simply to show that prices are stable, but rather to explore how oligopolies react to changes in demand. His testable hypotheses are clearly listed.

> As far as the cyclical behavior of oligopoly prices is concerned we might expect to find (1) that prices go up easily and openly, in time of upswing; (2) that prices resist downward pressure in times of recession and depression; and (3) that list prices become less trustworthy guides to real prices the longer bad times last. I think this analysis can be developed in such a way as to throw valuable light on the much debated problem of rigid prices, but to do so would be beyond the scope of this paper. (Sweezy, 1939: 572)

Stigler ignores what Sweezy wants to do, instead using the model as a device to attack the concept of rigid oligopoly prices. In doing so, Stigler fails to distinguish between price changes due to variations in cost versus variations in demand. Nor does he distinguish the varying market circumstances in the industries he investigates. In other words, his refusal to approach Sweezy's model as anything but an abstract, generalised, equilibrium construct completely runs counter to Sweezy's purposes.

> This leads to a famous criticism which appears, sadly enough, in most first year textbooks. The theory of the kinky demand curve explains why prices that have been stable should continue to be stable despite certain changes in demand or costs. But the theory does not explain why prices that have once changed should settle down, again acquire stability, and gradually produce a new kink. (Stigler, 1951: 417)

Sweezy is quite clear why he intentionally does not deal with this issue.

> No attempt is made to explain how the current price and output situation came about except as it may be explained by reference to a previously existing situation. This is unavoidable since imagined demand curves, unlike the ordinary demand curves of economic analysis, can only be thought of with reference to a given starting-point. That starting-point itself cannot, of course, be explained in terms of the expectations to which it gives rise. Once this is realised, it becomes very doubtful whether the traditional search for "the" equilibrium solution to a problem in oligopoly has very much meaning. Generally speaking, there may be any number of price-output combinations which constitute equilibriums in the sense that, ceteris paribus, there is no tendency for the oligopolist to move away from them. But which of these combinations will be actually established in practice depends upon the previous history of the case. Looking at the problem in this way the theorist should attempt to develop an analysis which will enable him to understand the processes of change which characterize the real world rather than waste his time in chasing the will-o'-the-wisp of equilibrium. (Sweezy, 1939: 572–573)

This sort of suggestion is exactly what Stigler seemingly dislikes and which he simply ignores. In Sweezy's case, models are seen as heuristics to aid analysis rather than applicable in some almost mechanical and universal way. The proposed methodological shift is too radical to even prompt Stigler to comment. Instead, Stigler seems more concerned with the paper Sweezy did not write. It is as though the most salient point to a literary critic about Dashiell Hammett was his glaring failure to write *Look Homeward Angel* rather than his influence on the genre of detective fiction. To reiterate, it seems somewhat peculiar to fault an author for the article he or she did not write. The issue is how well aims are accomplished and the importance of those aims.

Summary. Given economists as readers, it is no wonder that economists as writers flee from prose whenever possible. The sometimes-false precision of mathematical formulation is seen as a safe refuge when compared to the potential ambiguity inherent in discursive presentations. Economists, at times display an almost wilful desire to misinterpret. The result is an innate distrust of any deviation in style from the canonical standard. In this sense, economists follow Plato in seeking to remove poets and other rhetoricians from acceptable economic society. They are regarded as a threat to the rigorous standards of the tribe. If as Freud once remarked, ambiguity is a sign of maturity, then most economists are still in their swaddling clothes.

4. Hypocrite Lecteur

Hypocrite lecteur, mon sembable, mon frere. (Baudelaire, 1964: 16)

If journals have degenerated to a point where they consist of articles by people who cannot write, producing articles for people who cannot read, what then is to be done to change this depressing situation?

The first step would be an increased tolerance, the sort of tolerance that Donald McCloskey has called for elsewhere. The ubiquitous standard format is not forcibly discarded. This is not about substituting one inflexible standard for another, but rather a willingness among readers to view this as just one among many possible alternatives. From there we would hope to progress by demanding higher standards of writing no matter what the format chosen. This means that appropriateness and accuracy of expression are prized more than pure precision. Stylistics then are not to be ignored as some mere matter of form. The content conveyed speaks through the style in which it is conveyed. In fact it is a decisive element of whether the article speaks at all.

Unfortunately, it is praiseworthy but ineffective to call for better writers without first realising that we need better readers in this market-driven world. McCloskey urges a self-consciousness on the part of the writer[35]. But such a self-consciousness would only make the writer aware of why he or she was choosing a particular style. What incentive does this desired self-awareness present which would lead the writer to actually forego a readily accepted rhetorical form?

These articles are written for a particular audience. Would the rhetoric flourish if no one really wanted it? Much in the same way that everyone condemns the proliferation of mindless violence, we all in a similarly high-minded spirit call for the end of poor and unnecessarily obtuse writing. But deep down we do not want change. Posing costs very little. To actually attempt to change the standards of the economics profession is at best a frustrating endeavour. McCloskey does claim, 'If even economics can be shown to be fictional and poetical and historical, its story will become better'. (1990: 162). Why though should this change the stories economists want to read or make them into more critical readers?

Like small children, economists hate having their stories varied. A few plots and ways of telling the story seem to suffice. If then we agree with McCloskey that economists are storytellers, how do these tellers of tales decide which stories to tell and how to tell them? To fall back on the archetypal story of all, they must be giving their readers the narrative they want. For anyone then, but especially for an economist, to complain about the appalling writing appearing in the major journals is in reality to express dissatisfaction with the readership. The writing does have an obvious utilitarian basis. Since writing well takes time, a fill-in-the-blanks style is efficient if no objection is raised by the readership. If there were more discriminating readers, more would be demanded from the writers

---

[35] In a sense, McCloskey imitates the skilful psycho-analyst. Awareness precedes the cure, or to be more exact, the shedding of the old for the new personality. This process of therapy doesn't even start however until there is an initial desire for change. That is why Dr McCloskey's couch will remain largely unoccupied. The profession is still generally satisfied with itself.

of journal articles. The limitations of their prose reflect the limitations of their readers. Both proceed in an ungainly, mutually reinforcing tango that removes economists from the responsibility of developing critical reading abilities.

Change is unlikely despite the best efforts of McCloskey and others. If optimists see this as the best of all possible worlds and pessimists are afraid that it is, I suppose I know where to line up in this great division between hope and despair. Change could come only if the reviewers for the acknowledged major journals were to have an inexplicable change of heart. If we are honest, we must admit that the fate of the discipline is largely shaped by what these journals are willing to publish. Publication, more than anything else, holds the key to tenure and recognition in academic life. Economists write in a style they think will meet with acceptance. In other words, they mimic the existing style of those key journals. Reviewers would have to start demanding superior and cleaner presentations. But this smacks of the sort of dues-ex-machina that Euripides used to mock the pretensions of the human plight. Humans unable to rectify their situation look to miracles as their only hope.

> We know little of how traditions get established, while it seems clear that once established, a tradition does not get changed through calling attention to its absurdity or that of the factual assumptions upon which it rests. Such things happen 'when the time is ripe'. (Knight, 1955: 272)

References

Applebaum, E (1979). The Labour Market. In *A Guide to Post-Keynesian Economics*, AS Eichner (ed.), pp. 100–120. New York: ME Sharpe.

Baudelaire, C (1964). *Les Fleurs Du Mal.* Paris: Editions Gallimard.

Baumol, WJ (1979). On the folklore of Marxism. *Proceedings of the American Philosophical Society*, CXXIII(2): 124–128.

Blank, RM (1991). The effects of double-blind versus single-blind reviewing: Experimental evidence from *The American Economic Review*. *American Economic Review*, LXXXI(5): 1041–1067.

Bronfenbrenner, M (1990). Economics as dentistry. *Southern Economic Journal*, LVII(3): 599–605.

Caldwell, BJ (1991). Has formalization gone too far in economics: A comment. *Methodus*, III(I): 27–29.

Coase, RM (1937). The nature of the firm. *Economica*, IV(3): 386–405.
Coats, AW (1991). The learned journals in the development of economics and the economics profession: The British case. *Economic Notes*, XX(1): 89–116.
Ellis, EV and GC Durden (1991). Why economists rank their journals the way they do. *Journal of Economics and Business*, XLIII(2): 265–270.
George, H (1958). *Progress and Poverty: An Inquiry into the Cause of Industrial Depressions and of Increase of Want with Increase of Wealth — The Remedy.* New York: Robert Schalkenback Foundation.
Gleick, J (1987). *Chaos.* New York: Penguin.
Gopen, GD and JA Swan (1990). The science of scientific writing. *American Scientific*, LXXVII: 550–558.
Graves, R (1955). *The Greek Myths Volume 1.* Middlesex: Penguin.
Hoover, KD (1991). Mirowski's screed: A review of Philip Mirowski's more heat than light: Economics as social physics, physics as nature's economics. *Methodus*, III(3): 139–145.
Katzner, DW (1991). In defense of formalization in economics. *Methodus*, III(3): 17–25.
Keynes, JM (1973). *The Collected Works of John Maynard Keynes*, Vol. IV. London and Basingstoke: MacMillan.
Keynes, JM (1936). *The General Theory of Employment, Interest and Money.* London: MacMillan.
Keynes, J (1973). *The Collected Works of John Maynard Keynes*, Vol. XIII. London: MacMillan.
Klamer, A and D Colander (1990). *The Making of an Economist.* Boulder: Westview Press.
Kline, M (1980). *Mathematics and the Loss of Certainty.* Oxford: Oxford University Press.
Knight, FH (1955). Schumpeter's history of economic analysis. *Southern Economic Journal*, XXI(3): 261–272.
Mahoney, J (1985). *Marshall, Orthodoxy and The Professionalisation of Economics.* Cambridge: Cambridge University Press.
Marshall, A (1920). *Principles of Economics*, 8th edn. Philadelphia: Porcupine Press.
Marshall, A (1923). *Industry and Trade.* London: MacMillan and Company.
McCloskey, DN (1985). *The Rhetoric of Economics.* Madison: University of Wisconsin Press.
McCloskey, DN (1990). *If You're So Smart.* Chicago: University of Chicago Press.
McCloskey, DN (1983). The rhetoric of economics. *The Journal of Economic Literature*, XXI(2): 481–517.
Meltzer, AH (1981). Keynes's general theory: A different perspective. *Journal of Economic Literature*, XIX(I): 34–64.
Mill, JS (1965). *Principles of Political Economy.* New York: Augustus M. Kelley.
Mirowski, P (1989). *More Heat Than Light: Economics as Social Physics: Physics as Nature's Economics.* New York: Cambridge University Press.

Mongell, S and AE Roth (1991). Sorority rush as a two-sided matching mechanism. *The American Economic Review*, LXXXI(3): 876–891.

Montaigne, M (1965). An apology for Raymond Sebond. In *The Complete Essays of Montaigne*. Stanford: Stanford University Press.

Ricardo, D (1886). *The Works of David Ricardo*. London: John Murray.

Sowell, T (1960). Marx's 'Increasing Misery' doctrine. *The American Economic Journal*, L(1): 111–120.

Stigler, GJ (1951). The Kinky Oligopoly demand curve and rigid prices. In *Readings in Price Theory*, KE Boulding and GJ Stigler (eds.), pp. 410–439. London: Allen and Unwin.

Stigler, G (1961). Alfred Marshall's lectures on progress and poverty. *Journal of Law and Economics*, X(1): 181–183.

Sweezy, PM (1939). Demand under conditions of oligopoly. *The Journal of Political Economy*, XLVII(4): 568–573.

Thomas, A (1964). *Summa Theologiae*. Cambridge: Blackfriars McGraw Hill.

Turgenev, IS (1950). *Fathers and Sons*. London: Hamilton.

Varian, H (1991). More heat than light: A review article. *Journal of Economic Literature*, XXIX(2): 595–596.

Veblen, T (1976). On the penalty of taking the lead. In *The Portable Veblen*. Middlesex: Penguin Books.

Whitely, R (1991). The organisation and role of journals in economics and other scientific fields. *Economic Notes*, XX(I): 6–32.

Chapter 12

Shunning the Frumious Bandersnatch: An Unacknowledged Assumption of Coase's Theorem

Beware the Jabberwock my son!
The jaws that bite, the claws that catch!
Beware the Jub Jub bird, and shun
The frumious Bandersnatch!

(Carroll, 1956: 15)

Theories do not die easily. No carefully selected critical stake seems capable of laying them to rest. Instead, like the undead, they seem to thrive on and draw life from those very critics who seek to violate their invulnerability. Having long ago forsaken the romantic possibilities of performing as a fearless vampire killer, I see no purpose to be served by trying to demolish long established theorems. Any attempt to dramatically banish such immortals to the nether regions of some fancied academic inferno is in large part fruitless. Most well-conceived theorems, accepted on their own terms, prove invincible. Ideas do not vanish at the first sign of enlightened truth as vampires are obligingly said to do at those warning streaks of daylight. But, if any theorem is carefully scrutinised for the purpose of understanding rather than vanquishing it, sometimes such an examination can cause it to fade into a much-deserved obscurity or to be refashioned into a more pertinent formulation.

At times, economic ideas rest on unacknowledged assumptions. Such assumptions may be so standard in the prevailing academic work that any controversy surrounding a particular economic model swirls instead around other issues. This leaves the basic theoretical underpinnings inviolate. When however, new doubts arise as to the primacy of such assumptions, the relevant theorems can be usefully reassessed in this new light. Recent empirical work indicates that one of the evergreens of economic thought, Coase's Theorem, rests on a possibly untenable supposition. As such, this may cause a need to alter any evaluation of Coase's 1960 article as well as to rethink the academic call to arms that Coase provided and has continued to provide ever since.

Coase's original work was the first of the fire breaks built against the *market failure* literature, which legitimised government intervention. Strictly speaking, the brief of that article extended no further than to the undermining of an automatic justification for any such positive action. Yet the rhetorical formulation of the argument led many economists to advance it as a defence of the market *status quo*. The onus of proof shifted to those advocating intervention in lieu of pure market transactions.

A re-examination of Coase's Theorem can separate policy implications from rhetorical overtones. Moreover, Coase and his chosen opponent, Pigou, turn out not to hold such irreconcilable positions. Misunderstanding is largely the result of a careless use of economic benchmarks.

A more controversial issue is the unacknowledged dependence of Coase's position on the assumption of symmetry of choice. Adopting recent empirical evidence, which denies the consistent applicability of such an assumption, allows a certain stripping away of those often misleading rhetorical overtones in order to more carefully evaluate the content of Coase's work. In this way the policy implications of externalities can be analysed in a somewhat less-biased fashion.

1. Coase's Theorem

The fox knows many things, the hedgehog one big thing

(Archilaous quoted by Isaiah Berlin in Shackle, 1967: 135)

Coase has essentially championed one particular insight throughout his long career. *Arranging for economic exchange must necessarily entail a cost.* Starting with his 1937 article on the firm, he has consistently defined these as transaction costs. This one idea has permeated and transformed economics at many different levels. For my purposes I will only concentrate on the way in which these costs shape economic institutions. This can be explained as attempts to minimise the existing cost of initiating and executing economic exchange. In the case of a firm, administrative control substitutes for market coordination of the same activity[1]. To summarise, institutions and trading arrangements arise which will increase a society's total output. This reflects the long-standing economic assumption which places self-interested behaviour as working those levers yielding observed results[2].

Coase, by focusing on the problem of transaction costs, has developed a broadly applicable technique, which clarifies the trade-off defining any economic choice. He uses this technique to identify a fundamental flaw in what had become the standard accepted analysis of externalities. Previously, the identification of any unpaid service or disservice presented a *prima facie* case of market failure requiring the saving grace of non-market coordination to correct the resulting distortions. More generally, any deviation away from the accepted Pareto efficient standard automatically required the visible paw of governmental correction to improve economic results.

---

[1] For additional explanation see Coase's oft-cited article, *The Nature of the Firm* (1937).

[2] When backed against a theoretical wall, most economists will plead simplification or necessity while attempting to shift the responsibility for this assumption on to Adam Smith.

> The natural effort of every individual to better his own condition when suffered to exert itself with freedom and security, is so powerful a principle that it is alone, and without any assistance, not only capable of carrying on the society to wealth and prosperity, but of surmounting a hundred impertinent obstructions with which the folly of human laws too often encumbers its operations. (Smith, 1976, Vol. II: 49–50)

The obvious error in such a broad generalisation lay in assuming that governmental action, unlike private economic actions, was essentially costless to implement, devoid of any attendant transaction costs. Any change however must involve concomitant costs as well as associated gains. The transaction costs involved in a governmental intervention might then be so prohibitively high as to clearly overwhelm any presumed benefits. In such cases, the wise thing to do would be to opt for the *status quo*. At least as early as 1946, Coase was taking aim at this rather naïve justification for government interference in his analysis of the Marginal Cost Controversy[3].

But this proved to be a mere warm up for his collision with an economic icon. A. C. Pigou, Marshall's designated heir, becomes Coase's preferred bête noire in his seminal 1960 paper, 'The Problem of Social Cost' (Coase, 1988c)[4]. Repeatedly, he faults Pigou for engaging in empty theorising.

> The Pigouvian analysis shows us that it is possible to conceive of better worlds than the one in which we live. But the problem is to devise practical arrangements which will correct defects in one part of the system without causing more serious harm in other parts (Coase, 1988c: 142)

---

[3] See Coase (1988b) for the detailed argument. What Coase terms the Hotelling–Lerner approach for achieving efficient levels of production when faced with decreasing cost industries required the corrective of a governmental subsidy paid for out-of-tax receipts. The implicit assumption in this analysis is a government that casts virtually no shadows. Abstracting from the ever-present trade-offs that such an intervention must always incur, unfairly prejudices the preferred solution. For Coase, this is mere 'Blackboard economic', existing apart from any conceivably practical application. It is more an intellectual diversion than it is a potentially useful analytical exploration.

> Whatever its merits as a means of regulating the generation of harmful effects, the use of taxes had the added attraction that it could be analysed by existing price theory, that the schemes devised looked impressive on a blackboard or in articles, and that it required no knowledge of the subject. (Coase, 1988d: 179)

[4] He would continue to pursue this crusade against what he saw as Pigou's wrong-headed and misleading analysis. See his attempt to demolish the textbook notion of a public good in *The Lighthouse in Economics* (1998e).

The world for Coase is not constructed for the convenience of economists. Economic analysis must be done on a case-by-case basis. Direct application of any generality must as a result be highly suspect. Pigou's use of such abstractions heavily influenced the development of welfare economics[5]. The work of his followers proceeded to identify market failure with the need for government intervention. Coase rejects this approach as over-simplified and misleading.

Shuttling the train of investigation off on a theoretical spur line essentially caused this failure to distinguish between theoretical models and corrective policy prescriptions. Simply spotting an externality does not warrant a government intervention. Yet, in the frictionless world of optimisation that Pigou and his followers created, one can effortlessly erase any market failure by engineering a corrective tax or subsidy. Given Pigou's assumptions, this generalisation follows. Once the comfort of these assumptions is surrendered, no such generalisation can survive. The mere presence of an uncompensated service or disservice suggests a deviation from an idealised condition of efficiency but not the requirement for governmental mediation.

> Economist, following Pigou, spoke of uncompensated disservices and implied that those responsible for these harmful effects ought to be liable to compensate those they harmed. (Coase, 1988d: 179)

It does not take much thought to see that such generalisations can lead to economic absurdities. Harm inflicted by one individual on another does not necessarily invite correction. An externality, a disservice done by one economic agent in pursuit of his or her own benefit should not have to condemn the destructive properties of competition. Otherwise, the same economists would ironically have to condemn the destructive properties of competition. As Alchian

[5] See Pigou (1932). Coase's quarrel with Pigou actually goes back at least as far as his 1946 paper, 'The Marginal Cost Controversy'. Economies of scale in production led Pigou to advocate subsidising such industries to increase economic welfare. This approach was picked up and developed by subsequent economists.

(1977: 224) points out, greater harm can be done to the owner of a firm through competition than can come about through physical encroachments of that owner's property rights[6]. As a logical consequence, government ought to also intervene to restrain any harmful effects due to competition. Given that competition must involve some losers, governments would need to handicap all participants until they resembled the homogeneous firms of perfect competition, until in fact, competition as it is more commonly understood vanished[7].

In a similar fashion, since Pigou is obviously referring to a violation of property rights, such violations will undoubtedly occasion economic losses. But as Coase notes, this is not reason enough to change the *status quo*. The gain from correcting the harm must outweigh the costs of correction. Otherwise we are logically compelled to conclude, using parallel logic that just as all losses due to a violation of property rights must be corrected, so must economic losses due to competition. Both would require the obligatory intervention of government.

Coase's message is aimed in the broadest sense at all such generalities. Nothing of value eventuates from economists indulging an unwarranted nostalgia for the absolute. Useable applications rather than generalizable theorems are the imperative need.

The goal of what has become known as Coase's Theorem is to point out that the allocation of resources remains the same whatever the legal position regarding liability for harmful effects be. By erasing

---

[6] Despite a tendency to equate existence with efficiency, Alchian has always brought a certain level-headed approach to practical economic issues.

> If I open a restaurant near yours and win away business by my superior service, you are as hurt as if I had burned part of your building. (Alchian, 1977: 294)

[7] The competitive battle for market share engenders change. The result of that change is unlikely to yield an anonymous group of identical firms. To maintain this statically defined industrial structure of perfect competition, competition in the more dynamic sense must be constrained if not eradicated.

the impediment of transaction costs, reallocations of property rights cease to lead to an increase in the value of production[8].

> But the ultimate result (which maximizes the value of production) is independent of the legal position if the pricing system is assumed to work without cost. (Coase, 1988c: 104)

Following Coase's analysis we begin to understand his animus towards a Pigouvian formulation. Wrong starting points tend to wayward analysis. The focus of debate is shifted to more peripheral and less directly applicable territory.

> A better approach would seem to be to start our analysis with a situation approximating that which actually exists, to examine the effects of a proposed policy change, and to attempt to decide whether the new situation could be, in total a better course than the original one. (Coase, 1988c: 154)

Coase's article has generated almost uncounted commentaries, objections and critiques. It has arguably changed the way economists think about externalities, though Coase might evaluate the change as generating considerable heat while emitting only intermittent light. Doing the proposed heavy lifting involved in measuring all the relevant transaction costs often remains honoured mostly in the breach, leaving us to wonder how practical such an approach turns out to be.

---

[8] Coase is less clear as to what happens to the distribution of wealth given different endowments of rights. In his initial 1960 paper, he seems to admit that distribution is not independent of legal liability.

> ... such an agreement could not affect the allocation of resources but would merely alter the distribution of income and wealth between cattle raiser and farmer. (Coase, 1988c: 100)

On later consideration it seems that he realises that altering distribution can change underlying market demand and thus resource allocation. This causes a rather conditional denial of his previous position:

> ... a change in the liability rule will not lead to any alteration in the distribution of wealth. There are therefore no subsequent effects on demand to be taken into account. (Coase, 1988d: 171)

Both the article and the subsequent note are long and repetitious, perhaps indicating Coase's basic mistrust in the ability of economists to assimilate new ideas. It is not hard to argue that he is justified in this regard.

> The world of zero transaction costs has often been described as a Coasian world. Nothing could be further from the truth. It is the world of modern economic theory, one which I was hoping to persuade economists to leave. (Coase, 1988: 174)

Yet, despite the very moderate and reasoned tone of much of his writing, the almost subliminal impression that comes from reading the relevant articles is one of market efficiency. In defiance of the Pigouvian tradition, the onus is thrust back on those economists who advocate intervention to plead their case. Coase is far too careful to make such explicit claims. Much in the article and subsequent note denies any presuppositions. Why then does this widely held belief persist? There is after all a measurable step between stating that government actions have costs and claiming that these costs will usually make intervention prohibitively expensive. Since any change incurs transaction costs, the former claim is definitional while the latter conclusion needs to be argued.

Upon careful examination, that persistent, if possibly imagined, belief about the message of the article appears to be the result of rhetorical devices seemingly at odds with one another. One obvious aspect is a tendency for throwaway lines that create an initial impression, which is not entirely modified by subsequent analysis and discussion.

> It is my contention that the suggested courses of actions [Pigouvian remedies] are inappropriate in that they lead to results which are not necessarily, or even usually, desirable. (Coase, 1988c: 96)

But this contention largely remains unexamined. The argument takes great pains in demonstrating that these results are not necessary. The problem arises in determining whether such results are usually desirable or not. Coase does mention the presence of political pressures and the absence of competitive checks (1988c: 119). The former has provided the foundation for the political choice theory of Buchanan and Tullock, while the latter strain of argument has been developed by Alchian (1977). By the logic of his own article however, Coase is not justified in sliding into such market sentiments. He should rather remain staunchly agnostic about the preferred mode of operation[9]. As he makes clear, it is only his belief that the advantages of regulation have been oversold by economists.

> But this belief, even if justified, does not do more than suggest that governmental regulation should be curtailed. It does not tell us where the boundary line should be drawn. (Coase, 1988c: 119)

Coase can legitimately offer no firm judgement on this matter until the necessary empirical work is completed. In that case the reader is entitled to ask the reason for intruding such a belief into the article. It plays no necessary role in the core argument he constructs. Remove it and nothing is lost. Instead, the rhetorical point of market efficiency still remains implicitly in the very form in which Coase presents his argument.

2. Nivana Economics — The Problem of Benchmarks

> Just Dolly and me
> And Baby makes three
> We're happy in my Blue Heaven
>
> (Hammerstein and Harbach, 1926)

Some little thought allows us to realise that Coase and Pigou have quite different starting points and subsequently different policy prescriptions.

---

[9] There are a few such points of slippage. Coase seems to unnecessarily favour market solutions. Having pointed out that regulating will not necessarily give better results, he acknowledges that on occasion it might lead to greater economic efficiency (1988c: 119). The modifier, 'on occasion', relegates it to the exception rather than the rule. Though this may not be true in a strict definitional sense, this meaning is conveyed by the tone.

What is easy to overlook is that they share a common benchmark, the common standard of Pareto efficiency[10].

The comparative institutional framework that Coase advocates is not inconsistent with such benchmarks. These only provide a way of measuring performance against an ideal, which remains as a goal even if actually unreachable. Without such benchmarks we are in danger of reducing efficiency to a situational standard. We move from the comparative institutional framework of Coase (1988c) or Demsetz (1969) to the reductionist world of Jensen and Meckling (1976) where market solutions, given the existing constraints are by definition what is meant by efficiency. This simply erases the issue of whether a market outcome is efficient or not[11]. Though Coase means to subsequently investigate a world where transaction costs are inevitable, his theoretical starting point is a world devoid of any impediments.

What Coase is objecting to is not the benchmark itself. His world of costless exchange is identical to one of Pareto-efficient results.

---

[10] Over the years, some economists have railed against the use of such benchmarks. In this view, efficiency needs to be defined in a realistic fashion rather than following the never never land dictates of academic theory.

> Blackboard economics is undoubtedly an exercise requiring great intellectual ability and it may have a role in developing the skills of an economist, but it misdirects our attention when thinking about economic policy. (Coase, 1985a: 19)
>
> In practice, those who adopt the nirvana viewpoint seek to discover discrepancies between the ideal and the real and if discrepancies are found, they deduce that the real is inefficient. (Demsetz, 1969: 1)

[11] Jensen and Meckling (1976) accomplish this slight of hand by adapting a Social Darwinist approach to institutional change i.e. existing institutions are optimal or they would not continue to exist.

> If we could establish the existence of a feasible set of alternative institutional arrangements which would yield net benefits from the reduction of these costs we could legitimately conclude the agency relationship engendered by the corporation was not Pareto optimal. However, we would then be left with the problem of explaining why these alternative institutional arrangements have not replaced the corporate form of organization. (Jensen and Meckling, 1976: 328, ftn. 23)

Coase takes exception to Pigou's insistence that a deviation from that benchmark, in the presence of externalities, creates a *prima facie* case for government intervention due to market failure. Note that it does not follow that such a case will necessarily exist. The onus however is on opponents to demonstrate that in fact such an intervention, though well intended, is actually misguided. What Coase implies and others such as Demsetz and Alchian insist is that, to the contrary, the onus should be placed on those who wish to prove a case for meddling with the market mechanism.

The disparity here is not one of conflicting benchmarks, or benchmarks versus comparative institutional analysis, but of starting points. Coase starts by assuming the frictionless world of costless transactions, a world identical to that of his benchmark. Loosening assumptions to allow for transaction costs creates a deviation from the assumed norm, which may or may not be ameliorated through regulation, taxes, or a change of legal framework (reassignment of property rights). This is a matter of comparative costs rather than some *a priori* judgement.

In essence, Coase's theorem reduces to saying that were it not for those things which make markets inefficient, markets would be efficient. As always, it is impossible to argue against a tautology, the intellectual equivalent of shouting down a drainpipe. What lifts the theorem out of the realm of inherent insipidity is Coase's attempt to pinpoint the cause of any such deviation. Care must be taken. Simply intoning transaction costs may be less than illuminating. In a rather circular fashion, transaction costs, at least implicitly, become that which prevents markets from being efficient i.e. a catch-all phrase encompassing any possible contingency. The danger here is simply equating market exchange with efficiency. In a similar way, maximising behaviour may be equated to any and all human behaviours. It is doubtful that such vacuous formulations are capable of serving any ends other than ideological ones.

Granted that relevant transaction costs can be specified and content attached to this broad framework, we still must deal with why Coase chose to start his argument with the frictionless case. An article's rhetorical framework cannot be assumed to be either incidental or coincidental. By starting with a series of frictionless cases, Coase implicitly defines the *status quo*, the *laissez faire* condition, with economic efficiency. Rhetorically this is gaining the metaphorical high ground by defining what the norm is. Deviation from this norm is impossible without first somewhat arbitrarily defining that initial position. This starting point need not be identical to the accepted efficiency benchmark. Alternative assumptions yield other norms. But by starting with an immaculate market efficiency, transaction costs provide the only occasion for a deviation without providing any automatic support for governmental action.

Pigou failed to see that his model also assumes zero transaction costs. Otherwise, government action cannot achieve the presumed benchmark of Pareto efficiency. But given zero transaction costs, Coase's theorem also holds. This means that either market exchange or government action will costlessly eliminate any potential inefficiency due to the presence of externalities, in which case, the choice is more one of aesthetics than of necessity. An unbiased policy-maker would be indifferent to choosing either course of action. Coase, in that sense, is also not quite correct. In the absence of transaction costs there would be no need for governmental solutions, and there would equally be no compelling reason to avoid such options. Coase is placing the onus on the non-market alternative without providing any compelling basis for doing so.

Pigou however creates confusion by muddling a clear distinction. Either he can have costless exchange, in which case market failure due to externalities is self-correcting, or he can allow for transaction costs in market exchanges, in which case the market failure is due to the existence of transaction costs rather than the externality. The presence of both of these conditions makes Pigou's starting point a vehicle for imprecise thought.

> Nevertheless it is difficult to resist the conclusion, extraordinary though this may be in an economist of Pigou's stature, that the main source of this obscurity is that Pigou had not thought his position through. (Coase, 1988c: 149)

It is possible though to salvage Pigou's choice of a non-efficient starting point, if not entirely his complete reputation, by delving into an, until recently, unexamined question. Coase's justification of his efficient starting point, in the absence of transaction costs, rests in part on an assumption of rational choice, which is never articulated throughout Coase's work, not because he deliberately obfuscates the issue but because traditionally the assumption has been so widely accepted as to pass by without notice. Such an assumption is part of the subconscious of every professional economist. But by raising doubts, Coase's logical starting point, though more precise than Pigou's, becomes just as much of a dreamworld.

3. Acknowledging the Unacknowledged — Symmetrical Choices, Asymmetrical Results

> ... the disutility of giving up an object is greater than the utility associated with acquiring it. (Kahneman *et al.*, 1991: 194)

Like stability, symmetry of choice is one of several assumptions made about the preferences of rational economic agents that yield the reassuring map of convex, non-intersecting indifference curves familiar to most economic students. It is such a standard assumption that seldom is it explicitly articulated in the specification of most economic models. It remains at a less than conscious level of awareness. There lies the persistent danger attached to habits of wont and use. Through habitual use, assumptions fade into the back reaches of awareness. Custom becomes transmuted into reality. Like skilled Indian fakirs, having once ascended their ladders of abstraction, economists pull the rope rungs up after them, cutting themselves off from the source of their own abstraction.

Whether such unexamined acceptance is deliberate or not, unacknowledged assumptions continue to provide the foundations for all subsequent analyses. Seemingly innocuous assumptions like that of symmetry of choice need to be stripped of any pretence of innocence. The choice of assumptions is not as unarguable as would often appear simply based on a consensus of common usage. Economists tend to confuse behavioural assumptions made for analytical convenience with the observed behaviour. For instance, having spent their careers assuming self-interested motivation, some economists are capable of entertaining only such an explanation behind any action just as some public choice theorists can only see rent seeking when examining human behaviour.

Coase's analysis thus is correct only within the limitation of his own assumptions[12]. If we examine his ongoing morality play featuring farmers and cattle raisers, he starts by assuming that the price either party is willing to accept for an existing legal right is identical to what they would be willing to pay to acquire that right. Farmers would be willing to accept the same payment to allow damage to be done to their property, as they would pay to prevent the same damage from being done. From this it follows that the assignment of legal rights will not affect the outcome of market exchange. At a more generalised level, individual preferences are assumed independent of initial endowments, such as the endowment of a particular property right.

Symmetry of choice does not seem counter-intuitive but rather bears a certain logical attraction. It is most likely based on the appeal to introspection much as diminishing marginal utility owes its appeal to a similar thought experiment[13]. But unlike transitivity,

---

[12] Coase may be closer to Pigou than he would have chosen to be. In the absence of transaction costs, the all-healing balm provided by the imposition of government taxes is equivalent to the smooth working of the market mechanism. Coase does not fault Pigou's logic. Replying to Baumol he maintains that

> ... what Baumol meant by saying that, 'taken on its own grounds, the conclusions of the Pigovian tradition are, in fact impeccable', was that its logic was impeccable and that, if its taxation proposals were carried out, which they cannot be, the allocation of resources would be optimal. This I never denied. (Coase, 1988d: 185)

Pigou never imagines that such an optimal tax system can be implemented. Coase never assumes that transaction costs can equal zero. Even in the zero gravity-like world that both assume, the result would not be Pareto-efficient unless both assume symmetry of choice amongst economic agents. In a sense they both start off in similar dream worlds. The issue that differentiates their approaches is whether the existence of an externality does in fact create a *prima facie* case for government intervention. Is the onus of proof to lie with the defenders of the market or should it be shifted to the promoters of non-market coordination?

[13] See Mainwaring (1990) for a discussion of diminishing marginal utility.

positing the opposite assumption does not lead to a reductio ad absurdum. Other than for analytic convenience or because of *a priori* desired results, there is no *prima facie* case to be made for symmetry over its negation. Neither of these behaviours is irrefutably irrational. Individuals may simply view choices involving different endowments as distinct rather than equivalent. This may make any analysis more complex, but behaviour does not exist for the convenience of the analyst.

The assumption of non-symmetrical choice may not always be the relevant one to make. Though, in this case, Coase would be hard put to use his favourite conjurer's trick of dismissing this objection as a pure theoretical possibility unlikely to occur with any significant frequency[14]. The evidence there refutes any such cavalier dismissal.

Recent empirical work seems to indicate that in the absence of transaction costs there are still endowment effects which cause allocation results to deviate from a Pareto-efficient benchmark. Such seeming anomalies in economic theory, variously defined as loss aversion or *status quo* biases, are potentially widespread[15]. If so, the initial identification that Coase uses between this benchmark and a world with zero transaction costs is illegitimate. If such assumptions of symmetry and reversibility are reduced to possible but potentially non-useful

---

[14] Coase uses this tack to acknowledge Samuelson's objection to his argument while simultaneously relegating it to a perpetual Gulag circumscribing trivial academic quibbles.

> It is certainly true that his secretary might not agree to make these side payments, or, what comes to the same thing, to accept a reduction in salary even though this would make her (and Samuelson) better off; or Samuelson might worsen his situation (and hers) by taking up plumbing because in his view she was not willing to reduce her salary enough; but I would regard such outcomes as being, in these circumstances, most unlikely, particularly in a regime of zero transactions costs. (Coase, 1988d: 163)

[15] See Kahneman *et al.* (1991) for a recent survey of this literature.

normative assumptions, the identity between benchmarks and working assumptions is relinquished[16].

> If the existence of nonreversible indifference curves is pervasive then the assumptions of reversibility will represent a normative ideal but will not serve as a very useful description of actual economic behaviour in most circumstances. (Knetsch, 1989: 1282)

The results of any such behavioural tests can always be questioned. Nothing is resolved once and for all by such staged experiments. Methodologies can be labelled as faulty. Results are liable to alternative interpretations. Yet the results are strong enough to make us wonder whether the assumption of symmetry should remain as an implicit basis for applicable rather than benchmark models. If we return to Coase's theorem, the consequences of adopting either assumption are not trivial. Our starting point changes from efficiency to inherent inefficiency.

> An implication of this asymmetry is that if a good is evaluated as a loss when it is given up and as a gain when it is acquired, loss aversion will, on average induce a higher dollar value for owners than for potential buyers, reducing the set of mutually acceptable trades. (Kahneman *et al.*, 1990: 138)

---

[16] The shape of indifference curves and their corresponding contract curve would both logically depend on a given initial endowment if we assume non-reversible and non-symmetric preferences. Certainly given a set of endowments, the marginal rate of substitution between two goods would be dependent on the direction of exchange. Swapping x for y would not by definition be identical to the reverse process. The contract curve itself would not be generated purely by the given preferences but by initial endowments as well. Possible Pareto-efficient states would multiply as well, given this endowment effect. To retain reversible, symmetric preferences as some sort of a benchmark might entail a redefining of Pareto-efficiency. We might say that given the possibility, people would be better off in such an alternative world (or at least some would and no one would be worse off). But given a set of endowment-dependent preferences, trading no longer yields a Pareto improvement under these revised circumstances. They would move to that superior position if they could, but the possibility is sealed off by the nature of their preferences. In such a world, the change would not prove to be a Pareto improvement. At this point, one wonders whether the additional complexity is at all useful.

Coase observes 'Traits which lead to such an outcome have little survival value'. (Coase, 1988d: 162). By this he is referring to non-exchange due to differences in buying and selling prices. The issue though is whether the number of transactions is reduced from that predicted using a Pareto-efficient benchmark, not whether they are eliminated. Outcomes then will obviously vary according to the initial arrangement of legal rights. If individuals demand more to allow the polluting of a river than they are willing to pay to prevent pollution, then the composition of the river will change according to the way in which the pertinent property rights are initially assigned.

By taking the assumption of symmetry as a given but unacknowledged basis for what follows, Coase distracts the reader from an underlying difficulty. Once recognised, Coase's starting point becomes questionable. It is no more defensible for Coase to start with a world of efficient markets than for Pigou to assume inefficiency[17]. If in fact we are careful to distinguish between our benchmark assumptions and those of our working model, we might more usefully start with market inefficiency. The proper course of action would then be to explore whether such inefficiency could be successfully modified. This would depend on whether the potential gains in moving closer to our chosen benchmark outweigh the inevitable and concurrent cost of effecting any such change.

This is no trivial issue if only from a rhetorical standpoint. Implicitly the structure of Coase's article supports a belief in market efficiency as an automatic default position. Deviation from efficiency needs to be explained rather than the presumption of efficiency itself. Coase chooses transaction costs to account for inefficiency. Yet, at least in some instances, particularly where externalities are concerned, the pertinent costs are not merely due to the types of information

[17] Pigou in his work on social welfare (1932) formulated what became the standard treatment of externalities. The resulting deviation from Pareto efficiency created a *prima facie* case for governmental intervention. Coase's work aimed to remove any such presupposition from economic analysis.

asymmetries underlying transaction costs[18]. As Schelling (1984) as well as Coase have pointed out, it is important to understand clearly what the problem is before we evaluate any potential solution. In this case, concentrating on transaction costs alone can be as misleading as the Pigouvian presupposition of costless government intervention. Given an asymmetric valuation, we inevitably start with certain inertial costs (due to the aforementioned endowment effects), which impede successful exchange and by definition distort outcomes whether or not transaction costs exist.

Asymmetric valuation can be lumped together under wealth effects but this reduces two separable items to one indistinguishable effect. Distributional effects refer to differences in income flows resulting from different allocations of legal entitlements. This in turn will affect the allocation of resources to some degree, though perhaps only trivially. Asymmetric valuation is in its own way a wealth effect since legal entitlements of this type are by definition a scarce resource. But it is the valuation itself of these legal entitlements, which change according to whether one is buying or selling. The effect is on the initial terms of exchange and subsequent allocation of resources rather than the subsequent wealth creation and distributional effects previously described.

---

[18] Commonly, both the strategic nature of bargaining and the possibility of *ex post* distributional effects have been advanced as reasons for non-optimal results even in the absence of transaction costs. Coase rejects both these possibilities. Strategic bargaining in the form put forward by Samuelson is rejected as trivial in nature.

> Samuelson also lays stress on the indeterminacy of the final result. While this is true for purchases of all kinds and therefore applies to all of economic analysis, the existence of indeterminacy, as Edgeworth showed, does not of itself imply that the result is non-optimal. (Coase, 1988d: 163)

Nor will Coase accept that *ex post* distributional effects will change resource allocations in the absence of transaction costs.

> Any change in income flows, provided that the rule of liability is known, will be offset by changes in the relevant assets. I consider this argument to be wrong, since a change in the liability rule will not lead to any alteration in the distribution of wealth. There are therefore no subsequent effects on demands to be taken into account. (Coase, 1988d: 171)

In Coase's famous farmer/rancher example he contends that the end result, the actual social product, is independent of the initial distribution of rights. This implicitly assumes symmetric preferences. The endowment effect argues against such a conclusion, not due to a subsequent wealth effect, which Coase denies[19], but rather as the result of an *a priori* asymmetry in preferences. The end result of bargaining in the absence of transaction costs may change depending upon who is granted legal liability. The farmer's willingness to pay to prevent damage may not be identical to his price for permitting the cattle to do harm. Thus the amount of crops vs cattle raised will depend on where the legal liability rests. More to the point, the optimal preservation of wildlife or rainforests may also be to some degree a function of assigned legal liability.

4. Letting a Little Asymmetry into Coase's Theorem: Consequences and Prescriptions

> It appears to me that the most fatal of all errors would be general admission of the proposition that a government has no right to interfere for any purpose except for that of affording protection, for such an admission would be preventing our profiting from experience and even from acquiring it. (Nassau Senior quoted by Reisman, 1990: 55)

The consequences of rereading Coase's seminal article in light of asymmetrical choice are surprising. The core of his conclusions, stripped of any taint of ideological bias, remains. If anything, it is

[19] In *Notes on the Problem of Social Cost* (1988d), Coase explicitly respond to this criticism.

> I consider this argument to be wrong, since a change in the liability rule will not lead to any alteration in the distribution of wealth. There are therefore no subsequent effects on demands to be taken into account. (Coase, 1988d: 177)

Coase trots out his basic farmer/rancher scenario to demonstrate this. There will be no change in wealth distribution because the relevant asset values (farm and ranch land) will adjust to cancel out such supposed redistributions. Those interested in a detailed exposition of this argument can refer pp. 170–174 of Coase's article (1988d). This debate however is at best peripheral to the concerns of this article.

strengthened and perhaps clarified. Contrary to Coase's hypothesis, even in the absence of transaction costs, the assignment of property rights is all-important and cannot be changed without cost. The end result may be suboptimal since the cost of reassigning the rights may be greater than the potential gains[20]. History can condemn an economy to a valley of efficiency lower than that which would have occurred given an alternative set of events. The path to improvement is thus at least temporarily blocked by circumstances.

Coase then is certainly not entirely correct in asserting (1988d: 157) that if a cave is newly discovered, what that cave is ultimately used for will not depend on the law of property but rather on who is willing to pay more for its use. The value a party attaches to that cave depends upon whether or not that party owns a legal entitlement of that cave. Thus, whether the cave ends up being used for storing bank records, as a natural gas reservoir or for growing mushrooms may have important distributional antecedents. If resource allocation is not indifferent to initial distributions of legal entitlements, the task of the economist becomes more complex. Allocations must be compared, but so must the costs and benefits of changing existing legal entitlements. Policies that are cost-effective under one distributional environment may cease to be so under another. Such an analysis must logically precede any subsequent concern about Coasian transaction costs.

As Coase states, there is certainly no *prima facie* case to be made for governmental intervention due to the existence of a sub-efficient outcome. Market failure may not indicate the possibility for improvement. But neither is there a case to be made in general against such an intervention. If, as seems likely, human choice creates a certain

[20] Even measuring welfare losses becomes problematic given an inherent asymmetry of valuation.

> Nor will the traditional assumption of symmetry of valuations and complete reversibility of indifference curves seem as useful a basis for predicting economic behaviour or as defendable a basis for the common practice of substituting payment measure for compensation measures of welfare losses. The common practice of assessing losses in economic well-being by people's willingness to pay to avoid the change may result in significant understatements if indifference curves are not reversible. (Knetsch, 1989: 1282–1283)

allure for the *status quo*, a shunning of the imagined sharp beak and pointed claws of potential alternatives, the costs as well as the gains from change need to be re-evaluated. To the traditional costs due to arranging for successful market transactions are added those needed to overcome an inherent inertia, which resists changes to the *status quo*. It is unclear how the addition of inertial costs changes the balance between potential gains and costs of change[21]. As Coase would point out, this can only be decided on a case-by-case basis[22].

---

[21] Initially it might seem that inertial cost added to those more standard costs translates into a greater deviation from the benchmark measure of efficiency. Such costs though need not reinforce one another but rather may tend to cancel each other out. In a world of second best, distortions need not be additive.

[22] An example from Coase's original paper on social cost can be easily adapted to demonstrate this. Coase argues the following:

> Assume that a factory which emits smoke is set up in a district previously free from smoke pollution, causing damage valued at \$100 per annum. Assume that the taxation solution is adopted and that the factory-owner is taxed \$100 per annum as long as the factory emits the smoke. Assume further that a smoke-preventing device costing \$90 per annum to run is available. In these circumstances, the smoke-preventing device would be installed. Damage of \$100 would have been avoided at an expenditure of \$90 and the factory-owner would be better off by \$10 per annum. Yet the position achieved may not be optimal. Suppose that those who suffer the damage could avoid it by moving to other locations or by taking various precautions which would cost them, or be equivalent to a loss in income of \$40 per annum. Then there would be a gain in the value of production of \$50 if the factory continued to emit its smoke and those now in the district moved elsewhere or made other adjustments to avoid the damage. (Coase, 1998c: 151)

Suppose though that if the home-owner holds the legal entitlement, the value attached to that right is not the cost of relocating but something much higher, say \$95. The factory-owner thus installs the smoke-preventing device. On the other hand, if the factory-owner holds a right to pollute, the home-owner's willingness to pay the factory-owner to stop polluting may be much less than \$95. It may be only \$40, the opportunity cost of relocation. This is undoubtedly insufficient as it does not cover the cost of installing a smoke-preventing device. As a result, resource allocation alters depending on whether or not the factory-owner is liable for the smoke it emits. The home-owner is not irrational but merely judges the two situations as discernibly different. This will hold whether or not the home-owner is given to opportunistically motivated strategic bargaining.

There is a need for caution in presenting any economic judgement. No firm basis exists for the prevailing tendency to overpromise the potential benefits derivable from either a governmental or a market approach to allocation problems. Both approaches have fallen into the popular disrepute due largely to unwarranted promotional campaigns by their advocates. On this key issue, which has so long divided and defined economic analysis, agnosticism, on reflection, remains the only tough-minded approach. Otherwise, economists, like other investigators, are likely to discover only their preconceived ideas in any given situation. This does not resolve any of the century-long debates. It instead removes the contentious question from legitimate discussion, replacing it with problems of a more specific nature. Economics can make larger strides by providing approaches to problem-solving than by trying to settle unresolvable ontological questions.

This wearisome game of the King of the Mountain, pursued with great avidity by champions from both camps, serves only to foil claims and counterclaims of these matched opponents. Deny the validity of the debate and much unproductive confusion falls away.

Coase's 1960 article served to redirect economic conversation by redefining the terms of the debate. Recent empirical work on the nature of economic choice and valuation does much to control the excesses of those who developed Coase's original insight. If taken to heart, such a revaluation of Coase's Theorem can successfully separate what economists know from what they individually wish and desire.

References

Alchian, AA (1977). 'Some economics of property rights'. In *Economic Forces At Work*, AA Alchian (ed.), pp. 291–311. Indianapolis: Liberty Press.

Carroll, L (1956). *Through the Looking-Glass.* New York: Macmillan.

Coase, RH (1937). 'The nature of the firm'. *Economica, New Series*, 4: 386–405.

Coase, RH (1964). 'Discussion'. *American Economioc Review*, 54: 194–197.

Coase, RH (1988a). 'The firm, the market, and the law'. In *The Firm, the Market, and the Law*, pp. 1–31. Chicago: University of Chicago Press.

Coase, RH (1988b). 'The marginal cost controversy'. In *The Firm, the Market, and the Law*, pp. 75–93. Chicago: University of Chicago Press.

Coase, RH (1988c). 'The problem of social cost'. In *The Firm, the Market, and the Law*, pp. 95–156. Chicago: University of Chicago Press.

Coase, RH (1988d). 'Notes on the problem of social cost'. In *The Firm, the Market, and the Law*, pp. 157–185. Chicago: University of Chicago Press.

Coase, RH (1988e). 'The lighthouse in economics'. In *The Firm, the Market, and the Law*. pp. 187–213. Chicago: University of Chicago Press.

Demsetz, H (1969). 'Information and efficiency: another viewpoint'. *Journal of Law and Economic*, 12: 1–22.

Jensen, MC and WH Meckling (1976). 'Therory of the firm: Managerial behavior, agency costs and ownership structure'. *Journal of Financial Economic*, 305–360.

Hammerstein, O III and YIP Harbach (1926). 'The Desert Song'.

Kahneman, D, JD Knetsch and R Thaler (1990). 'Experimental tests of the endowment effect and the Coase theorem'. *Journal of Political Economy*, 98: 1325–1348.

Kahneman, D, JD Knetsch and R Thaler (1991). 'The endowment effect, loss aversion, and status quo bias'. *Journal of Economic Perspectives*, 5: 193–206.

Knetsch, JD (1989). 'The endowment effect and evidence of nonreversible indifference curves'. *The American Economic Review*, 79: 1277–1284.

Mainwaring, L (1990). 'Marginalism and the margin'. In *Foundations of Economic Thought*, J Creedy (ed.), pp. 87–124. London: Basil Blackwell.

Pigou, AC (1932). *The Economics of Welfare, 4th Edn.* London: Macmillan.

Reisman, DA (1990). 'The state and economic activity'. In *Foundations of Economic Thought*, J Creedy (ed.), pp. 28–58. London: Basil Blackwell.

Schelling, T (1984). *Choices and Consequences.* Cambridge, Mass.: Harvard University Press.

Shackle, GLS (1976). *Years of High Theory.* London: Macmillan.

Smith, A (1976). In *An Inquiry into the Nature and Causes of the Wealth of Nations*, E Cannan (ed.). Chicago: Chicago University Press.

Chapter 13

Animal Spirits in His Soup: A Look at the Methodology and Rhetoric of *The General Theory*

> Because, said Scrooge, a little thing affects them. A slight disorder of the stomach makes them cheats. You may be an indigestible bit of beef, a blot of mustard, a crumb of cheese, a fragment of an underdone potato. There's more of gravy than of grave about you, whatever you are! (Dickens, 1875: 27)

1. Introduction

More than fifty years since the initial publication of *The General Theory*, relatively little attention has been paid to the methodology and rhetoric which underlies this work. Only in the last decade such issues have really been afforded the serious attention they deserve[1].

[1] Methodological interest seems to have been boosted by the centenary of Keynes' birth (1983) which coincided with a general revival of interest in such questions. See Lawson and Pesaran (eds.) (1985), Carabelli (1988), Fitzgibbons (1988), or O'Donnell (1989) for a variety of methodological issues that Keynes' work raises.

Economists generally allowed the rhetorical aspects of the discipline to slumber until the profession was jolted out of its long dogmatic nap by Donald McCloskey. In the past, decade McCloskey has himself generated a veritable paper blizzard of articles and books (1983, 1985, 1990, 1993). Others have since jumped on this particular bandwagon creating one of the newest cottage industries in the economic

Its seeming lack of coherence, often dwelt upon by a variety of commentators, largely vanishes if we are willing to concede that Keynes tried to make a methodological as well as a theoretical break with his predecessors, a break partially assisted, but also at times completely muddled, by a deliberate rhetorical strategy. By taking this interpretive approach, Keynes's ideas cease to be so opaque.

Instead, most economists seem content to snipe at Keynes's arguments, or to concentrate on aspects of his thought that they find congenial. This approach may accurately reflect one's own predilections but it falls sadly short of describing the aims of the actual work. For these reasons, an alternative approach might prove to be more productive. (1) Start by extending some old-fashioned courtesy to the author of what is unequivocally a seminal work[2]. (2) Assume that

---

kingdom. Extensive works on the peculiarities of Keynes' own rhetorical devices are still rather underdeveloped. Keynes is perhaps unusual amongst economists in being conscious of his own rhetorical pose. See Brown (1991) and Boland (1985) for a short discussion of this point as well as Dow (1988) and Harcourt (1986).

[2] Keynes himself, though not easily swayed, never shut himself off from other approaches. When his perceived facts changed he did not venture out in search of more congenial facts.

> This means, on the one hand, that an economic writer requires from his reader much goodwill and intelligence and a large measure of co-operation; and, on the other hand, that there are a thousand futile, yet verbally legitimate, objections which an objector can raise ... (Keynes, 1973: 469–470)

Keynes consistently deprecated a typically non-generous spirit often demonstrated by his fellow economists.

> When one looks at Keynes's copy of the review [Hayek's review of Keynes's *Treatise on Money*] the most heavily annotated article in the surviving copies of his journals, one finds he wrote at the end: 'Hayek has not read my book with that measure of "goodwill" which an author is entitled to expect of a reader. Until he does so, he will not know what I mean or whether I am right." Perhaps a similar reaction to what he believed to be unsympathetic criticism helped to mar (from Keynes's side) the once pleasant and fruitful relationship between Keynes and D.H. Robertson in the course of the 1930s. (Moggridge, 1976: 34–35)

Keynes successfully presented a comprehensible and coherent theory. (3) Adopt the common law tradition that he is innocent of error until proven guilty.

Taken together as a basis for interpretation, these three steps strongly imply that the onus of proof rests no longer with Keynes but with the scrupulous reader. If we initially fail to grasp the intrinsic coherence of the work, the fault does not necessarily lie with *The General Theory*. The solution is not immediately to reject uncongenial pieces of the book or even to claim that the work is a poorly stitched together amalgamation of different threads. The thoughtful interpreter will prefer to redouble all efforts rather than carp at the difficulties involved. It is only by first making such an honest attempt to unlock the meaning and purpose of the author that we subsequently earn the right to adopt a more critical stance.

For many economists, it is far from clear that Keynes bothered to make the smallest methodological detour, let alone a significant break (Boland, 1985)[3]. The presumptive micro-foundations of *The General*

Those who sought to quibble over every potential sticking point without regard to the methodological or rhetorical framework employed, succeeded only in sidetracking the overall terms of debate.

> But it was an essential truth to which he [Marshall] held firmly that those individuals who are endowed with a special genius for the subject of economics and have a powerful economic intuition will often be more right in their conclusions and implicit presumptions than their explanations and explicit statements. That is to say, their intuitions will be in advance of their analysis and their terminology. Great respect, therefore, is due to their general scheme of thought, and it is a poor thing to pester their memories with criticism which is purely verbal. (Keynes, 1951: 211n)

[3] This would come as a surprise to Keynes himself who believed that his book was revolutionary both in its theoretical as well as in its policy implications.

> To understand my state of mind however, you have to know that I believe myself to be writing a book on economic theory which will largely revolutionize — not, I suppose, at once but in the course of the next ten years — the way the world thinks about economic problems. When my new theory has been duly assimilated and mixed with politics and feelings and passions, I can't predict what the final upshot will be in its effect on actions

Theory, given this position, diverge insignificantly from the familiar individual optimisation of the standard received theory, the 'habitual modes of thought and expression' (Keynes, 1960: viii) against which Keynes claimed to be struggling. This view necessarily explains a failure of markets to deliver full employment as a correctible market malfunction, not as an inherent characteristic of markets per se. But such a reading explicitly denies to Keynes not only his methodological break but also the rhetorical relevance of attaching the adjective 'general' to the theory he propounds. Interpretations of this type, by focusing on the price stickiness of variables such as wages, end by standing Keynes on his head[4]. *The General Theory* becomes merely a special case encompassed by what Keynes labels 'classical theory'[5].

Given the uncertainty that Keynes posits[6], the classical optimum is only one of many equally likely possibilities. Unregulated market

---

> and affairs. But there will be a great change, and in particular, the Ricardian foundations of Marxism will be knocked away.
>
> I cannot expect you or anyone else, to believe this at the present stage. But for myself I don't merely hope what I say, in my own mind I'm quite sure. (John Maynard Keynes in a letter to George Bernard Shaw, 1 January 1935, quoted in Shaw, 1988: vii)

[4] See among other work that of Applebaum (1979), Chick (1983, 1985), Lawlor *et al.* (1987) and Brown (1991) for convincing demonstrations of Keynes's intentions. For Keynes, price stickiness rather than presenting a problem, provided a market economy with stability.

[5] Please note that Keynes does not refer to any variant of Walrasian general equilibrium. Classical does not encompass quite the same ideas as those often associated today with the term neoclassical.

> 'The classical economists' was a name invented by Marx to cover Ricardo and James Mill and their *predecessors*, that is to say for the founders of the theory which culminated in Ricardian economics. I have become accustomed, perhaps perpetuating a solecism, to include in 'the classical school' the *followers* of Ricardo, those, that is to say, who adopted and perfected the theory of Ricardian economics, including (for example) J.S. Mill, Marshall, Edgeworth and Prof. Pigou. (Keynes, 1960: 3)

[6] It is important to be clear about the manner in which Keynes employs the term uncertainty, since the inclusion of uncertainty as the rule rather than the exception in

competition would not necessarily move the economy in that particular direction. Therefore, the classical case cannot in any sense of the word be general[7]. An all-encompassing theory would entertain a multitude of possibilities; much in the way that projective geometry includes Euclidean, Riemannian and Hyperbolic as special cases. In this mathematical example, projective geometry is the more general theory since it continues to hold without the necessity of more stringent assumptions.

The failure to see Keynes' methodological break seems tied up with a similar failure to recognise the rhetorical strategy Keynes employs to advance his aims. This is somewhat ironic. Keynes struggled to break loose from the mundane modes of thought which he saw as stifling the economics profession in much the same way that conventional modes of behaviour could retard an economy from generating employment. Unfortunately, standard analysis, by disregarding rhetoric as being irrelevant to economic theory would be lulled by

---

his theory is the starting point for the methodological break that he makes. Markets are inherently riddled with uncertainty. Given this assumption, the failure of a market system to insure high levels of employment is not an imperfection but rather a defining characteristic.

> By 'uncertain' knowledge, let me explain, I do not mean merely to distinguish what is know for certain from what is only probable. The game of roulette is not subject, in this sense, to uncertainty; nor is the prospect of a Victory bond being drawn. Or, again, the expectation of life is only slightly uncertain. Even the weather is only moderately uncertain. The sense in which I am using the term is that in which the prospect of a European war is uncertain, or the price of copper and the rate of interest twenty years hence, or the obsolescence of a new invention, or the position of private wealth-owners in the social system in 1970. About these matters there is no scientific basis on which to form any calculable probability whatever. We simply do not know. (Keynes, 1937: 213–214)

[7] For a discussion of what Keynes means by the term *general* see Kriesler (1993).

> I shall argue that the postulates of the classical theory are applicable to a special case only, and not to the general case, the situation which it assumes being a limiting point of the possible positions of equilibrium. (Keynes, 1960: 3)

the conventionality of Keynes's rhetoric into largely overlooking the methodological departures implicit in his work.

Words, as Keynes himself knew, are written in the hope of persuading potential readers. 'It was in a spirit of persuasion that most of these essays were written, in an attempt to influence opinion' (Keynes, 1963: v). He would no more choose his words and approach carelessly than he would the theories and policies he intended to forcibly advocate. Form and substance created a seamless whole. Keynes fashioned his rhetorical stance to focus on what he saw as the key element behind inadequate aggregate demand, the inherent volatility of investment. As a result, consistently high levels of employment would be forever in conflict with market determined levels of investment. More explicitly, Keynes's policy aims fashioned certain necessary stations which he saw as prophetically leading to the salvation of economic theory.

- (Step 1) to overthrow Say's law[8] and all it implies (Keynes, 1960: 4–22);
- (Step 2) to demonstrate that without assuming a fixed level of aggregate demand, flexible wages will not act to equilibrate the system through the demand and supply of labour (Keynes, 1960: 2–33, 257–271);
- (Step 3) to indicate the systemic origin of involuntary unemployment (Keynes, 1960: 245–254, 313–332);

---

[8] For simplicity, I will use the version which Keynes himself formulates.

> Thus Say's law, that the aggregate demand price of output as a whole is equal to its aggregate supply price for all volumes of output, is equivalent to the proposition that there is no obstacle to full employment. If, however, this is not the true law relating the aggregate demand and supply functions, there is a vitally important chapter of economic theory which remains to be written and without which all discussions concerning the volume of aggregate employment are futile (Keynes, 1960: 26).

Certainly Keynes constructs this law in a rhetorically convenient fashion. His aim is after all to demonstrate that a preoccupation with aggregate supply yields an insufficient depth of analysis. This provides his wedge for insisting on equal standing for aggregate demand.

- (Step 4) to show that its cause lies in the inherent instability and fluctuation of the investment process (Keynes, 1960: 245–254);
- (Step 5) and to conclude that since investment will only by chance be large enough to ensure full employment, this investment process must be socialised (Keynes, 1960: 372–383).

Keynes attempts to make this argument in a quite logical and coherent fashion. Evidence for this position lies in the way he sets about accomplishing these highly dependent steps. Keynes makes a methodological break from what he labels the classical tradition. He does this by arguing that an economic environment ruled largely by conventional judgments is not necessarily chaotic or resistant to analysis. It is not however the most conducive ground for the strict application of mechanical models, specifically those involving optimising agents. This is why Keynes cautions against the indiscriminate use of mathematical analysis. False rigour only provides the semblance of understanding[9]. Economics remains largely an art for Keynes, providing an approach to economic problems but largely dependent on the skill and intuition of the practitioner[10]. In doing so he implicitly takes issue with John Stuart Mill who though recognising the force of custom in economic matters saw such custom as impervious to rational analysis.

> Political economists generally, and English political economist above others, have been accustomed to lay almost exclusive stress upon the first of these

[9] Throughout his writing there are throwaway lines that seek to create a proper perspective for mathematical formulations.

> Too large a proportion of recent 'mathematical' economics are mere concoctions, as imprecise as the initial assumptions they rest on, which allow the author to lose sight of the complexities and interdependencies of the real world in a maze of pretentious and unhelpful symbols. (Keynes, 1960: 298)

[10] Keynes stressed the importance of economic intuition, a quality often these days more readily observed in the breach than the practice.

> Good economists are scarce because the gift for using 'vigilant observation' to choose good models, although it does not require a highly specialised intellectual technique, appears to be a very rare one. (Keynes in a letter to Harrod, 1938, quoted in Moggridge, 1976: 26)

agencies, to exaggerate the effect of competition, and to take into little account the other and conflicting principle [custom]. They are apt to express themselves as if they thought that competition actually does, in all cases, whatever it can be shown to be the tendency of competition to do. This is partly intelligible, if we consider that only through the principle of competition has political economy any pretence to the character of science. (Mill, 1965: 242)

Keynes's methodological break with the past came from a deliberate attempt to incorporate uncertainty into his economic models. The optimising calculator of traditional theory is necessarily transformed into a more recognisable individual leaning heavily on conventional judgments and evaluations.

We should not conclude from this that everything depends on waves of irrational psychology. On the contrary, the state of long-term expectations is often steady, and, when it is not, the other factors exert their compensating effects. We are merely reminding ourselves that human decisions affecting the future, whether personal or political or economic, cannot depend on strict mathematical expectations, since the basis for making such calculations does not exist; and that it our innate urge to activity which makes the wheels go round, our rational selves choosing between the alternatives as best we are able, calculating where we can, but often falling back for our motive on whim or sentiment or chance. (Keynes quoted in Dow and Dow, 1985: 48)

To understand the form that this methodological break took, we must first turn to a brief examination of Keynes's rhetorical strategy as well as to an initial attempt to define the use of convention in an economic framework.

2. Rhetorical Strategies, Conventional Actions

The point of Keynes' assault is that he wished to challenge the advocates of neoclassical economics *on their own terms* — namely, in a world where only individuals make decisions. If he were to try to criticise them on radically different terms, his views could too easily be dismissed as being irrelevant for questions addressed by neoclassical economics. (Boland, 1985: 192)

Success for Keynes, as for any other thoughtful author, depended not solely on the content of his work but at least partially on its presentation.

Accomplishing his aims required treading along a fairly restricted path. Knowing that his main points of contention could easily be buried if opponents could shift the terms of debate, Keynes was quite willing to grant 'classical theory' all but a minimum number of assumptions. Rhetorically, he concentrated the fury of his attack against previously entrenched positions regarding investment. There was deliberately and explicitly no attempt to offer an alternative set of micro-foundations in his discussion of investment or elsewhere in the book. The individual decision maker and the competitive market both serve as adequate starting points for his discussion. The points made were largely seen as independent of such considerations[11]. Though in this case, as in many of the points raised in his concluding chapter of *The General Theory*, it is far from clear how many of these issues are conceded to reassure his opponents, or more precisely, to remove a potentially controversial and distracting point of contention from their grasp. Certainly correspondence with Gerald Shove indicates that he was far from wedded to standard models of the firm[12].

---

[11] See Keynes (1960: 245, 377–379) for attempts to neutralise any such micro-foundation discussion. This did not stop contemporaries of Keynes from attempting to supply these missing underpinnings in the immediate post-war period. See Freedman (1995) for a summary of this attempt. More recently this long-abandoned search for micro-foundations consistent with the analysis cultivated in *The General Theory* has been taken up by a variety of post-Keynesian economists. See Weintraub (1979), Niman (1987), Katzner (1991), Taylor and Williams (1991–1992) and Kriesler (1993) for a few examples of this project.

[12] One of the earliest exchanges of letters Keynes had following the publication of *The General Theory* was with Gerald Shove of King's College who immediately recognised the micro-problem implicitly posed.

> I thought you were too kind to the 'classical' analysis as applied to the individual industry and firm. Unless very artificial assumptions (e.g. perfect and instantaneous fluidity of resources) are made, it seems to me either wrong or completely jejune. I have been groping all these years after a re-statement of it on lines similar in some respect to your solution for the system as a whole, stressing in particular 'expectations' and the influence of current and immediately past experience upon them. But I can't make it precise. (Shove, 1936: 1)

The rhetoric of the book deliberately tries to provoke potential opponents into responding to a few well-chosen points. Keynes wants to force them to rethink their own positions in the process of attempting to refute his own allegations. Otherwise, received wisdom would continue to be accepted in an unexamined fashion. Keynes's ability to shape an appropriate rhetoric to advance his particular theoretical points may at times have faltered. His well-known judgment on Marshall's unreasonable yearning after unachievable perfection[13] means that he was well content to put his own ideas out for publication well before perfection could have been achieved.

For rhetorical reasons alone, Keynes could not throw all of the bathwater out with the baby. Some soapy residue would necessarily have to cling to whatever theory he proposed. But this strategy ultimately helped to blur his fundamental methodological break. Keynes was evidently not overtly concerned with the 'elements of the system' (Keynes, 1936: 2) he created in *The General Theory* (see footnote 11). It does seem that he thought the micro-based issue to be at best of only secondary importance to the point he was trying to push across.

To which Keynes replied:

> What you say about the classical analysis as applied to the individual industry and firm is probably right. I have been concentrating on the other problem, and have not, like you, thought very much about the elements of the system. But you ought not to feel inhibited by a difficulty in making the solution precise. It may be that a part of the error in the classical analysis is due to that attempt. As soon as one is dealing with the influence of expectations and of transitory experience, one is, in the nature of things, outside the realm of the formally exact. (Keynes, 1936: 2)

It is difficult to square such remarks with any strong reliance on the type of marginalism that distinguishes mainstream analysis. Rigour is not necessarily a goal to be pursued but in fact may be counterproductive if expectations are a key component to any useful understanding of economic processes.

[13] See *Essays in Biography* (1951: 211–212) for this evaluation. Ironically it is for this very characteristic that Schumpeter takes Keynes to task. 'It is a thousand pities that the harvest was garnered before it was ripe. If only he had learning something from Marshall's craving for "impossible perfection" instead of lecturing him about it!'. (Schumpeter, 1946: 507).

By explicitly introducing an alternative set of micro-foundations, or even by discussing such issues, he would be deliberately constructing his theory's own Achilles heel. His approach to aggregate investment might then seem idiosyncratic to a specific micro-theory. This would not only undercut the generality of the proposed theory, but also allow the terms of debate to be sidetracked on to a discussion of competitive markets. Given his take on the campaign to be fought, as well as the terrain of the battle, his aims might more effectively be accomplished by not fighting simultaneously on two fronts[14]. Though as previously pointed out, Keynes's interest in such micro-based issues was at best limited.

In any case, a stronger rhetorical and perhaps theoretical case is to be made by showing that the presence of competitive or imperfectly competitive markets is not the issue. The problem of underinvestment remains whether or not markets are acting in a textbook prescribed manner. This makes the problem inherent in the working of markets themselves instead of some sort of potentially correctible market failure. In which case Keynes can rightfully stake a claim to the appellation 'general' as a description of his theory. Unfortunately, as with any rhetorical strategy, there is a price to pay. In retrospect this price might have been too great. Keynes did not largely succeed in keeping the discussion focused solely on issues of uncertainty and investment. Instead, by granting his opponents those traditional classical foundations, he allowed the debate to be shaped by the very elements he cavalierly accepted as being peripheral to the points in question.

As a result, the underlying methodological message went largely unheeded. Keynes, if only implicitly, rejects standard optimising micro-behaviour. Strictly marginalist tools sit badly with the role that uncertainty plays in his theory. What tends to get lost when discussing methodological issues is that taking uncertainty seriously allows for conventional judgments to come to the fore. Such infiltration into the realm of optimising behaviour[15] is more insidious

[14] See Harcourt (1986) and Kregel (1985) on this point.

[15] See Bateman (1988) for a discussion of non-optimising behaviour in Keynes's work.

than it might seem to be at first glance. Pushed to its logical conclusion, conventional decision making seriously undermines marginality as the guiding rule of economic analysis. Neither wage bargains nor investment decisions need to yield optimal results. Keynes's rhetorical strategy doesn't sufficiently allow this connection to become clear. On reflection, outside of the rhetorical context, it is hard to justify the need for much of the standard apparatus that Keynes retains in his work.

The non-optimising framework that dominates his approach serves to distinguish his theoretical position on investment from that of the classical tradition. This differentiation is impossible to accomplish without resorting to a methodological break. Keynes's failure to explicitly point this out is required by his rhetorical strategy of not fighting a multi-front campaign, especially on terrain which he find uncongenial. Passing remarks do make it clear that standard optimising behaviour runs contrary to his approach.

> The calculus of probability, tho mention of it was kept in the background, was supposed to be capable of reducing uncertainty to the same calculable status as that of certainty itself; just as in the Benthamite calculus of pains and pleasures or of advantage and disadvantage, by which the Benthamite philosophy assumed men to be influenced in their general ethical behaviour. (Keynes, 1937: 213)

Rejecting the standard Benthamite calculation when dealing with uncertainty (1937), leads Keynes, in *My Early Beliefs* (1949), to likewise reject the same approach when dealing with choice in general. Logically what is scuppered is not only Ricardian analysis but 'Marshall's contribution mainly consisting in grafting on to this the marginal principle and the principle of substitution, together with some discussion of the passage from one position of long-period equilibrium to another' (Keynes, 1937: 212). Or if Marshall's contribution does not have to go, at least its more rigorous Pigouvian translation does.

Keynes cannot maintain standard optimising behaviour and incorporate the sort of uncertainty which he see as lying fundamentally at the core of all investment decisions. This is clear in his use of liquidity as a linchpin of any decision process. Optimal liquidity must remain a contradiction in terms.

> Thus, when it comes to liquidity (which, in the face of uncertainty, is offered as a necessary short-run endogenous variable in *The General Theory*) there may not be any good reason to doubt the presumption that it has been chosen optimally — except one. If liquidity could be chosen like any other variable there would be no need for liquidity! (Boland, 1985: 192)

In arguing that any analysis should start by depicting markets as they are rather than as they should be, Keynes accepts the importance of convention as the basis for economic valuations.

> Knowing that our own individual judgment is worthless, we endeavour to fall back on the judgment of the rest of the world which is perhaps better informed. That is, we endeavour to conform with the behaviour of the majority or the average. The psychology of a society of individuals each of whom is endeavouring to copy the others leads to what we may strictly term a conventional judgment. (Keynes, 1937: 214)[16]

In simple terms conventions should hold sway as long as they seem to work, if they achieve a given set of aims based on past experience. Such rules of thumb reduce transaction costs by cutting down on search time. In this way, though not providing a purely optimal solution, they have a good bit of staying power. Why such conventions seem to work is largely irrelevant to their users. To investigate runs counter to their usefulness in reducing the time spent in making decisions. It is safe to say that a necessary if not sufficient reason for

---

[16] Robert Sugden (1989) has also tried to pin down the idea of a convention in a somewhat more technical sense.

> An *evolutionary stability strategy* (or ESS) is a pattern of behaviour such that, if it is generally followed in the population, any small number of people who deviate from it will do less well than the others. This, then, is a state of rest in the evolutionary process. I shall define a convention as any ESS in a game that has two or more ESS's. The idea here is that a convention is one of two or more rules of behaviour, any one of which, once established, would be self-enforcing. (Sugden, 1989: 91)

any convention's success lies in the shared belief in its status as a viable convention. Keynes is not particularly concerned with how or why conventions arise but rather the implication of living in an economy where so many estimates are conventional by nature[17]. Particularly, he focuses on the dual nature of conventions. While bestowing gifts, the unreflective nature of their use also extracts a cost. Stability may translate into a resistance to needed change. Moreover, the collapse of conventions which are badly out of sync with experience creates a cycle of volatility until an old convention is replaced with a new one.

For Keynes, markets do not deliver consistently high levels of employment due to the conventional basis that underlies much of economic decisions making. To see that this theme flows through *The General Theory* we can best focus on two aspects of the work: (1) the manner in which Keynes disposes of Say's Law, clearing a space for his alternative hypothesis; (2) his depiction of investment expenditure which demonstrates his methodological break.

3. Say's Law Does Not a Conventional Account Make

> I doubt if many modern economist really accept Say's law that supply creates its own demand. But they have not been aware that they were tacitly assuming it. (Keynes, 1937: 223)

Keynes doggedly demonstrates the inapplicability of Say's law to any existing complex economic system. He suggests an alternative approach and indicates how such a method might be applied. A perspicacious reader of the first three chapters of *The General Theory* can discover Keynes' complete project laid out in skeletal form. The remainder of the book serves only to explicate the implicit premises of the beginning. There is an underlying coherent logic as well as

[17] Those interested in the evolution of conventions can peruse either the work by Sugden (1989) and/or Elster (1989). The continuing revival of interest in the role that institutions play has led to an increasing focus on the role of conventions in economic theory (see Hodgson, 1988, 1993).

rhetoric to the work. Sections and chapters arise only as needed to carry Keynes to his final goal[18]. But one must bear in mind that this theoretical amplification is made possible only by the simultaneous development of his methodology. This is liable to be overlooked since it is never explicitly stated in the same way as the purely theoretical arguments.

Keynes is determined to shift the methodological focus from the classical equilibrium labour market to the more worrisome domain of aggregate supply and effective aggregate demand where full employment need not be guaranteed. This is coupled with a reconsideration of the role of money in a modern industrial economy. Money becomes both the result of and contributor to an underlying level of economic uncertainty which serves to undermine the validity of any general equilibrium analysis. Stability, when achieved, is largely the product of convention.

> In particular, it is an outstanding characteristic of the economic system in which we live that, whilst it is subject to severe fluctuations in respect of output and employment, it is not violently unstable ... since these facts of experience do not follow of logical necessity, one must suppose that the environment and the psychological propensities of the modern world must be of such a character as to produce these results. (Keynes, 1960: 249–250)

Keynes, more than many have allowed, breaks from a strict reliance on technical relations. He reintroduces the troublesome factor of human perceptions and expectations which relatively few economists are ever eager to include. Flexible wages will not bring full employment since they are only presented as a technical condition resting on a special set of circumstances which are unlikely to obtain at any given

---

[18] Economists trained to read only explicitly linear arguments tend to be led astray by the more subtle approach adopted by Keynes.

> It would have been an advantage if the effects of a change in money-wages could have been discussed in an earlier chapter ... It was not possible, however, to discuss this matter fully until our own theory had been developed. (Keynes, 1960: 257)

time or place[19]. A system of wage bargaining which does not necessarily mirror a movement towards an equilibrium real wage is not a traditional approach no matter how Keynes dresses up the analysis in marginal clothing and no matter how much he clings to a standard labour demand function (see Applebaum, 1979; Brown, 1991). Labour demand and supply curves more closely resemble the parameters of a bargaining game described by reservation prices.

Strict adherence to marginal analysis adds very little here. The resulting nominal wage has more to do with the conventional institutional arrangements of the bargaining process than with marginal decision making resulting in long-run equilibrium real wages[20]. 'Though the struggle over money-wages between individuals and groups is often believed to determine the real level of real wages, it is in fact concerned with a different object' (Keynes, 1960: 13–14).

---

[19] As with most of his rhetorical devices, Keynes's use of 'General' in his title is both deliberate and specific. The difference between a restricted and more general case is intrinsic to his analysis.

> Obviously, however, if the classical theory is only applicable to the case of full employment, it is fallacious to apply it to the problems of involuntary unemployment — if there be such a thing (and who will deny it?). The classical theorists resemble Euclidean geometers in a non-Euclidean world who, discovering that in experience straight lines apparently parallel often meet, rebuke the lines for not keeping straight as the only remedy for the unfortunate collisions which are occurring. Yet in truth, there is no remedy except to throw over the second postulate of the classical doctrine and to work out the behaviour of a system in which involuntary unemployment in the strict sense is possible. (Keynes, 1960: 16–17)

[20] One example of this is Keynes's explanation for sticky downward nominal wages.

> Since there is imperfect mobility of labour, and wages do not tend to an exact equality of net advantage in different occupations, any individual or group of individuals, who consent to a reduction of money-wages relatively to others, will suffer a *relative* reduction in real wages, which is a sufficient justification for them to resist it ... In other words, the struggle about money-wages primarily affects the distribution of the aggregate real wage between different labour-groups, and not its average amount per unit of employment ... (Keynes, 1960: 14)

This same shift in analytic focus also strikes at the classical conception of money. By definition, commodities are produced for exchange. Their entire use value lies for the producer in an ability to realise their exchange value. In a barter economy where all exchanges are made in terms of goods and services, the seriousness of this realisation problem is limited, as in fact is the type of economy in which such barter can operate[21].

For Adam Smith, money, at least in the long run, merely facilitated this bartering of goods. The sole use of money is to circulate goods (Smith, 1937: 323). Money could never affect any real quantities because money itself was merely a neutral tool, undoubtedly a necessary and useful commercial tool, but still only a tool and definitely not a determinative factor. However, if our starting point is aggregate supply and expected rather than actual aggregate demand, money will play a non-neutral causative role in our general economic drama. A short-run dynamic must be introduced and integrated with the more traditional long-run perspective[22].

---

[21] For Keynes like many who followed him, money is the link between the present and the future.

> It [money] thus greatly multiplies, and offers extensive leverage to, the basic fact of ignorance of the future, and enables what might, in a barter system be a large number of mostly unimportant discrepancies between the supply and demand of individual goods and the exertions and rewards of individual persons to become a unified, measurable and very large gulf between what has been deemed worth producing in hope and what, when market day comes at the end of a long period of speculative commitment of resources, actually proves to be exchangeable for money. Money enormously enlarges the hurtful power of uncertainty at the same time as it enormously facilitates the beneficial power of specialisations. (Shackle, 1967: 136)

Rotheim (1981) emphasises the key role that a monetary production economy plays in Keynes's analysis.

[22] Again, Keynes rhetoric seems often to be ignored. 'Classical economics' for Keynes has an almost teleological fixation on long run equilibrium. What must be crucial is the road taken that has led us to some specific destination. A different road must equate to an alternative end point. In economics at least, all road do not necessarily lead to Rome.

> But the long run is a misleading guide to current affairs. In the long run we are all dead. Economists set themselves too easy, too useless a task if in tempestuous seasons they can only tell us that when the storm is long past the ocean is flat again. (Keynes, 1973: 65)

Keynes refused to be lulled by that peculiar economic sedative known as Say's law. For Keynes, the underlying assumptions of that law, particularly its fixation with aggregate supply, made it largely irrelevant to any but the most rudimentary economy. In which case, if the economic profession was ever to rescue itself from Crusoe's Island, it must dispense with the elementary barter system underlying Say's law, for it could not lead to any useful heuristic model but rather only confirm one's own prejudices.

4. Investment Spending — The Conventions of Business

> These games can be played with zest and enjoyment, though all the players know that it is the Old Maid which is circulating, or that when the music stops some of the players will find themselves unseated. (Keynes, 1960: 156)

To understand Keynes' theory one must understand the methodological break he makes. But one must understand it in a context centred on the interplay of aggregate supply and demand. And it is only by turning to the investment process that both methodology and theory become a coherent whole. This is where many commentators become derailed.

For Keynes, the *laissez faire* investment process of modern capitalist countries is the deep rooted and necessary cause of involuntary unemployment. As long as demand does not entirely consist of consumption, the gap between consumption demand and total income must be filled by investment.

> Thus, to justify any given amount of employment there must be an amount of current investment sufficient to absorb the excess of total output over what the community chooses to consume when employment is at a given level. (Keynes, 1960: 27)

Since investment involves planning for the future, the yields from any such investment will be realisable only in the years to come. Because the future by its very nature is unknowable, there is no reason to expect planned investment to always and perfectly fill the gap between consumption and full employment output. Due to this underlying uncertainty and the resulting periodic failures in confidence, investment becomes the weak link upon which the health of such a market economy must hang. Though not the only factor determining aggregate output, it is the most unstable. This flow of production, propelled by expected aggregate consumption and investment demand, in turn determines the level of employment.

The decision to invest is not simply a product of cool calculation. It is heavily influenced by conventional business opinion. Business types, despite the knowing looks they are required to maintain, are guided largely by consensus wisdom. In a world where ignorance of the future must predominate, conventional ideas remain the major support underlying long-range investment decisions.

The level of aggregate investment is the result of an interplay between expected future returns from a myriad of investment opportunities and the monetary rate of interest. As an analytic, as much as a rhetorical device, Keynes initially separates these two determinative factors[23]. This should not be considered an arbitrary decision. The two have quite differing dynamics. Investment demand falters due to the frailties inherent in these two key components. While expectation of investment returns rides the roller coaster of business confidence, seemingly unable to avert periodic collapses, interest rates display a more phlegmatic character. Though not unruffled by the winds of speculation, the chief impediment these rates contribute to the failure of investment demand is a quality of being sticky downward. The instability reflected by an uncertain future finds its major causative impact among investors rather than in the combat staged between borrowers and lenders.

[23] Let us not forget that Keynes used broad strokes in painting his distinctions. When constructing a new approach to economic analysis, starting points and distinctions must initially be presented in a simplified mode to insure clarity. Carabelli (1988) and Dow (1991) have both used Keynes' approach to investment as a vehicle for exploring his methodological procedures.

The division is between those who invest in real capital assets, whether first hand or indirectly, and those concerned with holding money and/or debts who Keynes lumps together under the rubric of bondholders[24]. To fail to distinguish between the buyers of stock and those of bonds is to confuse the processes involved in calculating future yields from capital investment opportunities (the marginal efficiency of capital or m.e.c.) with those determining the interest rate.

To repeat, even though when further yields on capital investment may become mired in a slough of pessimism, together they exhibit a certain degree of symmetry. Both have an unfortunate downward stickiness or stability on the bottom end of the scale and an open-endedness on the other[25]. We must discriminate though, between the secondary influences on these two investment components. Or more exactly, we must distinguish between the separate starting points Keynes uses to analyse each in turn.

---

[24] As with so much else in Keynes, the distinction between monetary and non-monetary assets is largely conventional. Such assets can be ranked in terms of their relative liquidity. This continuum can then be divided at any number of convenient points. For further discussion see Freedman (1993).

> Without disturbance to this definition, we can draw the line between 'money' and 'debts' at whatever point is most convenient for handling a particular problem. For example, we can treat as *money* any command over general purchasing power which the owner has not parted with for a period in excess of three months, and as *debt* what cannot be recovered for a longer period than this; or we can substitute for 'three months' one month or three days or three hours or any other period; or we can exclude from *money* whatever is not legal tender on the spot. It is often convenient in practice to include in *money* time-deposits with banks and, occasionally, even such instruments as (e.g.) treasury bills. As a rule, I shall, as in my *Treatise on Money*, assume that money is co-extensive with bank deposits. (Keynes, 1960: 167n)

[25] Conventional belief in the case of expected returns proves too fragile to sustain a full-employment level of aggregate demand. On the other hand, conventional belief deters interest rates from falling far enough to spur investment. Stability for both exists at the bottom end of the scale, volatility on the other. The result is that conventional behavior yields stability which sustains slumps, yet is too fragile to maintain high levels of employment.

In the heroic age of capitalism, investment depended on the willingness of an entrepreneur to expand an enterprise through the use of accumulated profits[26]. It was unlikely to be an easily reversible action. No spot market existed to provide sufficient liquidity. An early pin factory either survived or shut its doors. The decision to invest was the result of expected future yields buoyed up by a certain dollop of optimism. As long as the operation remained a going concern, able to support the entrepreneur and his family, investment in real capital would continue. Further expansion ultimately required greater resources than these early entrepreneurs could be expected to command. To gain access to these funds, joint stock companies, along with the concomitant secondary markets in which such shares could be resold, developed to respond to this need, but at the price of placing an intermediary between the investors in and purchase of real capital assets[27].

---

[26] As always, Keynes focuses on the implicit costs of the modern investment process by using former practises to create a clear contrast.

> In former times, when enterprises were mainly owned by those who undertook them or by their friends and associates, investment depended on a sufficient supply of individuals of sanguine temperament and constructive impulses who embarked on business as a way of life, not really relying on a precise calculation of prospective profit. (Keynes, 1960: 150)

[27] This is representative of what Keynes sees as the two edged sword of efficiency. The cost of growth through better organised capital (money) markets is the injection of a greater degree of instability into an economy.

> Decisions to invest in private business of the old-fashioned type were, however, decisions largely irrevocable, not only for the community as a whole, but also for the individual. With the separation between ownership and management which prevails today and with the development of organised investment markets, a new factor of great importance has entered in, which sometimes facilitates investment but sometimes adds greatly to the instability of the system. In the absence of security markets, there is no object in frequently attempting to revalue an investment to which we are committed. But the Stock Exchange revalues many investments every day and the revaluations give a frequent opportunity to the individual to revise his commitments. (Keynes, 1960: 151)

The selling of a share of stock is not equivalent to issuing a corporate liability. There is no contractual obligation as there would be to a bondholder. Stockholders buy their shares in the hope of future dividends and/or capital gains. They are interested in corporate investment only in as much as it affects these concerns. Minsky (1975) assumes that the potential yields stockholders anticipate (q_1, q_2, ..., q_n) are for all practical purposes identical to those (Q_1, Q_2, ..., Q_n) which plant managers must consider. For Keynes, such an identity is not required. This difference in fact can prove to be essential[28]. Though the consensus judgment of the stock market is certainly connected to managerial decisions concerning equipment purchase and other investment, that connection is not direct. Ultimately the reigning conventions need not move the participants towards similar decisions. Stock prices (the evaluation of long-run future flows) are liable to fluctuate quite apart from any specific hard-headed cost-benefit analysis. Rather, they may be driven by speculative evaluations of a conventional nature which are quite distinct from managerial decisions[29]. In turn those managerial decisions may be largely constrained by conventional market estimations. The market, acquires an implicit veto over any action proposed by management. Captains of industry and their various lieutenants are playing to an audience more comprehensive than that defined by the dimensions of their boardrooms.

Managers are not immune to such speculation. An increase in the stock price, whether warranted or not, may jack up the m.e.c.

---

[28] See Pasinetti (1974: 36–41) for a discussion along these lines.

[29] The idea that key economic values are largely conventional is too often overlooked when examining the approach pioneered by Keynes. The very conventionality of any economic system underpins its basic instability.

> In practice we have tacitly agreed, as a rule, to fall back on what is, in truth, a *convention*. The essence of this convention — though it does not, of course, work out quite so simply — lies in assuming that the existing state of affairs will continue indefinitely, except in so far as we have specific reasons to expect a change. (Keynes, 1960: 152)
>
> Speculators may do no harm as bubbles on a steady stream of enterprise. But the position is serious when enterprise becomes the bubble on a whirlpool of speculation. (Keynes, 1960: 159)

schedule[30]. It does this by effectively reducing the cost of capital, in part by decreasing the number of shares necessary to float a new stock issue or to serve as a basis for leveraged investments. Access to cheaper funds means projects previously rejected may become viable. Though veteran executives will sometimes differ with market assessments, they will still be tempted to snatch up a bargain. Booms can build a momentum that will not be denied, or denied only at the risk of forfeiting one's reputation for good sense. Managers may expect the bubble to burst, for their stocks to be down-valued sometime in the future. They cannot, however, and never will be able to foretell when this will occur. Further, they know that, when the market is strongly disappointed, the resulting pessimism will undervalue future yields, unreasonably restricting additional capital investments. The pressure is to expand now under what may prove to be only temporarily favourable auspices.

The longer they resist this consensus view, the longer they stubbornly rely on their own judgment, the more such managers begin to fear that their reluctance to invest will cause them to miss the boat. They are afraid of watching those already on board outstrip their own performance. It is only when stock prices are consistently defined in terms of the cost of capital, leavened with the yeast of speculation that much of Chap. 12 of *The General Theory* (1960) makes sense.

---

[30] It is far too easy to blur Keynes' distinction between bond- and stock-holders. Remember, his discussion on the state of long-term expectations is conducted quite apart from any consideration of the interest rate.

> In my *Treatise on Money* I pointed out that when a company's shares are quoted very high so that it can raise more capital by issuing more shares on favourable terms, this has the same effect as if it could borrow at a low rate of interest. I should now describe this by saying that a high quotation for existing equities involves an increase in the marginal efficiency of the corresponding type of capital and therefore has the same effect (since investment depends on a comparison between the marginal efficiency of capital and the rate of interest) as a fall in the rate of interest. (Keynes, 1960: 151n)

It might be wise when reading Chap. 12 to ignore any repercussions in the bond market. Such complications are only analysable after the basic framework has been developed. Any connections between these investment components will most assuredly not rest on a simple linear cause and effect basis.

The basic layering effect should be clear. With the addition of intermediaries, ignorance is mounted on ignorance, allowing conventional evaluations to gain greater sway. The uncertainty inherent in the investment process becomes leveraged as the investor is separated from any managerial decision. Such a flimsy base of knowledge is highly vulnerable to the winds of speculation. It becomes more personally advantageous to try to anticipate the short-run market than to search for long-run profitability. As more and more investors participate in this game of Old Maid, a critical mass is reached. The bulls stampede the field in front of them. As a result, investment may flow into less than optimum avenues. 'There is no clear evidence from experience that the investment policy which is socially advantageous coincides with that which is most profitable'. (Keynes, 1960: 157)

An unstable m.e.c. schedule is a far cry from the sedate technical relationship of marginal physical product to interest rate. With this continuing potential for instability, it is not possible to think of movement as consisting entirely of swapping one equilibrium point for another. The very self-same endogenously generated motion may itself shift the direction of the economy by affecting expectations and confidence. Keynes substitutes these mutable and rather fragile conventions for the strict automatic stabilisers of the classical system.

Interest rates, the other major determinant of investment, are the rent necessary to induce wealth holders not to hoard, namely the opportunity cost of their perceived liquidity. As should be expected, the accepted rate is also a convention[31]. Usually, these rates will cycle

---

[31] The expectations derived interest rate reflects to a large extent the conventional wisdom of the money markets. Again the non-equilibrating nature of Keynes' system is apparent.

> It might be more accurate, perhaps, to say that the rate of interest is a highly conventional, rather than a highly psychological, phenomenon. For its actual value is largely governed by the prevailing view as to what its value is expected to be. Any level of interest which is accepted with sufficient conviction as likely to be durable will be durable; subject, of course, in a changing society to fluctuations for all kinds of reasons round the expected normal. (Keynes, 1960: 203)

in a rather narrow band, prevented by a combination of institutional and speculative conventions from ever falling by a sufficient amount to sustain a full employment economy[32]. 'John Bull can stand many things, but he cannot stand 2 per cent' (Keynes, 1960: 309n). When, as in recent years, that convention shatters for whatever concomitant reasons[33], the possibility for free fall becomes apparent. In the seventies and early eighties, the bond market exerted a destabilising influence on interest rates by rewarding bearish behaviour. Money was to be made by selling short. Bonds were dumped in fear of rising rates. This widespread belief motivated corresponding behaviour. A self-fulfilling prophesy worked to accelerate the subsequent sell-off. Between the breaking of one convention and the establishment of another, the possibility in the Keynesian system of widely fluctuating interest rates can always become a reality. There is no necessary stabilising element inherent in the interest rate mechanism itself outside of the power provided by a conventional system of belief.

5. Methodology — The Importance of Conventional Behaviour

> Economics is a science of thinking in terms of models joined to the art of choosing models which are relevant to the contemporary world. (Keynes in a letter to Harrod, 1938, quoted in Moggridge, 1976: 26)

---

[32] It might be noted in passing that Keynes mentions 'the intermediate cost of bringing the borrower and the ultimate lender together' (Keynes, 1960: 208) as one element which may keep interest rates from reaching a low enough level to support a sufficient amount of investment, one which sustains a full employment economy. This seems to anticipate the printed appearance of Coase's (1937) work on transaction costs and the theory of the firm.

What is dismissed as a mere theoretical possibility 'I know of no example of it hitherto' (Keynes, 1960: 207) is the problem of a liquidity trap (not so labelled by Keynes himself). The preciseness of this concept had more of an intrinsic appeal to Keynes' self-proclaimed apostles than more heavily stressed considerations such as lenders' risk.

[33] In the summer of 1979 Paul Volcker, the then Chairman of the Federal Reserve, announced what most market analysts believed to be a conversion to monetarist doctrine. Whether such a major policy change actually occurred was largely beside the point. It was the perception of events that proved to be crucial.

Keynes' methodological break with what he defines as the classical system can best be understood by examining his use of marginality throughout *The General Theory*. As previously stated, though he does not entirely throw out all of the bath water with the baby, at best only a sudsy residue remains. While dismissing traditional theory as no more than a highly restricted special case. Keynes has no intention of needlessly alienating his colleagues by also entirely rejecting the *lingua franca* of the profession. However, the actual use made of marginality is very loose and is largely supplanted by notions of conventional beliefs and expectations[34]. As such, it is to some degree a rhetorical tactic and to some degree a failure to fully wean himself from the formulas of his youth. In other words, remove the marginal apparatus and relatively little is lost, remove conventionality and expectations and the edifice of his argument largely collapses. Unfortunately, by adopting this approach, Keynes may have allowed too many economists to declare that Keynes was offering nothing new, or (almost as debilitating) to reframe his arguments into a more traditional configuration. The later alternative is perhaps the more insidious of the two since it allows practitioners to undermine Keynes' approach while seeming to support his argument.

The m.e.c. schedule does not measure the physical productivity of capital. It is therefore not a simple translation of micro-theory's diminishing returns to scale. The idea of short-run increasing costs remains, but its link with scarcity is augmented by the addition of expectations, both on the revenue and cost sides (see particularly Keynes' discussion of user costs). The context is not one of sedately and incrementally moving down an unchanging m.e.c. schedule until the current interest rate is reached. Movement along the curve can

---

[34] It is always a mistake to simply read Keynes too literally.

> The fact that the assumptions of the static state often underlie present-day economic theory, imports into it an element of unreality. But the introduction of the concept of user cost and of the marginal efficiency of capital, as defined above, will have the effect, I think, of bringing it back to reality, whilst reducing to a minimum the necessary degree of adaptation. (Keynes, 1960: 146)

cause the whole curve to shift. Interest rates also cease to move smoothly but instead proceed in discrete jumps[35]. Marginal ideas become merely a heuristic aid to the analysis, a way of talking about the problem. It does not serve as the underlying rationale behind a system of equilibrating and strictly stable curves.

Re-examining the central conceit of the classical system, Keynes finds the labour market to be the setting in which matters other than the level of real wages are decided. Workers cannot effectively bargain for such a wage without concurrently having the ability to set the level of aggregate output. Employers analogously find their production plans constrained by market expectations. The real wage workers receive is the result of contractual negotiations over the money or nominal wage coupled with the flow of output resulting from the interaction between aggregate supply and effective demand.

The agreed upon money wage, like so many other components of the theory, turns out to be largely based upon conventions, namely those describing the traditional patterns of negotiations. The nominal wage is acknowledged to be somewhat rigid. Contracts do extend over time while workers will resist any attempted cutback in their nominal wage. But this provides the system with stability rather than unemployment. The close kinship linking money wages to prices causes a volatility in one to translate back into a volatility in the other and leads to an ascending or descending wage/price spiral. Widely fluctuating prices accentuate the already existing uncertainty in a market economy (see Keynes' discussion on prices in Chapters 17 and 21 of *The General Theory* (1960)).

On examination, Keynes makes little use of the classical apparatus despite all the attendant superficial trappings and despite his obvious debt to his mentor, Marshall. Rather, in using the traditional language

---

[35] The reign of conventionality must undermine the convenient fiction of smooth and continuous economic functions.

> Changes in the liquidity function itself, due to a change in the news which causes revision of expectations, will often be discontinuous, and will therefore give rise to a corresponding discontinuity of change in the rate of interest. (Keynes, 1960: 198)

of economics he often finds himself entrapped by the very logic he seeks to overthrow. We must therefore pay even closer attention to the thread of his argument. His is not a system where the real wage automatically equates the marginal product of a worker with the marginal disutility of that worker. The decisive action lies somewhere in between.

In the neoclassical synthesis which tries to weld together Keynes with his traditional predecessors, after an exogenous shock to the system, a return to an equilibrium position is always the result of sliding back and forth along the appropriate IS-LM and/or labour market curves. The endogenous readjustments to equilibrium never change the parameters of the system. Unless we are willing to accept change as occurring in a largely unchanging fashion, such orderly quadrilles of mathematical curves must be either abandoned or vastly overhauled.

In Keynes' framework this very movement towards equilibrium sets up countervailing forces which may shift the direction of the system by changing parameter values over time. Nor will the same exogenous shock necessarily result in the same movements. Events carry with them their own distinct histories. Change should be seen as directed towards a moving equilibrium which itself shifts with events. We must talk of tendencies rather than equilibrium points. Thus, the fragility of the investment process means that any upward surges in the economy can carry within them their own collapse. Instead of a sedate readjustment back to full employment output, Keynes substitutes a yo-yoing motion within an ill-defined corridor. In place of convergence, we may find an indefinite and unsatisfactory fluctuation[36].

---

[36] See Runde (1991) for an analysis of the stabilizing role of conventions.

> Thus our four conditions together are adequate to explain the outstanding features, of our actual experience; — namely that we oscillate, avoiding the gravest extremes of fluctuations in employment and in prices in both directions, round an intermediate position appreciably below full employment and appreciably above the minimum employment a decline below which would endanger life. (Keynes, 1960: 254)

This is the message of Chap. 18 of *The General Theory* (1960). Its purpose is to explain why capitalism does not simply self-destruct. Though the investment process is fatally flawed, there remains enough stabilising conventional beliefs and influences within the system to keep it intact, giving us neither economic bliss nor destitution. But these stabilising elements are themselves the result of human institutions and like other human institutions are vulnerable to change[37].

6. Conclusion

> The extraordinary achievement of the classical theory was to overcome the beliefs of the 'natural man' and, at the same time, to be wrong. (Keynes, 1960: 350)

In a sense, we need to reinvent Adam Smith in a more conscious incarnation by stripping the market system of all of its mystical raiment. Such a mythology has only succeeded in obfuscating economic analysis. Instead, with Keynes, we must try to develop institutions capable of supplying an otherwise absent degree of stability. Investment, left to the atomistic landscape of private players, risks setting an economy adrift in an unpredictable game of blind man's bluff. For Keynes, the commitment to a socialised form of investment meant an end to this deliberate relinquishment of responsibility.

Many are surprised to find no carefully laid out blueprint of such a transformed economy in *The General Theory* or in his other works. But, the very nature of the ideas presented by Keynes precluded any such model. What we are after in this book is an approach to

---

[37] Thus, it is necessary to shift away from simple equilibrium analysis when reading Keynes.

> But we must not conclude that the mean position thus determined by 'natural' tendencies, namely, by those tendencies which are likely to persist, failing measures expressly designed to correct them is therefore, established by laws of necessity. The unimpeded rule of the above conditions is a fact of observation concerning the world as it is or has been, and not a necessary principle which cannot be changed. (Keynes, 1960: 254)

economic problems rather than a delineation of fixed theoretical principles. It is against this traditional standard that Keynes presses his opposition.

> The object of our analysis is, not to provide a machine, or method of blind manipulation, which will furnish an infallible answer, but to provide ourselves with an organised and orderly method of thinking out particular problems ... This is the nature of economic thinking. Any other way of applying our formal principles of thought (without which, however, we shall be lost in the wood) will lead us into error. (Keynes, 1960: 297)

It is true that he develops a very definite framework which underlies his approach. The framework though is never sacrosanct. As is well known when his facts changed, Keynes was willing to change his mind. He stayed committed to no inflexible model or even one rhetorical strategy.

> There are other criticisms also which I would be ready to debate. But tho I might be able to justify my own language, I am anxious not to be led, through doing so in too much detail, to overlook the substantial points which may, nevertheless underlie the reactions which my treatment has produced in the minds of my critics. I am more attached to the comparatively simple fundamental ideas which underlie my theory than to the particular forms in which I have embodied them, and I have no desire that the latter should be crystallized at the present stage of the debate. If the simple basic ideas can become familiar and acceptable, time and experience and the collaboration of a number of minds will discover the best way of expressing them. (Keynes, 1937: 211–212)

What remains vivid from a careful re-reading of *The General Theory* is this approach. It is here that Keynes made his methodological break with the past. Like Frank Knight (1969) before him, Keynes recognised the role of the random event in economic activity. By placing a limit on knowledge, the resulting uncertainty restricts the applicability of any overly elaborate system[38], even if such a system were to be enlivened by the addition of stochastic processes. Instead,

---

[38] Weintraub (1979) for one would disagree with Keynes on this point.

we are left with a system where conventional judgment plays a determinative role.

By allowing ambiguity and uncertainty to permeate the structure of economic decisions, Keynes forces such a radical approach. An investment process sensitive to the length of a hemline or fluctuating according to the vagaries of the breakfast table is not about to come under the purview of traditional classical economics.

> In estimating the prospects of investment, we must have regard, therefore, to the nerves and hysteria and even the digestions and reactions to the weather of those upon whose spontaneous activity it largely depends. (Keynes, 1960: 162)

Acknowledgment

I would like to thank Peter Kriesler (UNSW) for his help and pertinent comments.

References

Applebaum, E (1979). The labour market. In *A Guide to Post-Keynesian Economics*, AS Eichner (ed.), pp. 100–120. New York: M.E. Sharpe.

Bateman, BW (1988). GE. Moore and J.M. Keynes: A missing chapter in the history of the expected utility model. *American Economic Review*, 78(5), 1098–1106.

Boland, LA (1985). The foundations of Keynes' methodology: *The General Theory*. In *Keynes' Economics*, T Lawson and H Pesaran (eds.), pp. 195–208. London: Croom Helm.

Brown, V (1983). On Keynes's inverse relation between real wages and employment: A debate over excess capacity. *Review of Political Economy*, 3(4), 439–465.

Carabelli, AM (1988). *On Keynes's Method*. New York: St. Martin's Press.

Chick, V (1983). *Macro Economics After Keynes*. Cambridge, MA: MIT Press.

Chick, V (1985). Time and the wage-unit in the method of *The General Theory: history and equilibrium*. In *Keynes' Economics*, T Lawson and H Pesaran (eds.), pp. 195–208. London: Croom Helm.

Coase, RH (1937). The nature of the firm. *Economica*, New Series 4, 386–405.

Dickens (1875). *The Works of Charles Dickens: Volume I Christmas Stories*. New York: Hurd & Houghton.

Dow, A and S Dow (1985). Animal spritis and rationality. In *Keynes' Economics*, T Lawson and H Pesaran (eds.), pp. 46–65. London: Croom Helm.

Dow, S (1988). What happened to Keynes's economics? In *Keynes and Public Policy after Fifty Years Vol. I*, OF Hamouda and JN Smihing (eds.), pp. 101–111. Aldershot: Edward Elgar.

Dow, S (1991). Keynes epitomology and economic methodology. In *Keynes as Philosopher-Economist*, R O'Donnell (ed.), pp. 1443–1467. London: Macmillan.

Elster, J (1989). Social norms and economic theory. *The Journal of Economic Perspectives*, 3(4), 99–118.

Fitzgibbons, A (1988). *Keynes's Vision: A New Political Economy*. Oxford: Clarendon Press.

Freedman, C (1993). In defense of footnotes — A clarification of a misunderstanding of Keynes's definition of money. *Cambridge Journal of Economics*, 17, 241–244.

Freedman, C (1995). The economist as mythmaker — Stigler's kinky transformation. *Journal of Economic Issues*.

Harcourt, GC (1986). The legacy of Keynes: Theoretical and unfinished economics. *mimeo*, Department of Economics, University of Cambridge.

Hodgson, GM (1988). *Economics and Institutions: A Manifesto for a Modern Institutional Economics*. Cambridge: Polity Press.

Hodgson, GM (1993). *Economics and Evolution: Bringing Life Back into Economics*. Cambridge: Polity Press.

Katzner, DW (1991). Aggregation and the analysis of markets. *Journal of Post-Keynesian Economics*, 3(2), 220–231.

Keynes, JM (1935). Letter to G. F. Shove in Donald Moggridge (ed.) (1973) *The Collected Writings of John Maynard Keynes, Volume XIV, There General Theory and After, Part II, Defence and Development*, p. 2. London: Macmillan.

Keynes, JM (1937). The general theory of employment, interest and money. *The Quarterly Journal of Economics*, 51, 209–223.

Keynes, JM (1949). *Two Memoirs: Dr. Melchior, A Defeated Enemy, and My Early Beliefs*. New York: Kelley.

Keynes, JM (1951). *Essays in Biography*. London: Hart-Davis.

Keynes, JM (1960). *The General Theory of Employment, Interest and Money*. London: Macmillan.

Keynes, JM (1963). *Essays in Persuasion*. New York: Norton.

Keynes, JM (1973). In *The Collected Works of John Maynard Keynes, Volume IV*, D Moggridge (ed.). London: Macmillan.

Knight, FH (1969). *The Ethics of Competition*. Freeport: Books for Libraries Press.

Kregel, J (1985). Harrod and Keynes: Increasing returns, the theory of employment and dynamic economics. In *Keynes and His Contemporaries*, G Harcourt (ed.). London: Macmillan.

Kriesler, P (1993). Keynes and Kalecki on method. *mimeo*, School of Economics, University of New South Wales.

Lawson, T and H Pesaran (eds.) (1985). *Keynes' Economics*. London: Croom Helm.

Lawlor, MS, WA Darity Jr and BL Horn (1987). Was Keynes a chapter two Keynesian? *The Journal of Post Keynesian Economics*, 9(4), 516–528.

McCloskey, DN (1983). The rhetoric of economics. *The Journal of Economic Literature*, 21(2), 482–517.

McCloskey, DN (1985). *The Rhetoric of Economics.* Madison: The University of Wisconsin Press.

McCloskey, DN (1990). *If You're So Smart: The Narrative of Economic Expertise.* Chicago: University of Chicago Press.

McCloskey, DN (1993). *Knowledge and Persuasion in Economics.* Cambridge: Cambridge University Press.

Mill, JS (1965). *Principles of Political Economy.* New York: Augustus Kelley.

Minsky, HP (1975). *John Maynard Keynes.* New York: Macmillan.

Moggridge, DE (1976). *Keynes.* Glasgow: Fontana.

Niman, NB (1987). Keynes and the invisible hand theorem. *The Journal of Post Keynesian Economics*, 10(1), 105–115.

O'Donnell, RM (1989). *Keynes: Philosophy, Economics and Politics.* London: Macmillan.

Pasinetti, L (1974). *Growth and Income Distribution: Essays in Economic Theory.* London: Cambridge University Press.

Rotheim, RJ (1981). Keynes' monetary theory of value. *The Journal of Post-Keynesian Economics*, 3(4), 568–585.

Runde, J (1991). Keynesian uncertainty and the instability of beliefs. *Review of Political Economy*, 3(2), 125–145.

Schumpeter, JA (1946). John Maynard Keynes. *The American Economic Review*, 36(4), 494–518.

Shackle, GLS (1967). *The Years of High Theory.* Cambridge: Cambridge University Press.

Shaw, GK (ed.) (1988). *The Keynesian Heritage, Volume 1.* Aldershot: Edward Elgar.

Shove, GF (1938). Letter to J.M. Keynes. In D Moggridge (ed.) (1973) *The Collected Writings of John Maynard Keynes, Volume XIV, There General Theory and After, Part II, Defence and Development*, p. 1. London: Macmillan.

Smith, A (1937). *The Wealth of Nations.* New York: Random House.

Sugden, R (1989). Spontaneous order. *The Journal of Economic Perspectives*, 3(4), 85–98.

Taylor, WM and WW Williams (1991–1992). Market microstructure and post-Keynesian theory. *The Journal of Post Keynesian Economics*, 14(2), 223–247.

Weintraub, ER (1979). *Microfoundations: The Compatibility of Microeconomics and Macroeconomics.* Cambridge: Cambridge University Press.

Chapter 14

In Defence of Footnotes — A Clarification of a Misunderstanding of Keynes's Definition of Money

Neither Groucho nor Karl Marx considered puns to be a contemptible literary device. Yet today, scholars seem less tolerant of their appearance in academic writing. Much perhaps has been lost by the relentless attempt to upgrade scholarly output. Unfortunately, what we have lost in wit has not been counterbalanced by any significant gains in clarity.

Though humble like the pun, footnotes do have a role to play in written communication. That role, however, should not be that of a scenic detour taken only at the discretion of the reader. This note hopes, perhaps foolishly, to restore a modicum of respect to the modest footnote.

1. Keynes's Definition of Money

Since its first appearance, Keynes's *General Theory* has excited debate and spread confusion among defenders and critics alike. In some cases, though, the origin of that confusion is hard to discover. Considerable mystery of this type surrounds the common version of Keynes's definition of money. Somehow, a tradition has arisen that for Keynes, money does not earn interest. (I use the term 'tradition' to denote a piece of folk wisdom handed down either orally or in written form without any attempt made at first-hand verification.) Thus, Robert Gordon in the latest edition of his textbook insists that:

> ... Keynes' speculative motive for money holding has drifted out of favour as an explanation of the demand for M1. Why should speculators necessarily hold M1 during those periods when they are trying to avoid a capital loss? Other assets, particularly savings deposits and other components of M2, are not only free from the risk of capital loss but pay interest as well. (Gordon, 1990: 496)

Textbooks have a long history of upholding the traditions of the discipline. Perhaps their true purpose lies only in passing on these traditions to the next aspiring generation. If so, more should be expected of those claiming to be post-Keynesian economists. This group has deliberately and quite consciously refused to accept the many traditions clinging to Keynes's battered work. Instead they have insisted that much would be gained by rereading Keynes with fresh eyes, eyes unblinkered by the interpretations of the past.

What then do we find when turning to the work of Basil Moore, a self-confessed post-Keynesian, who deals with the field of monetary theory:

> Unlike the *Treatise* [*on Money*] the *General Theory* devotes very little analysis to the banking system ('technical monetary details fall in the background'). Keynes proceeded as if the return on deposits were zero, which led to his famous inquiry of why anyone would wish to hold such an asset? While it is true that lending rates had fallen to low levels, they were still sufficiently positive to be above the required spread of banking intermediaries, so that competition still maintained positive if low deposit rates. Yet "the" interest rate for Keynes was the rate in [sic] long-term bonds. Keynes was wrong in not following Wicksell and relating this to the return paid on deposits, especially since he did not want to rely on the effects of monopolistic market structures for his results. (Moore, 1988: 132)

Nor does the tradition flag when repeated by Sheila and Alexander Dow:

> Keynes in the *General Theory* (Keynes, 1936, p. 167) did equate money and liquidity with non-payment of interest. Nevertheless, liquidity preference

> explicitly encompassed demand for inactive as well as active balances (Keynes, 1973, p. 223). Therefore, translating Keynes's liquidity preference concept into an institutional context where money (in M_3 and broader definitions of the money stock) includes interest-bearing deposits, we arrive at a theory of choice between those assets and other less liquid assets. Indeed this is simply a translation of the Keynes of the simplified world of the *General Theory* back to the Keynes of the *Treatise on Money*, where he explicitly discusses the speculative demand for money as a demand for (interest-bearing) savings deposits. (Keynes, 1971A: 32, 223–230) (S Dow, and A Dow, 1989: 148)

Surely a tale so consistent in its telling cannot be incorrect. Yet it is only fair to let Keynes speak on his own behalf, even if reduced to the more modulated tones appropriate to a footnote:

> Without disturbance to this definition, we can draw the line between "money" and "debts" at whatever point is most convenient for handling a particular problem. For example, we can treat as *money* any command over general purchasing power which the owner has not parted with for a period in excess of three months, and as *debt* what cannot be recovered for a longer period than this; or we can substitute for "three months": one month or three days or three hours or any other period; or we can exclude from *money* whatever is not legal tender on the spot. It is often convenient in practice to include in *money* time-deposits with banks and, occasionally, even such instruments as (e.g.) treasury bills. As a rule, I shall, as in my *Treatise on Money*, assume that money is co-extensive with bank deposits. (Keynes, 1964: 167fn)

It is true this is uttered as an aside, but it should be clearly audible to all but the deliberately stone deaf. Where such a tradition arose and why it persisted are questions not within the scope of this note. That it has no discernible foundation is evident. More discouraging, perhaps, than the existence of such a tradition is that, in this case, authors returning to the source material chose to perpetuate, rather than eliminate, this tale for well-behaved infants.

What is most inexplicable is the purpose in replicating this tradition. Perhaps the majority of economists wish to point out that the speculative demand for money is a contradiction in terms, since the choice is not between money and financial instruments but between financial instruments of different term structures. This apparent contradiction only arises by accepting a definition of money traditionally attributed to Keynes but, as we have seen, totally inconsistent with his own footnote. Such a misconceived definition does allow a few simple points to be scored off this landmark work. Why post-Keynesian economists should feel obliged to reinforce such an easily dispelled misconception cannot be easily explained[1]. It is clear that when Keynes speaks of the rate of interest as a reward for parting with liquidity, in contradistinction to the neoclassical reward for postponing consumption, he means a complex of differential rates of interest, not just the rate on long-term bonds. Thus, for Keynes, a rush to liquidity, given the prevailing and expected interest rate, is not undermined by the existence of interest-bearing deposit accounts.

> In general discussion, as distinct from specific problems where the period of the debt is expressly specified, it is convenient to mean by the rate of interest the complex of the various rates of interest current for different periods of time, i.e. for debts of different maturities. (Keynes, 1964: 167fn)

---

[1] One can only hazard the guess that they looked to Keynes to provide authenticity for their theoretical views. Thus, a long line of reinterpretations of Keynes's work has, since the 1960s, been more a vehicle to support partisan positions than an exploration of Keynes's work. Like the *Wealth of Nations* or *Das Kapital* before it, *The General Theory* lends itself to such creative reconstructions.

> Is it possible that Homer meant to say all they make him say, and that he lent himself to so many and such different interpretations that the theologians, legislators, captains, philosophers, every sort of people who treat of sciences, however differently and contradictorily, lean on him and refer to him: the general master for all offices, works, and artisans, the general counsellor for all enterprises? Whoever has needed oracles and predictions has found in him enough for his purpose. It is a marvel what a friend of mine draws out of him in support of our religion; and he cannot easily let go of this opinion that this was Homer's purpose (yet he is as well acquainted with this poet as any man of our century). And what he finds in favour of ours, many of old had found in favour of theirs. (Montaigne, 1965: 442–443)

Perhaps since Keynes does identify the interest rate with a reward for parting with liquidity, one may mistakenly infer that money therefore earns no interest. This is true only if we assume all money to be equally liquid. In fact it is cash, the most liquid form of money, to which Keynes attributes a zero interest rate[2]. Bank deposits which involve some relative, though perhaps slight, loss of liquidity can be a component of money without requiring that money itself earn a zero interest rate. The portfolio decision that Keynes concentrates on is not the decision to hold cash but rather the choice between money and debt. Money, no matter how operationally defined, will not encompass all debt. The interest rate therefore can be understood as a price that balances the alternative desires to hold the existing stocks of debt and money, no matter how those stocks are defined.

2. The Perpetuation of Misunderstanding by Tradition

We learn our economics from textbooks and lectures. Later on we may extend our knowledge of earlier work by reading recent journal articles. Far too seldom do we make the time-consuming attempt to evaluate the interpretations we absorb. More dangerously, we sometimes seem incapable of recognising them as only interpretations, rather choosing to accept them as summarising indisputable conclusions. When the simplified interpretation supplants

---

[2] The confusion here is not totally inexplicable but not entirely necessary either. Keynes uses non-interest earning cash to question the idea that interest is earned as a reward for delaying consumption: 'For if a man hoards his saving in cash, he earns no interest, though he saves just as much as before. On the contrary the mere definition of the rate of interest tells us in so many words that the rate of interest is the reward for parting with liquidity for a specified period' (Keynes, 1964: 167). A preference for greater liquidity, which may include a greater desire for cash holding as well as a reduction of the term structure of debts, must lead to a higher rate of interest, *ceteris paribus*. It, therefore, is reasonable to question why anyone would hold cash for speculative purposes. It is quite another issue to deny that money is held for this reason. Keynes himself does not always make this distinction clear enough. He sometimes uses the term cash when money would be the more appropriate term.

the original, a tradition, a bit of folklore, becomes firmly implanted in the daily discourse of the discipline and nearly impossible to uproot.

References

Dow, A and S Dow (1989). Endogenous money creation and idle balances. In *New Directions in Post-Keynesian Economics*, J Pheby (ed.). Aldershot: Edward Elgar.

Gordon, R (1990). *Macroeconomics.* London: Scott, Foresman.

Keynes, JM (1964). *The General Theory of Employment, Interest and Money.* London: Macmillan.

Mantaigne, M (1965). *The Collected Essays*, D Frame (tr.). Stanford, CA: Stanford University Press.

Moore, B (1988). Unpacking the post-Keynesian black box: Wages, bank lending and the money supply. In *Post Keynesian Monetary Economics*, P Arestis (ed.). Aldershot: Edward Elgar.

Chapter 15

Economic Convictions and Prior Beliefs: Akerlof Wrestles with the Ghost of John Maynard Keynes

That may be very well in practice but will it work in theory? (Anonymous)

Jokes are, in a contradictory fashion more serious than most people like to acknowledge. They can give expression to unresolved issues, the incongruities that can often shape lives, even those which are seemingly untouched by humour. Economists, as the joke quoted above pinpoints, despite their predilection for mathematical precision, have yet to resolve the precedence that matter of fact, empirical arguments should have over their grander, theoretical relatives.

Ideally, economic questions, to paraphrase George Stigler (1949a: 103), should be no more than questions of fact. The post-war era endorsed this point of view by moving away from discursive arguments which set one theoretical explanation against another, to a system of statistical analysis which could resolve economic issues and questions on a generally accepted, fact driven basis[1].

---

[1] Stigler's 1964 Presidential address, given to the members of the AER, is tantamount to a call to arms.

> I am convinced that economics is finally at the threshold of its golden age — nay, we already have one foot through the door ... The historical evidence

Unfortunately, as McCloskey[2] has insisted on a number of occasions, empirical arguments tend not to convince unless their target audience is already predisposed towards belief, based upon some *a priori* theory, argument or experience. Stigler himself, never changed his mind as the result of any known example of statistical analysis. Economists, as a group, would in fact be hard pressed to name instances where the course of economics has been noticeably redirected as the result of decisive empirical evidence.

Failure to recognise the implicit limitations that economists attach to such evidence can lead to rather fruitless discussions. Like most academics, economists are adept at defending theoretical constructs against empirical bombardment. Evidence in contradiction to some

---

> that we are becoming good empirical workers is less extensive, but the last half century of economics certifies the immense increase in the power, the care, and the courage of our quantitative studies. (Stigler, 1982: 134–135)

Even close colleagues were, at the time, taken aback by the evangelical fervour of Stigler's sermon. (Personal conversation with Ronald Coase, October 1997).

[2] Since the appearance of the first article on economic rhetoric in 1983, McCloskey has tried to point out that economists are not simply persuaded by the accumulation of data.

> It is common in a seminar in economics for the speaker to present a statistical result, apparently irrefutable by the rules of positive economics, and to be met by a chorus of "I can't believe it" or "It doesn't make sense". (McCloskey, 1983: 413)

Demsetz to an extent has also made this point with understated eloquence,

> All policy preferences, of course, ultimately derive from a view of the world combined with one's preferences. The taste component remains a personal matter, but the view of the world can be convincing to others or not. Opposition to a tariff because of its impact on consumers is based on a convincing view of the world (to economists anyway!) because of our agreement as to the correctness of the underlying analysis. (Demsetz, 1982: 56–57)

One seldom articulated fact amongst volumes of empirical data is that economists rarely accept conclusions that run counter to their own experience, to anecdotal evidence.

deeply held belief will not be credible until and unless the core theory is itself replaced.

What happens instead is a variant of Akerlof's 'lemon' principle. Relevant discussion breaks down because the effective seller of a hypothesis shies away from stating, much less discussing, essential theoretical issues. Opponents can then successfully shift the debate to ground more salubrious to their particular agenda. In a parallel to Gresham's law, less relevant discourse fills the vacuum produced by such reluctance. Strategic approaches of this sort successfully drive out argument and analysis focused on the more direct, but difficult, theoretical construct at stake.

A recent paper by Akerlof *et al.* (1996) aptly demonstrates the problem of building a controversial model on a purely empirical foundation. In that paper, the authors' noticeable failure to cite Keynes as an influential source of their work, subliminally indicates the unresolved and even suppressed issues which undermine their own project and those of many New-Keynesian economists. The attempt to straddle inconsistent empirical and theoretical positions is simply not viable. Unless theories can be attacked at their roots, empirical evidence seems incapable of altering, let alone refuting, them. Empirical data are at best a complement to, not a substitute for, theoretical debate.

1. A Major in the Brave Army of Heretics

> We have not read these authors: we should consider their arguments preposterous if they were to fall into out hands. Nevertheless we should not, I fancy, think as we do if Hobbes, Locke, Hume, Rousseau, Paley, Adam Smith, Bentham and Miss Martineau had not thought and written as they did. (Keynes quoted in Routh, 1975: 1)

Sins of omission can reveal problems that economists would rather ignore, especially when they are of a glaring variety. Akerlof *et al.* (1996) argue against a policy of complete price stability. To do so they need to convincingly demonstrate that gains from such a pursuit would fall short of any associated costs, measured in the currency of unemployment. This is clearly the case if the cost is not a once-off boost in unemployment for a relatively short period, but rather a persistent increase in the level of those unemployed.

Their basis for believing in a more enduring boost in the level of unemployment lies in a persistent characteristic of the labour market. Without inflation, real wages (absolute and relative) would tend not to adjust throughout the labour market, yielding instead a level of involuntary unemployment[3]. Response to a drop in economic activity would in that case be of a quantity rather than a price variety. Adjustment is impeded by a widespread resistance to cuts in the nominal wage. This implies that the labour supply function is equally dependent on relative wages as on any absolute level.

In the minds of many economists, an insistence on downward sticky or rigid money wages is notoriously associated with the work of Keynes[4] (1964). Yet it is only an article by James Tobin (1972), rather than anything of Keynes (1964), which is briefly noted. But even a very preliminary investigation of the Tobin paper indicates that it is an attempt, whether misguided or not, to expand on the work of Keynes. Tobin himself clearly acknowledges this. Akerlof, Dickens and Perry seem deliberately and pointedly to ignore Keynes, pointedly since Akerlof has succinctly summarised Keynes' labour theory in a paper written with Janet Yellen (1987)[5].

Keynes's banishment from this particular paper, and perhaps others produced by economists with New-Keynesian leanings, seems to be quite deliberate. The reason cannot lie merely in the fact that Keynes has become discredited or at least irrelevant to most mainstream

---

[3] Think in terms of heterogeneous markets with distinctive labour supply and demand functions. Real wages will need to rise in some and fall in others to remove the disequilibrating effects of economic change. With nominal wages rigid downwards, real wage adjustments can be accomplished using inflation as a surrogate.

[4] For Keynes' own view of the labour market see the discussion below.

[5] *The General Theory* makes clear that money wage stickiness is not in Keynes' opinion the ultimate cause of involuntary unemployment; indeed, due to the adverse effect of falling prices on demand, involuntary unemployment might possibly be more severe in its absence ... What to Keynes was a minor assumption in a theory rationalizing business cycles is now interpreted as the key assumption. (Akerlof and Yellen, 1987: 137)

economists[6]. A lurking feeling of unrest reflects the subtle realisation that to invoke Keynes's name, no matter how tangentially, in an analysis of labour markets, is to implicitly question a key shared assumption of current day economists whether they be of the New-Classical or New-Keynesian persuasion. Flexible wages are widely viewed as market clearing. If nominal wages are sufficiently flexible then, at least in the long run, real wages adjust to clear the labour market[7]. The debate between New-Classical and New-Keynesian schools focuses on speeds of adjustment rather than on the relative desirability and inevitability of flexible wages. It is exactly Akerlof, Dickens and Perry's refusal to reconsider this core belief that ultimately helps to undermine their own argument particularly when applied to possible policy recommendations[8].

---

[6] Keynes may have joined Marx in that strange underworld where an idea proposed by either one is automatically an idea scorned.

> Indeed, new Keynesian economics may appear more similar to the classical economics of David Hume, or even to monetarist economics of Milton Friedman ... If new Keynesian economics is not a true representation of Keynes' views, then so much the worse for Keynes. (Mankiw, 1992: 560)

[7] Two contemporaneous surveys of macroeconomics both see the New-Keynesian project as providing micro-foundations for market failure. Remove such failures and New-Keynesians would be indistinguishable from their New-Classical counterparts.

> ... a large number of authors, young and middle-aged alike, in the past decade have produced an outpouring of research within the Keynesian tradition that attempts to build the microeconomic foundations of wage and price stickiness. The adjective new-Keynesian nicely juxtaposes this body of research with its arch-opposite, the new-classical approach. (Gordon, 1990: 1115)
>
> ... the short-run sluggishness of wages and prices was the key assumption of the consensus view of the 1960s. And the absence of an adequate theoretical justification for the assumption was one of the fatal flaws that undermined the consensus. (Mankiw, 1990: 1654)

[8] Unlike Akerlof *et al.* (1996), Tobin (1972) does not dodge the more fundamental theoretical issue. Tobin (1972) interprets Keynes' theory of labour markets so that '... what Keynes calls equilibrium should be viewed as persistent disequilibrium' (1972: 4). As a result '... with unending sectoral flux, zero excess demand spells inflation and zero inflation spells net excess supply, ... Unemployment in excess of vacancies'. (1972: 10)

The temptation that Akerlof, Dickens and Perry face is the hope that by resolutely sticking to a firm empirical basis they can start all analysis from an assumption that relative wages are important since workers do resist nominal wage cuts. They need not then consider the logic of standard, wage-adjusted labour markets, nor the desirability of flexible wages since these are not included in the range of relevant observations. Whether it would be preferable for such wages to exist simply has no need to enter into the conversation. Unfortunately, this attempt to circumvent the problem by constructing a model on a purely empirical base leads to an unresolvable tension within the theoretical core of their economics.

If you accept that perfectly flexible money wages would lead to the efficient use of labour resources, rigid wages, no matter what their cause, lead to sub-optimal results. However, market imperfections are implicitly correctable. To claim that resistance to nominal wage cuts is part of ingrained behaviour is to transfer the perceived problem from worrisome but manageable to the too hard to handle bin. This puts in doubt the usefulness of an economic model based on fundamentally flexible labour markets (whether short or long run). Such elaboration of a clear counterfactual seems a dubious effort at best. This is not a simplification, like a strong assumption of rationality, but rather an effort to create a parallel universe. The allure of such a model vanishes if you have reason to doubt the efficacy of flexible wages. In which case, no disjunction between theoretical and empirical beliefs need take place. Unless this theoretical issue is clearly faced, debate can be shifted to arguments over the validity of the relevant empirical data or into a rather fruitless debate over whether such behaviour is fundamental, or whether it is historically determined and hence likely to alter with changes in the economic environment. Clearly, if theoretical and empirical foundations are at odds, it is tempting to poke holes in empirical arguments to save the desired theoretical conclusions. Given their refusal to resolve this incompatibility, it is unsurprising that Akerlof, Dickens and Perry have faced such a determined opposition. Their critics have recognised that what is at stake is one of the pillars of modern economic theory[9].

2. Banquo's Bloody Ghost

> The effectiveness of your work ... is diminished if you try to eradicate very deep-rooted habits of thought *unnecessarily*. One of these is the supply and demand analysis. I am not merely thinking of the aged and fossilised, but of the younger generation who have been thinking perhaps only for a few years but very hard about these topics. It is doing great violence to their fundamental groundwork of thought, if you tell them that two independent demand and supply functions won't jointly determine price and quantity. Tell them that there may be more than one solution. Tell them we don't know the supply function. Tell them that the *ceteris paribus* clause is inadmissible and that we can discover more important functional relationships governing price and quantity in this case which render the s. and d. analysis nugatory. But don't impugn that analysis itself. (Harrod warning Keynes against his approach to the labour market, quoted in Chick, 1983: 132–133)

As Harrod warned, you can tell an economist almost anything except that price does not equate the demand and supply for a commodity. An unshakeable belief in supply and demand keeps many economists from fully understanding Keynes. Given an absence of market imperfections, prices must adjust to equate supply with demand. Wages must do this for labour markets except if the natural working of the markets is impeded by some institutional constraint. This is the reason for focusing on sticky or even rigid wages. It provides a convenient way of dealing with observed labour markets without needing to deny the theoretical building blocks of the economic craft. Imperfections

---

[9] The issue of money illusion (see below) is perhaps of secondary importance but far from negligible. It at least seems to question the basic rationality of individual decisions.

> Lebow noted that downward nominal wage rigidity is evidence of money illusion ... the distortionary impact of inflation on people's behavior is potentially far reaching, so it is unclear whether, on balance, money illusion is an argument in favor of moderate inflation. (Lebow in general discussion of Akerlof *et al.*, 1996: 73)

are palatable to most economists. They provide an analytic rationale without denying a core belief in price-adjusted (Walrasian) markets.

Unfortunately this inverts the analysis. Keynes intended to establish a more general theory which would replace restrictive classical (or neoclassical) thinking. Focusing on sticky money wages merely describes a special case of the more general classical theory. Keynes did not deny the existence of a real wage which would clear the labour market[10]. He did deny that market forces would necessarily lead to a real wage adjustment which could accomplish this market clearing equilibrium. In a quantity-adjusted world, movements in money wages would not automatically, or even probably, yield this expected result. It is not then the lack of flexible wages that keeps labour markets from clearing. Keynes is taking a more fundamental tack. Perfectly flexible wages would most likely lead only to instability, since wage changes are not a once off, across the board, instantaneous phenomenon. Therefore, in his view, it was fortunate that wages were downwardly rigid[11]. Ironically only a system of centralised wage setting

---

[10] This is more in the nature of a hypothetical point of equilibrium, not in any sense partaking of an operational reality. Given the derived demand for labour and a labour supply curve there must be some real wage which would equate the two curves. But changes in the real wage reflect more fundamental shifts in the determinants of aggregate demand and supply rather than a gravitational drifting toward market clearing.

> ... the volume of employment is not determined by the marginal disutility of labour measured in terms of real wages except in so far as the supply of labour available at a given real wage sets a maximum level of employment. (Keynes, 1964: 30)

[11] Flexible wages created the possibility for deflationary spirals:

> If, on the contrary, money-wages were to fall without limit whenever there was a tendency for less than full employment, the asymmetry would, indeed, disappear. But in that case there would be no resting-place below full employment until either the rate of interest was incapable of falling further or wages were zero. In fact we must have some factor, the value of which in terms of money is, if not fixed, at least sticky, to give us any stability of values in a monetary system. (Keynes, 1964: 303–304)

could hope to accomplish the assumed price adjustments taken for granted by mainstream models. For the most part, economists have dealt with Keynes' core objection by ignoring it.

It is a misfortune that this part of Keynes's theory disappeared since it was the focus of Keynes's attack on what he termed classical theory. Flexible wages could not and would not resolve employment problems. Unemployment was not simply voluntary. An economy characterised by truly flexible wages would not inexorably move out of depression into sustained growth but instead could be cursed with increased price and employment instability. For Keynes, just as a frictionless physical world would be unmanageable, so would one with perfectly flexible wages. It is the grit in the works that allows markets to operate.

Keynes seems to have had a premonition that classical theory would triumph if its foundation remained intact. Unless classical labour market analysis was flawed, no basis for his own work remained, other than resorting to empirical arguments. But if labour theory itself could be found wanting logically, empirical buttressing would certainly send such a theory into voluntary retirement. His failure to have this key point generally acknowledged, let alone accepted, eventually doomed his theory to neglect. Of his contemporary critics, only Jacob Viner (1937)[12] saw the pivot of his work as turning upon

---

Keynes considered it unfortunate that there was no analogous constraint to keep money wages upwardly sticky as well. Though deflationary spirals might be inhibited by institutional factors, no such restraint opposed any tendency for rising wages to lead to an inflationary spiral.

> ... factors of production, and in particular the workers, are disposed to resist a reduction in their money-rewards, and that there is no corresponding motive to resist an increase. This assumption is, however, obviously well founded in the facts, due to the circumstance that a change, which is not an all-round change, is beneficial to the special factors affected when it is upward and harmful when it is downward. (Keynes, 1964: 303)

[12] What I understand to be the current doctrine is different. It looks to wage-reductions during a depression to restore profit-margins, thus to restore the investment-morale of entrepreneurs and to give them again a credit status

his rejection of the standard labour market. Despite the many attempts to flesh out Keynes' labour theory, the received wisdom of the profession still focuses on the sticky wages aspect, leaving unquestioned the role, or at least the desirability, of flexible wages[13].

The now commonly accepted idea that *The General Theory* lacked any recognisable, let alone rigorous, micro-foundation stems from this failure to understand Keynes' objection to neoclassical labour theory. Micro-foundations built upon non-clearing, long-run labour markets could only raise the profession's profound antipathy. He does in fact provide for heterogenous labour markets, each with different characteristics and responses to economic factors[14]. This was

---

which will enable them to finance any investment they may wish to make. It relies upon the occurrence of a lag between the reduction in wage-rates and a response in reduced volume of sales at the previous prices, during which interval entrepreneurs find prices to be higher than marginal costs and extension of output therefore profitable, provided buyers can be found for the increased output ... They do not contend that this is certain to occur, but on the ground that the chief factor in governing the action of entrepreneurs with respect to postponable expenditures is the current profit status of their operations as compared to their immediately preceding experience, they say that it is a reasonable probability. (Viner, 1937: 162–163)

Dennis Robertson makes a similar argument defending the position jointly held by Pigou as well as himself (see Robertson, 1973: 319). It is surprising how very little debate there was about Keynes' central tenet. Either this point slipped by most critics or they were reluctant to engage Keynes on this terrain.

[13] That very little has been done with Keynes' suggestions regarding the labour market prior to Akerlof *et al.* (1996) is indicated by Allan Meltzer's recent remark

> ... Keynes' attempt at a theory of employment or unemployment has not been fruitful. In the sixty years since the publication of the *General Theory*, neither Keynes' suggestions about the theory of labor supply nor the various interpretations of that theory have produced an empirically successful theory of the labor market or unemployment. (Meltzer, 1996: 39)

[14] If, for example, the increased demand is largely directed towards products which have a high elasticity of employment, the aggregate increase in employment will be greater than if it is largely directed towards products which have a low elasticity of employment. (Keynes, 1964: 286)

expanded by Tobin but largely left to drift until formalised by Akerlof, *et al.* (1996) employing monopolistic competition as their particular modelling vehicle. Keynes himself stuck with a Marshallian notion of competitive markets, possibly to avoid controversy over whether markets were or were not imperfectly competitive[15]. Such empirical debates could serve only as distractions. Gardiner Means long-running attempt to provide suitable micro-foundations for Keynes's macro-driven models floundered in sustained but inconclusive squabbles over how to define competitive markets and flexible prices as well as how to interpret the available market data. Keynes wanted to uproot the logical foundations of neoclassical theory not merely to appeal to data for justification.

Keynes himself declined to be sidetracked. He brushed aside Leontief's[16] comment concerning the homogeneity postulate. This attempt to steer clear of the briar patch of irrationality failed as other such attempts have since. The charge of money illusion stuck as a way to close off rather than enlarge economic discussion. Moreover, it became transformed from a side issue of empirical validation to an *ad hoc*, *a priori* assumption underpinning the entire edifice and

---

[15] It seems unlikely that Keynes had any real attachment to a Marshallian construct involving competitive markets. Though a contentious issue, it seems probable that Keynes' avoidance of imperfect market structures was largely dictated by reasons mostly rhetorical in nature.

> ... Keynes was aware that his theory did not take account of the behavior of administered prices. At the time he was writing the *General Theory*, we had some correspondence on the inflexibility of administered prices, and when I talked with him in the summer of 1939 he repeatedly referred to the unreality of the classical assumption of flexible prices he had made in the *General Theory*. (Means, 1959: 453)

[16] Leontief (1937) somehow fastens on the idea of rigid wages as Keynes' core theoretical departure.

> One of these fundamental assumptions — that which Mr. Keynes is ready to repudiate — defines an important universal property of all supply and demand functions ... supply and demand functions, with prices taken as independent variables and quantity as a dependent one, are homogeneous of the zero degree. (Leontief, 1937: 192–193)

undermining the generality of Keynes's theory. The implicit and damning allegation in this and other cases is that necessity, rather than observation, was the mother of this assumption. Claiming that money wages were sticky downward became analogous to believing in money illusion. The idea that there was an asymmetry between a real wage lowered through a wage cut versus a parallel price increase was considered irrational. Such a charge was deemed pejorative simply because of the *a priori* assumption of economic rationality. No empirical evidence seemed required, though even casual observation would indicate that people do make decisions based on nominal values. The use of the phrase 'sticky downward' prejudges the case. It implies that wages ought to adjust but are, for some non-economic reason, due to some institutional constraint, prevented from doing so, much as a door that sticks is automatically assumed to need maintenance of some sort. If instead, the emphasis was on the importance of relative wages, the issue of money illusion would not arise so readily.

For Keynes, his casual observation of workers' behaviour rendered such arguments non-starters. He felt no need to square actual behaviour with *a priori* behavioural assumptions. Such objections were side issues quite distinct from the main sermon he was determined to preach.

Tobin (1972), focusing more on relative wages, takes on the money illusion indictment directly[17]. His argument, though incorporating

[17] If expansion of aggregate demand brings both more inflation and more employment, there need be no mystery why unemployed workers accept the new jobs or why employed workers do not vacate theirs. They need not be victims of ignorance or inflation illusion. (Tobin, 1971: 13)

Concern with relative wages is not mere foolishness. Inflation does not affect the opportunity cost of leaving one's current job or accepting another. The same cannot be said for cuts in the nominal wage for selected industries. Given the costs of switching jobs, such cuts will be resisted. Failure to achieve a gain is not valued equally with the loss of an existing asset. Economists have defined this as loss aversion (see Kahneman *et al.* (1991) for a survey of such non-traditional assumptions). A nominal increase, which runs behind the rate of inflation, is not viewed as gravely as a nominal wage cut even though the real effect might seem equivalent. A concern over fairness also plays a part. Inflation does not stem from an employer's decision in the

relative wages, does not strictly depend on an assumption of downward sticky wages. Drawing out the heterogeneity assumption underlying labour markets is sufficient. Reminiscent of Keynes, the existence of a market clearing equilibrium wage is irrelevant outside of a central wage setting mechanism. In other words, the logic of neoclassical theory requires a non-market mechanism to assure market efficient solutions[18].

The three models by Keynes (1964), Tobin (1972) and Akerlof *et al.* (1996) represent distinct stages of development. The empirically testable assumption of downward sticky money wages moves from a peripheral assumption, dictated by casual observation, to centre stage. By resting on an empirically verifiable, but theoretically unnecessary assumption, Akerlof *et al.* (1996) construct a highly provocative model, one that questions the sanctity of stable prices[19],

---

same way that a nominal wage cut does. One is in the way of an act of God. The other is deliberate and directed. Inflation affects workers differently depending on their consumption basket and willingness to substitute. Nominal wage cuts hit everyone equally. There is necessarily more of a common ground on which to resist such cuts in the latter rather than the former case.

[18] Tobin (1972) points out that aggregation is not a simple magnification of the functional relations characterising the representative economic agent. Markets are heterogeneous. In the case of labour markets, this becomes particularly important since economic shocks will inevitably create vacancies in some job markets (excess supply) and unemployment (excess demand) in others. Unemployment retards money wages less than vacancies accelerate them. Added to this, wage elasticity of demand will also vary between specific labour markets and over time. Given such heterogeneous markets, and shocks in the form of the usual suspects (innovation, changes in tastes, etc.), zero inflation must imply that unemployment remains in excess of vacancies.

> Criteria that coincide in full long-run equilibrium — zero inflation and zero aggregate excess demand — diverge in stochastic macro-equilibrium. Full long-run equilibrium in all markets would show no unemployment, no vacancies, no unanticipated inflation. But with unending sectoral flux, zero excess demand spells inflation and zero inflation spells net excess supply, unemployment in excess of vacancies. (Tobin, 1972: 10)

[19] Curiously, Akerlof *et al.* (1996) face the same sort of rancour by suggesting that low inflation may be beneficial as Keynes (1964) met by pointing out that saving in and of itself might not necessarily be advantageous. In both cases, dissenting economists

but provides at best a makeshift foundation attractive only to like minded economists.

3. The Thought Police

> The classical theorists resemble Euclidean geometers in a non-Euclidean world who, discovering that in experience straight lines apparently parallel often meet, rebuke the lines for not keeping straight — as the only remedy for the unfortunate collusions which are occurring. (Keynes, 1936: 16)

Physicists do not sit around and grumble because the world is not frictionless. Nor do they assume that it would be a preferable alternative. Keynes took the world as he found it. He saw no reason to deny or overlook a convenient empirical observation which buttressed his own approach. But it clearly remained in a designated supporting role. Still, if workers do resist wage cuts then every analysis which chose to ignore this constant would be fruitless as far as policy implications go. It would be specifically contradictory for neoclassical economists, proponents of individual choice, to expect individuals to be re-educated so as to conform to these economists' desired results. Yet until the very recent work by Akerlof *et al.* (1996) relatively little systematic work sought to determine whether or not nominal wages were in fact cut with any frequency.

The three authors analysed existing studies and undertook an extensive survey of their own. They furthermore are able to cite historical studies of wage movements prior to World War II. The data seems to strongly support the claim that except when a firm is distressed over an extended period, nominal wages are rarely reduced. Given this evidence of human behaviour, Akerlof *et al.* (1996) use this

---

find themselves engaging in what are essentially moral rather than strictly economic debates.

> No wonder that such wicked sentiments [Mandeville] called down the opprobrium of two centuries of moralists and economists who felt much more virtuous in possession of their austere doctrine that no sound remedy was discoverable except in the utmost of thrift and economy both by the individual and by the state. (Keynes, 1964: 363)

as their starting point. To engage in what Demsetz has termed nirvana economics seems fruitless.

> This *nirvana* differs considerably from a *comparative institution* approach in which the relevant choice is between alternative real institutional arrangements. In practice, those who adopt the nirvana viewpoint seek to discover discrepancies between the ideal and the real and if discrepancies are found, they deduce that the real is inefficient. (Demsetz, 1969: 1)

The issue now becomes whether starting with a classical labour market is in a sense either a simplifying or heuristic assumption. If it ultimately leads further analysis and suggested policy astray then it is far from an innocent theoretical starting point. This becomes evident in the discussion that follows the paper (as is customary with the Brookings series). Both Gordon and Mankiw sidetrack the discussion to some extent by claiming that wage rigidity could very well be time specific[20].

> In addition, even if there is downward wage rigidity in our economy it might well decrease in a regime of price stability. To some extent, downward wage rigidity is based on workers' sense of what is fair treatment by their employers. Yet notions of fairness surely depend on the environment. In a world of price stability, falling nominal wages would be more common, and aversion to them would be reduced, at least to some extent. (Mankiw commenting on Akerlof *et al.*, 1996: 69)

---

[20] There are also a number of spurious comments concerning historical occurrences of near-zero inflation (or even deflation) concurrent with relatively low unemployment. This misses the point of the paper. Akerlof *et al.* (1996) are questioning whether an explicit government policy aimed at price stabilisation is beneficial. They do not deny that price stability can occur without generating economic costs in terms of unemployment. But as Perry replies

> While industrial countries have experienced stretches of time with inflation rates near zero, these generally occurred in periods of rapid productivity growth. (Perry replying in Akerlof *et al.*, 1996: 72)

Reading the comments of these well-known economists, makes one wonder if economists actually listen to each other.

Akerlof, Dickens and Perry unintentionally have crafted their own Achilles heel here and displayed it as a target for critical barbs[21]. A shared belief in the inevitable market clearing ability of flexible wages shifts the terms of debate. The nature of wage rigidity (fundamental versus historically specific) is unessential if labour markets lack the undisputable ability to predictably clear. There would then be no compulsion to save the theoretical *status quo*. The danger of fashioning an empirical foundation for economic analysis becomes clear. Particularly since these authors are deliberately wandering on to controversial terrain. At a time when perhaps a majority of economists raise worries about expected inflationary comebacks, they are intent on looking at the other, or cost side of policies that aim to eliminate inflation. Despite the lack of empirical evidence supporting price stability and the increasing volume of published work doubting the damage that low levels of inflation inflict[22], fighting inflation, in whatever form it occurs, has become a motherhood issue for economists, the equivalent of a moral tenet. As a result, the profession is left largely unmoved by models based solely on empirical evidence. Even if there is a general acceptance of the existing data, such empirical evidence can either be dismissed as inconclusive or time specific. It does nothing to change any fundamental thinking about labour markets. Only by significantly altering an economist's theoretical perspective can any progress be made.

4. Revolution and Reform

> And nowhere outside the 1920s and early 1930s tradition of what may be called, by contrast with its contemporary counterpart, 'the methodology of

---

[21] One has only to look at a number of rebuttals of the Akerlof *et al.* (1996) paper to see that this has in fact happened. Most of the attacks have come from economists attached to central banks or government treasury departments who are eager to defend a standard policy tool. The interested reader can look at Lavoie (1997) for a typical attempt to shift the terms of debate.

[22] Recent work seems to indicate that the costs associated with low-level inflation is at best negligible. See Barro (1995), Sarel (1996) or Cameron *et al.* (1996) for some recent empirical studies.

> negative economics' — the belief that one can refute a theory of how the world works by exposing the unreality of its assumptions rather than the falsity of its conclusions ... would it be considered an important political strategy for the destruction of capitalism and the triumph of the revolution to insist stridently on an alleged logical flaw in the logic of the competitive system. (Johnson and Johnson, 1968: 168)

Harry Johnson was only half right. It is also true that you cannot refute a theory by exposing the falsity of its conclusions without also demonstrating the unreality of its assumptions. Like assumptions, empirical evidence has to be sifted and evaluated. Facts never speak for themselves. Here as well, there is seldom only one true course to pursue. In a world where arguments of any sort are unlikely to be decisive, the process of persuasion has to be undertaken on a number of fronts simultaneously.

The inconsistency between inherent wage rigidity and the ability of flexible wages to clear (at least in the long-run) means that either one path or the other needs to be chosen. If Akerlof, Dickens and Perry intend to depart from standard labour theory, they have to be prepared to do so on a fundamental basis rather than squabbling about adjustment speeds. They cannot save appearances by dint of a clever compromise that turns a blind eye to any theoretical issues and tries to lever up its economic analysis from an empirical data set, no matter how good such a set may be. They give away the game by elegantly sidestepping a more fundamental debate concerning long-run market equilibrium which would compel them to question not only the world view of the economics fraternity but their own basic beliefs as well. As we have seen, debate shifts back to familiar but less fertile territory. Implicitly, both sides have agreed to informational barriers which narrowly define the issue.

Empirical and theoretical starting points need to be consistent, even if only one aspect is explicitly stressed. Straddling conflicting positions will always be an uncomfortable and unsustainable pose. It cannot be enough to pragmatically take empirical observations as the groundwork for further analysis. Trying to simply duck theoretical issues will not succeed even if you are convinced further discussion is counter-productive. These frameworks inform any serious discussion of empirical work and often prejudge it.

Since 1972, economists have learned 'more about labour markets, mobility, and search, and more about the social and distributive costs of both unemployment and inflation' (Tobin, 1972: 18) as Tobin required. But as Keynes suspected, none of this new knowledge has shaken the profession's core acceptance of equilibrating labour markets. As a result, the flood of knowledge Tobin anticipated has failed to forward Tobin's own objectives. Where is the bright future of welfare economics he envisioned? Lost amongst the long-run assumptions concerning aggregate labour markets. Akerlof and company undermine the effectiveness of their own work by forgetting the very lesson that Akerlof taught the economics profession when he was still a young man. The 'lemon' principle has come back to haunt its progenitor.

> *For 'tis sport to have the engineer*
> *Hoist with his own petard.* (William Shakespears, *Hamlet*, Act 3: Scene 4)

References

Akerlof, GA (1970). The market for lemons. *Quarterly Journal of Economics*, 84(3), 488–500.

Akerlof, GA and JL Yellen (1987). Rational models of irrational behaviour. *The American Economic Review — Papers and Proceedings*, 77(2), 137–142.

Akerlof, GA, WT Dickens and GL Perry (1996). The macroeconomics of low inflation. *Brookings Papers on Economic Activity*, 1, 1–76.

Barro, RJ (1995). Inflation and economic growth. *Bank of England Quarterly Bulletin*, 35(2), 166–175.

Berle, AA and GC Means (1932). *The Modern Corporation and Private Property.* New York: The Commerce Clearing House.

Cameron, N, D Hum and W Simpson (1996). Stylized facts and stylized illusions — inflation and productivity Revisited. *Canadian Journal of Economics*, 29(1), 152–162.

Chick, V (1983). *Macroeconomics After Keynes.* Cambridge: Cambridge University Press.

Demsetz, H (1982). Barriers to entry. *The American Economic Review*, 72(1), 47–57.

Friedman, M (1969). The role of monetary policy. *The American Economic Review*, 58(1), 1–17.

Gordon, RJ (1990). What is New-Keynesian economics? *Journal of Economic Literature*, 28(3), 1115–1171.

Hoover, K (1995). Relative wages, rationality, and involuntary unemployment in Keynes's labor market. *History of Political Economy*, 27(4), 653–686.

Johnson, ES and HG Johnson (1978). *The Shadow of Keynes*. Chicago: University of Chicago Press.

Kahneman, D, JL Knetsch and R Thaler (1986). Fairness as a constraint on profit seeking: Entitlements in the market. *The American Economic Review*, 76(4), 728–745.

Kahneman, D, JL Knetsch and R Thaler (1991). The endowment effect, loss aversion, and status quo bias. *Journal of Economic Perspectives*, 5(1), 193–206.

Keynes, JM (1937). The general theory. *Quarterly Journal of Economics*, 51(2), 209–223.

Keynes, JM (1964). *The General Theory of Employment, Interest, and Money*. New York: Harcourt Brace Jovanovich.

Keynes, JM (1979). Letter to J.T. Dunlop 9 April 1938. *The Collected Writings of John Maynard Keynes Vol. XXIX; The General Theory and After — A Supplement*, D Moggridge (ed.), p. 284. London: Macmillan Press Ltd.

Lavoie, C (1997). Nominal wage rigidities and the Phillips surve, an application of the Akerlof, Dickens and Perry model to Canada. *Economic Studies and Policy Analysis Division of the Department of Finance Working Paper*. Department of Finance: Ottawa.

Lee, FS (1995). Philanthropic foundations and the rehabilitation of big business, 1934–1977: A case study of directed economic research. *Discussion Papers in Economics*, pp. 95–108. De Montfort University: Leicester.

Leontief, WW (1937). The fundamental assumption of Mr. Keynes' monetary theory of unemployment. *The Quarterly Journal of Economics*, 51(1), 192–197.

Mankiw, NG (1990). A quick refresher course in macroeconomics. *Journal of Economic Literature*, 28(4), 1645–1660.

Mankiw, NG (1992). The reincarnation of Keynesian economics. *European Economic Review*, 36(3), 559–566.

McCloskey, DN (1983). The rhetoric of economics. *Journal of Economic Literature*, 21(2), 481–517. Reprinted in *The Philosophy of Economics*, DM Hausman (ed.), pp. 395–445. Cambridge: Cambridge University Press.

Means, GC (1935). *Industrial Prices and Their Relative Inflexibility*. 74th Congress, 1st Session, Senate Document No. 13, Washington.

Means, GC (1959). Administered prices reconsidered — discussion. *The American Economic Review — Papers and Proceedings*, 49(2), 451–454.

Meltzer, AH (1996). The general theory after sixty years. *Journal of Post Keynesian Economics*, 19(1), 35–45.

Robertson, DH (1973). Letter to John Maynard Keynes, October 1933. In *The General Theory and After — Part I Preparation; Vol. XIII of The Collected Writing of John Maynard Keynes*, D Moggridge (ed.), p. 319. London: The Macmillan Press.

Routh, G (1975). *The Origins of Economic Ideas.* London: Macmillan.

Sarel, M (1996). Nonlinear effects of inflation on economic growth. *IMF Staff Papers*, 43(1), 199–215.

Stigler, GJ (1949a). A survey of contemporary economics. *The Journal of Political Economy*, 57(2), 93–105.

Stigler, GJ (1949b). Competition in the United States. *Five Lectures on Economic Problems*, pp. 37–46. London: Longmans, Green and Co.

Stigler, GJ (1982). The economist and the state. Reprinted in *The Economist as Preacher*, pp. 119–145. Chicago: University of Chicago Press.

Stigler, GJ and C Friedland (1983). The Literature of economics: The case of Berle and means. *Journal of Law & Economics*, 26(2), 237–268.

Stigler, GJ and J Kindahl (1970). *The Behavior of Industrial Prices.* National Bureau of Economic Research. New York: Columbia University Press.

Stigler, GJ and J Kindahl (1973). Industrial prices, as administered by Dr. Means. *American Economic Review*, 63(3), 717–721.

Tobin, J (1972). Inflation and Unemployment. *The American Economic Review*, 62(1), 1–18.

Viner, J (1937). Mr. Keynes on the causes of unemployment. *The Quarterly Journal of Economics*, 51(1), 147–167.

Chapter 16

When Truth is Not Beauty, Nor Beauty Truth: A Review of Econ Art — Divorcing Art from Science in Modern Economics

Rick Szostak (1999). London: Pluto Press. pp. xv + 256. ISBN 0-7453-1447-3 (HB), 0-7453-1442-1 (PB)

Rick Szostak's latest effort has at its core an entertaining conceit. Economists are too much immersed in economics to fully comprehend what they are doing. Shock tactics are required to shake the profession out of its dogmatic sleep. This can only happen if economists are willing (or forced) to don alien lenses when reflecting on their own endeavours. (Though, economists under the best of circumstances are not much given to introspection.) When suggesting a new perspective from which to view the economics profession, modern art (specifically painting) has to be as far afield from an economist's normal concerns as picnicking on Mars.

This approach establishes two quite interesting fields for further exploration. Those collateral background events which fostered the revolution in the art world *circa* the 20th century very well might help to explain the path modern economics chose during that selfsame century. It is not inconceivable that a common culture should show similar results. Surely, the 19th century philosopher Hegel was correct in stating that:

> Whatever happens, every individual is a child of his time; so philosophy too is its own time apprehended in thoughts. It is just as absurd to fancy that a philosophy can transcend its contemporary world as it is to fancy that an individual can overleap his own age, jump over Rhodes. If his theory really goes beyond the world as it is and builds an ideal one as it ought to be, that world exists indeed, but only in his opinions, an unsubstantial element where anything you please may, in fancy be built. (Hegel, 1967: 11)

Even economists live very much in their own time-specific world with its own peculiar set of beliefs and concerns. Yet this cultural aspect has been vociferously denied by a wide spectrum of the profession who are loath to admit that something potentially smacking of ideology should in some way channel the investigations of scientists[1]. George Stigler is quite definite in consigning cultural influences to the bin of half-baked ideas, fanciful and lacking any foundation. More recently only a few professional dissenters like Arjo Klamer, and in her own way Deirdre McCloskey, have been willing to discuss the effect of Modernism on the economics profession.

The second, even more contentious idea is that economics has grown more to resemble modern art rather than modern science. By this Szostak seems to mean that economists revere technique over content. As a consequence, modern economics has lost its relevance.

---

[1] This would seem to be at odds with the core theory of neoclassical economics, choice according to individual preferences. If we appropriate the argument first advanced by Becker and Stigler (1995), then the market for ideas is no different from the market for any other commodity. A producer sells an idea by appealing to potential buyers' existing preferences. As Becker has confirmed in a private conversation with me (October 1997), this process will not necessarily lead us to the truth, though we of course hope that it will. One of Stigler's close colleagues, Harold Demsetz, perhaps put it most clearly by claiming that

> All policy preferences, of course, ultimately derive from a view of the world combined with one's preferences. The taste component remains a personal matter, but the view of the world can be convincing to others or not (1982: 56–57).

It has come to be an inward-looking, narcissistic art form rather than a useful applied science.

Ultimately, I think that Szostak falls down and fails to fully accomplish either objective, especially the second. However, this does not make his book any the less worthwhile. As the years slog past me, I find myself more drawn to books and articles that challenge my thinking and economic beliefs. I will even admit to a sneaking fondness for the Chicago School. Not because I am often in agreement with their conclusions, but rather because they force me to rethink my own positions when I try to lay out grounds for disagreement. This is quite different than simply rejecting an argument because you like neither its conclusions nor its implications.

Szostak's book made me range over a large and varied terrain of issues. It gave me the pleasure of thinking about art and the structure of Modern Art (a sufficient reason by itself for any economists to have a read through the volume). Just the conceit of Friedman as a disciple of the artist Piet Mondrian (the Phillips curve as Mondrian knock-off)[2] is by itself, enough of a delight to justify purchasing Szostak's book[3]. Added to this, we have Friedman's (1953) attempt at methodology reduced to a manifesto, parallel to the apologias favoured by seemingly every revolutionary group of ambitious, but largely unknown, artists[4].

---

[2] The connection is clear enough if the reader has studied a few Mondrian paintings. To Szostak both represent a pursuit of linearity or an almost obsessive urge to simplify.

> If we were to find an urge toward linearity in econ-art, might that not lead us to suspect that this was more than just a technique for both Mondrian and econ-artists alike? ... The long-run Phillips Curve is — wait for it — a vertical line. (Szostak, 1999: 65–67)

[3] In fact, I wish Szostak had done more of this type of analysis. I can start to see Robert Lucas as a later day Dadaist (the Man Ray of Chicago) or Gerald Debreu as an imagíste in the style of Odilon Redon. Unfortunately, Szostak's dominant agenda does not leave room for such extended flights of fancy.

[4] Szostak, as is his wont in this particular work, pushes the point a bit too far. Friedman's (1953) philosophic effort owed as much to his close colleague, George Stigler. Evidence of their synchronicity of thinking goes back to the late 1940s. Friedman himself is generous enough in his acknowledgment of the part Stigler

Unfortunately, the problem with the book begins when the choice is made to focus more on what Szostak perceives to be the difference between art and science and much less on the common cultural impulses that show up in different manifestations of human endeavour. This is a rather regrettable decision, since some additional detailed case studies (much as McCloskey did in his original work on the use of economic rhetoric) could have been eye-opening. There are undoubtedly common themes that dominate the 20th century, particularly those dealing with time and space. The end of the Newtonian universe is seen not only in physics but in mathematics as well with the rise of non-Euclidean geometry. In different ways, Cubist and Futurist painters grappled with new concepts of time. The rise of photography and motion pictures freed artists from the seeming obligation to reproduce sense perceptions. In economics, Keynes (an economist with a particularly well-developed appreciation of the arts) struggled to present dynamic economic cycles in a static framework (an almost Cubist objective).

Szostak, however, glides by a number of potentially interesting byways. His heart seems captured by his central obsession. Economics in his opinion has turned inward, more concerned with developing ever more elaborate models than in attempting to understand the world we are forced to inhabit. He is a congenital reformer. But before he can trot out his proposed ten-step plan to a better profession, he needs to demonstrate what is wrong with the economics profession today. To capture the heart of this issue he constructs what I consider to be a false dichotomy between art and science. This is where a potentially interesting analysis gets shunted off to a less interesting and fruitful discussion.

It must be remembered that Szostak is trying to shock his audience out of a largely self-imposed stupor (though those most needing

played in this particular work (Conversation with Milton Friedman in August 1997). Friedman's methodology was not merely meant to provide narrow support to his work on monetary theory. It betrays more the common concern that these two eminent economists shared concerning the appropriate application and testing of economic theory.

a good, sharp shock are those least likely to pick up this volume). He uses satire and exaggeration to deliberately provoke. It is then no use in pointing out those very deliberate exaggerations or the resulting discrepancies. Szostak is angling for a response, no matter how angry, in order at least to push his concerns on to centre-stage[5].

Still, even acknowledging this framework, Szostak's discussion seems at times far too glib. It is bad enough when he feels compelled to talk about Truth with a capital T. Without venturing to become a professional Pontius Pilate, I must admit that I start to squirm a bit when someone is so adamant about concepts of Truth[6]. 'But surely there is a Truth out there toward which we scrabble, if we have but the guts and integrity to do so' (Szostak, 1999: 145). I feel the same as when preachers insist on talking about sin and redemption. Articles of faith and belief can be unobjectionable, but the subsequent claim that science brings us truth while art yields only beauty is not a formula I am conditioned to swallow easily. A reflex action causes me to gag.

This unease is amplified when the term 'the real world' is spread almost carelessly across the pages of this volume. Science (in Szostak's estimation) deals with the real world while art is self-obsessed. Art constructs a utopian reality, where the chief concern manifested reflects issues of technique, more than anything else. Szostak is reasonable enough to allow for some overlap between science and art, but maintains that there is a clear and definable difference boiling down to whether the endeavour is outward-looking (scientists unravelling the

[5] Two quite different economists, John Maynard Keynes and George Stigler, were fond of deliberate distortions. By putting forward a case, using the strongest of possible images, the sought for response was at least a lively, even if hostile, discussion. If it is (at least initially) impossible to get opponents to relinquish deeply held positions, it is essential to at least provoke them into defending their theoretical fortifications. The worst possible response for such economists would have been for their ideas to be met by stony silence.

[6] At this point, I would have felt more comforted had Szostak not been so readily to dismiss the epistemological concerns of Feyerabend (1978).

real world) or artists steadfastly gazing inward (creating beautiful objects of the imagination).

> Science, to be sure, may not be immune to cultural influences, but if these come to dominate a discipline it ceases to be science. If economists aren't using scientific standards to judge their work, what are they doing? They are creating works which satisfy some other faculties of appreciation, at least among themselves. What are castles in the sky, if not art? (Szostak, 1999: 118)

This view of science and art refuses to rest comfortably with me. It seems to miss equally what scientists do and what artists (read painters) seek to achieve. I get the sneaking suspicion that the sensibilities described are those more common to engineers, than to scientists *per se*. In contrast, Szostak's artists seem to inhabit a Hollywood back lot. The sharp differentiation between scientist and artist is a creation of the past century (especially the second half that followed World War II, which C. P. Snow (1993) described with great insight). As late as the 19th century the difference was much more muddled, with artists and scientists engaged in reciprocal activities[7].

Szostak's core mistake is to think that artists are concerned with utopian visions. This is not necessarily the way to read either Surrealism or Cubism (the two art movements that Szostak almost exclusively analyses). Artistic endeavours, like their scientific counterparts, are trying to make sense of the world we inhabit. Just as dreams provide insights into the human condition, so do surrealist paintings. It is not simply a benchmark for otherworldly experience. For that reason, scientists and artists are both storytellers, although the form their stories may take can be quite different (more so in the modern age than in prior eras)[8]. Scientists, like artists, provide insights into the

[7] In England of that time certainly Coleridge was as interested in physics as Faraday and others were interested in poetry. See Johnson (1991) for an interesting viewpoint of this era.

[8] Think of Kepler's use of the music of the spheres in his astronomical explanations. Religion itself was often featured (if not acting as a central character) in most scientific explanations until quite recently. Even in present terms, theoretical physics often engages in discourse that is somewhat poetical and certainly metaphorical in nature.

human condition and the environment in which they live. Do artists employ the scientific method that so captivates Szostak? I'm not sure. But then again, I'm not sure that scientists actually abide by such a limited approach. They are not strangers to intuition, serendipity and repeated attempts to achieve their objectives. Undoubtedly, both self-proclaimed artists and scientists are firmly in the world, as they perceive it. Certainly you can take the position of the small boy keen to point out that Franz Marc's blue horses do not exist anywhere in the 'real world', but to do so would be to miss the point.

Szostak's vision of econ artists and econ scientists will, as a result, not fly[9]. I am strongly reminded of Fritz Machlup's (1963) discussion of *weasel words* in economics. For example, *statics* is what you do and what makes your work inferior, while *dynamics* is what I do and what makes my work superior. Szostak offers his own stark contrast of the 'good versus bad' economics. Such simplistic categories mislead, rather than illuminate. Like any other discipline, most work produced by economists has little or no impact. But that is true of the work done by artists and by scientists as well.

At times, Szostak appears almost unaware of the fact that he shares quite a bit of common ground with the Chicago school whom at times he seems to label as econ artists. Yet it was Stigler who rallied the troops in his AEA presidential address to applying economics to test economic theories. Many at Chicago dismissed much pre-war work as worthless, composed of untested theories and outright assertions. Economists at Chicago have been traditionally averse to purely theoretical work (whether general equilibrium theoretics or game theory)

---

[9] The strict opposition that Szostak presents, along with the emotive connotation that he employs, is not unlike the approach that Mayer (1993) utilises in his similarly excellent work. However, Mayer's distinction between 'formalist economics' and 'empirical science economics' has similar problems. As Robert Solow points out in his review of Mayer's work:

> The proper target is not 'formalist theory' nor is it even the use of heavy technical artillery where a pocket-knife would do. The right target is the rigid, narrow-minded, doctrinaire application of particular formal models, with technical fireworks used to cover up the poverty of irrelevance or the assumptions underlying the formal model itself. (1994: 169–170)

if it is equivalent to mathematical self-absorption. Of course, at Chicago, testing meant statistical analysis. Szostak rightly points out the limitations of such an approach. However, ineptness in common practice does not automatically invalidate an approach. Like many of his other condemnations, the fault lies essentially in application and performance rather than in any inherent characteristic.

Moreover, like both scientists and artists, a range of objectives and incentives also motivate economists. This means that the majority of ordinary foot soldiers serving in the profession will opt to tackle problems that more readily lend themselves to definitive solutions. Much published work is simply small (and not always fruitful) extensions of already existing efforts. Essentially, risk-averse toilers will choose to polish the strongest existing theoretical links[10]. Often it is not an aesthetic imperative but rather a pragmatic limitation that dominates the choices made by working economists.

Szostak is correct in asserting that economics tends to be highly limited in its approach to problem solving. This narrowness must be galling in the extreme, given his aspirations as an economic historian. Economic history has diminished into a backwater where only cliometricians are allowed any shred of respectability. We cannot conclude, however, that either mathematical formulations or statistical analyses are inherent signposts of artistic self-indulgence. There is no more legitimacy for such thinking than the animus against such approaches that previously motivated the top academic journals in the pre-war era.

---

[10] To once again revert to Solow's (1994) review of Mayer's (1993) work, there is a rather simple explanation for the trivial nature of much of the work that is ultimately published.

> In any moderately complex argument aimed at a genuine problem of economic interpretation or policy, the strongest part of the argument is likely to be the formal part. It is just easier than trying to capture a complicated reality in a useful model, and when it has been done right one knows it. But this very fact, together with the overvaluation of formal work, tempts the economist (or a succession of economists) to polish and extend and improve and refine the strongest part of the argument although this can contribute very little to the strength of the argument as a whole. It is the weak links that need shoring up, but they are unglamorous and neglected (1994: 170).

What Szostak has accomplished is to provoke our thought without really convincing us of his idiosyncratic dichotomy. At its core lies a fixation with what Szostak terms the 'real world'. Yes, there are economists who develop an obsession with techniques, just as there are artists who revel in technical experimentation for its own sake[11]. But this alone should not lead one to dismiss the attempts to model markets using the benchmark of perfect competition as mere artistic (or autistic) abstraction. If, as many economists (especially those with Chicago affiliations) believe, competitive markets dominate individual choices or institutions, then such an approach cannot simply be dismissed out of hand. Economists must learn to be more tolerant of alternative approaches, but labelling some economists 'artists' (and sneeringly dismissing them) will not accomplish this end, or even throw much light on the problem.

References

Becker, G and G Stigler (1995). De Gustibus Non Est Disputandum. In *The Essence of Becker*, R Frebrero and P Schwartz (eds.), pp. 184–208. Stanford: Hoover Institution Press. Previously published 1977.

Demsetz, H (1982). Barriers to entry. *American Economic Review*, 72(1), 47–57.

Feyerabend, P (1978). *Against Method*. London: Verso.

Friedman, M (1953). *Essays in Positive Economics*. Chicago: University of Chicago Press.

Hegel, GF (1967). *Philosophy of Right*. Oxford: Oxford University Press.

Johnson, P (1991). *Birth of the Modern*. London: Weidenfeld & Nicolson Limited.

Machlup, F (1963). *Essays on Economic Semantics*. Englewood Cliffs, NJ: Prentice-Hall.

Mayer, T (1993). *Truth Versus Precision in Economics*. Aldershot: Edward Elgar.

Snow, CP (1993). *The Two Cultures*. Cambridge: Cambridge University Press.

Solow, R (1994). The whole truth and nothing but the truth — A review of Thomas Mayer's *Truth Versus Precision in Economics*. *Journal of Economic Methodology*, 1(1), 167–171.

---

[11] I am always surprised by how many comments in a given seminar (especially by younger members) are devoted purely to technical issues. At times it seems such economists lose sight of any inherent economic intuition, which (in my opinion) should form the core of economic practise.

Chapter 17

Court Jesters, House Gadflies and Economic Critics

Craig Freedman*

Colander, D (2001). *The Lost Art of Economics: Essays on Economics and the Economics Profession*, pp. x+203. Cheltenham UK: Edward Elgar. ISBN 1-84064-694-2.

> *Thou should'st not have been old till thou hadst been wise.*
> (The Fool to King Lear)

In the medieval court of *King Lear*, the fool seems to have been granted an extraordinary liberty to speak truthfully, without resorting to guile or subterfuge. Why was there a tradition that permitted a seemingly incendiary figure license to speak his mind (assuming the role of professional as opposed to amateur fool was limited to those of the male persuasion)? We might reasonably assume that, from a fool, home truths served only to increase the innocent merriment of the established court players, providing a reasonable release from the more serious strivings of daily life. Truth amuses since court life (the life of a successful courtier) is very much about keeping true thoughts and observations safely out of sight. Fools, or at least authorised fools,

* Department of Economics, Macquarie University, Sydney NSW 2109, Australia. Email:craig.freedman@efs.mq.edu.au

are allowed such privileges because they deliberately put themselves outside the intrigues and political competition of the Court.

The profession of economics is not without its own versions of unofficially sanctioned fools, gadflies and critics. They are allowed to speak the truth (sometimes even in the very journals dedicated to perpetuating orthodoxy) because in some sense, to use the Hollywood terminology, they are not considered to be serious players. Although such critics enter into some of the inner sanctums, are allowed to sup and dine with the elect, as a class they are perceived as having no impact on the profession itself. Economists may listen to what they have to say, read what they write, even in principle agree with many of their arguments. But for all intents and purposes, they are largely ignored. Professional gadflies of this sort create only the gentlest of ripples on the placid surface of mainstream economics. These domesticated critics generate no noticeable upheavals and perhaps not even the most modest of changes. (To be honest, this is in many ways preferable to the treatment almost inevitably doled out to those carpers who resist the necessary potty training that would make their presence tolerable. Such deliberate outcasts are simply ignored.) Among those allowed to loiter in the anteroom of prestige and power, David Colander represents one of the best known and accomplished of this species: widely respected, widely read, largely without impact. In one of his many disarming moments, he himself admits his own limitations.

> For these students the graduate program in economics is a hoop they must jump through to reach what they want to do. This group is the group I hang around with; it has, however, very little influence in the profession; you won't see its members on the executive committee of the AEA or in one of the AEA offices. (Colander, 2001: 5)

The fact of being able to observe and publish the profession's shortcomings without having a reasonable hope of influencing that development creates a core tension that provides Colander's overall thought-provoking and often entertaining volume with a rather schizophrenic foundation. The problem itself is very accurately detailed by a blurb on the inside dust jacket of the book. (Being well acquainted with the publishing practices of Edward Elgar, I feel confident that the actual words are those of David Colander.) 'The essays are written in a highly accessible style, and can be enjoyed by most non-economists, as well as by those economists who don't take themselves too seriously. It can be usefully read by all economists, even those who do take themselves too seriously'. If only those economists who do not take themselves seriously can enjoy the book (those whom Plato once described as the only truly serious individuals), then not all that many accredited economists are going to be capable of enjoying this collection. Nor is it likely that those economists who do take themselves seriously will benefit from reading this book, even though they are exactly the audience that can best be served by a serious consideration of the ideas contained in Colander's work. They will be too busy going about what they consider to be the true business of an academic economist and, by doing so, advancing their careers and their own importance. Why should they choose to read or take seriously any analysis of economics and economists that cuts against their own self-interest? Given the human capital already invested (and the subsequent sunk costs), are they likely voluntarily to wave good-bye to their currently appropriated quasi-rents?

Even those economists who find themselves with the time and the proclivity to think about what Colander has said will find that he or she are still residing in that same criticised academic discipline with the same existing incentives in place. The cost of changing the *status quo* is simply prohibitive. Before a newly minted economist becomes established, outward rebellion is at best suicidal. Afterwards, there is noticeably less of an incentive to attack a system that now seems capable of providing adequate nourishment and sustenance. As Frank Knight pointed out in his minimalist defense of conservatism, while the faults of an existing system are readily known, the faults of a new one are not[1] (see Patinkin, 1972: 801)

---

[1] Patinkin makes it clear that though Knight was a trenchant critic of the market system, his radicalism was conservative by nature. Rather than trying to insist upon any unalloyed virtue for competitive economic systems, he was content to claim that whatever grave failings it might have, alternatives offered the risk of even worse outcomes:

> Primitive society was wise in its conservatism, for it knew at least that the group had previously lived somehow, both as individuals and as a group. (Knight quoted by Patinkin, 1973: 801)

It is possible to pursue this line of thought further, but the heart of the problem is clear. The paradox is not unlike the one that Camus presents to Sisyphus. Why bother rolling the boulder up the hill if it must only inevitably trundle back down? Ostensibly nothing is accomplished by such exertions and struggles. Like all such sanctioned critics, Colander never manages to resolve this core contradiction. This does not say that the sermon is not worth preaching; instead one rather wonders how many deaf ears make up the relevant target audience (those who might be most assisted by such wisdom). Only the already converted will readily lend their full attention. True, Colander's collected articles are not simply a sermon depicting the evils of vegetarianism, forcefully delivered to an enthusiastically cheering congregation of cannibals. That would be a largely unfair characterisation. However, while recognising that the incentives within the profession make the changes he advocates unlikely, Colander at times displays the same sort of optimism that tends to infect many similar critics (whether authorised or officially beyond the pale). The necessary trick seems to be an ability to simultaneously know, yet deny one's own knowledge[2].

---

[2] Colander clearly realises that any endogenous change must reflect a change in graduate education. He frankly does not see this happening nor does he expect it to happen in the future. Instead, he sees change in the economics profession coming by means of external competition:

> I am a realist; I do not expect graduate economics programs to change. Thus I see applied economists gravitating more and more to public policy schools and interdisciplinary programs. As the rigor and selectivity of these schools and programs increase, more and more of the demand for applied economists will come from them, not from graduate economics programs. (Colander, 2001: 146)

This is a clear reiteration of his stance 10 years earlier:

> There is no easy way out of the current state of economics. It is a self-reinforcing state that will require Herculean efforts to change, because change goes against the very interest of individuals who would be required to make that change. Unfortunately, history provides few examples of such changes from within. Instead institutions go through the motions of implementing change, but they do not change. That seems to be the path chosen by the economics profession. (Colander, 1991: 79–80)

Self-appointed reformers of the profession seem to tether their optimism to an unarticulated belief that all that is ever required for such change to take place is a sufficiently clear explanation. (Notoriously, the archetypal American tourist holds a firm belief that foreign inhabitants will understand English if it is spoken in a very loud and slow fashion.) This is the sort of 'reasonable chaps will agree' prejudice that is just below the surface of Keynes's own work and underlies the stirring end of the *General Theory*[3]. But in that given case, the profession promptly excised the most disruptive aspects of his work and went about the requisite domestication of Keynes's theory. Much the same spirit imbues the work of Deirdre McCloskey. Over the last decade and a half she has repeatedly explained what seems obvious to her about the way in which economists argue and so go about doing their work. Despite the apparent impenetrability of economic opinion to such analysis, McCloskey has persisted in her criticism. When they are at their worst, such reformers resemble those evangelists who always see indications that the tide is turning and that good is about to triumph over evil. True, this slightly Pollyannaish position is preferable to the sort of pessimism that leads to a combination of defeatism and cynicism. But I find a consistently pragmatic approach more appealing. As Colander himself admits, change can occur only by appealing (at least in some sense) to the self-interest of the practitioners. Serious attempts to produce change will go astray if the underlying imperative is to change economists' preferences. It is perhaps more strategic to demonstrate that an alternative path will better fulfill their existing preferences, than to try to imbue the flinty bosoms of hard-headed economists with a

Yet there are other points in the volume where at least an impression is created that economists will inevitably listen to sweet reason no matter what the relevant issues of self-interest may be.

[3] The quote is well known in the profession:

> But, soon or late, it is ideas, not vested interests, which are dangerous for good or evil. (Keynes, 1972a: 384)

This is a real Cambridge call to arms. It is not the sort of clarion call you would expect to hear coming from the environs of Chicago.

crusading spirit. By this I mean that you cannot expect academic economists, whether at their incubation, fledgling or full flight stage to cease to be careerist, at least to a certain extent. After reducing human motivation largely to a narrow level of self-interest, economists, more so than any other conceivable group, cannot conveniently dodge their own self-interested motives. That of course is what makes change from within so difficult. Old economists die but they don't fade away[4]. They train others to take their place.

1. Colander's Second Voyage

> Well then, it seemed to me next, since I'd wearied of studying the things that are, that I must take care not to incur what happens to people who observe and examine the sun during an eclipse; some of them, you know, ruin their eyes, unless they examine its image in water or something of that sort. I had a similar thought: I was afraid I might be completely blinded in my soul, by looking at objects with my eyes and trying to lay hold of them with each of my senses. So I thought I should take refuge in theories, and study in them the truth of the things that are. (Plato, 1975: 51)

David Colander has made a very comfortable career for himself as an outsider, an economist who examines other economists as a profession in much the same way that anthropologists put under observation the customs and practices of isolated (and what was previously characterised as primitive) tribes. Am I envious of Colander's success? You bet. Do I think it is well deserved? Absolutely. So perhaps what I harbor isn't true envy. I wouldn't mind being in the same position, but I don't think for a moment that I am in any sense more deserving.

As Colander himself explains in his latest collection of essays, he stumbled on to his current path after having failed to engage the profession on issues relating to his own particular macroeconomic ideas. Like a disappointed debutant, he was puzzled by the almost complete

---

[4] Life may be brief, but not that of many economists. I admit to having made no rigorous investigation, but consider the age reached by many well-known economists, starting with Friedrich von Hayek.

indifference with which much of his work was met. What was it about economists that led to such strongly enforced professional norms?

> What is not understandable to me, and what led me to start looking at the economics profession rather than economics, was that I couldn't even get most economists to understand my arguments informally. Somehow thinking informally about very abstract issues was not something that most economists could do. Their minds seemed compartmentalized. They thought about economic theory in a highly formal way, but when they thought about economic policy, they often left their abstract analysis aside and relied on pedestrian analysis. (Colander, 1991: 11)

In this sense, Colander has embarked on a second career parallel to the second voyage Socrates declares he took when faced with the failure to find truth directly through the observation of natural phenomena. Colander decided to analyse the actual practices of economists (what they do and don't do) rather than tackling economics in a more direct fashion. Lest such an enterprise be sneered at by successful or wannabe doers (those who can, do; those who can't, write about doing), observers of the economic tribe must be as steeped in their lore as ever an anthropologist was or is about the relevant kinship rites in their own preferred *clan du jôur*.

His career as an economics watcher really began with a study done in association with Arjo Klamer (1987) detailing the way in which graduate education was conducted (or misconducted) at top-ranked departments in the United States (being at that time, and still, the relevant economic universe for the profession). He stumbled on to the obvious. Much of what Colander found to be annoying about economics could be recognised clearly, as in the sharp depictional lines of a miniature, when examining the way in which economists were not only trained for, but also socialised into, the profession. The incentives driving the activities of its members were inculcated into its apprentices. It was here that the MIT categorical imperative was honoured; thou shalt employ only simple formal models:

> The MIT approach is ... sterile and highly limiting for most economists ... it eliminates the passion in doing economics and instead directs economists'

> goals toward financial gain and institutional success. Economics becomes a job, not a vocation. (Colander, 2001: 95–96)

This core insight arose largely from the responses provided by surveyed graduate students. The puzzle it presented (how did this come about? what purpose does it serve?) provided the impetus for Colander's further investigations. The initial article was in fact widely read (and largely ignored since the same set of incentives within the profession continues to dominate). Though individually and as a profession we may have at best a very limited attraction to outsiders, those who toil within its confines tend to be more than a bit self-absorbed (as are all those of any profession). Generalised, this only demonstrates what the tabloids have known for years: gossip sells. Yes, we do want to pretend that we are reading the material for high-minded reasons, but at some basic level idle curiosity does rule. However, like most gossip, although it is largely read, it tends to have little impact on the lives or habits of those who read it. Gossip about the profession does not change the inherent institutional incentive structure that dominates that same profession.

This current collection of articles follows the success of a previous collection published a decade ago. A casual reader might be tempted to dismiss Colander's current effort by saying that he has said all this and more in his previous books and articles (including books consisting of past articles). Even worse, the current effort just consists of recycled (republished) articles cobbled together with the aid of an introduction. In effect we are asked to purchase (theoretically, since few individuals can afford Elgar's prices), the product of academic double-dipping, squeezing new out of old publications. Such charges would be entirely unfair. By collecting his work of the last decade, consistent themes in all of Colander's anthropological studies of economists become clear. These links are illuminated when the separate pieces are presented as a whole. Not only are connections clarified, but the current volume also takes forward issues and themes previously explored in a more tentative fashion in earlier work. As it should, Colander's thinking on the issues is evolving, though not largely changing course. Even people already familiar with much of

Colander's work should gain from reading this volume. Those coming to his work for the first time will find that they are able to profit greatly from a careful consideration of the ideas in this volume, despite lacking any previous familiarity.

The book itself might be better titled *Keeping Economists (and Other Drunks) Away From Lamp Posts* in honour of the joke often attributed to James Tobin (who needless to say, did not win a Nobel Prize for humour)[5]. What Colander constructs is an overarching argument based on his observation and analysis of the profession itself. In a very deft way, his own approach to the economist's trade illustrates his proposed model for analysing economic activity in general. An understanding of Colander's one over-reaching theme provides insights into both the strengths and the weaknesses of all his work in this vein.

2. Positive, Normative or Artistically Bent — The Madness in Method

> As the terms are here used, a *positive science* may be defined as a body of systematized knowledge concerning what is; a *normative* or *regulative science* as a body of systematized knowledge relating to criteria of what ought to be, and concerned therefore with the ideal as distinguished from the actual; an *art* as a system of rules for attainment of a given end. The object of a positive science is the establishment of *uniformities*, of a normative science the determination of *ideals*, of an art the formulation of *precepts*. (Keynes, 1890: 34–35)

The pity is that Colander uses John Neville Keynes's slick-sounding tripartite prescription to judge modern economics and find it wanting. The fallen nature of the profession then is the result of not only tasting, but also swallowing whole, Milton Friedman's update of this Keynesian recipe. Though quoting Keynes correctly, Friedman's methodological cake contains only the positive and normative elements. Accepting

[5] The punch line of the joke, quoted on the book's dust-jacket, has a drunk telling a policeman that he is looking for his house keys under the street lamp, not because they are there, but because the light is better.

this unstable version of the original led post-war economics astray. Colander thinks that the inherent contradiction between what Friedman preached and what he actually did, destroyed his ability to influence, let alone maintain, a benchmark for method. However, the illegitimate division between positive and normative continued to rule the thinking of practitioners as well as the textbooks training the successive generations of economists. Such an analysis provides Colander with a powerful tool for dissecting economics and economists, but it is ultimately a tool that indiscriminately damages critic and object alike:

> In reality, Friedman and other post-1950s Chicago economists were enormously interested in the art of economics, but because they did not distinguish between the methodology appropriate to the art of economics and methodology appropriate to the science of economics, post-1950s Chicago economists were heavy-handed in drawing policy conclusions from scientific laws. They certainly did not follow Neville Keynes's conclusion that the art of economics would "have vaguely defined limits" and be "largely non-economic in character". Their art of economics was photographically sharp and used only an economic lens. (Colander, 1992b: 114)

Methodology is a subject that makes the eyes of most economists cross. As Colander would admit, economists do not have any incentive to be introspective. There are no clear, tangible rewards for trying to understand what one is doing and why. Too much introspection and we become like so many millipedes worrying about which foot to put down first. Economists want to get on with their work. They do not want to analyse either what they are doing, or what they might be doing in a far better world. Acting upon this very pragmatic stance, questions of methodology and epistemology are best left to take care of themselves. Unfortunately, since Friedman's one great and influential effort at methodology forms the launching pad for Colander's criticism and recommendation, we need to understand, at least at some level, what Friedman (1953) was both reacting against and promoting in those dim days, some 50 years ago.

Though awarded sole credit for articulating this now canonical approach of the profession, the self-named positive methodology of Milton Friedman is perhaps equally the responsibility of Friedman's close colleague George Stigler[6]. While graduate students at Chicago, both (along with Allen Wallis) had come heavily under the influence of Frank Knight. Knight's determining characteristic was his all-embracing skepticism. This is clear in his reaction to those who wished to turn economics into a science with a capital *S*:

> The author (T.W. Hutchinson) is a positivist, i.e., one of those who always think of "science" with a capital *S*... and use it in a context which conveys instructions pronounced in the awe-inspired tone chiefly familiar in public prayer ... The attempt to build a social science on these foundations suggests that the human race ... having at long last ... found out that the objects of nature are not like human beings-are not actuated by love and hate and caprice and contrariness, and subject to persuasion, cajolery, and threats — have logically inferred that human beings must be like natural objects. (Knight, 1956a: 151)

The staking out of a strident positivistic methodology reflects *a long struggle of escape* on the part of Knight's most admiring students. Friedman's manifesto included an undeniable imperative, which insisted on deciding issues of fact by means of empirical testing. This clearly rejected Knight's use of deductive logic aided and abetted by the institutional structure in which the economy operated[7]. "Knight

[6] This can be traced in letters written between the two in the years leading up to the publication of Friedman's article. Certainly, a version of the positivist position is presented in Stigler's (1949) lecture on monopolistic competition. Milton Friedman willingly admits his debt (conversation with the author, August 1997). According to Mark Blaug (conversation with the author, June 1998), one of Stigler's former students, George Stigler always felt a bit miffed about the lack of recognition accorded to him.

[7] Empirical testing became an almost religious tenet of the Chicago School, charted from Milton Friedman's laying out the path to righteousness to George Stigler's (1965) AEA Presidential Address whose evangelistic tone reveals the coming promise of salvation through data. Such attitudes were poles apart from that of their teacher, Frank Knight:

> Insistence on a concretely quantitative economics means the use of statistics of physical magnitudes, whose economic meaning and significance is uncertain and dubious... In this field, the Kelvin dictum very largely means in practice, 'if you cannot measure, measure anyhow!" That is, one either performs some other operation and calls it measurement or measures something else instead of what is ostensibly under discussion, and usually not a social phenomenon. (Knight, 1956a: 166)

taught economic theory in a loose, 'literary', philosophical fashion — and was antipathetic to mathematical economics" (Patinkin, 1973: 789)[8]. Such an approach, however, became fundamentally unsatisfactory to Friedman (and Stigler) for at least two reasons. Much of economics, when judged by pre-war published articles, seemed decidedly *ad hoc*[9]. In reaction, both were pushing for more empirical testing of what might otherwise seem to be pure assertion. Had this not been the case, they might have been quite happy to bury all and any methodological issues. As previously pointed out, practicing economists, like any other group of practicing researchers, want to get on with their work. They tend not to be particularly introspective about what they are doing. Stigler would have dismissed any such fixation as so much navel gazing.

We can see here a yearning for the precision and decisiveness of a true science (with a capital *S*). Furthermore, the breakthroughs in statistical testing and a burgeoning increase in available data sets seemed to provide an empirical grounding to what had been largely a discipline with scatty bits of data presented according to the preferences of the individual author. More hidden is what I believe to be a second reason for this particular methodological approach. Knight's critical

---

[8] This extended to questioning the rationality proposition in economics:

> Another basic element of Knight's teaching was the view that the study of man-including economic man-could not proceed within the same deterministic framework as the study of nature. For the behavior of man must also express his freedom of will-to which there is no counterpart in the physical world. (Patinkin, 1973: 790)

[9] Armen Alchian (conversation with the author, October 1997) characterised much of this output as garbage (or words to that effect). Similar sentiments were expressed to the author by a number of other Chicago School types. (Though Alchian never was connected officially with Chicago, Samuelson, for one, has termed him 'more Catholic than the Pope' in terms of Chicago style doctrine (conversation with the author, October 1997).) As Colander points out:

> In many ways the modern movement to applied modeling is laudable. It is empirical and is an attempt to avoid the pontificating which characterized earlier periods. Modern applied modeling looks to the empirical evidence through models. (Colander, 2001: 164)

stance did not provide even an approximate defense of market competition[10]. Meaning that a defense of such a system could not be provided by Knight's version of *a priori* reasoning. Friedman's goal was to eliminate such an obvious Achilles heel, while putting to rest further methodological debate. David Colander should not find it ironic, then, that Milton Friedman's essay created a lack of interest in taking the methodological debate any further. The purpose of the paper was in part an attempt to leave such issues behind (Get behind me Satan!) so that theories could be tested against available data.

Friedman's methodological approach seems to have met a prevailing demand within the profession because it closely agreed with the pre-existing preferences held by many good economists. It was also officially or quasi-officially adopted in a wide range of textbooks. An encapsulated approach of this sort could be brought up as an officially sanctioned stance, result in a multiple-choice question on an exam, but then be entirely left behind and forgotten for the rest of any course. Even today, it remains in many textbooks because it is easy to teach and to test if anyone feels obliged to do so. In any case, most academic economists find such discussions not to be a particularly congenial chore, if a chore performed at all. Given the low payoff to teaching, most academic economists are more than willing to deal with the issue by avoidance. As a result, there is not really a strong need by textbook writers to present any sort of digression on methodology. On this point, Colander goes off track a bit. Dethroning positivist methodology would have little impact. If methodologists could agree on an alternative (in essence seizing the high ground), it is likely

---

[10] The defense that Friedman and Stigler eventually would erect ended up equating market outcomes with ethical results. Like Knight, they maintained 'freedom of choice' as an objective in and for itself. Unlike Hayek (as well as Knight), they would not accept that individual freedom could be inconsistent with distributive justice. Such an allowance naturally brings in questions of trade-offs and possible state intervention:

> Moreover, neither the income distribution which we observe, nor that which would result from the perfect competition of theory is to any great extent in conformity with any acceptable ethical standard. (Knight, 1956b: 95)

that methodology questions in textbooks would simply vanish, as they already have in some recent texts. It is not therefore any degree of accuracy that has made Friedman's encapsulation such a textbook fixture, but rather the way in which it dismisses such issues while leaving an impression of scientific precision.

At the same time, Colander is perfectly correct in claiming that Milton Friedman never employed his own prescribed methodology. Coase (1994a) comes even closer to the truth in saying that no one, including Milton Friedman ever used the method he propounded, because the approach was essentially impossible to apply even if someone had desired to do so[11]. Instead, the Friedman article served the purpose of dismissing the need for further methodological discussion. By fusing the prescriptive with the descriptive it shut off any meaningful (anthropological?) examination of how economists actually go about their work. In his article, Friedman indicates how he believes economists should act and then proceeds as if this is in fact how they could or even did act:

> When I was a graduate student we were taught a paradigm of how you do research. I've got to tell you, it's all wrong. It's not the way we operate. We don't sit up here and develop hypotheses and go out and test them. That's just not what we do. George taught me that. Milton taught me that. They're wrong! And I understand that. I'm old enough now to figure out that's not the way we do work. (Sam Peltzman, conversation with the author, October 1997)

---

[11] Coase, like Colander, is bothered (perhaps for different reasons) by a seeming confusion between positive and normative standards. But even as a prescription only, Coase cannot see how it could be a fruitful one:

> If choosing theories in accordance with Friedman's criteria is to be treated as a positive theory, economists would need to adopt a procedure somewhat similar to the following. When a new theory is advanced, economists would compare the accuracy of its predictions, preferably about "phenomena not yet observed", with that of predictions of the existing theory and would choose that theory which gave the best predictions ... An insistence that the choice of theories be made in accordance with Friedman's criteria would paralyze scientific activity. (Coase, 1994: 23–24)

Colander, though, claims that the wheels came off Milton Friedman's methodology when (faced with the impossibility of using his own stated methods) he opted to follow something like a Marshallian straddle. This desire to claim the status of positive economics for what was essentially applied policy objectives eventually brought him down:

> I argue that Friedman, like Alfred Marshall before him, tried to straddle a fence between policy and logical-deductive theory, combining the artistic science of the historical and institutional school with the logical-deductive science of economics under a single category — which Friedman called positive economics. This combination worked for Marshall, in part because in Marshall's day formal logical-deductive economic analysis was still in its infancy, and didn't need to be separated from applied policy economics, and in part because of Marshall's proclivity to avoid taking strong policy stands, hence avoiding normative issues in the art of economics. (Colander, 2001: 28)

Colander is clear that, had Friedman resorted to John Neville Keynes' tripartite categorisation instead of getting bogged down in the morass of a Marshallian muddle, Friedman could have found a way out of his dilemma. It is here that I feel compelled to disagree with Colander's analysis. (Although I suspect, that Friedman did not perceive any such muddle, but that is not the issue here.) The pristine tripartite approach that so attracts Colander's interest has the appeal of abstract clarity but the reality of concrete confusion. Though I could wholeheartedly support returning art to economics in the sense Colander uses the term, I do not see Colander's particular categorisation as furthering this aim.

How the approach works is actually clearer in the original Keynesian version than in Colander's adaptation. Keynes presents the example of tax incidence. Determining the incidence of a tax belongs to the positive branch of economics. It is concerned with finding out what is, meaning ferreting out the facts of what the case actually is. We then move from fact in this scheme to what ought to be, namely the normative issue. The debate over what ought to be (normative science) is every bit as important as the fact-finding stage. In the case of tax incidence, what should be the ideal system? Keynes would not accept the implicit (and sometimes quite explicit) assumption held by some

Chicago-type economists that what is, is what ought to be[12]. Moreover, positive science (in the case of economics) makes no sense to Keynes if pursued as an end in itself[13]. The art, or applied aspect, of this tax issue, requires us to determine the appropriate rules to achieve our desired tax incidence objective. Keynes labels this endeavor as an art in distinction to a science, because more than a simple mechanical application of economic theory is required:

> But more usually when we pass, for instance, to problems of taxation ... it is far from being the case that economic considerations hold the field exclusively. Account must also be taken of ethical, social, and political considerations that lie outside the sphere of political economy regarded as a science. (Keynes, 1890: 56–57)

As presented in the paper, the division sounds intuitively obvious. Colander then can make his plea for an appropriate division of labour based on the tasks at hand[14]. Specialisation of separate tasks always

---

[12] This implicit position can be seen in much of the later work of George Stigler and Gary Becker. It is best formulated in Armen Alchian's dictum that 'What is, is efficient'. The onus then becomes one of arguing that a seemingly inefficient result should be a desired objective.

[13] It is important to keep in mind that, under Keynes's tripartite scheme, no one division is privileged. The point of economics is ultimately (for Keynes and Colander as well) to achieve certain objectives (economics being a distinctly applied discipline). The positive branch provides the basis for discussing normative objectives and guiding practical policy applications:

> No one desires to stop short at the purely theoretical enquiry. It is universally agreed that in economics the positive investigation of facts is not an end in itself, but is to be used as the basis of a practical enquiry, in which ethical considerations are allowed their due weight. (Keynes, 1890: 47)

[14] Colander does intend specialisation to be understood in the strictest sense of the word. What I doubt is the possible gains from trade by groups that share no core language or understanding (or perhaps just enough to seriously misunderstand each other). No common medium of exchange (the role that money plays in standard commerce) exists to overcome this basic lack of knowledge. The inherent transaction costs attached to such exchange would then become simply prohibitive:

> Such specialization opens up the possibility of trade, and ideally economics would have two types of economic researchers making trades-formal theorists

appeals to economists. But specialisation would not do, if we are essentially talking about output that is to a significant degree a joint product, divisible in theory but not in practice. This would make Marshall's muddle more sensible than Colander would care to admit[15]. Implicit in any discussion of a single aspect of economics are the other two. It is to Keynes's credit that he at least wrestles with this problem, though ultimately arguing that such a division is eminently practicable despite some inherent problems. In fact, in Keynes' discussion the problem is not quite as acute since he does not argue for different types of economists based on his categorisation. Part of Colander's problem is that he sincerely wants to present his prescription as an entirely doable approach. Given the current composition of the profession, along with its incentives and prejudices, Colander realises that he will be unable to interest economists unless he retains a positive branch that does science with a big *S*. Colander would put off too many of his potential readers, if the idea of economics as positive science (big *S*) were to be given a much-deserved funeral.

> dealing with highly complex and abstract analysis almost devoid of institutions, and intuitive institutionally-based theorists dealing with real-world institutions and informal abstract analysis. The MIT approach of simple formal models would make sense if there were not increasing returns to scale in research, but it seems obvious that there are increasing returns, so not to take advantage of them and not to encourage specialization is, in my view, a highly inefficient approach to understanding. If you are going to be formally abstract, then go all the way and don't let the real-world issues contaminate the purity of your analysis. If you are going to be concerned with the real world, don't formalize more than the least precise real-world element. (Colander, 2001: 98)

[15] Marshall, writing his *Principles* at the same time that John Neville Keynes was writing his volume, disagreed with Keynes sharply, though, given his nature, Marshall tried to minimise those differences. Still, he saw little use for the sharp divisions as set up by Keynes:

> I never discuss any line of division or demarcation except to say that Nature has drawn no hard & fast lines, & that any lines Man draws are merely for the convenience of the occasion: & shld never be treated as though they were rigid. (Marshall writing to Keynes, quoted in Coase, 1994b: 168)

Certainly the idea that the truth is out there to be discovered and tested was never part of Adam Smith's approach. For Smith, the order we find in nature is not an existing order but rather an order that we impose to relieve the mental discomfort caused by what, otherwise, would be chaotic observations. For example, using this perspective, Newton did not discover the laws of Nature but rather invented them. They arose out of Newton's imagination rather than being results dictated to him by his own observations:

> Philosophy is the science of the connecting principles of nature ... [It] endeavours to introduce order into this chaos of jarring and discordant appearances, to allay this tumult of the imagination, and to restore it ... to that tone of tranquility and composure, which is both most agreeable to itself, and the most suitable to its nature. Philosophy, therefore, may be regarded as one of those arts which address themselves to the imagination. (Smith, 1980: 45–46)

The use of the science term (especially science with a big *S*), makes me want to slip into something more comfortable, like a highly starched lab coat. However, I doubt that this insistence on science can be reduced entirely to an underlying core of insecurity, like that which provokes a teenager into attempting to grow a wispy moustache to assert his masculinity. It is more (again consistent with Friedman's objectives) a desire to emphasise the precision and certainty of economics, even if implicitly sacrificing something in terms of accuracy. Chicago could not make space for anything resembling economics as an art, since that could have undermined a basic belief in the assured effectiveness of the price system and the efficiency of the market. Truly understanding what is (in this view), allows you to understand that it is what should, or at least what can, be. Who then needs an artistic sensibility to accomplish policy objectives? The development and subsequent promotion of an approved methodological approach complemented the marketing of a particular Chicago type view and its associated set of policy recommendations. Effective promotion necessitated claiming a certain scientific vision, in this case involving verifiable predictions:

> There's a lot of salesmanship, there's a lot of taking positions, defending them. The facts will win out. I'm not saying that we're not in that sense correct.

> The facts do win out. But the process by which that happens is not the clean one of scientific method rigorously applied all the time. I've come to understand that, and George [Stigler] had a big part in that process. He staked out a position. People attacked it. The empirical work goes back and forth and after a while it does sort itself out. (Sam Peltzman, conversation with the author, October 1997)

Coase (1994a) points out that understanding rather than predictive accuracy is what is required. Making sense of what we observe is the prescriptive requirement, rather than simply correctly guessing some next-period scenario. In this regard, assumptions do matter. Though, in his famous essay, Milton Friedman dismisses any consideration of the underlying reality of theoretical assumptions (a most un-Marshallian stance), it is doubtful that he ever regarded any of his own assumptions in that same dismissive light. Certainly his close colleague George Stigler did not. But, in quite an essential sense, Friedman did not want a discussion that focused on the relative accuracy of assumptions when it came to competing theories. This would have had the unfortunate consequence of shifting the terms of debate to what Friedman would see as sterile territory. Meaning, he would place himself on rather treacherous ground, forced to defend an inherently weaker position. Certainly on such terrain, the assumptions forming the foundations of perfect competition would face an uphill battle against those comprising monopolistic competition[16].

The core problem is that the sort of positive science that Colander accepts demands an outside objective observer. Here, in a strange fashion, Colander is guilty of the same category of transgression that he cavalierly assigns to Milton Friedman. By blurring

---

[16] Bronfenbrenner (1962), a Chicago contemporary of Friedman and Stigler, points out their tendency to favour the simplest over relatively more realistic hypotheses:

> As an indication of the relative downgrading of "realistic" hypotheses H_2, one finds at Chicago a correlative underemphasis on what the detailed facts are (as distinguished from the figures), and on the narrative or insightful history of how the facts developed to be what they are. (Bronfenbrenner, 1962: 75)

the supposed division between positive and normative, conservative scholars (like Friedman) were able to identify what is (in terms of market competition) with what ought to be and recommend policies accordingly. But, in order to counter the worst excesses of such an approach, Colander insists on a strict categorical separation. Unfortunately, he does not feel any need (unlike Keynes) to provide a reasonable defense for his stance. In both cases, expediency seems to be driving the logic of the debate. A more effective way to counter ideological-based presentations might be simply to admit the impossibility of moving with any convincing rigor beyond one's underlying preferences[17].

What is worse is that Colander is never clear-cut about the exact nature or extent of the positive end of economics. At times, it seems to consist purely of deductive logic, like much of the work involving general equilibrium theory. However, Colander strongly indicates that positive economics involves empirical testing. Two problems quickly arise (both of which he acknowledges to a certain extent). Much of the theoretical work cannot be tested and much of the empirical work fails to convince[18]. Nor can a purely positive basis exist

---

[17] Demsetz does not deny the role that individual preferences play in policy positions. He does claim that such elements can be sifted out, at least to some degree, based upon underlying analysis. But this simply takes the argument back a step. Acceptance of certain forms of argument and evidence has to be predicated once again (at least to a given extent) on deep-rooted preferences:

> All policy preferences, of course, ultimately derive from a view of the word combined with one's preferences. The taste component remains a personal matter, but the view of the world can be convincing to others or not. Opposition to a tariff because of its impact on consumers is based on a convincing view of the world ... because of our agreement as to the correctness of the underlying analysis. (Demsetz, 1989: 38)

[18] Clearly Colander agrees that econometrics as it is currently practiced has failed to live up to its early post-war promise. But he is not sufficiently clear as to what sort of empirical evidence would be a convincing substitute. Simulations and data mining seem similarly flawed. The problem is in thinking that there can be a knock-down test or body of evidence. As McCloskey has insisted, a resort to empirical argument is simply another form of rhetoric, and not necessarily the most convincing form (see

for choosing the appropriate evidence with which to test these general theories of fact. Data to start with are never generic or abstract but rather specific by definition[19]. But the type of data mining that

McCloskey, 1994b for just one example). In a complementary fashion Solow indicates that:

> The austere view is that "facts" are just time series of prices and quantities. The rest is hypothesis testing. I have seen a lot of those tests. They are almost never convincing, primarily because one senses that they have very low power against lots of alternatives. There are too many ways to explain a bunch of time series. (Solow, 1997: 202)

Similarly Coase maintains:

> ... I doubt whether such studies have often led to a change in the views of the authors. My impression is that these quantitative studies are almost invariably guided by a theory and that they may most aptly be described as explorations with the aid of a theory. In almost all cases, the theory exists before the statistical investigation is made and is not derived from the investigation. (Coase, 1994a: 26)

Taking this one step even further, it is hard to site even one theory in economics that has been discredited once and for all. Unfashionable theories bide their time, are eventually resurrected, tarted up and described as new breakthroughs. In this way they gain another lease on life. This may be true to a certain extent in all the sciences, natural as well as social, but not to the same extent as in economics.

[19] Unfortunately, I do not find that Colander's explanations provide sufficient clarity to dispel the problems raised by his strict categorisation of positive economics versus the art of economics. I quote an extended passage to give you some of the flavour of the underlying confusion. At least in my mind, Colander's arguments and explanations raise more questions than they answer. At a sufficiently deep level, I'm not at all sure what the following statement actually means:

> In the art of economics one accepts the general laws and models that have been determined by the profession and one tries to apply the insights of economic models to real-world problems. Applied policy economics has nothing to do with testing a theory; it has to do with applying the insight of that theory to a specific case ... Similarly, once a generalized model is developed, it makes little sense to test specific implications of that generalized model, other than as an educational exercise. If one believes the generalized model, one believes it applies; applied policy economics has nothing to do with empirically testing theories; it has to do with applying

Colander champions as a substitute for more traditional statistical methods does not seem an overly productive route to explore. Too often, the heavy use of computer analysis and simulation acts as a substitute rather than as a complement to economic intuition and thought. An even more fundamental issue is that Colander divorces future specialists in positive economics from the type of economic intuition demanded of those practicing the art of economics or framing the normative objectives of the discipline. Equally, applied workers would lack much of the rigorous foundations needed to handle the fruitful output of the positive division (if any should exist). Thus, models would be handled mechanically and perhaps incorrectly (as econometric packages often are today)[20]. You could caricature Colander's approach as involving billions of monkeys grinding out billions of theories like so many multi-flavoured sausages, while billions of orang-outangs throw billions of these sausage theories against brick walls to see if any of them stick:

> ... my approach calls for two increasingly polar branches of economics; a positive branch — a highly abstract, deductive, branch in which work is subject to rigorous empirical tests before it allows an insight to become a law,

---

> theories-theories that one is willing to tentatively accept as true-to the real world. To do that, one must add back into the model all the assumptions that were made as it was being generalized. The question in applied policy economics concerns whether the theory fits the application, not whether the theory is true. The applied policy issue is: How can the insights of positive economic theory be translated into real-world policies which achieve society's goals. (Colander, 2001: 49, 51)

[20] Colander's partial solution to the lost art of economics requires quarantining applied mathematicians to a reservation he labels positive economics and shrinking their numbers by cutting down funding for their projects. They could only survive as pure researchers, since they would be incapable of teaching the art of economics (the new standard economics curriculum). But the usefulness of their work would then seem to me extremely limited. In this regard, Solow observes:

> What I am saying is that the economist cannot dispense with keeping his or her eyes open, looking around, and forming judgments about what makes sense and what is simply farfetched. Those cannot be uncritical judgments, but judgments to be defended by appeal to observation and to logic. (Solow, 1997: 203)

> and an art branch: a loose, non-formal, application of the theoretical insights to the real world ... In the art of economics one accepts the general laws and models that have been determined by the profession and one tries to apply the insights of economic models to real-world problems. Applied policy economics has nothing to do with testing a theory; it has to do with applying the insight of that theory to a specific case. (Colander, 2001: 52, 48)

Colander is simply trying too hard. The cool, clear divisions he adopts from John Neville Keynes undercut rather than advance what I would concede to be an excellent aim, reviving economic intuition (the art of economics). A more congenial environment in which to advance such goals might be just that Marshallian muddle which, at times, Colander seems to scorn. By prescribing what remains an impracticable and too complex set of rules for reforming economics, he is in danger of generalising his own preferences. A more productive option would be for him to observe how economists actually operate, an ability he possesses and repeatedly demonstrates in the highest degree. No wonder that Marshall shied away from all and any such detailed methodological discussions!

Instead of John Neville Keynes, Colander should keep in mind the working methods of his son John Maynard Keynes, who ultimately aligned himself more with his teacher Alfred Marshall than with his father:

> He [Keynes] was a student of Marshall, and he said, "The theory of economics is a method rather than a doctrine, an apparatus of the mind, a technique of thinking which helps its possessor to draw correct conclusions". ... This quotation is the epitome of the Marshallian method. It tells us to use economics as an engine of analysis, not as a set of principles. If we keep that Marshallian method in mind, we will be giving our students a good foundation in understanding macroeconomics and we will be treating Keynes the way he should be treated as an economist who carried on an important tradition in Classical economics. (Colander, 2001: 90)

McCloskey has made the same point about Keynes, though from the perspective of rhetoric:

> I would claim that Keynes is one of a long if thin line of economic sophists as against the massed phalanx of economic Platonists. Most economists have been Platonists. The Platonists believe that Truth is out there on the

> blackboard somewhere, or less commonly out there in the econometrics or in the experiment. That their program has failed repeatedly does not discourage them any more than it has discouraged Platonists in philosophy these two-and-a-half millennia past. They carry on seeking the one immutable Truth for the ages, and scorn the practical sophist like Maynard Keynes making arguments for the day. (McCloskey, 1996: 233)

This represents a more pragmatic approach that identifies economics as an art employing a number of tools and methods. Its inherent messiness explains why John Maynard Keynes thought that, despite the commonplace nature of the subject matter, a good economist (like a *good* man) was hard to find. Rather than employing any rigid categorisation, it can be more helpful to adopt Robert Solow's simple division of economists into system builders and puzzle solvers. By doing so, much of the debate then centres on the way in which economists solve puzzles. For instance, Chicago economists largely felt no need to build systems since, to Friedman or Stigler, Adam Smith had already accomplished all that needed to be done in that respect. Their challenge was to show how any observation, no matter how seemingly aberrant, could be explained by means of the self-interested choice of rational economic agents. For Solow, then, economics is not Science with a capital *S*:

> ...economics should try very hard to be scientific with a small *s*. By that I mean only that we should think logically and respect fact ... My hunch is that we can make progress only by enlarging the class of eligible facts to include, say, the opinions and casual generalizations of experts and market participants, attitudinal surveys, institutional regularities, even our own judgments of plausibility. My preferred image is the vacuum cleaner, not the microscope. (Solow, 1994: 202–203)

Such an approach lacks the glamour of an elegant categorisation, but captures much of what Colander wants to accomplish without introducing a counterproductive definitional straightjacket.

3. David Colander's Brave New World

> We shall once more value ends above means and prefer the good to the useful. We shall honour those who can teach us how to pluck the hour and the

> day virtuously and well, the delightful people who are capable of taking direct enjoyment in things, the lilies of the field who toil not, neither do they spin. (Keynes, 1973b: 331)

True, Keynes allowed some 100 years for this to occur and placed caveats concerning war and population growth as hedges against his predictions. But even with some 30 years still to run, very few people are looking forward to such a millennium. The economic problem is not close to being solved (though progress, whatever that may mean, has been made).

The quote from Keynes, though, should be a warning to all economists concerning the dangers of peering too confidently into the future. As Galbraith is said to have remarked, 'Economists forecast, not because they know, but because they are asked'. No matter how enticing, no matter what inducement, the black hole of pontification should be avoided at all costs. Strength of character comes from resisting all and any opportunities to offer accurate glimpses of the future, as well as avoiding these obvious occasions on which to pronounce dubious judgments. Colander fails to let the fateful cup pass by. Because he does in fact give in to the allures of prognostication, of being wise before his time, the last two chapters of his current volume inevitably remind me of one of Keynes's essays in persuasion (*Economic Possibilities for Our Grandchildren*). These are all essentially economic bedtime stories for well-behaved infants. Needless to say, I think such attempts weaken, rather than strengthen, what until this final section has been an excellent collection.

In particular, the last chapter is fey where it means to be fun. This may reflect simply my own distaste for science fiction as my choice of pulp reading material (favouring detective novels instead). Nonetheless, when economists wax lyrical about some achievable golden age for the economics profession, I feel queasier and more embarrassed than if the same person were to wax lyrical about his or her sex life. The major difference is that the later might be of more interest and certainly of more practical applicability (though this is possibly a stretch given some members of the profession).

The problem as stated in the first five parts of the volume certainly exists. The profession tends to take abstract models and jumps from the implications of those general (but at the same time highly restricted models) to policy conclusions. This makes no sense, displaying instead finely attuned symptoms of what Colander labels 'artiphobia', essentially a hard-core contempt for serious policy analysis. The remaining challenge, then, is the way in which the *status quo* might be changed. What is interesting in much of this attempt at constructing a future vision is that it is clearly at odds with Colander's well-honed skill of looking for and locating prevailing economic incentives. Instead, he seemingly abandons his concrete practicality and opts for unwarranted flights of fancy.

Usually, the all too sensible Colander takes the only consistent approach to understanding what economists do and why economics is as it is today. This also provides the only reasonable basis for trying to peer into the future, if we cannot be persuaded to refrain from all such activity. Colander is at his best when he searches for and locates those dominant incentives that motivate individual economists. Certainly, we can wish that those incentives were different. But, in reality, the self-selection that goes on in graduate school, and on the job market thereafter, almost ensures that those who do succeed will be comfortable (for the most part) with what they are doing. This would make change from within unlikely:

> The below-age-45 professors are now almost all highly technical economists who are comfortable with the existing situation. Given current selection procedures, in 20 years almost all criticism of the profession will come from without rather than within since potential critics will never enter the profession. (Colander, 2001: 145)

This inconsistency in his approach (between wish and reality) becomes apparent when Colander seems to think that preaching to the existing congregation of largely self-satisfied economists will initiate tangible, discernable change. At this point, he comes close to agreeing with Stigler that the internal dynamics of the profession must dominate. 'On my reckoning, the immediate stimulation to advances in economics has overwhelmingly been the attempt to improve on other economists' work' (Stigler 1997: 106). Colander is certainly leaning this way when he somehow assumes that grabbing the methodological high ground and imposing the fruits of victory on the leading squadron of textbook writers will shape a new generation of economists. This, as I have previously pointed out, seems more of a flight of fancy than a calculated likelihood.

Where Colander is on stronger ground is when he ironically resorts to standard Chicago reasoning. At the moment, the economics profession has a monopoly on granting accreditation to practicing economists. This unofficial licensing procedure is done via the awarding of PhDs. As Colander carefully argues, the profession selects out all but those who fit the prevailing mode of theorising. If, though, the market for economists (teachers, policy makers, business analysts) expresses sufficient dissatisfaction with the existing model, alternative sources of producing economists more suitable to the appropriate market will appear. In simple terms, clear potential for gain will produce academic competition.

It is also true, as Colander points out, that one clear venue of change lies in the type of teaching we do. As it now stands, undergraduate teaching is often regarded as a necessary evil. According to Colander, it is an awkward compromise; a series of badly related models with enough flesh slapped on to make it palatable in a very loose sense. In its place, Colander would prefer to substitute teaching the art of economics. The drastic nature of such a reform should not be underestimated. This is just the sort of economic thinking that John Maynard Keynes found to be in such scarce supply.

I have tried to teach something like the art of economics to my final-year undergraduates. I persist due to what must be an ingrained and improperly acknowledged streak of pure masochism. First, you have to try to disabuse students of what economics is. (No, it is not simply memorising pointless models.) Next, you have to supplement whatever text you use with relevant case study material. Then, you have to be firm against the whining of students who simply do not want to put in the requisite time and effort. They have become acclimatised to a mindless level of committing to memory meaningless material the week before an exam. (Colander (1992d) himself points this out in some of his earlier writings.) I suspect that students may walk away with something from my efforts. This is not difficult, since they often walk away from standard courses with absolutely nothing. But McCloskey ultimately may be right: perhaps you cannot teach undergraduates the art of economics. At best, you can only hope to provide a glimpse of what that process is:

> Our undergraduates, and most of our graduate students, can learn a lot *about* economics that they can use in life. But unless they join us in that slog up the spiral they are not going to think like economists. Perhaps we should redirect our energies, teaching them economic facts and stories, say, or inspiriting them for later study. (McCloskey, 1992: 239)

Despite some purple prose, flights of fancy and the dreaded sin of pontification, David Colander once again provides us with a nourishing and welcome diet. His work is thought-provoking and should (but probably will not) cause both those in the mainstream and those critical of the profession to reassess their thoughts. What more could anyone desire? I await with some anticipation David Colander's next census of the economics trade in 2011. He looks forward to some noticeable changes in the profession with what I would describe as measured optimism. Being less buoyant by nature, I would expect after canvassing whatever changes are wrought over the next decade simply to respond, 'Plus ça change, plus la même'.

> If a discipline changes, it is because of informed complaints about what the discipline is doing and because of what critics of the discipline are doing. I see my challenges as part of the process through which the invisible hand of truth operates. (Colander, 2001: 14)

References

Brenner, R (1992b). Truth in teaching microeconomics. In *Educating Economists*, D Colander and R Brenner (eds.), pp. 97–111. Ann Arbor: University of Michigan Press.

Bronfenbrenner, M (1962). Observations on the "Chicago school(s)". *Journal of Political Economy*, 70(1), 72–75.

Cannan, E (1893). *A History of the Theories of Production and Distribution in English Political Economy from 1776–1848*. London: Staples Press.

Coase, RH (1994a). How should economists choose? In *Essays on Economics and Economists*, pp. 15–34. Chicago: University of Chicago Press.

Coase, RH (1994b). Marshall on method. In *Essays on Economics and Economists*, pp. 167–176. Chicago: University of Chicago Press.

Colander, D (1991). *Why Aren't Economists as Important as Garbagemen?* Armonk, NY: M. E. Sharpe.

Colander, D (1992a). Truth in teaching macroeconomics. In *Educating Economists*, D Colander and R Brenner (eds.), pp. 153–167. Ann Arbor: University of Michigan Press.

Colander, D (1992c). Reform of graduate economics education. In *Educating Economists*, D Colander and R Brenner (eds.), pp. 213–231. Ann Arbor: University of Michigan Press.

Colander, D (1992d). Reform of undergraduate economics education. In *Educating Economists*, D Colander and R Brenner (eds.), pp. 231–243. Ann Arbor: University of Michigan Press.

Colander, D (2001). *The Lost Art of Economics*. Cheltenham, UK: Edward Elgar.

Colander, D and A Klamer (1987). The making of an economist. *Journal of Economic Perspectives*, 1(2), 95–111.

Demsetz, H (1989). Barriers to entry. In *Efficiency, Competition, and Policy — The Organization of Economic Activity Volume II*, pp. 25–40. Cambridge and Oxford: Blackwell.

Friedman, M (1953). The methodology of positive economics. In *Essays in Positive Economics*, pp. 3–43. Chicago: University of Chicago Press.

Friedman, M (1997). Milton Friedman. In *Lives of the Laureates*, W Breit and RW Spencer (eds.), pp. 79–94. Cambridge MA: The MIT Press.

Keynes, JN (1890). *The Scope and Method of Political Economy*. London: Macmillan.

Keynes, JM (1972a). *The General Theory of Employment Interest and Money: The Collected Writing of John Maynard Keynes (Volume VII)*. London: Macmillan Press.

Keynes, JM (1972b). Economic possibilities for our grandchildren. In *Essays in Persuasion: The Collected Writings of John Maynard Keynes (Volume IX)*. London: Macmillan Press.

Knight, FH (1956a). "What is truth" in economics? In *On the History and Method of Economics*, pp. 151–179. Chicago: University of Chicago Press.

Knight, FH (1956b). Historical and theoretical issues in the problem of modern capitalism. In *On the History and Method of Economics*, pp. 89–104. Chicago: University of Chicago Press.

Loasby, BJ (1989a). On scientific method. In *The Mind and Method of the Economist*, pp. 15–30. Aldershot: Edward Elgar.

Loasby, BJ (1989b). Knowledge and organization: Marshall's theory of economic progress and coordination. In *The Mind and Method of the Economist*, pp. 41–71. Aldershot: Edward Elgar.

McCloskey, DN (1992). The natural. *Eastern Economic Journal*, 18(2), 135–137.

McCloskey, DN (1994a). Economics: Art or science or who cares? *Eastern Economic Journal*, 20(1), 117–120.

McCloskey, DN (1994b). Why don't economists believe empirical findings? *Eastern Economic Journal*, 20(3), 357–360.

McCloskey, DN (1996). Keynes was a sophist, and a good thing, too. *Eastern Economic Journal*, 22(2), 231–234.

Patinkin, D (1972). Frank Knight as teacher. *American Economic Review*, 63(5), 787–810.

Plato (1975). *Phaedo*. Oxford: Clarendon Press.

Smith, A (1980). The principles which lead and direct philosophical enquiries; illustrated by the history of astronomy. In *Essays on Philosophical Subjects (1795)*, W Wightman (ed.), pp. 33–105. Oxford: Oxford University Press.

Solow, R (1997). Robert Solow. In *Lives of the Laureates*, W Breit and RW Spencer (eds.), pp. 183–203. Cambridge Mass: MIT Press.

Stigler, GJ (1949). Monopolistic competition in retrospect. In *Five Lectures on Economic Problems*. London: Longmans, Green.

Stigler, GJ (1965). The economist and the state. *American Economic Review*, 55(1), 1–18.

Stigler, GJ (1997). George Stigler. In *Lives of the Laureates*, W Breit and RW Spencer (eds.), pp. 95–113. Cambridge, MA: MIT Press.

Index

A priori beliefs 385
A priori objectives 263
A Survey of Contemporary Economics 119, 135, 150
Absolute liquidity preference 250–254
Academic 1–3, 14, 52, 53, 72, 77, 78, 89, 106, 112, 158, 161, 168, 170, 172, 177, 186, 192, 196, 204–206, 219, 220, 234, 239, 259, 268, 269, 272, 287, 290, 295, 300, 302, 318, 321, 322, 330, 335, 379, 412, 417, 420, 422, 427, 441
Academic exchange 52
Achilles heel 73, 141, 217, 313, 355, 400, 427
Ad hoc basis 242
Adaptive expectations 215
Adjustment 214, 248, 341, 388, 389, 392, 393, 401
Administered price inflation 15, 113
Administered pricing 89
Adversarial approach 8, 28, 53, 147, 175, 220, 239
Adversarial approach of the courtroom 147
Adversarial style of debate 113
AEA Presidential Address 26, 95, 411, 425
Aggregate demand 142, 242, 248, 350, 359, 361, 364, 392, 396
Aggregate output 30, 44, 363, 371
Alchian, Armen 163, 426, 430
Altruism 190
American Capitalism 133, 137
American Economic Review 53, 87, 288, 289
Anecdotal evidence 64, 113, 114, 386
Animal spirits 345
Anti-semitism 204, 205
Antitrust 60, 98, 103
Antitrust legislation 98
Aquinas, Thomas 231, 242, 300
Arrow, Kenneth 80, 97, 102
Art 138, 277, 351, 369, 405–410, 415, 423, 424, 429, 430, 432, 435–438, 441, 442
Articles of faith 54, 409
Asking the right question 20, 21, 212, 221, 245
Assumptions 48, 59, 90, 91, 163, 179, 318, 322, 325, 331–337, 349, 351, 353, 362, 370, 395, 396, 401, 402, 411, 433, 436

Austen, Jane 138, 225, 228

Backwaters 157, 232
Bank deposits 364, 381, 383
Bath water 370
Baudelaire, Charles 316
Becker, Gary 8, 13, 26, 46, 98, 106, 160, 169, 183, 189, 190, 208, 238, 239, 263, 430
Behaviour 11, 13, 16, 48, 53, 57, 82, 101, 127, 134, 172, 174, 175, 248, 269, 323, 331, 333–336, 340, 349, 355–357, 360, 369, 390, 396, 398
Benchmarks 322, 329–336
Bilateral monopoly 143
Bishop Berkeley 305
Blackboard economics 330
Blaug, Mark 50, 65, 90, 159, 183, 192, 193, 219, 425
Bondholders 364
Bonds 235, 248, 255, 268, 364, 369, 380, 382
Bubbles 366
Businessman 116, 126

Cambridge Quantity Theory 246
Capitalism 37, 116, 133, 137, 151, 237, 365, 373, 401
Capitalism and Freedom 237
Capitalists 35, 36, 41
Caricature 138, 214, 234, 247, 258, 436
Carroll, Lewis 275
Case-by-case basis 325, 341
Cash 9, 76, 249, 253, 383
Central power 29, 147
Centralised wage setting 392
Chalk and talk 187
Chamberlin, Edwin 86, 88
Chicago oral tradition 9, 264, 267, 269
Chicago School 5, 21, 65, 74, 81, 86, 95, 96, 98, 102, 107, 112, 132, 169, 191, 201, 205–208, 216, 226, 227, 256, 261, 277, 407, 411, 425, 426
Chicago School counter-revolution 95, 226, 277
Chicago tradition 125, 234, 276
Chick, Vickie 348, 391
Choice 5, 13, 16, 21, 22, 26, 28, 30, 40, 41, 43, 45–47, 51, 55, 60, 61, 82, 90, 101, 116, 119, 147, 189, 202, 203, 205, 206, 215, 227, 244, 265, 269, 285, 302, 306, 322, 323, 329, 332–335, 339, 340, 342, 256, 381, 383, 398, 399, 406, 408, 427, 428, 438, 439
Classic liberal society 29, 74, 85, 102, 146
Classical economist 83, 84, 92, 93, 178, 258, 302, 308, 348
Classical equilibrium labour market 359
Classical tradition 351, 356
Coase, Ronald 26, 38, 49, 50, 166, 172, 178, 179, 185, 386
Coase's theorem 321, 322, 326, 331, 332, 336, 339, 342
Colander, David 416, 417, 420, 427, 438, 442
Cold war 5, 6, 11, 16, 19, 63, 73, 86, 127, 206, 237, 243
Collectivism 5, 51, 52, 64, 73, 126, 202, 206, 237
Collectivists 63, 201
Collusion 127, 129, 398
Columbia University 74, 119, 133, 139, 183
Communication 184, 225, 226, 286, 287, 296, 303, 304, 379
Communism 58, 65, 243
Communist sympathisers 261

Competitive markets 2, 15, 22, 23, 60, 63, 84, 85, 91, 101, 102, 126, 130, 140, 141, 202, 237, 355, 395, 413
Concentration ratios 99, 126, 128, 130, 131, 141
Conclusion 2, 11, 49, 54, 65, 91, 94, 95, 103, 105, 107, 116, 130, 149, 163, 175, 178, 226, 252, 258, 262, 275, 276, 285, 289, 299, 307, 308, 310, 313, 314, 328, 332, 334, 339, 347, 356, 373, 383, 386, 390, 401, 417, 424, 437, 440
Conservative 6, 28, 43, 46, 62, 76–78, 103, 107, 115, 120, 121, 126, 139, 148, 178, 201, 203, 205, 207–209, 221, 237, 301, 417, 434
Consumer preference 46, 105
Consumer sovereignty 45, 309
Consumption function 10, 160, 172, 210, 211
Controversy 9, 28, 93, 179, 233, 239, 257, 258, 277, 322, 324, 325, 395
Conventional judgments 351, 352, 355
Conventional system of belief 369
Core contradiction 418
Counter-revolution 4, 9, 23, 71, 74, 77, 86, 95, 97, 101, 201, 205, 210, 213, 214, 218, 220, 226–228, 231, 236, 237, 243, 246, 249, 252, 260, 261, 268–270, 276, 277
Countervailing force 30, 60, 372
Countervailing power 126, 129, 133, 138–146, 194
Court jesters 415
Court room tactics 65
Cowles Commission 79, 80, 96, 97, 207, 266
Critical Reading 170, 293, 295, 297, 301, 303, 305, 310, 314, 318
Criticism 8, 41, 91, 112, 113, 120, 122, 126, 142, 143, 192, 236, 240, 250, 269–271, 275, 315, 339, 346, 347, 374, 419, 424, 440
Cubist 408
Currie, Laughlin 262, 264
Curve, Phillips 210, 215, 216, 407
Custom 123, 242, 283, 333, 351, 352
Cycle of volatility 358
Cynicism 419

Dadaist 407
Darwinian process of evolution 294
Das Adam Smith problem 172
Das Kapital 382
Data 11, 13, 53, 64, 65, 99, 104, 124, 127, 130, 134, 151, 164, 200–202, 215, 216, 219, 220, 242, 254, 255, 261–263, 304, 386, 387, 390, 395, 398, 400, 401, 425–427, 434, 435
Debreu, Gerard 96, 407
Deflationary spiral 392, 393
Deliberate muddle 264
Demand for money 191, 210, 212, 214, 235, 245, 246, 248, 249, 250, 260, 261, 269, 276, 381
Demsetz, Harold 10, 60, 86, 90, 102–104, 166, 172, 174, 210, 406
Die Meistersinger 301
Differential rates of interest 382
Diminishing marginal utility 334
Director, Aaron 6, 12, 14, 22, 26, 45, 62, 76, 77, 81, 125, 137, 185, 201, 204, 209, 237

Discrete jumps 371
Dishonesty 2, 265
Disillusionment 270
Dissertation student 183
Dissertation supervisor 159, 183, 187
Dogma 107, 139, 269
Dominant market structure 107, 130, 135, 139
Don Quixote 4, 13, 27, 201
Dynamics 363, 411, 440

Easy to teach 9, 427
Econometrics 79, 151, 160, 163, 434, 438
Economic choice 28, 323, 342
Economic critics 415
Economic framework 31, 40, 78, 173, 352
Economic history 8, 92, 158, 162, 163, 187, 191, 214, 238, 240, 247, 254, 277, 412
Economic intuition 15, 21, 96, 97, 161, 179, 212, 245, 347, 351, 413, 436, 437
Economic Journal 212, 245, 285, 286, 288, 290
Economic literature 6, 172, 238, 284, 303
Economic man 174, 426
Economic power 15, 28–38, 40–43, 45, 55, 60, 120, 125, 133, 134, 150
Economic questions 57, 131, 385
Economic system 15, 57, 84, 85, 116, 146, 165, 243, 312, 358, 359, 366, 417
Economic textbooks 166, 383
Economic theology 107, 139
Economics 2, 3, 5–8, 10, 11, 13, 16, 19, 21, 22, 25–28, 30, 32, 40, 44, 46, 47, 50, 51, 54, 55, 58, 59, 61, 63, 65, 66, 72–74, 77, 78, 80–82, 84, 86, 87, 89, 90, 92, 93, 95, 96, 100–105, 107, 111, 112, 114, 117–125, 127, 128, 131–133, 141, 146, 150, 151, 158–168, 171–174, 177–179, 184–186, 191, 193, 194, 200–203, 209, 210, 216–218, 220, 221, 227, 229, 236, 240, 243, 259, 262, 266, 268, 272, 283, 284, 286, 287, 291, 292, 294, 297, 301, 302, 304, 309, 312, 313, 317, 323, 324, 329, 330, 342, 347–349, 351, 352, 361, 369, 372, 375, 383, 385, 386, 389, 390, 399, 401, 402, 405, 406, 408, 411, 412, 415, 416–418, 421–426, 429–432, 434–442
Efficiency 15, 22, 28, 32, 43, 48, 56, 58, 59, 61, 84, 90, 97, 101, 105, 113, 125, 126, 137, 176, 204, 227, 242, 248, 252, 254, 325, 326, 328–332, 336, 337, 340, 341, 364, 365, 367, 370, 432
Eminence grise 112, 201
Empirical basis 390
Empirical bombardment 386
Empirical findings 13, 131, 132, 296
Empirical foundation 387, 390, 400
Empirical testing 26, 65, 81, 425, 426, 434
Empirical work 16, 26, 50, 81, 95, 96, 103, 113, 166, 168, 203, 262, 263, 322, 329, 335, 342, 386, 401, 433, 434
Endogenous 59, 309, 357, 372, 418
English classical economist 308
Entrepreneur 39, 42, 85, 126, 365
Entrepreneurial economists 214, 247
Epistemology 424

Equality 29, 35, 44, 57, 83, 86, 101, 147, 227, 237, 360
Equilibrium 13, 15, 16, 56, 73, 79, 80, 84, 87, 91, 96, 97, 112, 137, 204, 207, 216, 217, 227, 235, 252, 253, 309, 310, 312, 315, 348, 349, 356, 359, 360, 361, 368, 372, 373, 389, 392, 397, 401, 411, 434
Equity 15, 28, 43, 48, 72, 90
Essays in Persuasion 241, 277, 439
Ethical considerations 47, 430
Evolutionary nature of knowledge 170
Externality 325, 332, 334

Fear of prose 308
Field courses 162
Finance motive 213, 245
Fiscal instrument 212
Fisher, Irving 163
Five Lectures on Economic Problems 17, 68, 108, 109, 154, 404, 444
Fixed exchange rates 210
Flexible prices 126, 127, 252, 395
Floating exchange rates 210
Fluctuations 249, 312, 359, 368, 372
Folklore 309, 314, 384
Fools 149, 189, 415, 416
Footnotes 379
Free to Choose 43, 46, 73, 91, 206
Freedom 2, 5, 16, 28, 29, 41, 43–45, 47, 48, 52, 61, 62, 64, 72, 73, 76, 78, 82, 86, 89, 91, 101, 106, 175, 202, 206, 219, 237, 244, 323, 426, 427
Free-market economic liberalism 206, 261
Freud, Sigmund 316
Friedland, Claire 51, 60, 62, 103, 104
Friedman, Milton 2, 5, 7, 10–12, 14, 21–23, 42, 62–64, 73–81, 83, 86–93, 95, 101, 105, 111, 149, 165, 172, 176, 191, 197, 199, 200, 202–213, 215, 217–222, 226–228, 234, 237, 243, 244, 246, 255, 256, 265, 266, 268, 270–272, 275, 291, 300, 389, 408, 424, 425, 428, 433

Galbraith, Kenneth 5, 14, 45, 81, 106, 111, 113, 114, 118, 146, 203, 301
Goldwater, Barry 29, 210
Good eggs 63, 77, 209
Good teachers 185
Gossip 422
Government intervention 28, 40, 43, 60, 61, 80, 84, 85, 91, 92, 97, 98, 101–104, 134–136, 145, 147, 209, 211, 214, 264, 322, 325, 331, 334, 338
Government regulation 22, 61, 105
Graduate education 158, 159, 162, 184, 189, 418, 421
Graduate students 6, 7, 62, 76, 84, 160, 161, 184, 186–188, 191, 196, 204, 228, 258, 296, 422, 425, 442
Great Depression 58, 72, 88, 94, 98, 143, 262
Growth theory 58, 59

Handicap 170, 177, 326
Harberger, Arnold 44, 75, 183, 194
Harcourt, Geoffrey 111
Hard-headed economist 419
Harrod, Roy 59, 351, 369, 391
Harvard University 48
Hayek, Friedrich von 62, 76, 77, 420
Hegel, Gottfried 406
Henry V 255
Heresy 89, 97, 265
Heretical views 28
Heretics 89, 226, 387

Heuristic 315, 362, 371, 399
Heuristic assumption 399
Hicks, John 195
History of Political Economy 157
History of Thought 3, 4, 7, 158, 159, 164, 167, 170, 175, 178, 184, 232, 233, 238, 257, 267
Hobbes, Thomas 25, 29, 387
Hobbesian 29, 82, 101
Hollywood 410, 416
Homer 173, 203, 311, 382
Hoover Institute 256
How to read 3, 167, 170, 172, 285
Human institutions 373
Humility 149

Ideological imperative 14, 27, 74, 206, 261
Ideology 2, 6, 10, 11, 16, 27, 31, 46, 48–52, 54, 62–65, 74, 101, 107, 221, 255, 256, 406
Illiteracy 2, 96
Impatience 4, 160
Imperfect competition 55, 206, 216, 261
Incentives 3, 12, 15, 47, 55, 271, 412, 417, 418, 421, 422, 431, 440
Income distribution 47, 57, 84, 136, 137, 142, 227, 427
Indifference curves 74, 207, 333, 336, 340
Individual 2, 6, 15, 16, 29, 40, 43, 45, 52, 55, 57, 60–64, 74–76, 79, 82–84, 86, 87, 89, 90, 101, 106, 114, 116, 117, 126, 146, 147, 186, 188–190, 202, 206, 211, 214, 216, 227, 237, 244, 288, 323, 325, 334, 348, 352–354, 357, 360, 361, 365, 391, 398, 406, 413, 426, 427, 434, 440
Individual choice 40, 43, 45, 55, 60, 61, 82, 90, 101, 116, 202, 206, 227, 398, 413
Industrial organisation 61, 116, 124, 184, 193, 201
Inequality 118, 263
Inflation 15, 113, 142, 201, 208, 210, 215, 216, 268, 388, 389, 391, 396, 397, 399, 400, 402
Inflation-unemployment trade-off 210, 215
Initial endowments 334, 336
Institutional framework 47, 330
Integrity 11, 65, 112, 121, 149, 220, 257, 260, 409
Intellectual history 92, 159, 170, 171, 179, 254, 256
Interdependence 127, 146
Interest rate 39, 210, 235, 248, 249, 251–254, 276, 309, 310, 363, 364, 367–371, 380, 382, 383
Introduction 85, 94, 228, 234, 267, 288, 289, 299, 300, 345, 370, 422
Investment 35, 45, 59, 134, 136, 191, 242, 248, 249, 254, 264, 309, 312, 350, 351, 353, 355, 356, 358, 362–369, 372, 373, 375, 393, 394
IS/LM framework 215
IS-LM analysis 179

Johnson, Harry 11, 213, 219, 246, 256, 265, 268, 401
Jokes 4, 62, 193, 385
Journal of Economic Literature 238, 284, 303
Journal of Political Economy 121, 262, 271, 286, 288
Journalism 138, 301
Justice 44, 48, 229, 234, 240, 264, 273, 427

Kahnneman, Daniel 333, 335, 336, 396
Keynes, John Maynard 92, 202, 209, 240, 244, 348, 385, 409, 437, 438, 441
Keynes, John Neville 423, 429, 431, 437
Keynesian macroeconomics 10
Keynesian revolution 55, 72, 73, 80, 121, 213, 246, 255, 256, 260, 265, 268–270, 277
Keynesianism 23, 77, 87, 205, 206, 214, 215, 217, 237, 261
Kindahl, James 19, 50, 81
King Lear 415
Kinked demand curve 5, 9, 53, 86, 87, 89, 124, 178, 314
Klamer, Arjo 406, 421
Knetsch, Jack 336, 340
Knight, Frank 3, 6, 13, 15, 56, 62, 77, 84, 149, 159, 162, 167, 189, 190, 191, 193, 204, 234, 258, 292, 374, 417, 425
Kriesler, Peter 375
Kuznets, Simon 203

La Guerre est Finie 255
Labour demand 80, 360
Labour market 94, 216, 359, 371, 372, 388, 389–394, 397, 399, 400, 402
Laidler, David 233, 271, 276
Laissez faire 158, 206, 253, 261, 332, 362
Lamp posts 423
Landlords 35, 36
Law or Economics 61
Laws of Nature 432
Lectures 9, 16, 26, 27, 48, 75, 77–80, 82, 83, 93, 101, 187, 193–195, 217, 287, 308, 383
Leeson, Robert 233
Legal entitlements 338, 340
Legal liability 327, 339
Leibenstein, Harvey 30, 56
Leijonhufvud, Axel 311
Lester, Richard 80
Letters 25, 60, 77, 208, 217, 225–229, 353, 425
Levels of employment 349, 350, 358, 364
Liberty 16, 28–30, 41, 43, 46, 52, 55, 61, 62, 64, 72, 73, 76, 82, 101, 227, 237, 415
Linearity 407
Liquidity preference 213, 235, 245, 246, 250–254, 261, 269, 276, 380, 381
Liquidity trap 9, 235, 249, 250, 253, 309, 369
Literature review 289, 299, 300
Logic 2, 28, 47, 114, 117, 127, 141, 142, 186, 214, 219, 248, 300, 305, 312, 313, 326, 329, 334, 358, 372, 390, 397, 401, 425, 434, 436
Lombardi, Vince 177, 272
London School of Economics 27, 77, 78, 93, 217
Long struggle of escape 425
Look Homeward Angel 316
Loyalty 7, 209, 254–256, 260, 262, 266, 268, 271, 272
Loyalty oaths 7

M.E.C. schedule 368, 370
Machlup, Fritz 151, 266, 411
Mainstream economists 62, 76, 146
Marginal cost 87, 92, 131, 324, 325, 394
Marginal efficiency of capital 242, 248, 252, 364, 367, 370

Marginal productivity theory 29, 32, 40, 41, 48, 55, 119, 123, 137, 147
Marginal revenue 87, 89, 92
Marginalist tools 355
Market distributions of income 84
Market efficiency 32, 58, 97, 105, 126, 176, 204, 328, 329, 332, 337
Market failure 58, 80, 97, 102, 212, 216, 322, 323, 325, 331, 332, 340, 355, 389
Market force 8, 29–31, 72, 137, 392
Market place of ideas 147
Market price 32, 33, 126, 127, 134
Market principles 72, 226
Market processes 28, 298
Marketing 7, 8, 46, 47, 49, 60, 106, 169, 175, 216, 238, 239, 254, 290, 306, 432
Marketplace for ideas 45
Markets 2, 15, 16, 22, 23, 28, 29, 41, 43, 45, 48, 60, 63, 64, 73, 82, 84, 85, 88, 90, 91, 97, 101, 102, 105, 107, 115, 116, 121, 124, 126, 130, 131, 133, 136, 139–142, 186, 188, 202, 203, 211, 212, 216, 217, 220, 227, 237, 272, 284, 331, 337, 348, 349, 355, 357, 358, 365, 368, 388, 389–395, 397, 400, 402, 413
Marshall, Alfred 33, 37, 38, 240, 287, 429, 437
Marshallian 9, 80, 96, 122, 227, 395, 429, 433, 437
Marshallian partial equilibrium 80, 96, 227
Marx, Grouch 379
Marx, Karl 307, 379
Mathematical economist 96, 97
Mathematical formalisation 292, 294, 297, 303, 305
Mathematical theorists 206
Mayer, Thomas 411, 412
McCarthy, Joe 29, 64, 65
McCarthyism 52, 65
McCloskey, Deirdre 114, 163, 174, 238, 406, 419
McCloskey, Donald 162, 284, 316, 345
Means, Gardiner 8, 89, 98, 106, 107, 113, 395
Measurement 26, 116, 131, 187, 425
Memoirs of an Unregulated Economist 17, 23, 68, 109, 153, 181, 196, 223, 229, 280
Methodological break 348, 349, 351, 352, 354, 356, 358, 362, 370, 374
Methodology 6, 9, 11, 12, 64, 90, 91, 105, 125, 126, 217, 218, 220, 227, 281, 345, 359, 362, 369, 400, 407, 408, 424, 425, 427–429
Microeconomics 55, 73, 160
Micro-foundations 55, 73, 214, 347, 353, 355, 389, 394, 395
Mill, John Stuart 283, 351
Minimalist defense 417
Mints, Lloyd 234
Mirowski, Philip 302
Mises, Ludwig von 62
Misplaced loyalty 272
MIT 79, 103, 151, 183, 421, 431
MIT approach 421, 431
Modelling 395
Modern economics 405, 406, 423
Modernism 406
Modigliani, Franco 213
Mondrian, Piet 407
Monetary authorities 251, 262, 308
Monetary policy 208, 214, 249, 250, 252, 262, 264, 275

Monetary theory 9, 151, 212–214, 228, 233–236, 241, 245, 247, 248, 259, 260, 264, 266–268, 273, 276, 380, 408
Money illusion 16, 391, 395, 396
Money neutrality 361
Money supply 201, 214, 215, 262
Money velocity 249, 269
Money-wages 310, 359, 360, 392
Monopolistic competition 15, 79, 86, 87, 90, 113, 119, 166, 193, 205, 217, 395, 425, 433
Monopoly 13, 22, 60, 61, 98, 100, 101, 102, 118, 120, 125, 129, 134, 143, 150, 441
Montaigne, Michel 173, 311, 382
Moral aims 83
Moral imperative 82, 84, 202
Movement along a curve 370
Mt. Pelerin Society 16, 128, 209
Multiple equilibrium 15

Natural rate of unemployment 210, 215, 216
Natural sciences 304
Neoclassical price theory 13, 15, 49, 60, 65, 73, 86, 91, 97, 99, 103, 104, 113, 127, 128, 133, 214, 260, 302, 348, 352, 372, 382, 392, 394, 395, 397, 398, 406
Neoclassical synthesis 372
Neo-mercantilist 259
New-Classical 389
Newtonian 135, 408
Nirvana economics 399
Nobel Prize 5, 21, 25, 115, 202, 221, 289, 423
Nominal interest rate 248, 249, 254
Non-equilibrium 10, 15, 56, 87, 101
Non-Euclidean geometry 408
Non-market alternative 332
Non-market mechanism 397
Non-money assets 248
Nonsense 14, 98, 193, 201, 220, 272
Normative science 423, 429

Obituaries 199
Objective observer 433
Oedipus 188
Ohlin, Bertil 212, 245
Old Maid 362, 368
Oligopoly 22, 60, 102, 118, 119, 126, 127, 130, 137, 142, 146, 314, 315
One-sided 123, 213, 246
Optimism 105, 365, 418, 419, 442

Pareto efficient 323, 330, 334, 335–337
Partisan arguments 50
Partisanship 271
Patinkin, Don 11, 96, 193, 206, 256, 265
Peltzman, Sam 47, 48, 55, 56, 98, 105, 177, 183, 184, 190–192, 218, 428, 433
Perfect competition 13, 22, 41, 43, 55, 56, 73, 206, 216, 256, 261, 326, 413, 427, 433
Permanent income hypothesis 211, 212
Persuasion 46, 168, 169, 184, 232, 238, 241, 277, 304, 308, 350, 389, 401, 415, 425, 439
Petard 268, 402
Phelps, Edmund 216
Philosophical fashion 426
Pigou, Alfred 239, 240, 265, 322, 324–326, 329, 332, 334, 337, 348, 394
Pigouvian 324, 327, 328, 338, 356
Planners 72, 73, 89, 91, 92, 94, 97, 201, 227
Plato 316, 417, 420

Platonists 437, 438
Polemics 10, 172, 210, 237
Policy 6, 9, 10, 22, 48, 51, 53, 57–59, 63, 66, 72–74, 76, 81, 83–86, 93, 94, 97, 100, 105, 112, 119, 120, 125, 126, 128, 129, 150, 172, 191, 208, 210, 211, 212, 214, 215, 219, 221, 234–236, 238, 240–243, 249, 250, 252, 254, 255, 257, 261, 262, 264, 265, 271, 275, 276, 289, 310, 311, 322, 325, 327, 329, 330, 332, 347, 350, 368, 369, 386, 387, 389, 398–400, 406, 412, 418, 421, 424, 429, 430, 432, 434, 435–437, 440, 441
Policy debates 9, 74, 93
Policy preferences 386, 406, 434
Political market 22, 23, 105, 176
Pontificating 426
Poor writing 291, 317
Popular writing 138
Portfolio adjustments 214
Positive science 423, 430, 431, 433
Positive sum game 52, 239
Positivism 93, 217, 268
Post-Keynesian 353, 380, 382
Post-war 4, 9, 21, 22, 26, 27, 29, 54, 55, 57–59, 63, 72, 73, 77, 79, 96, 116, 120, 124, 127, 133–135, 141, 148, 166, 169, 179, 201, 212, 217, 226, 227, 237, 238, 241, 245, 266, 297, 301, 353, 385, 424, 434
Post-war economy 134
Power 15, 25, 28–38, 40–45, 55, 60, 61, 63, 76, 82, 84, 86, 91, 94, 101, 107, 120, 125, 126, 129, 133–147, 150, 163, 194, 195, 202, 206, 236, 237, 268, 283, 286, 289, 308, 357, 361, 364, 369, 381, 386, 416, 435
Preaching 106, 210, 418, 440
Preciseness of mathematical models 297
Predictive accuracy 433
Prejudices 92, 193, 201, 239, 259, 305, 308, 324, 362, 431
Prescriptive requirement 433
Pre-war published articles 426
Price rigidity 15, 113
Price stability 387, 399, 400
Prima facie case 323, 331, 334, 335, 337, 340
Procrustean bed 305
Production and Distribution Theories 85
Professional gadflies 416
Professional output 202
Profit 32–34, 36–39, 41, 125, 126, 136, 142, 307, 365, 393, 394, 423
Property rights 29, 34, 36, 41, 42, 84, 163, 326, 327, 331, 337, 340
Protestant Father figure 190
Psychology 116, 173, 188, 352, 357
Public appearances 11
Puns 379

Quantification 26, 81, 95, 159
Quantification of Economics 81
Quantitative methods 26
Quantity theory of money 206, 211, 212, 228, 233, 235, 261, 267
Quarterly Journal of Economics 121, 262, 286
Questions of fact 131, 385

Rational explanation 142
Rationality 13, 306, 390, 391, 395, 396, 426
Reading skills 3
Real wage 360, 371, 372, 388, 389, 392, 396
Realist 418
Reder, Melvin 13

Redistribution 15, 36, 44, 45, 55–57, 82, 85, 102, 105, 147, 339
Relative power 137
Rent 25, 32–35, 39, 41, 44, 145, 307, 334, 368
Rent seeking 25, 44, , 145, 334
Reviewers 120, 133, 273, 287, 290, 299, 318
Rhetoric 136, 138, 163, 240, 243, 284, 296, 297, 299, 301–303, 314, 317, 345, 349, 350, 354, 359, 361, 386, 408, 434, 437
Rhetorical strategies 238, 352
Rhetorical trick 123
Ricardo, David 31, 35
Right wing intellectuals 237, 261
Rigid wages 310, 390, 391, 395
Road to Serfdom 44, 62, 75, 201
Robbins, Lionel 27, 77, 195
Robertson, Dennis 121, 394
Robinson, Joan 89, 111, 219, 244
Roofs or Ceilings 227
Rosen, Sherwin 7, 11, 15, 158, 169, 172

Salesman 205, 218
Samuelson, Paul 6, 8, 10, 28, 30, 51, 52, 53, 62, 63, 97, 125, 163, 183, 189, 197, 199, 201, 204, 205, 208, 209, 215, 217, 220, 222, 228, 248, 255, 258
Sancho Panza 4, 201
Savage, Jimmy 42, 255
Say's law 166, 178, 290, 350, 358, 362
Schumpeter, Joseph 30, 95, 117, 120, 145, 151, 161, 166, 167, 270, 354
Schwartz, Anna 262
Science 31, 59, 79, 97, 121, 138, 149, 161, 162, 164–166, 175, 211, 217, 286, 287, 296, 306, 358, 369, 405–411, 423–426, 429–433, 438, 439
Scientific format 304
Scientific literature 169
Scientific precision 428
Scientific work 10, 48, 167, 172, 210
Self-interest 22, 50, 51, 65, 102, 105, 149, 173–176, 242, 168, 417, 419, 420
Self-interested action 176
Sesame Street dropouts 293
Sheltered workshop 164
Short run 102, 264, 312, 313, 357, 361, 368, 370, 389
Shove, Gerald 353
Simon, Herbert 173, 306
Simons, Henry 60, 191, 234, 235, 263
Sins of omission 387
Slumps 364
Smith, Adam 50, 74, 81, 85, 93, 144, 157, 164, 166, 171, 172, 174–176, 323, 361, 373, 387, 432, 438
Social Darwinism 148
Social engineering 30, 58, 84
Social welfare 102, 131, 337
Solow, Robert 192, 411, 438
Soviet Union 63, 72
Sowell, Thomas 192
Specialisation 161, 184, 185, 361, 430, 431
Specialist 133, 158, 160, 162, 232, 233, 436
Speculators 248, 366, 380
Spencer, Herbert 3, 148, 294
Stability 58, 59, 135, 141, 142, 253, 312, 315, 333, 348, 357–359, 364, 371, 373, 387, 392, 399, 400
Stabilizing role of conventions 372
Statics 217, 411

Statistical analysis 8, 104, 113, 385, 386, 412
Statistical Research Group 228
Status quo 23, 36, 214, 241, 247, 284, 301, 322, 324, 326, 332, 335, 341, 400, 417, 440
Steindl, Frank 271
Sticky downward nominal wages 360
Stigler, George 2, 6–8, 10, 12, 14, 19–21, 23, 26, 27, 30, 31, 42, 46, 47, 49, 50, 53, 62, 65, 74–78, 80, 81, 83, 86, 87–92, 95, 101, 102, 105, 111, 112, 114, 117, 118, 119, 121, 133, 139, 157–160, 164, 166, 168, 169, 171, 174, 175, 177, 183–185, 188, 190–193, 195, 196, 199, 201, 202, 204, 205, 207, 208, 210, 212, 217, 221, 226–228, 238, 243–245, 255, 258, 265, 266, 271, 291, 314, 385, 406, 407, 409, 425, 430, 433
Stock prices 366, 367
Stockholders 366
Strategic bargaining 338, 341
Strawman 242
Sugden, Robert 357
Summa Theologica 231
Supervisor 159, 183, 184, 187, 189, 192, 195
Surrealism 410
Sweezy, Paul 5, 53, 89
Swift, Jonathan 286
Symmetry of choice 322, 333, 334
Szostak, Rick 405

Teaching 158, 167, 177, 184–187, 189, 193–195, 204, 226, 242, 244, 258, 259, 304, 426, 427, 436, 441, 442
Technical economists 440
Techo-structure 146
Telser, Lester 193
Terms of debate 113, 200, 211, 213, 214, 245, 247, 257, 265, 347, 353, 355, 400, 433
Testable hypothesis 48, 57, 64, 90, 167
Testing 26, 65, 81, 95, 131, 132, 255, 408, 412, 425, 426, 434, 435, 437
Textbooks 9, 63, 178, 308, 314, 315, 380, 383, 424, 427, 428
The Economic Consequences of the War 240
The Economics of Information 13, 22, 127
The Economist Plays with Blocs 138
The Ethics of Competition 56
The General Theory 9, 121, 212, 235, 241–243, 245–252, 258, 273, 276, 309, 345, 347, 348, 353, 354, 357, 358, 367, 370, 371,. 373, 374, 380–382, 388, 394, 395, 419
The Intellectual And The Market Place And Other Essays 228
The Journal of Excluded Middles 299
The Marginal Cost Controversy 324, 325
The Moral Sentiments 50
The Problem of Social Cost 324, 339
T*he Quantity Theory of Money – A Restatement* 233
The Theory of Economic Regulation 22
The Theory of Moral Sentiments 173, 174
The Theory of Oligopoly 109
The Theory of Price 87, 195, 208, 243
The Treatise on Money 241, 381
The visible paw 323
The Wealth of Nations 50, 173, 174, 382
Theology 39, 107, 139, 206
Theoretical constructs 386
Theoretical framework 111, 264

Theoretical results 97, 296
Theorists 16, 51, 73, 79, 95, 99, 127, 187, 206, 234–236, 269, 287, 334, 360, 398, 430, 431
Theory of distribution 40, 41, 42, 85
Tight Prior Equilibrium 13, 16, 112, 204
Tobin, James 213, 267, 388, 423
Toqueville, Alexis de 85
Totalitarian collectivists 206
Tract on Monetary Reform 241, 250, 273
Tradition 9, 32, 62, 72, 81, 84, 89, 93, 118, 122, 125, 141, 173, 177, 178, 187, 193, 204, 233, 234, 236, 246, 250, 257, 260, 264, 266, 267, 269–271, 274–276, 295, 308, 314, 318, 328, 334, 347, 351, 356, 379–381, 383, 389, 400, 415, 437
Transaction costs 135, 248, 284, 309, 323, 324, 327, 328, 330–335, 337–340, 357, 369, 430
Transitivity 334
True believer 19, 28, 200, 220, 263

Uncertain knowledge 349
Unemployment 59, 135, 210, 215, 216, 266, 350, 360, 362, 371, 387–389, 393, 394, 397, 399, 402
Unintended consequences 92, 94, 101, 233, 274
University of Chicago 21, 23, 51, 52, 62, 74, 76–78, 122, 133, 158, 163, 183, 203, 205, 206, 209, 220, 258, 261, 263, 266, 269
Unscientific 123, 296, 302
Utilitarian 293, 299, 317

Value and Distribution 120, 125, 150
Vampires 321
Varian, Hal 303
Veblen, Thorstein 146, 283
Viner, Jacob 62, 150, 178, 190, 191, 204, 206, 234, 259, 261, 393

Wage reductions 393
Wage rigidity 309, 391, 399–401
Wallis, Allen 53, 151, 204, 228, 425
Walrasian general equilibrium 96, 227, 348
Walrasian system 211
Weasel words 411
What Can Regulators Regulate? The Case of Electricity 22
Wilcox, Claire 99, 100, 128, 129, 131
Wilde, Oscar 157
Winner-take-all 8, 220

X-efficiency 15, 113

Yellow pages approach 103

Zero inflation 389, 397
Zero sum game 52, 239
Zero transaction costs 328, 332, 335